THE
SPANISH CIVIL WAR AND
THE BRITISH LABOUR
MOVEMENT

TOM BUCHANAN

University Lecturer in Modern History and Politics, Department for Continuing Education,
University of Oxford

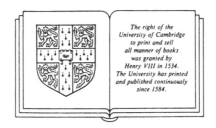

The right of the
University of Cambridge
to print and sell
all manner of books
was granted by
Henry VIII in 1534.
The University has printed
and published continuously
since 1584.

CAMBRIDGE UNIVERSITY PRESS

CAMBRIDGE

NEW YORK PORT CHESTER

MELBOURNE SYDNEY

CAMBRIDGE UNIVERSITY PRESS
Cambridge, New York, Melbourne, Madrid, Cape Town, Singapore, São Paulo

Cambridge University Press
The Edinburgh Building, Cambridge CB2 8RU, UK

Published in the United States of America by Cambridge University Press, New York

www.cambridge.org
Information on this title: www.cambridge.org/9780521393331

First published 1991
This digitally printed version 2008

A catalogue record for this publication is available from the British Library

Library of Congress Cataloguing in Publication data
Buchanan, Tom, 1960–
The Spanish Civil War and the British labour movement/Tom
Buchanan.
p.   cm.
Originally presented as the author's thesis (D.Phil.).
Includes bibliographical references (p.   ) and index.
ISBN 0-521-39333-7
1. Spain–History–Civil War. 1936–1939–Public opinion.
2. Public opinion–Great Britain–History–20th century.   3. Spain–
History–Civil War, 1936–1939–Participation, British.   4. Trades
Union Congress–Political activity–History–20th century.
5. Labour Party (Great Britain)–History–20th century.   6. Spain–
Relations–Great Britain.   7. Great Britain–Relations–Spain.
I. Title.
DP269.8.P8B83   1991
946.081–dc20   90-35461   CIP

ISBN 978-0-521-39333-1 hardback
ISBN 978-0-521-07356-1 paperback

For Julia

CONTENTS

Preface   *page* xi

List of abbreviations   xv

Introduction: 'The Spanish problem'   1

1 'The best that could be done at the time...': Non-
   Intervention, 17 July–28 October 1936   37

2 Breaking with Non-Intervention: October 1936–October 1937   73

3 The failure of the left: October 1937–April 1939   107

4 'A demonstration of solidarity and sympathy...': The Spanish
   Workers' Fund and its competitors   137

5 Opposition: Catholic workers and the Spanish Civil War   167

6 Rank-and-file initiatives   196

   Aftermath and conclusion   221

Bibliography   229

Index   241

PREFACE

During the course of this research I became inured to the comment that nothing new could be found to be said on this subject, yet in fact no detailed analysis of the response nationally of the labour movement to the Spanish Civil War has so far been published.[1] This surprising lacuna in the literature of both the Civil War and the British labour movement is perhaps due in part to a lack of documentation, and I have been fortunate to have access to a number of previously unavailable sources (in particular the TUC archives) which have greatly informed my argument. However, the reason goes deeper than this and is, I would suggest, primarily historiographical. In the aftermath of the fall of the Spanish Republic, and in the absence of any sustained investigation into labour's role in the conflict, two conclusions became widely accepted. Firstly, that the response of the Labour Party and trade unions to the Civil War had been an unmitigated failure and, secondly, that this failure was due to a weakness in leadership, with the result that criticism was primarily directed at individuals rather than at institutions or bureaucratic procedures. Significantly, labour's leaders did little to counter this impression – after all, for most of them criticism of their role in the Civil War did not hinder their advance to grand and lengthy ministerial careers. The one major leader who did not progress to high political office, Sir Walter Citrine, who emerges from this study as the central figure in labour's response to Spain, could have responded to the attacks directed against him on this question but opted in his autobiography for silence: 'I have had to leave out much that I think interesting, including chapters about my

---

[1] The subject has, of course, been dealt with in books which examine Britain's reaction to the Civil War more generally; there have also been regional studies of the labour movement and the Civil War, and a number of dissertations on the response of the Labour Party. This literature is discussed below, pp. 3–6.

activities at the Ottawa Conference in 1932 and the Spanish Civil War in the later thirties; this has been inescapable '.[2]

Thus, virtually no attention was devoted, either at the time or since, to assessing the performance of labour's institutions: in fact, the dominant historical interpretation of this subject has almost negated the need for any analysis of them. According to this view the Civil War was seen by many in Britain as a struggle between democracy and fascism and generated a mass movement of solidarity with the Spanish people within which the Communist Party played a leading role. However, the leaders of the labour movement, especially the trade union leaders Walter Citrine and Ernest Bevin and Hugh Dalton in the Labour Party, blinded by anti-communism, refused to give adequate support to the Spanish Republic and frustrated those who wanted to do so. The problem with this approach is that it has always been rooted in caricature – Citrine, Bevin and Dalton's actions have been read off from their political position on labour's right wing without any recourse to analysis of their personal motivations, let alone the institutional constraints on their actions.

Hence, this interpretation leaves many questions unanswered. Why, for instance, if the leaders were so out of sympathy with their members did their viewpoint prevail throughout the course of the Civil War? Why was the labour movement not torn apart by the passions generated by the conflict? Moreover, in the creation of a convenient argument many inconvenient facts have been passed over. To take one example, Bevin has been seen as one of the most obdurately obstructive trade union leaders, whose performance at the TUC Congress in September 1936 was instrumental in persuading the unions to accept the British government's policy of 'Non-Intervention' in the Civil War. Yet, barely a week later Bevin was involved in a very different mission. His mainly Catholic members in Ireland were outraged at his union's £1,000 grant for humanitarian relief in Spain and there was a danger that their conference might repudiate the leadership. Bevin, in the face of threats and intimidation, went to Ireland to confront his critics and persuaded them to support the grant.[3] This episode illustrates two of the main themes of this book. Firstly, that even reviled figures such as Bevin were willing to go to considerable lengths to defend solidarity with the Spanish workers: however, this was very much on their own terms and in order to protect their institutional interests. Secondly, that the dominant view from the apex of the labour movement was not one of united support

---

[2] Lord Citrine, *Men and Work: The Autobiography of Lord Citrine*, (1964), p. 10; Lord Citrine briefly discussed the Civil War on pp. 357–60.

[3] This episode is discussed below p. 193.

for Republican Spain. Quite apart from the special case of Ireland, many Catholic workers in Britain felt profoundly discontented on this issue. Thus, Spain was a problem to leaders of the labour movement. Not only did the left want to push it towards more active solidarity with Spain, but a distinct section of the movement was critical of what had already been achieved.

This book should not be taken as an attempt to prove that yet more of the left's most hallowed achievements were, in fact, mythical. There was nothing illusory about the commitment or sacrifice of those who fought for the International Brigades or collected money on behalf of the Spanish Republic. However, what it does take issue with are the patterns which politicians at the time and historians since have sought to impose on these activities. Thus the intention of this book is to provide a unifying argument that will reconcile all of these disparate threads into an overall explanation of why the labour movement responded to Spain in the way that it did. The core of this argument is provided by an analysis of labour's bureaucratic internationalism, the importance of which has regularly been overlooked by historians. More generally, I have judged it necessary to make the 'labour movement' the focus for the book because to take either the Labour Party or the trade unions on their own would distort the interpretation. In the 1930s a unique combination of Labour Party weakness, trade union strength and a joint structure of decision-making ensures that neither can realistically be studied in isolation. However, this is particularly important in the case of the unions because so often in the past Citrine and Bevin have been dismissed as *eminences grises* who effectively controlled the Labour Party, and yet whose motivation has remained impenetrable.

The book falls into two main parts. The first three chapters are broadly chronological, charting the evolution of the labour movement's response to the Civil War. It is argued that this response was conditioned by a shifting balance of factors such as perceptions of events in Spain, the mediating role of the international labour movement, and pressures from below, either for or against the Spanish Republic. This section shows how the balance of these factors changed in importance during the course of the conflict. Chapter 3 also begins a discussion of the left's Popular Front strategy which is developed in the second half of the book, especially in chapter 4 which studies the politicisation of relief work. More generally these later chapters study themes which span the Civil War period: these also include opposition to the Spanish Republic within the labour movement, and the alternative forms of solidarity suggested by the 'rank-and-file' activists within the unions.

I would like to record my gratitude to the British Academy and the Marquis of Lothian's Award for the grants which made possible the doctoral research on which this book is based. Of the archive centres that I have visited a particular debt is owed to Rosie Stone and the staff of the TUC's Filing Department and Richard Storey, Alistair Tough and Nicholas Baldwin at Warwick University's Modern Record Centre who gave invaluable assistance with archival sources. I would also like to thank the staff at all of the many other libraries and trade union offices that I visited in the course of my research for their hospitality and helpfulness. I am grateful to the following institutions and individuals for permission both to consult and to quote from documentary material: the Trades Union Congress; the Warden and Fellows of Nuffield College, Oxford; Sir John Cripps; the Master, Fellows and Scholars of Churchill College, Cambridge; The Honourable Francis Noel-Baker; Ruskin College, Oxford; The Trustees of the National Library of Scotland; the Labour Party; The Public Record Office, Kew.

Without the hospitality of the following friends this research would have been difficult to contemplate: Penny Gorman, Richard East, Nicola Pyke, Richard Lake, Keith Jacobs, Richard and Barbara Lowndes, Jos de Putte, David Lewis, Tracy Parr, Ben Lockwood.

I owe special thanks to Dr Frances Lannon who supervised my DPhil thesis and whose advice, both then and since, on all aspects of my work has been invariably helpful. I am also grateful to Professor Ben Pimlott and Dr Ross McKibbin who examined the thesis and made many pertinent criticisms. I would finally like to thank the following who have helped at various stages of this project: A. F. Thompson, Sir Raymond Carr, Mary Vincent, Martin Conway, all the members of the Oxford Spanish Studies Seminar group, Andy Buchanan, Helen Arthur, Angus Buchanan, Brenda Buchanan, and Julia Lowndes. Of course, the responsibility for the conclusions reached in this book remains entirely my own.

ABBREVIATIONS

AESD	Association of Engineering and Shipbuilding Draughtsmen
AEU	Amalgamated Engineering Union
ASLEF	Associated Society of Locomotive Engineers and Firemen
ASSNC	Aircraft Shop Stewards' National Council
ASW	Amalgamated Society of Woodworkers
AUBTW	Amalgamated Union of Building Trade Workers
BLPES	British Library of Political and Economic Science
CEDA	Confederación Española de Derechas Autónomas
CGT	Confédération Général du Travail; the French trade union centre
CNT	Confederación Nacional del Trabajo; the Spanish anarchist trade union centre
CPGB	Communist Party of Great Britain
CSCA	Civil Service Clerks' Association
ETU	Electrical Trades Union
HCLA	Home Counties Labour Association
IFTU	International Federation of Trades Unions
IISG	International Institute of Social History, Amsterdam
ILP	Independent Labour Party
ISF	International Solidarity Fund
ITF	International Transport Workers' Federation
ITGWU	Irish Transport and General Workers' Union
ITUC	Irish Trades Union Congress
LCC	London County Council
LPCR	Labour Party Annual Conference Reports
LSC	Labour Spain Committee
LSI	Labour and Socialist International
LTC	London Trades Council

MFGB	Miners' Federation of Great Britain
MHIWU	Mental Health and Institutional Workers' Union
MRC	Warwick University, Modern Records Centre
NAFTA	National Amalgamated Furnishing Trades Association
NATSOPA	National Society of Operative Printers and Assistants
NAUSA	National Amalgamated Union of Shop Assistants
NCL	National Council of Labour
NEC	Labour Party National Executive Committee
NFBTO	National Federation of Building Trades Operatives
NJCSR	National Joint Committee for Spanish Relief
NLS	National Library of Scotland
NUBSO	National Union of Boot and Shoe Operatives
NUC	National Union of Clerks and Administrative Workers
NUDAW	National Union of Distributive and Allied Workers
NUFW	National Union of Foundry Workers
NUGMW	National Union of General and Municipal Workers
NUR	National Union of Railwaymen
NUS	National Union of Seamen
NUSM	National Union of Scottish Mineworkers
NUTGW	National Union of Tailors and Garment Workers
PKTF	Printing and Kindred Trades Federation
PLP	Parliamentary Labour Party
POUM	Partido Obrero de Unificación Marxista; the Spanish communist left opposition party
PRO	Public Records Office (Kew)
PSOE	Partido Socialista Obrero Español; the Spanish Socialist Party
PSUC	Partit Socialista Unificat de Catalunya; the united Catalan Socialist–Communist Party
RCA	Railway Clerks' Association
SCC	Spain Campaign Committee of the Labour Party NEC
SFIO	Section Française de l'Internationale Ouvrière; the French Socialist Party
SMA	Spanish Medical Aid Committee
STUC	Scottish Trades Union Congress
SWMF	South Wales Miners' Federation
T&GWU	Transport and General Workers' Union
TUC	Trades Union Congress
TUC CR	TUC Annual Congress Reports
UGT	Unión General de Trabajadores; the Spanish Socialist trade union centre
VIASC	Voluntary Industrial Aid for Spain Committee

NOTE ON ABBREVIATIONS FOR TUC SUBJECT FILES

For convenience in the footnotes the following abbreviations have been adopted for the TUC Subject Files held at Congress House.

Box 430, File 946/520, 'Spanish Rebellion, General Correspondence': TUC, Correspondence 1

Box 430, File 946/520, 'Spanish Rebellion, General Correspondence, 2nd File': TUC, Correspondence 2

Box 430, File 946/520, 'Spanish Rebellion, Correspondence, 3rd File': TUC, Correspondence 3

Box 432, File 946/521, 'Spanish Rebellion, General – Documents': TUC, Documents 1

Box 431, File 946/521, 'Spanish Rebellion – General Documents (2nd File)': TUC, Documents 2

Box 431, File 946/521, 'Spanish Rebellion – 1936, Documents (3rd File)': TUC, Documents 3

Box 431, File 946/521, 'Spanish Rebellion Documents from 1938': TUC, Documents 4

Box 432, File 946/523, 'Spain – March Conf. 1937': TUC, International Conference 1

Box 432, File 946/525, 'International Conference on Spain, London March 10–11 1937': TUC, International Conference 2

Box 432, File 946/524, 'Spanish Rebellion, Catholic Aspect': TUC, Catholic Aspect

Box 433, File 946/530, 'Spanish Rebellion, Fund (Important), July '36–March '37': TUC, Fund 1

Ibid. 'Spanish Rebellion – Fund – 2nd File': TUC, Fund 2

Box 436, File 946/530, 'Spanish Rebellion, Fund, 3rd File': TUC, Fund 3

Ibid. 'Spanish Rebellion. Fund. November 1938–1942': TUC, Fund 4

Box 434, File 946/535, 'Spanish Rebellion, Aid – International Brigade': TUC, International Brigade

Box 435, File 946/537, 'Basque Children's Committee – Minutes and Documents': TUC, Basque Children 1

Ibid. 'Spanish Conflict; Basque Children': TUC, Basque Children 2

Ibid. 'Basque Children's Committee 1938 – Correspondence': TUC, Basque Children 3

File 90241, '1938, International Situation, Special Conference': TUC, File 90241

INTRODUCTION: 'THE SPANISH PROBLEM'

The fall of the Spanish monarchy in 1931 and its replacement by a progressive, democratic Republic was welcome news to the British labour movement, coming at a time of world economic depression and political failure for governments of the left.[1] The appointment of three leading Spanish socialists as ministers in the first Republican government and the rapid expansion of Spanish trade unionism appeared to herald not only a new era in Spain's history, but also a transformation in the international standing of Spanish labour. For the leaders of British labour, who for years had seen it as a marginal European nation – poor, socially and politically backward – Spain could seemingly no longer be ignored. For the Spanish, the Republic brought the opportunity to extend their previously slender links within the confraternity of international labour. Yet this new dawn proved illusory. By 1933 the socialists were out of office and, within a year, had participated in a failed insurrection against the new centre-right government. By the time the left had returned to power by legal means in February 1936, as a broad Popular Front stretching from the anarchists to the middle-class Republican parties, it was too late to resolve Spain's appalling social and political tensions bloodlessly. The civil war that erupted with an army revolt on 17 July 1936 lasted until April 1939; it cost up to a million lives and at its end the Republic lay in ruins. General Franco's authoritarian regime ruthlessly repressed all independent workers'

---

[1] *TUC Congress Reports* (hereafter *TUC CR*), 1931, p. 232; 1932, p. 172. On 8 July 1931 the Labour Party NEC sent the following telegram to the Spanish socialist congress: 'The Spanish Revolution is a ray of light in these dark days of tyranny and oppression. The British workers are proud of the part played by the Labour and Socialist Movement in the Spanish people's great act of liberation. We are confident that the Spanish Socialist Party will be equally energetic in the maintenance of those free political institutions within which alone Socialist Democracy can flourish and develop' (*Labour Party Conference Reports*, hereafter *LPCR*, 1931, p. 43).

organisations, and Spain's socialists and trade unionists were scattered in exile to the corners of the earth.

It is not surprising that, in the light of such a disaster, the record of the British labour movement's response to the Civil War should be seen as a failure. Not only had it failed to force the British government to change its policy of Non-Intervention in the conflict, so injurious to the Republic, but it had even initially supported that policy. It had failed to mobilise its own resources in defence of Spanish democracy and spurned the offer of united action with other left-wing forces. Indeed, for the left 'Spain' became a metaphor for the inability of labour's leaders to confront political reality on all the crucial questions of the 1930s, just as 'Spain' also came to symbolise the inevitability of war between fascism and democracy. These feelings were reinforced when the same leaders, in government after 1945, failed miserably to take decisive action to foster the restoration of Spanish democracy. Such failure should, rightly, raise the question of whether it is worth studying the response of British labour at all? After all, a recent author has contrived to write a study of British government policy towards the Civil War in which the Labour Party and the trade unions figure hardly at all. She concludes by endorsing the verdict of the then French ambassador that the Labour Party appeared 'not much interested' in Spain,[2] the same picture of an ineffective and uninterested labour movement drawn by contemporary critics on the left.

And yet, what labour did, and did not do, about Spain is important. Its voice was taken seriously in Whitehall, and had it taken a strong line against Non-Intervention, especially in the crucial early months, the British government would have faced a most difficult task in implementing that policy. Hence the reason why it acted as it did is of more than antiquarian interest. Moreover, British labour played a decisive role in determining the response of the trade union and socialist internationals, and hence affected labour movements throughout Europe. Finally, even in failure, the institutions of the labour movement were still central to the reaction of the British working class to the Civil War: thus, an understanding of this subject opens a window into the nature, if not the soul,[3] of the labour movement in the 1930s.

This book is not intended as an apologia for labour's leaders. Indeed, as it points out, they made many mistakes and sometimes deliberately misled

[2] Jill Edwards, *The British Government and the Spanish Civil War, 1936–1939* (1979), p. 199.
[3] A consideration that troubled some of the participants during the debates over Spain: 'Mr Bromley said that what concerned him was that no one seemed to think about the soul of the British Movement' (TUC, Documents 1, Labour Movement Conference, 4 September 1936, verbatim report, p. 7).

their followers. However, no real attempt has yet been made to understand the Civil War from their perspective. The usual context for studying this subject has been one that portrays the Civil War as the 'last great cause', a radicalising force uniting intellectuals and workers which generated mass enthusiasm in Britain, and which the leaders resisted out of cowardice or stupidity. In this sense it is easy to see the response of the labour movement as a succession of missed opportunities – to unite with the rest of the left in overthrowing the government which sponsored Non-Intervention; to defeat fascism in Spain and thus to avert European war.

For the leaders this all looked very different. Spain was not an opportunity but a problem. It had the potential to undermine the structure of the labour movement and to force it off the course on which they had set it, by stimulating independent action by rank-and-file members. Moreover, the impact of the Civil War on the British working class was far more complex than has generally been accepted, and at no point was it fully united in support for the Spanish Republic. Indeed, the impact of the war, by emphasising the presence of a strong Catholic minority which acted as a storm-centre for opposition to the Spanish Republic within the working class, casts a different light on claims that the homogeneity of Britain's labour movement sets it apart from its continental counterparts. While never facing a situation such as that in Belgium and, to a lesser degree, France where the conflicting passions aroused by the Civil War ripped apart the socialist movements,[4] one of the minor, and unrecognised, achievements of British labour was to avert similar damage. Thus, when the debates from the 1936 TUC Congress on Non-Intervention were published under the title of *The Spanish Problem*, the title was more revealing than might have been realised. Until the end of the conflict the prime objective would be to prevent Spain from damaging the labour movement, instead of using the power of organised labour to support Spanish democracy.

This primacy of the defensive, institutional imperative is the context which previous historians have tended to ignore when assessing the impact of the Civil War on British labour. One of the first to study this subject at length was the late K.W. Watkins who presented a Britain divided by the conflict between 'right' and 'left', within which the left was in turn divided into its own 'left' and 'right'. Thus, Spain became 'the battlefield on which

---

[4] On Belgium see Adrian Poole, 'A Note on the Belgian Socialists and the Spanish Civil War' in Eric Cahm and Vladimir Claude Fisera (eds.), *Socialism and Nationalism in Contemporary Europe*, vol. 3, (Nottingham, 1980); on France see Nathanael Greene, *Crisis and Decline: The French Socialist Party in the Popular Front Era* (Ithaca, New York, 1969) pp. 167–84.

right and left contested for control of the Labour Movement'.[5] Such Manichean certainties do scant justice to the real complexities of the problem and are only discernable when one concentrates, as Watkins did, only on the published records of the set piece debates at the Labour Party and TUC conferences. In fact the definition of a 'right' and 'left' on purely political lines is of limited value, and at times positively unhelpful, when analysing the labour movement. However, both the main subsequent lines of interpretation have persisted with this idea of a central division within labour, positing either a responsible leadership and an irresponsible membership, or a near-traitorous leadership refusing to give a lead over Spain even though the rank and file were ready and waiting to follow.

One approach has been to treat the Civil War as the crucial episode in the conversion of the labour movement from the pacifism of the 1920s and early 1930s to support for rearmament against the growing danger of fascism. Because historians who follow this line of argument have tended to regard rearmament as both justifiable and essential for Britain's survival, the labour leaders emerge quite favourably from this treatment – sympathetic towards Spain while never losing sight of the more important domestic political issues. In the case of Ernest Bevin, for instance, Bullock argues that, while 'all Bevin's sympathies lay with the Republicans', he refused to succumb to the 'emotion' generated by Spain, and the Civil War merely reinforced his belief in 'the need for the Labour Party to face the issue of arms for Britain as well as Spain'.[6] This approach mimics the language of contemporary leaders (especially Hugh Dalton) who used the term 'emotion' to belittle rank-and-file members who, for quite rational reasons, opposed the policy which the leaders wished to impose on them.[7] Yet, in practice, it will be argued that the conversion to rearmament, while genuine, was often incidental to labour's response to the Civil War. The leadership was too concerned with short-term problems arising from the war's impact to make a priority of such high-minded objectives, however justifiable.

Conversely, the other main interpretation, dominant amongst recently

[5] K.W. Watkins, *Britain Divided: The Effect of the Spanish Civil War on British Political Opinion* (1963), p. 145.
[6] Alan Bullock, *The Life and Times of Ernest Bevin, Volume 1: Trade Union Leader, 1881–1940* (1960), pp. 586 and 588. The most sustained exposition of this argument is John F. Naylor, *Labour's International Policy – The Labour Party in the 1930s* (1969), especially chapter 6, 'For Spain and Rearmament'. However, Naylor later adopts a more Popular Frontist position when he criticises the Labour Party for not leading a Popular Front in 1939 when it could have relegated the Communist Party to 'a minor role, in which they could neither divert nor disgrace the movement' (p. 269).
[7] Hugh Dalton, *The Fateful Years; Memoirs 1931–1945* (1957), p. 100. Dalton wrote of the Labour Party's Edinburgh conference that 'a large number of the delegates were now wildly wallowing in sheer emotion, in vicarious valour'.

published material, takes seriously the preoccupations of ordinary workers and treats those of the leaders with marked scepticism. It views the impact of the Civil War through the perspective of the campaign for a British 'Popular Front' (a rallying of anti-government forces), and assumes that Popular Front activity was the only way to deliver practical support to Spain. According to this argument the Civil War gave rise to a mass movement of solidarity in Britain, that has been given the umbrella title of the 'Aid Spain movement', in which the Communist Party played the leading role. However, most labour leaders were opposed to helping Spain in any meaningful way due to their anti-communism and innate conservatism, and prevented the Aid Spain movement from developing into a genuine Popular Front. According to Jim Fyrth, and again to use Bevin as an example: 'Bevin's lack of enthusiasm... sprang not only from his lack of interest in the Spanish war, but also from his belief that the "left's" real interest in Spain was as a lever for moving the British Labour Movement towards a "People's Front" policy'.[8]

Yet this approach too is unsatisfactory. Inconvenient facts are omitted: for instance the very considerable role that the labour movement played in the care of Basque refugee children finds no place in these histories.[9] The effect is to conceal the fact that the labour movement did have its own, very concrete, policies for supporting the Spanish workers, even if these differed markedly from the Popular Front. Moreover, the emphasis on the Popular Front as an alternative pole of attraction to the labour movement exaggerates the importance of the Communist Party at this time. It is certainly true that, within the Labour Party and the trade union movement, the leaders and sections of the rank and file had very different perceptions of the Civil War and of how to respond to it. It does not follow, however, that the rank and file were the only ones capable of genuine internationalist action, nor that their activities were all subsumed by an amorphous and, in historical terms, elusive, Aid Spain movement.[10] And to understand why Spain caused so many problems for the leadership it is more instructive to look to the existing tensions within the labour movement rather than the counter-attractions of communist policy.

---

[8] Jim Fyrth, *The Signal was Spain: The Aid Spain Movement in Britain, 1936–39* (1986), p. 266. For a similar interpretation see Noreen Branson, *History of the Communist Party of Great Britain, 1927–1941* (1985), pp. 220–39.

[9] This point is made more fully in my article 'The Role of the British Labour Movement in the Origins and Work of the Basque Children's Committee, 1937–39', *European History Quarterly*, vol. 18, April 1988.

[10] See my forthcoming article in *History Workshop Journal*, (1990) 'Britain's Popular Front? Aid Spain and the British Labour Movement'.

The most illuminating work on this subject has been concentrated in regional studies. Hywel Francis has shown how, in industrial South Wales with an active and well-organised Communist Party and a highly politicised miners' trade union, the Popular Front could take an effective form around the question of Spanish Aid. Francis argues convincingly that a distinctive form of 'proletarian internationalism' existed in South Wales: witness the unusually high number of volunteers for the International Brigades from the Welsh valleys. However, beyond alluding to the long-standing inter-nationalist tradition in Wales, he does not develop his contention that South Wales miners lay 'beyond the mainstream of British labour history'[11] with an explanation of why they should have been so distinct, even though many other coalfields experienced the same extremes of political militancy and economic dislocation. This mystification of the Welsh miner is unhelpful for understanding labour responses in other, less militant, areas of the country. A more comprehensive approach is attempted in the other main regional study, Peter Drake's (sadly unpublished) thesis on the impact of the Civil War on the Birmingham and West Midlands labour movement, in which he presents an already declining and divided movement further troubled by the demands made by the Civil War and the competition from a much more active local Communist Party.[12]

This book follows on from this latter approach in its aims if not its conclusions. It assumes that the response of the Labour Party cannot be understood in isolation from its relations with the trade unions (and *vice versa*), but nor can either be fully understood in isolation from the broader concerns of the labour movement in the country. Thus, the 'labour movement', both in the specific sense of a form of political decision-making combining party and unions, and in the sense of a nation-wide organisation of the working class, forms the core of the study. In turn, this movement's response to the Civil War cannot be understood simply in terms of relations between unions and party, but has to be seen within a series of contexts including relations with the international labour movement; perceptions of what was occurring in Spain and contacts with Spanish socialists; opposition to the Spanish Republic within the British labour movement; and pressures for greater assistance from the left. Within this framework the objectives are twofold: firstly, to show the limitations of internationalism as a form of political action within the labour movement; secondly, to show the inability

---

[11] Hywel Francis, *Miners Against Fascism: Wales and the Spanish Civil War* (1984), p. 29.
[12] Peter Drake, 'Labour and Spain: British Labour's Response to the Spanish Civil War with particular reference to the Labour Movement in Birmingham', unpublished MLitt thesis, Birmingham University, 1977.

of the left to find an adequate strategy of opposition to official policy over Spain.

The 1930s mark a period of flux in the history of the labour movement. After the First World War the Labour Party had shot from relative obscurity to form two minority administrations and to replace the Liberals as the main alternative to the Conservatives, at the same time differentiating itself from its trade union sponsors. Yet the collapse of Ramsay MacDonald's second government in 1931 and his decision to form a 'National' government with Conservative support left the party decapitated and intellectually shattered, facing a decade of hesitant policy change in opposition. With the bitter passing of MacDonald and Snowden, and the subsequent death or retirement of other old guard leaders such as Henderson and Lansbury, the party had definitively cast itself off from its founders and was yet to define a new politics or discover a new set of hero figures. This vacuum was partially filled by the trade unions, already further advanced along the revisionist path than the Labour Party. Accordingly this was a decade in which the concept of the labour movement as two separate 'wings' defending the political and industrial interests of the working class, always problematic, became increasingly devalued as the trade union leaders decided that politics was simply too important to be left to a weakened Labour Party.[13]

The result was not simply a shift towards more pragmatic, social democratic, policies, but also the creation of more hierarchical forms of organisation which set up profound tensions throughout the movement. Thus, the labour movement of the 1930s presented a series of disjunctures – between how the leaders wanted the movement to behave and the form of political expression which the members themselves wanted to exercise; between the movement's continuing strength in the nation and its weakness in parliament; and between the radicalising potential of issues such as the fight against unemployment or fascism and the studied moderation of labour's official response. The reason for this lay primarily in the intersection of the transformation of trade unionism with the trauma of 1931 and its aftermath for the Labour Party.

Before 1914 the trade union movement had lacked strong central institutions and authority was divided between the TUC, the General Federation of Trade Unions (GFTU: an organisation for mutual financial

---

[13] Soon after the fall of the Labour government in 1931 Citrine was already making clear his modified view of party–union relations. 'The TUC did not seek in any shape or form to say what the Labour Party was to do, but they did ask that the primary purpose of the Labour Party should not be forgotten. It was created by the Trade Union Movement to do those things in Parliament which the Trade Unions found ineffectively performed by the two-party system' (V.L. Allen, *Trade Unions and the Government*, (1960), p. 258).

support founded in 1899) and local trades councils. However, the First World War profoundly affected trade unionism. For the first time the government was willing to seek the unions' co-operation in production; this in turn stimulated the growth of autonomous shop-floor organisation in the shop stewards' movement. Union membership and militancy both reached a peak in the immediate post-war years and this gave the unions a double incentive to devise a new structure for the exercise of authority, both to preserve the war-time gains from a government and business class which wanted to revert to pre-war conditions, and to protect their own authority from an assertive rank and file. In 1921 the 17-member TUC Parliamentary Committee was replaced by a 32-member General Council, annually elected from trades groups and endowed with powers of administration and co-ordination as well as research facilities. Although portrayed as a putative 'General Staff of Labour' to co-ordinate forthcoming industrial conflicts, the council's brief also included the resolution of inter-union disputes and the handling of relations with international bodies. Yet this centralisation was flawed from the outset by the unions' refusal to grant the General Council the right to interfere with their internal affairs. Hence, the power of the reformed TUC was essentially a confidence trick, ultimately dependent on the ability of individual TUC leaders to win respect.

The process of centralisation was facilitated by a burgeoning committee system – the Finance and General Purpose Committee, for instance, developed into an executive body where the TUC General Secretary met with an inner circle of General Council members. According to the original blueprint the General Council had also been expected to enjoy close links with the Labour Party through a National Joint Council of Labour and joint departments for publicity, research and international affairs. However, this arrangement appeared increasingly unsatisfactory to the unions and from March 1926 the departments were again separated. Reorganisation had not produced a more militant trade union centre, but rather a more efficient and bureaucratised system so that, according to V.L. Allen 'by 1927 the TUC had the making of a trade union bureaucracy akin to the Civil Service', in function if not in size.[14]

However, the fact that centralisation could be as effective a basis for moderation as for militancy was initially concealed by the advance of the left. After the formation of the Communist Party in 1920 the communist-led Minority Movements sought to organise militants from inside the unions, while the non-communist left was initially well represented on the General Council. This phase was abruptly ended by the General Strike in May 1926,

[14] V.L. Allen, *Sociology of Industrial Relations* (1971), p. 184.

when the General Council led a national strike in sympathy with the miners but soon backed down and left them to fight on alone. The strike was at once a peak of union solidarity and a turning point towards greater moderation. It clarified the relationship between unions and the state and finally buried all talk of 'direct action' (independent political action by the unions). In one sense this was a moderation imposed by government action – the 1927 Trades Disputes and Trades Unions Act outlawed any sympathetic industrial action which attempted to coerce the government by harming the public interest. As union leaders in the 1930s were all well aware, this would make sympathy action with Spanish workers just as illegal as action in sympathy with another union.[15]

However, moderation was not only imposed, but was also generated from within the movement, particularly through the influence of Walter Citrine and Ernest Bevin, the dominant figures of the new era. Citrine (1887–1983) had risen rapidly through the electricians' union, where he displayed a peculiar talent for office administration, and then moved to the TUC as Assistant General Secretary when the organisational changes created an opening for his managerial skills. He was precipitated into the General Secretaryship in 1925 at the tender age of 37 on the premature death of Fred Bramley. Although by his own terms not an intellectual,[16] Citrine was much more than the mere 'apparatchik', obsessed with filing cards,[17] that his reputation would suggest. Bureaucratisation was central to his vision of the British working class winning its rightful position in society through the strength of its institutions, something which could only be achieved by sound administration and centralised lines of command. In opposition to the left's representation of the General Strike as a betrayal by the General Council, Citrine fostered an alternative history in which the strike had forged a new *modus vivendi* between organised labour and the government. 1926, he claimed, had given even the most reactionary Conservatives ample evidence of the unions' continuing powers of resistance, and effectively drew a line around such gains as union recognition and collective bargaining. The

---

[15] See below, pp. 111 and 131. The 1927 Act also changed the conditions governing the trade unions' Political Funds, replacing 'contracting out' by individual members with 'contracting in', so that the number of trade unionists affiliated to the Labour Party fell dramatically in the 1930s. Further clauses restricted picketing and forced the Civil Service trade unions to disaffiliate from the TUC and international bodies.

[16] Lord Citrine, *Men and Work: The Autobiography of Lord Citrine* (1964), pp. 300–1.

[17] The term 'apparatchik' comes from Kenneth Morgan, *Labour People: Leaders and Lieutenants, Hardie to Kinnock* (Oxford, 1987); according to John Saville, Citrine was a 'super bureaucrat', 'May Day 1937' in J. Saville and A. Briggs (eds.), *Essays in Labour History 1918–39* (1977), p. 262. W.J. Brown, the Civil Service trade union leader, wrote that 'Citrine was the precise pedant, who always had the appropriate files and references handy, but who never on any account saw the wood for the trees', *So Far...* (1943), p. 131.

General Strike marked the unions' arrival as a respected force in British politics and it was their duty to use that position with responsibility.[18] Hence, the TUC's new course which Citrine championed after the General Strike implied the recognition of the capitalist system and the need for effective bargaining within it. Moreover, the unions had to be able to deal with governments of any party, and Citrine appealed for a strict separation of political and industrial responsibilities within the labour movement. In practice, however, in the changed conditions of the 1930s this did not prevent the unions from interfering almost at will in the party's sphere while jealousy guarding their own against left-wing calls for industrial action in support of political objectives.

Citrine's growing influence beyond the confines of the TUC was apparent when he played a major role in deciding the fate·of MacDonald's second government.[19] During the 1930s he became a powerful figure in both the Labour Party and the unions when, as a consummate committee politician, he was at the centre of all the decade's important debates. Yet Citrine's rise to prominence (and his close identification with controversial new policies) was not without personal cost, making him perhaps unduly sensitive to criticism even though, for instance, when he became one of the first trade union leaders to accept a knighthood, he had come to expect it.[20] This led him to treat even humorous criticism as an act of *lèse majesté*. He was disproportionately angered by a public comment by Ellen Wilkinson that, from her own experience, the Spanish workers were 'not cut to a pattern that would suit Sir Walter Citrine'[21] and demanded an apology. This tetchiness did little to win him friends in the movement, but perhaps reinforced the respect, and even fear, with which he was regarded, especially by those who confronted him in debate.

Bevin (1881–1951), by contrast, had earned his reputation as a tough negotiator and through his success in welding the disparate unions representing the dockers and other general workers into one of the most powerful organisation in the TUC. His Transport and General Workers' Union (T&GWU) was also a model of centralisation with little tolerance for local autonomies. He played a more formal role in Labour Party politics and reached the height of his power in the inter-war labour movement when his

---

[18] Lord Citrine, *Men and Work*, pp. 216–17.
[19] Ross McKibbin, 'The Economic Policy of the Second Labour Government', *Past and Present*, 68, 1975, pp. 118–20.
[20] Lord Citrine, *Men and Work*, chapter 19, pp. 310–22.
[21] BLPES, Citrine papers, III/2/2, 12 November and 27 November 1936, Citrine to Ellen Wilkinson; 25 November 1936 for her reply. Ellen Wilkinson was unrepentant: 'It does happen incidentally to be true. I cannot think of any Trade Unionists who would be less likely to conform to your desires than members of the C.N.T.'

year as Chairman of the General Council in 1936-7 coincided with Hugh Dalton's chairmanship of the Labour Party's National Executive Committee. Self-consciously working-class and often contemptuous of the middle-class intellectuals in the Labour Party, Bevin's often clumsy self-expression concealed a powerful intellect. His blustering rhetoric contrasted with Citrine's more forensic approach yet, despite an apparent lack of personal rapport,[22] their differing styles combined effectively in steering the trade union movement towards conciliation.

Thus, by the 1930s, the combination of strong leadership, well-researched briefs and the voting power of the large amalgamated unions left the General Council, and in particular Bevin and Citrine, almost unchallenged in directing the policy of the trade union movement. Their domination was both resented and admired. Even the critics who railed against their 'dictatorship' at Congress took pride in their achievements as genuine products of the working class, able to hold their own against middle-class socialists.[23] Such sentiment formed an important undercurrent in the debate on Non-Intervention at the 1936 TUC Congress, when delegate after delegate reported to his union that the sweet reason of Bevin and Citrine's speeches had swung a conference more affected by the 'emotion' of the moment.[24] Bevin had already softened up his audience by pointing out how privileged they were that they, as working men, could even be debating such weighty matters as foreign policy.[25] Thus, as with all forms of leadership, at the root of this 'dictatorship' lay a desire to be led. A new mystique of leadership was growing within the TUC according to which the members were supposed to yield readily to their more able, and better informed, superiors. Hugh Clegg has identified both the strengths and dangers inherent in this new style of leadership when he describes it as 'elitist': it 'emphasised negotiations and the skills of the negotiator'.[26] Yet, the trust placed in such a negotiator could easily be abused when not carefully monitored.

The logical concomitant of the new industrial policy was a more tightly controlled labour movement organisation, a trend towards centralisation that was occurring throughout the British left at this time.[27] The local trades

[22] Lord Citrine, *Men and Work*, pp. 238–40; BLPES Library, Dalton papers, Diary, 1/19, 11 May 1938, Citrine had commented that Bevin was 'more difficult than ever to do business with'.
[23] *AEU Monthly Journal*, October 1936; see also Ellen Wilkinson's article on 'The Secret of Citrine's Power over Congress', *Tribune*, 16 September 1938.
[24] See for instance, *Railway Service Journal* (RCA), October 1936; University of Warwick, Modern Records Centre (MRC), Mss 41/NUFW/4/1, National Union of Foundry Workers, *Quarterly Reports*, October 1936.   [25] *TUC CR*, 1936, p. 367.
[26] Hugh Armstrong Clegg, *A History of British Trade Unions Since 1889: Volume 2, 1911–1933* (Oxford, 1985), pp. 470–1.
[27] Raphael Samuel, 'Staying Power; The Lost World of British Communism, Part 2', *New Left Review*, 156, March/April 1986, p. 95.

councils, for instance, were subordinated to the TUC. Their collective voice was muffled in the TUC-dominated Joint Consultative Committee set up in 1926; their power to take independent political action (such as support for 'unofficial' hunger marches) was circumscribed; and the notorious 1934 TUC 'Black Circulars' required them, along with affiliated unions, to ban communist delegates.[28] Yet this control was far from complete. Shop-floor organisation was reviving in the early 1930s as distant trade union leaderships appeared unable to protect their members from 'speed ups' in production or cuts in wages and conditions, and a new generation of rank-and-file movements was emerging amongst engineering workers, railwaymen and London's busmen. The continuing struggle between the traditions of workplace organisational autonomy and the centralising tendency of the TUC and certain unions formed a distinct line of tension in the later 1930s.

Thus, mainstream trade unionism in the 1930s was essentially cautious and defensive. In many respects, however, this was a rationalisation of its straitened circumstances imposed by recession and mass unemployment after 1929. Strike activity was minimal and the level of the TUC affiliated union membership rose steadily but undramatically from a trough of 3,613,273 in 1931, to some 4 million in 1936, in contrast with the explosions of membership in France and the USA in the mid-1930s (although from much lower base lines). British trade unionism appeared somewhat complacent and even self-congratulatory at its achievements and unwilling to press for anything more than a better deal for those in work. The organisation of the unemployed, and even of those in new industries, was largely left to the Communist Party.[29]

The relative stability of leadership and policy in the trade unions after 1926 contrasted strongly with the experience of the Labour Party. The watershed was the debacle of 1931 which left Labour shorn of its best-known leaders and shaken by the government's failure adequately to confront the economic crisis. The party's virtual annihilation at the polls in October 1931 (when only fifty-two members were returned), only partially recouped in 1935 when 102 more seats were won, put an end to the conflicts that had dogged relations between the party and the unions in the 1920s. For the remainder of the decade the Labour Party was doomed to parliamentary insignificance and increased pressure from the unions. Indeed, the memory

[28] Alan Clinton, *The Trade Union Rank and File: Trades Councils in Britain 1900–40* (Manchester, 1977), pp. 152–3.
[29] On the unemployed see Richard Croucher, *We Refuse to Starve in Silence: A History of the National Unemployed Workers' Movement* (1987); on the new industries see Ross Whiting, *The View from Cowley: The Impact of Industrialization Upon Oxford, 1918–1939* (Oxford, 1983).

of 1931 gave the union leaders a clear edge in their dealings with the party – for instance, the initial confusion over how to respond to the Spanish Civil War drew instant comparisons with that earlier humiliation.[30]

A tangible example of this changed relationship was the revival in December 1931, on Bevin's initiative, of the National Joint Council (in 1934 renamed the National Council of Labour (NCL) as a policy co-ordinating body meeting on a regular basis), immediately prior to the party's National Executive Committee (NEC). Representation was weighted in favour of the General Council which sent its chairman and six other members, while the Parliamentary Labour Party (PLP) and the NEC each sent only their chairmen and two other members. The revival of the NCL was widely apprehended by Labour Party politicians as an extension of trade union power, and resented as such.[31] It compounded the existing influence of the unions on policy formation through their block votes at the Labour Party conference, based on affiliated membership, and their representation on the NEC. The NCL was, however, particularly significant because it removed policy discussion to a new tier that was above any direct intervention from members or constituent bodies.

Another legacy of 1931 was ferment on the left of the party with the disaffiliation of the Independent Labour Party (ILP), still a powerful force in its Glasgow strongholds, and the creation of the Socialist League as a left-wing ginger group within the party. The alleged extremism and the undeniable factionalism of the left increased Bevin's exasperation with the party – at the height of the debates over Spain in the summer of 1936 he would exclaim that: 'You couldn't afford Socialist Leagues if you are going to fight Fascism... The key thing was, could they as Trade Unionists go on any longer trying to keep in step with Political Labour? He didn't think they could'.[32] However, such outbursts also reflected the fact that the Labour Party could not be controlled as effectively as the unions. The trades councils could be shackled, communist fronts could be proscribed, but the grass roots organisation of the party in the divisions and constituencies retained a large measure of independence at a time of rapid growth in individual party membership. In 1937 the constituency parties won a significant concession by being allowed to select their own representatives on the NEC instead of their being elected by conference as a whole (and thus

---

[30] See Greenwood's comments at the 25 August 1936 NCL, TUC Documents 1, verbatim report, p. 45.

[31] See, for instance, Bernard Donoughue and G.W. Jones, *Herbert Morrison: Portrait of a Politician* (1973), p. 597, fn 35.

[32] TUC, Documents 1, NCL, verbatim report, 25 August 1936, p. 41.

by the unions).[33] The constituency parties would, like the rank-and-file movements in the unions, form a centre for opposition to official policy over Spain.

The party's parliamentary weakness, exacerbated by the absence of a formal 'Shadow Cabinet' which could have concentrated its powers of opposition,[34] and the often rebellious mood of the membership conspired to reduce the authority of the Labour leader. Clement Attlee (1883–1967), appointed leader as Lansbury's deputy in 1935 and confirmed in office after that year's General Election, was widely seen as a stopgap. His unassertive style of leadership, later an asset when in government, was taken as a sign of weakness: the General Council apparently dubbed him 'Clam' Attlee for his reticence on the NCL.[35] The jealousy with which he refused to divulge information that he had gleaned in confidential meetings with government ministers only served to annoy his NCL colleagues further.[36] Apart from some significant parliamentary interventions, Attlee's most lasting contribution to the Spanish Civil War was his visit to the International Brigades in 1937 which resulted in part of the British Battalion being renamed the 'Major Attlee Company'. Attlee was often unfavourably compared to two more charismatic figures within the party whose contributions to the debate on the Civil War were more striking; Hugh Dalton (1887–1962) and Herbert Morrison (1888–1965). Morrison enjoyed a power base in the London Labour Party which he had organised and led to victory in the London County Council (LCC) elections of 1934 and 1937. Although easy to typecast as a political 'boss', Morrison was also an intelligent and independently minded socialist, the only labour leader to oppose Non-Intervention from the outset.[37] His influence during the Civil War was, however, hampered by two factors, a perceived lack of facility in dealing with foreign affairs[38] (later to be cruelly exposed during his brief spell as

[33] Ben Pimlott, *Labour and the Left in the 1930s* (Cambridge, 1977), pp. 111ff.
[34] Instead, parliamentary spokesmen were appointed from the PLP's Parliamentary Committee composed of *ex officio* members and twelve MPs elected from the PLP.
[35] Lord Citrine, *Men and Work*, pp. 367–8.
[36] *LPCR*, 1936, p. 258; BLPES, Dalton Diary, 11 April 1938, p. 7.
[37] Morrison was understandably aggrieved when his speech at a Trafalgar Square rally for Spain in February 1939 was drowned out by cries of 'We want Cripps', following Stafford Cripps' recent expulsion from the Labour Party. Morrison pointed out to the *Daily Herald* journalist Hannen Swaffer that Cripps had refused to support his own principled opposition to Non-Intervention in August 1936, *Daily Herald*, 27 February 1939. See below p. 60.
[38] Hugh Dalton, *The Fateful Years*, p. 138. Dalton wrote that by 1937 Morrison was 'already a disappointment to me in foreign affairs and arms policy ... international affairs were for him a comparatively unknown field'. Donoughue and Jones write that Morrison's 'views on foreign affairs were superficial', *Herbert Morrison*, p. 249.

foreign minister) and poor relations with the unions, and in particular with Bevin.

Dalton did not share this problem – as chairman of the NEC 1936–7 he worked closely with Bevin in tackling the biggest source of friction between the union leaders and the Labour Party, the question of defence and rearmament. Partly as a consequence of the First World War there was still an ingrained pacifism in the party in the early 1930s. Labour MPs, for instance, habitually voted against the defence estimates. Labour's 1934 policy document *War and Peace* advocated war resistance if the British government were designated the aggressor. Similarly, the General Council was endowed with a standing order (number 8) which stipulated the recall of Congress should war threaten. While still paying lip service to the anti-war doctrines, however, a group of leaders, most notably Citrine, Bevin and Dalton, chipped away at the pacifist case and tried to swing the movement towards a greater realism (or pragmatism) and to support rearmament. At the 1935 Labour Party conference Bevin's brutal verbal assault on the then party leader, the venerable George Lansbury, succeeded in discrediting the strict pacifist case which he embodied. However, the left's case, that rearmament could not be entrusted to a reactionary National Government which could as equally use the weapons against the Soviet Union as in defence of democracy, continued to be widely supported and the party did not fully endorse rearmament until 1937. However, the union leaders' use of Labour's vacillations on defence as further proof of the party's unreliability was hypocritical – as late as 1938 the most obdurate resistance to rearmament came not from the Labour Party but from the skilled engineering unions who feared a recurrence of the wartime 'dilution' of their privileged status.

The exact nature of the relationship between the trade unions and the Labour Party in the 1930s has continued to excite debate amongst historians. At one extreme Henry Pelling had characterised Labour as 'The General Council's party', subservient to trade union influence on all important points of policy. After 1931 the General Council had 'abandoned its usual role of being the sheet-anchor of the party and instead moved in to take the helm'. In particular, it used the NCL to set the policy guidelines for the party's NEC to implement.[39] In challenging this view, however, Ben Pimlott has gone too far in asserting the primacy and independence of the party. For instance, he gravely underestimates the significance of the NCL, portraying it as secondary to the NEC and designed merely to give greater authority to

---

[39] Henry Pelling, *A Short History of the Labour Party* (1961), pp. 77 and 79.

party pronouncements rather than as a vehicle for trade union control.[40] Similarly, in his biography of Dalton he contrasts his subject's role in the rearmament debate favourably with that of Bevin: 'Bevin was an influential general secretary who could speak for a large section of trade union opinion. Dalton spoke for the Labour Party, even for the Movement as a whole'.[41] Within the strict parameters of this debate, this study tends towards Pelling's view. On the question of Non-Intervention, one of the most crucial political issues of the decade, policy was clearly decided within the NCL, and the dominant figures were the trade unionists Citrine and Bevin. However, it diverges from both arguments on two points; firstly, on the concept of the labour movement, and secondly, on the nature of trade union influence.

Very little attention has been paid by historians to the idea of the 'labour movement'[42] – it has been common to present it as a hollow conceptual shell within which the trade unions and the Labour Party compete for dominance. Yet it would be wrong to underestimate the degree to which both sides believed themselves to be partners in a larger movement that transcended their immediate membership. The unions were certainly loath to bludgeon the Labour Party into obedience and preferred to be seen to come to an agreement representative of 'the movement', even if only to legitimate their influence. It is significant that the unwieldy 'Labour Movement Conference', an irregular meeting of the General Council, NEC and the whole PLP on which the trade unions lacked formal control, was called in August 1936 to endorse the NCL's acceptance of Non-Intervention prior to the conferences of the TUC and the Labour Party – Citrine greeting the delegates with the comment that 'you are the most representative men in the movement'.[43] Thus the 'labour movement', enjoyed tangible existence in the 1930s as an, admittedly unequal, institutionalised form of joint decision-making. The movement also existed in the sense of a national organisation of the working class through a network of union branches, local Labour Parties, and the Co-operative movement, membership of which would often overlap. Despite its humiliation in October 1931 the Labour Party's vote held

[40] Ben Pimlott, *Labour and the Left*, pp. 19 and 111.
[41] Ben Pimlott, *Hugh Dalton* (1985), p. 247.
[42] Although there has been a spate of interesting interpretive studies in recent years, they have not greatly advanced the understanding of the particular question of the relationship between unions and party, either nationally or locally. See, for instance, John Saville, *The Labour Movement in Britain: A Commentary* (1988); James Hinton, *Labour and Socialism. A History of the British Labour Movement, 1867–1974* (Brighton, 1983).
[43] TUC, Documents 1, 28 August 1936, Labour Movement Conference, verbatim report, p. 23.

up surprisingly well and its 6 million voters represented an absolute bedrock of support. By 1935 the 1929 figure of over 8 million had been regained.

It was this very gap between the numerical presence of the movement in the nation and its under-representation in Parliament that constituted the main source of the unions' influence over the party. There was certainly more involved than their block votes alone. Labour Party conferences were highly volatile and, as the debate on Non-Intervention demonstrated in October 1936, the victories won by block votes were worthless if delegates immediately changed their minds. At root the influence was psychological. It was inherent in the contrast between a strong union leadership sure of its own base of support and a party leadership dependent on the unions to overawe its own members; between a party treated with contempt by government and a trade union movement which the National Government recognised as the voice of responsible labour.[44] The imbalance in the relationship would only be fully corrected with the election of Labour's first majority government in 1945. Yet this union representation was fraught with dangers. For the union leaders brought with them the ingrained caution and defensive instincts of British trade unionism, backed up by their understanding of a mass membership that was often apathetic about politics, was possibly not socialist, and was certainly anti-extremist. The decision to accept Non-Intervention that caused such grief to a 'socialist humanist' such as French premier Léon Blum would come quite happily to Britain's trade union leaders.

The same processes that were transforming the inter-war labour movement also created a tension between the three distinct conceptions of labour internationalism as, firstly, a set of ideals, secondly, a tool of practical action, and, thirdly, a radicalising force within labour politics. It is widely agreed that in the absence of an indigenous British socialist internationalism, a hybrid ideology had emerged that was a compound of the radical tradition of Cobden and Bright and the Liberal ideas transfused into the Labour Party when many prominent Liberals joined after the First World War. Ramsay McDonald and the dissident Liberals came from the same progressivist stable and had worked closely during the war in the Union of Democratic Control. This marked the Labour Party's post-1918 internationalism, practised in government by MacDonald and Henderson, as pacific and idealist: belief in the rule of international law, the League of Nations and anti-imperialism co-existed, often uneasily, with varying degrees of support for the Soviet Union in the aftermath of the 1917

[44] Ross Martin, *TUC – Growth of a Pressure Group, 1868–1975* (Oxford, 1980), p. 240.

revolution.[45] Thus the radical tradition formed a common set of references in international policy, even though their meaning had perhaps become somewhat blurred – in September 1936 Bevin was to invoke the names of Bright and Campbell-Bannerman in support of Non-Intervention.[46]

However, although these internationalist ideals were carried forward into the 1930s, notably by politicians such as Philip Noel-Baker, their immediate value was increasingly questioned at a time when fascism was openly flouting international law, when the League was exposed as a paper tiger by Italian aggression in Abyssinia, and when belief in pacifism was yielding to an acceptance of 'necessary murder' in self-defence.[47] In this context the second strand of labour internationalism, the structuring of international relations between labour movements, came strongly to the fore. Hence, if the internationalist world view broadly conditioned the way in which labour's leaders looked at the Spanish problem, it was the structures of internationalism, which would provide a framework for their response.

The third, more politicised, form of internationalism had flickered briefly in the immediate post-war years of labour militancy. In 1920 the Labour Party and the TUC joined in sponsoring a Council of Action which threatened Lloyd George's government with a General Strike if it should intervene militarily on Poland's side in the Russo-Polish war. Despite subsequent revision by historians who point out that the Council was motivated more by anti-war than pro-Soviet sentiment, it is clear that it involved the unparalleled encroachment of the trade unions into the political arena, and for the labour movement as a whole entailed extra-parliamentary action of considerable novelty. The local councils of action survived to play an organising role in the General Strike.[48] Subsequently these events, symbolised in the name of the ship the 'Jolly George', the blacking of which by dockers had initiated the action, were to inspire militants calling for more aggressive action to help Spain. However, comparisons between 1920 and

---

[45] For example, see Michael Gordon, *Conflict and Consensus in Labour's Foreign Policy, 1914–1965* (Stanford, 1969), pp. 13–19.

[46] TUC CR, 1936, p. 369: 'I know that in the American civil war conflicts raged in this country as to the claims of the North and the South, but I will never forget, notwithstanding the appeal to Lancashire which was then suffering due to that war, the voice of the old Radical John Bright rang out on that occasion, and I claim that this Movement is the inheritor of the best Radical tradition on these issues... We are maintaining the spirit that Bannerman would have maintained had he been in office, and we are standing out as he stood out as the last of the Radicals in the case both of South Africa and Russia.'

[47] The phrase used by W.H. Auden in 'Spain', first published 1937, and notoriously later changed to the 'fact of murder'.

[48] L.J. Macfarlane, 'Hands off Russia – British Labour and the Russo-Polish War, 1920', *Past and Present*, 38, December 1967; S. White, 'Labour's Council of Action, 1920', *Journal of Contemporary History*, vol. 9, no. 4, October 1974, pp. 112–14.

1936 were cruelly deceptive – if anything a better guide to the labour movement's response to Spain was its reaction to the 1913 Dublin lock-out when financial aid was deliberately preferred to industrial solidarity action. On both occasions moderate union leaders were alive to the danger that a sympathy strike could be used 'not just as a tactic to secure traditional trade union demands, but as a tactic to pose revolutionary ones'.[49]

Just as the labour movement rapidly put the aberration of the Council of Action behind it, its internationalism also became more bureaucratised and limited itself to the task of organising bodies of workers around specific objectives across national boundaries. This left an unresolved tension between the means of internationalism as a simple mechanism for structuring relations between the representatives of workers, and its ends as a (potentially revolutionary) force for the mobilisation of workers through solidarity action. Moreover, the idea of solidarity with all workers clashed with the practice of solidarity with a specific group of them. This practice created peculiar problems for the British because by the 1930s Britain was almost unique in Europe in possessing essentially hegemonic 'centres' of trade union and political organisation at a time when workers' organisation in most European countries was divided on religious or political lines. The frequent identification of the Spanish socialist party and its trade union centre as the Spanish 'Labour Party' and 'TUC' was inevitably misleading to British workers, and concealed the fact they only represented sections of the Spanish working class. Hence, during the Spanish Civil War the NCL's 'Spanish Workers' Fund' was directed not at all Spanish workers, as its title suggested, but at that particular section of Spain's working class who happened to be members of its sister organisations. Similarly, the institutions of the labour movement would view their prime political commitment as being towards these organisations rather than to the Spanish Republic or to the Spanish people as a whole.

Both the wings of British labour came comparatively late to formal involvement in international structures. Although the ILP and the Marxist Social Democratic Federation had been members of the Second International (founded in 1889) since 1904, the Labour Party did not apply to join until 1907, and its affiliation was delayed for a year by continental parties perplexed at Labour's lack of socialist doctrine. When the Labour Party did join it accepted the Second International's doomed policy of war resistance, although continuing to dissent on major points of socialist theory such as the necessity of class struggle. The first sustained effort at trade union

---

[49] See W. Moran, 'The Dublin Lockout – 1913', *Bulletin of the Society for the Study of Labour History*, 27, Autumn 1973, p. 15.

organisation began in 1901 in Copenhagen, and until 1913 there were regular meetings of the leaders of national trade union centres. Discussion was strictly limited to trade union matters, to the chagrin of the French who wanted to raise political questions such as anti-militarism and the revolutionary General Strike. Until 1913, however, the British representative was the Secretary of the GFTU. In 1913 the International was renamed the International Federation of Trade Unions (IFTU) and the TUC was represented for the first time, although not finally displacing the GFTU as the single recognised British centre until 1920.[50]

Almost immediately the system was ruptured, internationally by the outbreak of the First World War and internally by the Russian Revolution and the formation of rival communist parties and trade union centres affiliated to the Moscow-based Third International (the Comintern). Although the IFTU was revived in 1919, having moved from Berlin to Amsterdam, socialist internationalism was not resumed until 1923 when a new organisation, the Labour and Socialist International (LSI), was created. However, although British labour had been instrumental in the revival of the Internationals, its behaviour in the early post-war years at times seemed designed to undermine them. The establishment in 1924 of an Anglo-Russian Joint Advisory Committee linking the TUC and the Russian unions, not officially wound up until 1927, placed great strain on British relations with the IFTU.[51] The ILP, meanwhile, had briefly supported the Vienna Union (or 'Two and a Half International') which sought to find a middle way between the undemocratic Comintern and the allegedly class collaborationist Amsterdam International.

The vulnerability with which international labour emerged into the post-war world, challenged to the left by communism and to the right by fascism and by authoritarian regimes, gave it the peculiar characteristics – defensive, anti-communist and bureaucratic – which were later apparent in its response to the Spanish Civil War. Internationalism took the form of limited exchanges between national centres with the effect of making these relations both highly personalised and formalistic.[52] Accordingly the British TUC was linked by the IFTU to centres such as the French CGT and the Spanish

---

[50] John Price, *The International Labour Movement* (Royal Institute of Historical Affairs, 1945); Marjorie Nicholson, *The TUC Overseas: The Roots of Policy* (1986), chapter 2; Alice Prochaska, *History of the General Federation of Trade Unions, 1899–1980* (1982), pp. 150–7.

[51] This subject is extensively treated in Daniel Calhoun, *The United Front – The TUC and the Russians, 1923–1928* (Cambridge, 1976).

[52] For instance, when the 1937 TUC Congress received a telegram of solidarity from the anarchist CNT trade union centre, Citrine had to return the compliment through the UGT centre (TUC, Correspondence 2, 9 September 1937, Citrine to Caballero).

UGT; similarly the Labour Party was linked by the LSI with the SFIO and PSOE. In direct contrast to the Comintern, the IFTU and LSI had no formal control over their affiliates, and the autonomy of the national centres was guaranteed by their rules. For the trade unions there was a further tier of organisation, the Trade Secretariats which linked nationally-grouped unions by sectional interest. The most powerful of these, the International Transport Workers' Federation (ITF), numbered some of the most influential British unions amongst its affiliates.

By the 1930s labour internationalism had become bureaucratised to the extent that careers could be made in it. Although the majority of these career internationalists were continentals (especially Belgians), there were some Britons among their ranks. John Price, for instance, who returned to Britain in 1937 as Secretary of the T&GWU Political and Research Department, had worked for the LSI as its 'English Correspondent' from 1929 and ran its office for six years. In 1934 he organised relief work in Austria and in 1936 was sent to Spain as part of the LSI/IFTU delegation to set up the relief committee there.[53]

Yet, although it aspired to international horizons, and despite the affiliation of trade union centres in countries as diverse as Argentina and India, the world of international labour was still primarily a north European and Scandinavian club. Moreover, as the 1930s progressed the voices of French and, in particular, British labour became decisive. The LSI was increasingly filled with exiled political parties fleeing both fascist and communist repression; there was a similar imbalance in the IFTU with the Russians excluded, the Americans holding aloof and the German, Italian and Austrian, movements crushed. Significantly, the Spanish were never quite accepted into the club which, indeed, they had never paid much attention to in the past. As the Secretary of the ITF, Edo Fimmen, put it in 1937:

> God knows I am whole-heartedly with the Spanish people in their fight against Fascism, and I wish them all God's blessings, provided that I am free to curse them roundly every day from early morn to dewy eve for their God damned lack of energy, responsibility and other qualities which we of the Nordic race possess.[54]

Thus, an understanding of the internationalism of the British labour leaders requires an appreciation of the structures of inter-war internationalism, and in particular of the dominant role of the trade unions

---

[53] TUC International Committee minutes, 12 November 1930; *The Record* (T&GWU), August 1937.
[54] MRC, ITF records, 159/3/c/6/13, 20 October 1937, Fimmen to Henson.

within that structure. Whatever his shortcomings as an internationalist, Citrine was later to recall that 'I was perhaps more internationally minded than most people, as a consequence of my connections...'[55] Indeed, at the time of the Spanish Civil War Citrine was by far the most prominent British figure in the international labour movement, having been President of the IFTU since 1928 – long before the current leaders of the Labour Party had risen to prominence. He was well travelled, having most recently visited the Soviet Union,[56] and was personally well acquainted with all the leading figures in the international movement. This made him a natural channel for information and influence during the Civil War, not least because by the later 1930s the TUC was (by default) the dominant body within the IFTU with a virtual right of veto. By contrast, Bevin was by no means so involved in this system, as his international contacts centred on the International Labour Organisation at Geneva and the ITF. Citrine had made himself both personally and institutionally central to the world of international labour in a way that none of the other labour leaders even attempted to emulate.

Therefore, the structural function of official British labour internationalism was clearly preponderant over any overtly political function: it was not designed to involve, let alone to mobilise, rank-and-file members. The only point at which the international structures coincided with the mass of members was the fleeting appearances of fraternal delegates at conferences. In particular, this was an internationalism which defined itself against its rivals – most notably the Comintern and the Profintern (the communist trade union international). Hence, at the time of the Civil War two systems of internationalism, strangely similar in their lack of democratic accountability, were competing for influence in Spain.

This conception of internationalism differs considerably from that described by Hywel Francis in his studies of the response of the South Wales miners to the Spanish Civil War. Placing their response in the context of broader Welsh internationalist traditions he argues that the miners' internationalism was not an artificial phenomenon stimulated from above, but rather 'a re-emergence of class politics, centred on foreign affairs and thus expressing itself in feelings of international class solidarity'.[57] For this group at least internationalism was able to serve a politicising function and, hence, its response was out of harmony with the broader institutional structure within which it was located. Yet this disharmony was by no means restricted to South Wales. Indeed, it could be argued that the great mass of

[55] Lord Citrine, *Two Careers – A Second Volume of Autobiography* (1967), p. 35.
[56] This resulted in Citrine's *I Search For Truth in the USSR* (1936).
[57] Hywel Francis, 'Welsh Miners and the Spanish Civil War', *Journal of Contemporary History*, vol. 5, no. 3, 1970, p. 177.

the labour rank and file had no real understanding of the internationalist structure which ostensibly represented them: nor was any effort made to clarify the situation. Much of the leadership's power during the Spanish Civil War stemmed precisely from this gap, so that internationalism became a form of mumbo-jumbo, intelligible only to the initiated. The rare successes of the discontented members came when they were able to demystify this structure and assert their own interests.

This demonstrates the proposition that will be argued below that there was no single form of internationalism within the labour movement. There was a nice contrast between the shop worker's branch secretary who argued that campaigning for Spain would bring the union to the notice of many unorganised workers who 'had never thought it "did anything" before',[58] and the union leader who recommended that his union should support a rally for Spain as an opportunity for some of the union's younger members to develop their talent for public speaking.[59] In fact, just as one might distinguish between the central bureaucracy, the individual unions and the rank and file when analysing the trade unionism of the 1930s, or between the leadership and the constituencies in the Labour Party, similarly these separate layers of organisation had their own forms of internationalism. Often these different internationalisms would clash, in which case bureaucratic instincts generally triumphed over political ones.

It is perhaps inevitable that the Spanish Civil War should be seen as a conflict between fascism and democracy because the importance of foreign intervention and its strategic position as a curtain-raiser to the Second World War allows of no other simple construction. Yet since the Civil War historians have increasingly emphasised the indigenous origins of the conflict and sought to push them back into Spanish history.[60] Hence, 'democracy' and 'fascism' come to appear as labels of convenience rather than as genuine tools of analysis. This distinction is important to this study because the argument over whether the Spanish conflict was *sui generis* or part of a wider fascist challenge lies at the root of the differing responses to the Civil War between the labour leaders and their critics.

Spain had entered the twentieth century as a marginal European nation, humbled by defeat in war with the USA and the loss of the last significant remnants of its empire, yet strangely detached from the rest of the continent.

[58] *The Shop Assistant*, (NAUSA), 19 September 1936.
[59] General, Municipal, Boilermakers' and Allied Trades' Union archives, NUGMW NEC minutes, 29 July 1937.
[60] Gerald Brenan's *The Spanish Labyrinth: An Account of the Social and Political Background of the Spanish Civil War* (Cambridge, 1943), will continue to be regarded as a landmark in this respect.

During the first decades of the new century, when the rest of Europe was absorbed in the struggles of the Great Powers, the Spanish army was blooding its future generals in a bitter colonial war in Morocco. A monarchy ruled by the house of Bourbon, restored after the brief First Republic of 1873–4, Spain possessed a weak parliamentary system dominated in the areas of large estates by corrupt *caciquismo* (rule by political bosses). Government was based on the alternation in power of almost indistinguishable parties to little discernible effect. Social and political power were marked by massive inequalities, especially on the land, and the forces of reaction were usually supported by the two most important and enduring institutions – the army and the church. These conditions gave rise to a radical critique of Spanish society which recognised the need for the overhaul of Spain's institutions and enjoyed support not only from the working class but also from middle-class liberals. In 1931 it was hoped that the aspiration for radical, but peaceful, change could be embodied in the Second Republic: however, entrenched resistance from the old order and divisions on the left conspired to prevent this.

Beyond the liberal left was the Spanish working class, historically divided between the two great mass movements of anarchism and socialism. Anarchism, a movement committed to the establishment of libertarian communism, bitterly opposed not only the state and institutions identified with the ruling class (such as the church and the army) but all forms of political compromise, amongst which it numbered parliamentary politics. Its main strongholds were amongst the agricultural workers in the south, where it had become established in the later nineteenth century, and amongst the working class of Catalonia. Here a distinctive Anarcho-syndicalism (revolutionary trade unionism) found expression in the National Confederation of Labour (CNT) established in 1910. Anarchism, however, suffered from internal divisions during the 1920s and early 1930s between those who saw the CNT as a semi-respectable organisation of labour which should be willing to work within the existing system, and those who argued that the anarchist movement should stay true to its revolutionary beliefs. The FAI (Iberian Anarchist Federation) was founded in 1927 to achieve this latter goal, and continued to represent the clandestine and violent *demi-monde* of anarchist leaders such as Durutti who were to play a crucial role in the early period of the Civil War.[61]

Spanish socialism can be traced back to 1879 with the foundation by Pablo Iglesias of the Socialist Workers' Party (PSOE) and, subsequently, of

[61] These tensions are detailed in John Brademas, *Anarcosindicalismo y revolución en España, 1930–1937* (Barcelona, 1974).

its trade union centre, the General Workers' Union (UGT), the historic rival of the CNT. The socialists were strongest in Madrid and in the big industrial cities of the north. Although an avowedly Marxist party the PSOE, unlike the anarchists, generally followed a parliamentary path with some success. However, lack of definition over ideology and tactics were to haunt the socialists until the Civil War and after.[62]

Spain had remained neutral during the First World War and prospered economically – hence the post-war depression hit the country very harshly. The Spanish workers fought back, inspired by the example of the Russian revolution, in a period known as the *trienio bolchevique*. As in other European countries, the socialist movement divided at this point over support for the Second or Third Internationals, although the resultant Spanish Communist party (PCE) was a sickly organisation lacking in political significance. Increasingly subservient to the Comintern and repeatedly purged of its leaders, the PCE was unable to pose a serious challenge to the dominant working-class organisations until thrust into prominence by the Civil War. Social conflict was particularly intense in Barcelona in the years 1919–21, where assassinations by anarchist gunmen or their rivals became commonplace. The military pacification of Catalonia was followed by the *coup d'état* of General Primo de Rivera. Primo's regime offers an interesting insight into the development of Spanish socialism because, although a military dictator, he possessed a vision of a corporatist Spain which the leader of the UGT, the opportunist Largo Caballero, was willing to exploit if it could further his struggle against the anarchist CNT. Thus, while the CNT was ruthlessly repressed, the UGT gained representation on *comités paritarios* that arbitrated wage claims. However, not for the last time Caballero's actions opened a breach with his great socialist rival Indalecio Prieto who felt that the PSOE should have no truck with the dictator and should aim for the revival of liberal democracy.

However, Primo's regime proved unable to resolve the conflicting demands of capital and labour and he was toppled from power in January 1930. The monarchy, which had supported him, was discredited in his fall and the municipal elections of 1931 resulted in the bloodless creation of the second Spanish Republic. Although also tainted by collaboration with Primo, Caballero's socialists were a major force in the new regime, and his appointment as Minister of Labour in the first Republican government allowed him to continue to bolster the UGT's position. The new government

[62] See Paul Heywood, 'Marxism and the Failure of Organised Socialism in Spain', unpublished PhD thesis, LSE, 1988, and 'De las dificultades para ser marxista: el PSOE, 1879–1921', *Sistema*, 74, September 1986, by the same author.

pushed ahead with a programme of reforms which were particularly concerned with redressing the imbalance of power on the land. By 1933, however, it was seriously divided and had lost popular support (not least following the brutal repression of some rural anarchist risings) and, after a heavy electoral defeat, gave way to a government of the centre-right under the Radical Lerroux.

Already, however, the Republic was crystallising the bitter divisions within Spain. Projected land reform, although pursued with little zest, antagonised the powerful landowners and inspired the labourers to act on their own through land seizures. The attempts to reform education and to reduce the power of the church impelled the Catholic hierarchy to deny legitimacy to the Republic. Although this had little impact in areas where religion was weak or almost extinct, in areas of strong religious observance, such as the heartlands of Castile, religion was a vital component of the right's mobilisation against the Republic.[63] This was especially the case in Navarre where Carlism, a heady combination of religious and monarchist traditionalism, provided a ready-primed weapon against the Republic. A further area of contention was the aspiration of certain Spanish regions for self-government. Already Catalonia had been granted its own Generalitat, and the Basque country was also keen to revive its medieval *fueros*. To the army, however, this appeared to threaten the territorial integrity of Spain of which it felt itself to be the ultimate guardian.

The creation of Lerroux's government contributed to these tensions, particularly because the left viewed with suspicion and fear the growing role of a relatively new political force, the CEDA movement led by the charismatic young lawyer Gil Robles, which sustained his minority government in power. The CEDA, which was rooted in Catholic social organisations, successfully tapped the disarray of the right in the aftermath of the fall of the monarchy, by mobilising its disparate forces in opposition to the Republic. There is perhaps little reason to dub the CEDA fascist; indeed, it soon became clear that Gil Robles had no real strategy for seizing power, and there were many more overtly fascist organisations on the fringes of politics. Even so, it is understandable that the left should have been alarmed by the CEDA's well stage-managed mass meetings, its thuggish youth movement and Gil Robles' dictatorial style as *Jefe*; all this at a time when Hitler had recently come to power and when Austrian clerical fascism, which the CEDA closely resembled, had smashed the

---

[63] See Frances Lannon, 'The Church's Crusade Against the Republic' in Paul Preston (ed.), *Revolution and War in Spain, 1931–1939* (1984). See also Mary Vincent's forthcoming thesis on politics and the Catholic church in the Salamanca region during the 1930s, St Antony's College, Oxford.

Austrian socialists. By 1934 neither right nor left in Spain had any respect for the other's democratic credentials, a polarity that has carried into the subsequent historical debate.[64] Thus, the entry of three CEDA deputies into government in September 1934 touched off an insurrectionary general strike led by the socialists. The 'October revolution' would have been a total fiasco, however, had not the miners of Asturias, organised in a united front of communists, socialists and anarchists, achieved a degree of local success and held out for some weeks until succumbing to massive military repression.

The October rising presented the Spanish right with an opportunity which it failed to take. With the working class temporarily cowed, the right allowed itself to squabble over how to punish the socialist leaders, while Lerroux's Radical party became discredited by financial scandal. Yet, the harsh repression after 1934 had given all the forces on the left the incentive to unite, even if only to secure the release of imprisoned comrades and restore regional self-government. Thus, the socialists joined in a *Frente Popular*, or electoral pact, with the communists and middle-class Republican parties in late 1935, and triumphed over a divided right in the election of February 1936. Even the anarchists agreed to recommend that their followers break with tradition and vote.

However, the victory of the Frente Popular solved little, not least because in the aftermath of the 1934 rising the socialist movement had undergone a major transformation. Largo Caballero, whose role in the October revolt had been inglorious, embarked on a process of 'bolshevisation' egged on by the communists and earning him the inappropriate soubriquet 'The Spanish Lenin'. This left-turn widened the gap between him and his moderate rival Prieto, who favoured working with the Republican parties. Paradoxically, Caballero's revolutionist rhetoric, which did much to deter international support, concealed a pragmatic and opportunist trade union leader. However, his almost millenarian zeal at this time brought him little long-term benefit, and allowed the communists to win control over those parts of the socialist movement which were willing to form a united front, namely the socialist youth and the Catalan socialists, both of whom formed joint organisations.

Under Caballero's pressure the socialists remained aloof from the new government which was drawn entirely from the Republican parties, and prepared for a purely working-class seizure of power. In the months before July 1936 there was a steady increase in political tension with land seizures,

---

[64] See the debate between Richard Robinson, *The Origins of Franco's Spain: The Right, the Republic and Revolution 1931–1936* (Newton Abbot, 1970) and Paul Preston, *The Coming of the Spanish Civil War: Reform, Reaction and Revolution in the Second Republic*, (1978).

strikes and assassinations. Disillusioned with the failure of the CEDA's essentially electoral tactics the right began to look either to the fascist Falange party, led by Primo de Rivera's son José Antonio, or to the army to intercede and restore order. After months of plotting a clear, if unplanned, signal for sections of the army and their civilian supporters to rise in revolt came on 17 July 1936 when the Monarchist leader Calvo Sotelo was slain in revenge for the assassination of a captain of the loyalist Assault Guards.

The attempted *coup d'état* achieved only patchy success and in many parts of Spain resistance by armed workers merged almost imperceptibly into a social revolution. This was particularly evident in Barcelona where the support of the anarchists was vital to the crushing of the military revolt, yet left real power in their hands, alongside the anti-Stalinist POUM party (Workers' Party of Marxist Unity). In the aftermath, columns of anarchist militia fanned out into the hinterland of Catalonia and Aragon, securing the countryside and imposing collectivisation where the villagers had not already done so. The revolt was also successfully resisted in Madrid, in central and eastern Spain and much of Andalusia. The other Republican stronghold was in the north where the Basques, although dominated by the Catholic and conservative Basque Nationalist Party, saw the chance to assert regional independence within the Republic. Cantabria and most of Asturias also resisted the rising. The army received widespread support in areas such as Navarre, Castile and Galicia, and these served as bridgeheads until the army of Africa (including the Foreign Legion and many Moroccan troops) under Francisco Franco had crossed over to the mainland and begun its seemingly inexorable advance on Madrid, stopping to slaughter the defenders of Badajoz on 14 August.

The essential characteristic of the early stages of the conflict was its utter confusion and savagery. Throughout the country old scores were settled and many were massacred on both sides. Life became very cheap. In the rebel areas people were killed for possession of a union card or support for the Popular Front: in the Republican areas for their wealth, membership of the *guardia civil*, or any association with the Catholic church. Although there was a degree of symmetry in the bestiality of the conflict, this last point outweighed all the others. The massacre of priests and nuns, and the burning of churches, horrified foreign opinion and sowed dissent even amongst potential supporters of the Republic. Moreover, it presented Franco's apologists with a *post hoc* justification for the rebellion as they claimed that they were merely forestalling a bloody and atheistic communist revolt.

The central government in Madrid was shorn of authority, and there was a rapid succession of prime ministers. José Giral held the office of premier for a month, but his position was undermined by a series of military defeats and the Republic's international isolation under the system of 'Non-Intervention'.[65] In the first week of September the socialists decided to enter the government with Largo Caballero becoming prime minister, and the six new socialist ministers were joined by two communists. However, Caballero appeared unable to stem the tide. Attention was centred on the Alcázar of Toledo where a small force of rebels held out against heavy odds until relieved by Franco's forces on 26 September 1936. The Republican disaster was compounded by the loss of the Toledo munitions factories. As Franco's forces bore down on Madrid in the autumn of 1936 an early end to the war appeared imminent.

The Civil War inevitably constituted a crisis for inter-war labour internationalism. The rise of fascism threatened the annihilation of all forms of self-organised labour, yet the system of internationalism was just as unsuited for fighting fascism as its predecessor had been powerless to prevent war in 1914. Indeed, the only reason that it was able to cope with the previous crises of the 1930s was because the Nazi victory in Germany in 1933 and the defeat of the workers' movements in Austria and Spain in 1934, was sudden and decisive. Thus, the immediate response entailed fund-raising and relief work for the victims of fascism, in practice the only form of response of which it was capable. To this end the Matteoti fund (from 1934 known as the International Solidarity Fund) was established by the LSI and IFTU. Yet in Spain between 1936 and 1939 the problem was of a quite different magnitude. The Spanish Republicans were not hapless victims but were engaged in bitter war against a better armed and disciplined enemy. Moreover, the PSOE and UGT were, from September 1936, the pivot of the Republican government. Suddenly there was no limit to the amount or type of relief that could be supplied, especially as the large amounts of military equipment supplied by international communism threatened to undermine the influence of the IFTU and LSI in Spain. How could the Internationals hope to compete with the communist support, and should they commit themselves to support the Republic in general or simply their own affiliates in Spain?

Time and again it was the leaders of British labour, and especially of the trade unions, who spoke out in favour of more limited action and against broadening the scope of solidarity by means, for instance, of opposing Non-Intervention more aggressively or co-operating with the Comintern. In fact they never envisaged solidarity with Spain in any terms other than humanitarian relief for their Spanish colleagues on an almost charitable

[65] See chapter 1 below, pp. 37–72.

basis. As Bevin put it in March 1937: 'nobody in the world could do more than what the TUC was doing *on humanitarian grounds* in that terrible catastrophe'.[66] Underlying such attitudes was a belief that the Civil War was simply that: a faction fight in a backward and feudal society which could have little relevance to Britain and which distracted attention from the real threat of a resurgent Germany. Thus, the Civil War had merely exposed Spain as an innately violent and undemocratic society. A confidential memorandum produced for the TUC in August 1936 argued that Spain was 'oscillating between the Anarchists and military government'. It concluded that should the rebels win there would be 'an authoritative [*sic*] regime, but not like that of Germany, deifying the state'.[67] Indeed, in these circles Spain was often seen as a terrible example of the conflictual social relations which Britain had managed to avoid through its democratic institutions and strong trade unionism. Thus, at the root of labour's insularity was the feeling that in a very real sense the Spanish conflict 'couldn't happen here'.[68]

In this respect the Spanish working class was paying the price for its cultural and political isolation. This was, of course, partly due to British ignorance of Spain. There were occasional examples of British proletarian solidarity with Spain prior to the 1930s. The Sheffield socialist Bert Ward, for instance, had corresponded with the famed anarchist and educationalist Francisco Ferrer, and in 1909 campaigned against his judicial murder. In 1934 he offered his services as a translator to the TUC.[69] Jack Tanner, the future president of the engineering worker's union, had visited Spain in 1912 to interview imprisoned revolutionaries in Barcelona, and in 1917 travelled to Bilbao to observe a General Strike.[70] But Spain remained *terra incognita* to British labour, and perceptions were often coloured by the persistence of unhelpful stereotypes of the Spaniard as, variously, cruel, anarchistic and lazy. After the victory of the Popular Front the correspondent of the official TUC journal felt compelled to explain that:

> The average Spaniard, despite his sometimes ferocious appearance, his devotion to the national blood sport and the fact that his country still breeds anarchists, is a very ordinary, kindly-disposed human being, heartily sick of the disorder which exists on his doorstep.[71]

[66]. *The Record* (T&GWU), March 1937 (my emphasis).
[67] TUC, Documents 1, 26 August 1936, memorandum entitled 'The Spanish Struggle'.
[68] *Labour*, September 1936, article by Alexander Thompson.
[69] TUC, Box 431, 946/510, 'Spain – Political Situation 1934', 30 October and 14 November 1934; John Saville and Joyce Bellamy (eds.), *Dictionary of Labour Biography, Volume 7* (1984), pp. 236–45.   [70] *Daily Worker*, 6 November 1934.
[71] *Labour*, May 1936. This question is developed in my as yet unpublished paper 'A Far Away Country of Which we Know Little...? The Spanish Civil War in British Politics'.

Such perceptions had, if anything, been reinforced by the Spanish socialists' rising of October 1934, the previous point at which Spain had forced itself upon British attention. Unlike in 1936, the fighting was soon over and the main response was confined to financial help and intercession for the lives of imprisoned socialist leaders. Subsequently the Labour Party had sent humanitarian aid to the PSOE, although there is no evidence to support the allegation that it was funding the PSOE's political activities.[72] The Labour MP Ellen Wilkinson and Lord Listowel, sponsored by the 'Friends of New Spain', went on a mission to Asturias to investigate allegations of atrocities, and fell equally foul of the Spanish authorities and the Labour Party, which deemed her visit 'unofficial'.[73] She remained one of the few Labour Party politicians to sustain an interest in Spain prior to the outbreak of the Civil War.[74] For leaders such as Citrine and Dalton, however, the rising tarnished the image of Spanish socialism by exposing its contempt for constitutional politics. Caballero in particular came to be seen as a maverick, unreliable figure and unrepentant in his commitment to revolutionism. Indeed, immediately prior to the Civil War he had attended the triennial conference of the IFTU in London and had ominously asserted that 'if the Fascists attempted to seize power again, he and his colleagues would repeat what they did in 1934'.[75]

Such foreign forays were, however, comparatively rare, and Spain still lay largely outside the world of the LSI and the IFTU. The PSOE and UGT had made little effort to build contacts outside Spain. In the aftermath of the October 1934 rising the Labour Party International Secretary commented that 'in the past they have communicated very little. Indeed, for many months they sent no news at all'.[76] This could in turn spark a more extreme reaction that the Spanish were somehow presumptuous in demanding assistance once civil war had broken out.

These attitudes were quite alien to the proponents of the Popular Front for whom the Civil War served as the main recruiting sergeant and who saw in the conflict the first round of the European war against fascism. The origin of the Popular Front was a fundamental change in communist strategy, whereby the ruinous sectarianism of the Comintern's 'Class

---

[72] PRO, FO 371, 20520, W2868/62/41, 24 March 1936, communication from Sir H. Chilton (British ambassador in Madrid).
[73] Betty Vernon, *Ellen Wilkinson 1891–1947* (1982), p. 163.
[74] Another example was the former Labour MP Leah Manning who joined a delegation to Spain in 1934 and subsequently wrote *What I Saw in Spain* (1936) (see K.W. Watkins, *Britain Divided*, p. 25). In May 1937 she oversaw the evacuation of Basque refugee children from Bilbao. [75] *TUC CR*, 1936, p. 191.
[76] Labour Party archive, William Gilles papers, WG 1/69, 12 December 1934.

against Class' policy, so damaging to workers' resistance in Germany, was finally abandoned in 1935. The Popular Front was the child of fascism – it stood for the abandonment of socialist objectives in the short term to allow for a cross-class appeal to all progressive forces to unite in defence of democratic liberties. The basis of such a movement would be the united front of all working-class organisations, and to facilitate this the Profintern was dissolved in 1935.

The Popular Front, and the Spanish Civil War in particular, set the seal on the Communist Party of Great Britain's (CPGB) rehabilitation after its arid years of sectarian isolation. Founded in 1920, the CPGB was unusual in that it did not derive from a profound split in the British labour movement, but rather from an amalgam of left-wing and syndicalist groupings, many of whom soon departed when confronted with the rigours of bolshevisation. Its numerical weakness, subservience to the contortions of Comintern policy and peculiar relationship with the labour movement all posed problems for the CPGB. Initially seeking to build an alternative leadership within the unions through the Minority Movements while offering critical electoral support to the Labour Party, the experience of political persecution after 1926 pushed some of the leaders (in particular Rajani Palme Dutt and Harry Pollitt) to welcome the Comintern's new Class against Class policy by which the communists would distinguish themselves from the 'social fascist' Labour Party.[77] Yet the extension of this policy to the industrial field was utterly counter-productive. Despite the limited success of a CPGB-sponsored breakaway union, the United Mineworkers of Scotland,[78] for many it simply eroded the base that communist militants had built up in the unions, and as early as 1931 Pollitt was arguing in Moscow for a return to working within the existing trade unions.

Pollitt's shift reflected an underlying reality of British communism – the degree to which it was rooted in the trade union movement. Indeed, it is clear that many communist militants found it impossible to follow the new line. Arthur Horner, future leader of the South Wales miners, recognised the absurdity of attempting to bypass the miners' lodges and to offer 'independent leadership'. The communist-led National Unemployed Workers' Movement appears to have fought a successful rearguard action against the ravages of sectarianism. The local vitality of communism in its strongholds ranging from the 'Little Moscows' of the Scottish and Welsh coalfields to the East End Jewish radicals gave communism a continuity at

[77] Noreen Branson, *History of the Communist Party of Great Britain*, pp. 17–30.
[78] *Ibid.*, pp. 41–2. The London-based United Clothing Workers' Union was a much less successful breakaway, see Shirley Lerner *Breakaway Unions and the Small Trade Union* (1961), pp. 85–143.

the heart of the British labour movement which allowed it to ride out the breezes of Comintern fashion.[79]

Thus, by the time of the international adoption of the united and Popular Fronts in 1935, the CPGB was ready and equipped to exploit it. Although its campaign for affiliation to the Labour Party fell at the 1936 conference, the CPGB was already engaged on a rapid expansion of (declared) membership from 6,500 in February 1935, to over 11,000 in 1936 and 17,750 in July 1939.[80] It was greatly aided by its ability to present itself as the party that truly fought fascism – the party of Cable Street (where Mosley's blackshirts were successfully confronted in October 1936), of the International Brigades and of Spanish Medical Aid. Yet this new membership left the CPGB with a strangely split personality. Many of the recruits were drawn from the ranks of the middle class – students and intellectuals attracted by the image of anti-fascism and through such original departures as the Left Book Club[81] but possessing little in common with the enduring tradition of industrial communism.

The Civil War helped to stimulate repeated and unsuccessful campaigns to forge both types of 'front' in Britain, ranging from the Unity campaign of 1937, which resulted in the disbandment of the Socialist League, to the United Peace Alliance, sponsored by the *Reynolds' News* newspaper in the spring of 1938. The Cripps Manifesto campaign of 1939 followed the expulsion of the leading Labour Party left-winger Sir Stafford Cripps and many of his allies from the party. Yet although different elements of these demands gained widespread support among certain unions and the constituency parties, 'unity' was always staunchly resisted by almost the entire labour leadership.

This attitude appears, and is usually presented as, wilful and inexplicable. After all, given the Labour Party's electoral weakness, surely any accretion of strength was to be welcomed? More generally it feeds the perception that it was the communists who took all of the initiatives in these years while anti-communist labour leaders desperately struggled to prevent their supporters from falling in behind them. In fact, however, there was political logic behind Labour's stance. Where the Popular Front had been created the two main factors had been, firstly, a perceived internal threat of fascist takeover and, secondly, the existence of potentially damaging divisions

[79] The local culture of communism has been captured by two excellent studies: Stuart MacIntyre's *Little Moscows* (1980) and Raphael Samuel's studies of the 'Lost World of British Communism' in *New Left Review*, especially 'Staying Power; The Lost World of British Communism, Part 2', p. 95.

[80] Noreen Branson, *History of the Communist Party of Great Britain*, pp. 130 and 188.

[81] See Stuart Samuels, 'The Left Book Club', *Journal of Contemporary History*, vol. 1, no. 2, 1966.

within the working class. In France the trigger for the Popular Front had been the anti-democratic rioting of the right-wing Leagues in February 1934 which convinced the communists, the socialists and even the middle-class Radicals of the need for united action to defend democracy. In Spain the Popular Front grew out of the harsh repression of the 1934 rising, which left many activists languishing in jail, and the continuing perceived danger from the CEDA.

In Britain, however, neither of these factors was decisively present. The National Government was no great friend of civil liberties and, especially after Neville Chamberlain became Prime Minister in 1937, was seen as dangerously sympathetic to Hitler and Mussolini. Yet in no way was it fascist. Oswald Mosley's blackshirts were violent and anti-democratic but were too close to the lunatic fringe to build a mass political following so long as the middle class continued to support the National Government. The Labour Party believed that Mosley could be best contained within the existing system and opposed the Communist Party's call for popular mobilisation against him.[82] Moreover, the relationship of the Labour Party to the left-wing parties was too unequal to make unity attractive on any terms other than Labour's. This was even truer for the trade unions which, since the failed breakaway unions of the early 1930s, had enjoyed complete hegemony over industrial organisation.

Thus, 'unity' was not a straightforward political proposal: in fact it was a metaphor for fundamental changes in the structure and political methods of the labour movement. In France it had resulted in the reunification of the communist and the pro-socialist trade union centres, while in Spain there had been a merging of parties in Catalonia and of youth movements nationally. In both cases British labour would regard these new formations with suspicion, as unreliable communist fronts. The united front appeared to require the dismantling of the existing labour movement for little tangible political advantage.

Thus, anti-communism was a more complex determinant in labour's response to the Civil War than many authors have allowed. In fact, it is helpful to distinguish between distinct types of anti-communism. Firstly, there was the McCarthyite sense of opposition to the CPGB as the representative of a foreign government, an alien virus seeking to infect labour's organisation, This was the anti-communism expressed by the list of proscribed organisations, and the 1933 pamphlet *The Communist Solar System*. Intolerant as this may seen, it is worth recalling the scars that had been inflicted on Citrine, Bevin and others by the years of fruity, often

---

[82] Michael Newman, 'Democracy versus Dictatorship: Labour's role in the struggle against British Fascism, 1933–1936', *History Workshop Journal*, 5, Spring 1978.

grotesque, invective poured upon them by the communists, which carried on into the Popular Front period.[83] If their anti-communism had a peculiarly personal touch to it this was not so surprising. Moreover, the coincidence of the new communist tactic with the first show trials in Moscow reinforced a sense of caution. Yet, despite the obvious hatreds and suspicions on both sides, there was a paradox here in that the actual practice of anti-communism rarely matched the rhetoric. Arthur Horner, although for years excluded from the General Council, was tolerated as leader of the SWMF within the TUC, and many lesser communists held high posts in their unions. Many unions ignored the Black Circulars banning communists from union office. Although things were not made easy for them, British communists were implicitly accepted within the trade union movement and could continue to influence the Labour Party from that position. Thus, throughout the 1930s, there was a wide discrepancy between the failure of the Communist Party to influence labour movement policy, and the prominent role that individual communists continued to play within it.

This suggests that the main function of anti-communism was one of externalising real political tensions that occurred primarily not between the labour movement and a small (if active) party to its left, but within the movement itself as the unions and the Labour Party sought to fasten greater discipline on their members and exclude them from policy making. As has been indicated above, there was already the basis for such tensions in the 1930s, whatever the role of the CPGB: indeed, communist historians have been much too ready to claim the credit for developments such as the rank-and-file movements which would probably have occurred, in some form, anyway.[84] The communists were seen as militants able to give a lead to the rank and file, but in many respects anti-communism served as an effective way of de-legitimating a swathe of dissenting voices inside the labour movement. Indeed, if the communists had not existed, Citrine and Bevin would have had to create them.

Thus, resistance to 'unity' was rooted not so much in fear of communism as in a desire to maintain the existing organisation and leadership of the British labour movement. Bevin put this very clearly when he told a gathering of international socialists in March 1937

---

[83] In April 1937 Noel-Baker criticised the 'ineffable stupidity' of the 'idiotic but unceasing attacks which the communists make on Bevin and Citrine every day in the *Daily Worker* and elsewhere', which he took as evidence of Pollitt 'sabotaging' Moscow's strategy in order to win adherents from the left of the Labour Party. Churchill College, Cambridge, Noel-Baker papers, NBKR 4/660, 21 April 1937, Noel-Baker to Zilliacus.

[84] Noreen Branson, *History of the Communist party of Great Britain*, p. 174: 'As one of the means towards changing the trade unions, the Party...had in the early 1930s initiated a number of rank-and-file movements.'

let us have unity in trying to help Spain, and do not force some philosophy on us that we do not want. We, in Britain, have a United Front – we represent the Co-operative Movement, the Trade Union Movement and the Labour Movement, that is the most solid Labour organisation in the world.[85]

When Britain's labour leaders gathered in the summer of 1936 to discuss the military rebellion in Spain it is clear that, beyond issuing general statements of support for Spanish democracy, the issues were far from clear-cut. What they knew of Spain, and of Spanish labour, they did not much like. However, the fact that Spain was so little known gave them considerable latitude in creating a structure for their solidarity. Even so, there were limitations to bear in mind. The authority of the leadership had to be maintained and therefore support for Spain could not be allowed to generate its own momentum within the movement. On the other hand, Britain's Catholic workers were shocked by the outrages against the Spanish church and their numerous voices in opposition to the Republic could not be totally ignored. However, all of these problems were overshadowed by the British government's adoption of the policy of Non-Intervention in the Civil War which changed the nature of the problem from a question of internationalism into one of diplomacy, with the threat of war as the price of failure. If the debate over Non-Intervention was to provide British labour with months of acrimonious division, it also saved it for over a year from exposure of the movement's fundamental weakness in its duty of delivering international solidarity.

[85] TUC, International Conference, 2, report p. 51.

1

'THE BEST THAT COULD BE DONE AT THE TIME...': NON-INTERVENTION, 17 JULY–28 OCTOBER 1936

As soon as Spain had erupted into civil war both sides turned immediately to their presumed allies for assistance and found them initially receptive.[1] Léon Blum's newly elected Front Populaire government in France sanctioned the delivery of arms to its Spanish counterpart and the Radical Air Minister Pierre Cot prepared a consignment of aircraft. However, almost immediately Blum's resolve was shaken by a combination of factors. On 23 July he had visited the British Foreign Secretary Anthony Eden who cautioned him as to the wisdom of sending arms. By the time he returned news of his intentions had been leaked to the right-wing press and some of his Radical ministers were in revolt. Worried that France might be forced to stand alone against Germany at a moment of internal chaos Blum agreed to an arms embargo on 25 July. Whatever the full extent of British pressure on Blum, a matter for interminable debate amongst historians,[2] it is clear that such a move chimed with the wishes of Baldwin's government. Already ill-disposed towards the Spanish Popular Front on ideological grounds,[3] for the duration of the conflict the British government would believe that Britain's best interests lay in preventing Spain's civil war from becoming a general

---

[1] See John Coverdale, *Italian Intervention in the Spanish Civil War*, (1975); Denis Smyth, 'Reflex Reaction: Germany and the Onset of the Spanish Civil War', in Paul Preston (ed.), *Revolution and War in Spain, 1931–9* (1984); Julian Jackson, *The Popular Front in France: Defending Democracy 1934–38* (Cambridge, 1988), pp. 202–9.

[2] The case against British culpability has been argued most forcefully by David Carlton in 'Eden, Blum and the Origins of Non-Intervention', *Journal of Contemporary History*, vol. 6 (3), 1971. The counter-argument has been restated by Glyn Stone, 'Britain, Non-Intervention and the Spanish Civil War', *European Studies Review*, vol. 9, 1979. See also M.D. Gallagher, 'Leon Blum and the Spanish Civil War', *Journal of Contemporary History*, vol. 6 (3), 1971.

[3] See Douglas Little, 'Red Scare, 1936: Anti-Bolshevism and the Origins of British Non-Intervention in the Spanish Civil War', *Journal of Contemporary History*, vol. 23, April 1988, 291–311.

European conflict, and staying on friendly terms with the eventual victors, rather than defending Spanish democracy.[4]

However, an embargo was difficult to explain to the rank and file of the Front Populaire, particularly as it became apparent that the rebels were continuing to receive foreign assistance. The embargo was thus only half-heartedly enforced and Cot's aircraft were allowed to leave for Spain on 2 August. At this point it is alleged that British pressure reached a new level of intensity with an ultimatum from the British ambassador in Paris, Sir George Clerk, and on 8 August Blum agreed to close the French frontier to all war material and to extend the embargo to aircraft. The decision would, however, be reviewed if no general Non-Intervention agreement was concluded. On 15 August the British and French governments exchanged notes and two days later Britain imposed its own embargo, although no significant amounts of war material had left this country for Spain.

The real key to Non-Intervention, however, was to involve the other European powers and genuinely to isolate the conflict. The main sticking point was the position of Germany and Portugal. Germany had sent aid since 26 July and already provided invaluable assistance by ferrying Franco's troops from North Africa to Spain by air. Much of the support for the rebels was being channelled through Portugal, itself a dictatorship under Salazar. On 30 July Italian planes sent to aid the rebels were forced to crash-land in French Morocco in dramatic proof of further lines of supply. Portugal finally accepted the principle of Non-Intervention on 21 August after prolonged British diplomatic pressure, and was soon followed by the Soviet Union and Germany. Even so, the future of Non-Intervention was in doubt until a Supervisory Committee could be convened. This met for the first time on 9 September in London, its home for the rest of the war, under the chairmanship of Lord Plymouth, although Portugal held aloof until the end of the month.

Thus, the diplomatic edifice of Non-Intervention was in place by the autumn, and from the spring of 1937 a multi-national naval patrol was intended to enforce it. Yet what was lacking was any real intention on the part of Germany and Italy of abiding by the agreement and for this reason Non-Intervention has been commemorated as a hollow sham more often than as a monument to international co-operation. Arms continued to pour into Spain and, despite the decision of the Soviet Union to send tanks and

---

[4] Eden defined British interests in January 1937 as follows: 'First that the conflict shall not spread beyond the boundaries of Spain; and second that the political independence and territorial integrity of Spain shall be preserved.' *Hansard*, 5th series, vol. 319, 19 January 1937, col. 95. As the war progressed he became convinced that the second goal was not being attained.

aircraft in October 1936 which saved the Republic from immediate military collapse, many more of them found their way to the rebels than to the democratically elected government. Moreover the Soviet support was a mixed blessing. The Civil War was an embarrassment for Stalin as he feared that a successful social revolution in Spain would undermine his attempts at *rapprochement* with the western democracies. Thus, his strategy dictated that the Spanish Republic should be sent enough weapons for its survival but not for victory: meanwhile, the increasingly powerful Spanish communists, and their Comintern allies, would work assiduously to tame the revolutionary forces unleashed by the military revolt.

With the advantage of hindsight it seems almost inconceivable that British labour could ever have supported this disastrous policy which starved the Spanish government of arms whilst weapons and military personnel poured into Franco's Spain from the fascist powers. Moreover, the fact that only Soviet Russia provided substantial military assistance to the Republic had the effect of boosting the formerly insignificant Spanish communists and undermining the political position of the socialists. Yet, for almost a year labour's leaders were able to convince themselves, and many of their members, that Non-Intervention was in the best interests of their Spanish comrades. This chapter is intended to show how this situation arose.

Three main factors conditioned labour's attitude. Firstly, the labour movement reached its decision on Non-Intervention through collective agreement with its international counterparts. However, within this decision-making structure, it is vital to stress the importance of the British trade unions and, within them, of Walter Citrine. Secondly, the interpretation of the Civil War as a struggle between fascism and democracy was regarded as simplistic in the upper echelons of the labour movement. The leaders were acutely aware of the divisions within the Spanish left, and the breakdown of government in Spain following the military rising, and this left a permanent imprint on their response to the conflict. Finally, although the Spanish Republic received strong support amongst sections of the British labour movement from the beginning of the conflict, this was not initially articulated into a form of pressure that could significantly influence the leadership. The members were not directly involved in the debate over Non-Intervention until after the crucial decisions had been taken, and in the first few months of the war a small group of leaders enjoyed a virtual free hand in devising the movement's response. This explains the unsettling impact of the Labour Party's 1936 Edinburgh Conference where a policy that had taken so long to formulate and justify was thrown out, quite literally, overnight.

Shortly after the start of the Civil War Parliament went into recess and many of the leaders of the Labour Party were scattered overseas on holiday.[5] Even so, it is unlikely that events would have unfolded very differently had they been present. The influence of the trade union leaders on labour movement policy towards Spain was by no means accidental and there were important structural reasons for this inherent in the nature of international labour movement decision-making. As Bevin put it: 'Our conception of international action is for Internationals to meet and come to decisions and then be loyal to their decisions'.[6] This framework, however flawed in practice, accentuated trade union influence because Citrine, as President of the IFTU, was the only British figure of stature in the international labour movement and was usually present at the joint meetings of the IFTU and LSI. Moreover, his regular deputy was another leading trade unionist, the builders' leader George Hicks. By contrast, the Labour Party's usual representative was William Gillies who, as International Secretary, was not a major political figure in the party. The party's Deputy leader Arthur Greenwood sometimes attended but had no permanent international post. Thus, not only did Citrine play a role in the formulation of international policy – which had repercussions for national decisions – but also formed the main channel for communications between the national and international bodies. The monopolisation of information emanating from Spain and (equally importantly) from France by Citrine and a coterie of trade union and Labour Party officials is crucial to an understanding of the acceptance of Non-Intervention, especially at the decisive meetings of the National Council of Labour (on 25 and 27 August 1936) and of the broader Labour Movement Conference (on 28 August, and 4 and 9 September 1936).

There was, however, nothing particularly sinister about the influence of the trade union leaders. Contrary to some accounts Citrine and Bevin were not motivated by malice towards the Spanish Republic.[7] Nor were they seeking to use Non-Intervention, as some feared, to lay the basis for broader collaboration with the National Government. Konni Zilliacus, for instance, wrote to Philip Noel-Baker in September 1936 that Non-Intervention was

> merely Citrine and co's first steps to committing the Labour Movement to a United Front with the Tories in preparing for the next world war. I've known

[5] Naylor, *Labour's International Policy*, p. 143. Dalton was in Lapland and Attlee in Russia. A.V. Alexander, another prominent leader, was in California.

[6] *TUC CR*, 1936, p. 385.

[7] See, for instance, Bill Alexander, *British Volunteers for Liberty: Spain 1936–1939* (1982), pp. 37 and 142.

for some time that Citrine and Gillies were in the pockets of the FO [Foreign Office]·and that Hugh [Dalton] was moving in the same direction.[8]

Yet the evidence presented below suggests that their objectives were in practice more limited. Given that the Civil War had taken all of the leaders by surprise, Citrine's main aim was simply to formulate a policy that all could agree on and that would fulfil his two main objectives, which the structures of internationalism were then manipulated to support. These objectives were, firstly, that the response to the Civil War should conform to his perception of Britain's national interest, and thus nothing should be done which might precipitate Britain's involvement in a war for which it was unprepared. Secondly, that the authority of the General Council and the other institutions of the labour movement must be maintained and, thus, the leaders should not become too isolated either from their members or internationally. However, it is argued below that the second, defensive, objective took clear priority: Citrine was far from doctrinaire in his support for Non-Intervention and quite willing to abandon it when it threatened the second of these goals.[9]

At the same time, however, it was certainly damaging to the interests of the Spanish government that the dominant force in the labour movement was a narrow and bureaucratic internationalism. Within the main decision-making bodies only the comparatively uninfluential Herbert Morrison would argue what seemed self-evident to many outside; that there was a clear socialist duty to oppose Non-Intervention. Citrine had many great strengths – he was alert, capable of rapidly assimilating detailed information and outstanding in debate. In short, he was admirably suited to the bureaucratic policy-making that had thus far characterised the labour movement's response to fascism. But he was not a campaigning political leader and his skills were not well suited to the special demands made by the Spanish crisis in the summer of 1936. None of the labour leaders was less temperamentally equipped to lead a mass campaign in challenge to the British government over Non-Intervention, and at no point did he even consider this as an option. Although he was willing to question the government on specific aspects of the policy, he readily accepted its main

---

[8] Churchill College, Cambridge, Philip Noel-Baker papers, Spain Correspondence volume 1, NBKR 4/656, 19 September 1936, Zilliacus to Noel-Baker. On the same day Noel-Baker was writing to Attlee warning that collaboration on Non-Intervention would lead to a 'sort of national union with the Tories on armaments and foreign policy generally. That, I believe, is what Citrine and some others really want, at least sub-consciously, and therefore I know that it is no use talking to them.' [9] See below p. 71.

premises. Certainly, with Citrine in charge the mood was essentially reactive, and the initiative was surrendered to Blum and to the British Foreign Office.

The perception of events inside Spain was a second crucial determinant of labour's policy during the first months of the Civil War. Bevin's assured comments at the 1936 TUC Congress that contacts with Spain were 'regular... active and constant'[10] belied the very limited information actually available to the leaders. Indeed, on 14 August Citrine admitted that 'we are getting daily news of the fighting from the newspapers, of course, but that is not sufficient'.[11] Moreover, tight control was kept on what limited information was available and it was certainly not shared with the members at large. On 27 August 1936 the NCL decided to issue no letters of recommendation to visitors to Spain other than for those specially delegated on its behalf.[12] Yet it would be wrong to think that British labour leaders were ignorant of or uninterested in the events in Spain, even though Hugh Dalton's memoirs have been influential in creating this impression. Apparently, Dalton personally valued France above Spain and was 'not a great admirer of the Spanish approximation to democracy'. In comparison with the French socialist leaders, amongst whom were 'many personal friends', he argued, his colleagues knew little of the Spanish leaders who 'did not, until now, attend meetings of the LSI.'[13] While Dalton's conclusions are doubtless correct, the picture that he presents is misleading in many respects. Citrine, for instance, was well acquainted with Caballero and other Spanish leaders, and suspicious of them through familiarity rather than ignorance.

All of the British labour leaders found what confronted them in Spain profoundly uncongenial. The moderate core of Spanish working-class organisation, on which they hoped to build their solidarity, simply did not exist in their terms. The Spanish socialists were deeply divided between the supporters of Caballero and Prieto, and Pietro Nenni, the LSI representative in Spain, reported to Citrine that these divisions formed 'un obstacle jusqu'ici insurmontable' to the formation of a strong government.[14] Moreover, their Frente Popular allies, the anarchists and communists, were both considered inimical to the international labour movement. One

[10] *TUC CR*, 1936, p. 388.
[11] TUC, Correspondence 1, 14 August 1936, Citrine to Schevenels.
[12] NCL minutes, 27 August 1936. There were echoes here of the action taken against Ellen Wilkinson for her unauthorised visit to Asturias in 1934, see above p. 31.
[13] Hugh Dalton, *The Fateful Years*, p. 94.
[14] TUC, Correspondence 1, 31 August 1936, Adler to Citrine enclosing Nenni's report.

consequence was that Citrine approached any dealings with Spanish labour with deep suspicion. For instance, when a UGT delegate from Barcelona, a former communist, arrived at the 28 July LSI/IFTU meeting, Citrine alone refused to accept his credentials as a representative of the Spanish workers, although bowing to the will of the meeting to hear him speak.[15] Similar reservations conditioned his treatment of a telegram which he received on 10 August from Comorera, leader of the joint communist/socialist Catalan PSUC party, urging him to visit Barcelona for a 'most important matter'.[16] Walter Schevenels, General Secretary of the IFTU, investigated the request and found it *bona fide*, although suspecting that the sympathies of the mass of Catalan labour were 'doubtless with Moscow'.[17] However, the Spanish representatives in Paris advised against Citrine's acceptance of the invitation because Barcelona was 'acting independently of Madrid and it was undesirable that there should be any intervention in the internal affairs of the Spanish movement'.[18] Citrine later revealed that he was warned not to go because 'there was a domestic situation bubbling up by the anarchists, and it would be very difficult for any outsider to interfere. "As I have no wish to shuffle off this mortal coil..." '[19] He excused himself on the grounds that he was busy with trade union work.[20]

In the absence of official representatives in Spain, Citrine and his colleagues relied for their intelligence on first-hand accounts and on semi-official sources, most of which confirmed the unhappy picture that was emerging. However, the effect was magnified by the Spanish representatives' habit of exaggerating the anarchist threat in order to win support, a tactic that was generally counter-productive because it simply emphasised the lack of any central control. At the 28 July LSI/IFTU meeting the UGT delegate had said that they were hard pressed to control the anarchists in Catalonia and that one of the main reasons why they should receive arms was so that they could guard against an 'anarchist putsch'.[21] This impression was confirmed by the reports of other prominent international figures. When Louis De Brouckère, President of the LSI, visited Madrid he was strongly influenced by the moderate socialist Prieto who persuaded him that the anarchists were 'public enemy No. 2' after fascism.[22] Léon Jouhaux,

---

[15] TUC, Documents 1, IFTU/LSI meeting, verbatim report, 28 July 1936, p. 9.
[16] TUC, Correspondence 1, 8 August 1936, Comorera to Citrine.
[17] TUC, Correspondence 1, 11 August 1936, Schevenels to Citrine.
[18] TUC, Documents 1, memorandum, p. 5.
[19] TUC, Documents 2, Labour Movement Conference, verbatim report of Citrine's speeches, 4 September 1936, p. 6.
[20] TUC, Correspondence 1, 11 August 1936, Citrine to Comorera.
[21] TUC, Documents 1, IFTU/LSI meeting, verbatim report, 28 July 1936, p. 11.
[22] TUC, Documents 1, IFTU/LSI meeting, verbatim report, 21 August 1936, p. 1.

Secretary of the French CGT trade union centre, who had visited Barcelona and Madrid, felt that the situation in Catalonia was 'temporarily normal', but feared that trouble would flare up as soon as the war ended. Caballero had told him that after the war there would be no return to the old form of government, but that 'the Socialists and Communists would take control themselves'. Jouhaux feared that Caballero 'did not seem to understand the importance of not fighting the anarchists just now'.[23]

Citrine was particularly influenced in his appreciation of affairs both in Spain and France by confidential despatches from the *Daily Herald* correspondents, most notably the Barcelona-based Victor Schiff. One such piece, which arrived in mid-August, was written at the urging of Comorera and recommended the supply of arms so that the anarchists could be crushed, as well as vilifying the POUM (the anti-Stalinist communists).[24] In a covering note the editor said that he had decided not to publish the piece 'partly because it would furnish arguments to sympathisers of the rebels and partly because it would dishearten sympathisers with the Government by suggesting serious divisions amongst the Government supporters' – he also found it unconvincing.[25] Despite these reservations Schiff's despatches reinforced Citrine's suspicions of Caballero at the very time when he was being appointed as the new prime minister. Already Citrine had opposed Caballero's claim for the control of the distribution of international labour

---

[23] *Ibid.* pp. 1–4.   [24] TUC, Correspondence 1, 16 August 1936. According to Schiff:

Comorera said to me that I should let you know that they urgently need arms for the test of power which he considers as unavoidable between the constructive Socialist, Communist and Trade-Union forces and the F.A.I. If the IFTU found it impossible to supply them with arms, they would like to get at least the money for purchasing them.

I must add that the communists, who have their own experience with the Anarchists in Russia, are no less determined than the Socialists to crush them.

There is also another problem, which seems to me very nasty, that of the Trotskist P.O.U.M., which responsable T.U. quarters describe as comparatively negligible. But I have the impression that they are very active and successful in touting for supporters among the dregs of the population round the port [in Barcelona], and among international adventurers. Communists at the front told me that they were behaving the worst in the villages which they occupied, and even anarchists speak scornfully of their low morals. [All spelling as in original.]

Schiff was a German socialist in exile. Citrine had previously met him in Berlin in 1933 (*Men and Work*, p. 342). Later in the war Schiff fell foul of the Labour Party for his reporting of Attlee's visit to Spain. William Gillies claimed that his allegations of profiteering in food were most 'unfortunate…there is a general impression among informed persons that your articles were unfortunate seen through the spectacles of propaganda' (Labour Party archives, WG/SPA, 296, Gillies to Schiff, 20 December 1937).

[25] TUC, Documents 1, 17 August 1936, Inter-Departmental Correspondence from Publicity Department to Citrine.

relief on the grounds that in Spain 'there were anarchists on the one hand and Communists and Socialists on the other. We felt that it would increase those difficulties if we allowed that sort of distribution to take place'.[26]

Addressing the Labour Movement Conference on 4 September Citrine elaborated on the dangers of division in Republican Spain. He reported that Catalonia was in the hands of the anarchists and acting independently of the central government, and had been the scene of atrocities. A 'united front' had been patched up there but 'it was only a veneer'.[27] Referring to Schiff's reports Citrine summarised his view that 'the greatest danger that now existed in Spain [in mid-August] was not the Fascists, but the internal divisions, the anarchists, Socialists and Syndicalists'. He then attacked Caballero:

> Caballero, whom most of them know, apparently is taking a different point of view from the Socialists and the Government. His idea is that the Trade Union force should be armed separately. But Sir Walter told them that for a very considerable time there had been differences, to say the least, between Caballero and Prieto, and indeed the whole of the central group, [and] they would realise that [this] was significant. *Indeed, one could say that there was a shrewd suspicion that if the Fascists had not started trouble, Caballero and his friends would have done. This was prior to the actual fighting taking place.*[28]

Interestingly, this view was countered by Bevin who argued that the main question was how to help Spain – 'he was not concerned about the divisions because where one found revolts there were always divisions'.[29]

Thus, in the early months of the Civil War, far from finding a moderate and reliable labour movement with which to co-operate, Citrine and his colleagues were confronted with a fractured and revolutionary movement with even more unsavoury political allies. It was not surprising, therefore, that, along with Dalton, the two leading trade unionists offered perceptions of the Civil War in private which differed markedly from their public pronouncements and which would have been anathema to their rank-and-file activists. Citrine, for instance, believed that

> there was a great deal more than just a [simple] issue, between Fascism and Democracy. In Spain as everybody knows there are groups and cliques who

---

[26] TUC, Documents 1, NCL, verbatim report, 25 August 1936, p. 7.
[27] TUC, Documents 2, Labour Movement Conference, verbatim report of Citrine's speeches, 4 September 1936, p. 5.   [28] *Ibid.* p. 7. My emphasis.
[29] TUC, Documents 2, Labour Movement Conference, verbatim report, 4 September 1936, p. 15.

are ready tomorrow [at] the first opportunity to set up a dictatorship in Spain, but it will be a Communist dictatorship.[30]

As to the argument that the Spanish government deserved arms as a democratically elected body Citrine had reservations about 'laying down too strongly the rights of Constitutional Government'. Somewhat facetiously referring to the Asturian revolt against the Lerroux government in 1934[31] he asked whether it would have been justified to send arms to that democratic government to help it to quell a workers' rising. Bevin too held an idiosyncratic view of the nature of the conflict, once depicting it as a clash between 'two great powers':

> Russia on the one side with her policy, and who could deny that all the temporal power of the Vatican is the driving force behind this business... One works through the red International and the other through the Pope, and it is those great forces getting to grips.[32]

Although there is no evidence that labour leaders did not support the Spanish government, however critical of it in private, it is clear that they found the situation bewildering: a dangerous morass of factions and ideologies which could endanger their own position (they were well aware of the revulsion against the anti-Catholic outrages amongst their Catholic constituency). Spain should be handled with care. Not surprisingly, therefore, the survival of Blum's government was made a priority over that of the Spanish Frente Popular. Moreover, Citrine and the others were hindered in their dealings with the British government by their scepticism over the credibility of the Spanish government.[33] Ironically, the one section of the Frente Popular to benefit, in their estimation, from the excesses of the anarchists and the socialist divisions were the Spanish communists who preached an attractive creed of unity and discipline. This was to be an important factor after Caballero's fall from power when cracks began to appear in the united front.

It has been easy to condemn the decisions of labour leaders in retrospect, once the shortcomings of Non-Intervention had become brutally obvious. In August 1936, however, these were by no means self-evident and, given the fear that Italy and Germany (or, indeed, the British government) would intervene openly on behalf of the rebels, some merit was initially seen in the idea of neutrality as a way to help the Spanish people. Thus, the debate over

---

[30] TUC, Documents 1, NCL, verbatim report, 25 August 1936, p. 44. Similar sentiments were expressed in TUC Documents 2, Labour Movement Conference, verbatim report of Citrine's speeches, 4 September 1936, p. 12.   [31] *Ibid.*

[32] TUC, Documents 2, Labour Movement Conference, verbatim report, 28 October 1936, p. 24.   [33] See below p. 51.

Non-Intervention has also to be seen in the context of continuing confusion within the labour movement. One of the first unions to respond was the building workers' (AUBTW) which passed a resolution supporting the Spanish workers at its annual conference. On 5 August its Executive Council decided to write to the Prime Minister stressing the danger of war if any help were given to the rebels from individuals in Britain, and 'insisting that our Government maintains the strictest neutrality during this frightful Civil War'.[34] Similarly, the Secretary of London Trades Council, prompted by a correspondence with Caballero, wrote to the Foreign Office expressing concern at the position of Portugal *vis-à-vis* the shipment of arms to the rebels, and concluded that: 'My Council appreciates the action taken by H.M. Government...in the matter of an international policy of Non-Intervention'.[35]

Non-Intervention also sowed confusion amongst the political left. The Communist Party had rapidly launched a campaign of solidarity with the Spanish people, seeing in Spain's Popular Front the perfect retort to those who opposed the tactic in Britain. However, the party's newspaper the *Daily Worker*, in an editorial of 5 August, concluded that the Non-Intervention proposals might be beneficial because the Spanish government would soon win the war 'if supplies could be stopped from the Fascist countries and if the Baldwin Government can be forced to give up its moral support for the Fascists'. Hence, it demanded that the British government should 'support the French government to stop all supplies of aeroplanes and munitions for the fascist militarists in Spain'. This surprising stance was partly explained by the paper's zeal in attacking the *Daily Herald* which had treated Non-Intervention with initial hostility on the grounds that it would 'only penalise the constitutional forces'.[36] Within a few days these positions had been reversed. As late as 28 August, however, the leading Labour Party left-winger Stafford Cripps, publicly outspoken against Non-Intervention, was arguing in private that the agreement had at least 'immobilised intervention'

---

[34] MRC, UCATT records, Mss 78/AU/1/2/10, AUBTW July 1936 Conference minutes, pp. 80–3; Mss 78/AU/1/1/15, AUBTW Executive Council minutes, 5 August 1936, p. 31.
[35] TUC, Correspondence 1, 7 August 1936, Wall to Foreign Office.
[36] This evidence suggests that Noreen Branson's statement that 'the moment "non-intervention" was mooted it was denounced' (*History of the Communist Party of Great Britain*, p. 222) is too sweeping. Although the CPGB had called for 'necessary supplies for [Republican Spain's] armed forces' as early as 27 July (*Daily Worker*), it was inevitable that the party's response to Non-Intervention was bound to be influenced both by the attitude of the Soviet Union and by the stance of the labour movement. Indeed, at the Plymouth Congress, Bevin was to claim that the CPGB 'scarcely said a word' about Non-Intervention until the NCL had decided its own position, and only then made their attack (*TUC CR*, 1936, p. 385); this point was disputed by Pollitt in *Spain and the TUC* (1936), p. 11.

against the workers' side and that they should not apply pressure to end it 'because it would be against the interests of the Spanish workers' to do so'.[37] Thus, there was initially a large area of ambiguity which leaders of the labour movement were able to exploit in not challenging Non-Intervention.

The first official response to the military revolt came from a 'Conference against the Means Test' on 20 July, where an emergency resolution was passed in support of the Spanish workers. Subsequently the TUC General Council and the Labour Party NEC met to pass similar resolutions and parted, in Citrine's words, 'without any feeling that the needs in Spain were such as to necessitate any immediate action' on their part.[38] However, steps were taken to initiate a fund for humanitarian relief, and the need to launch an international relief effort to compete with the communist 'Red Aid' formed the main item on the agenda when the IFTU and LSI met jointly in Brussels on 28 July.

At this meeting the British representatives, Citrine and Gillies, learnt for the first time that Blum had refused to sell arms to the Spanish government. Walter Schevenels of the IFTU had had a lengthy meeting with Fernando de los Ríos, the unofficial Spanish ambassador in Paris and a leading member of the socialist party, according to whom Blum had bowed partly to internal pressure from his Radical colleagues. This had been compounded by representations from the Italian and German embassies to the effect that, should the arms deliveries go ahead, these governments 'would feel freed from their obligations of neutrality, and this might lead to an outbreak of war'. De los Ríos had asked the CGT leader Léon Jouhaux to put pressure on Blum and the Radicals to reverse this decision and was later assured that 'a way would be found to send the arms to Spain'. When asked by Schevenels what aid in particular the two Internationals could provide, de los Ríos was adamant that their main priority was 'arms and aeroplanes',[39] a message that was reinforced when the UGT delegate from Catalonia, Sr Airlandis, addressed the meeting. A draft manifesto was drawn up which, despite the French government's action, affirmed the Spanish government's right to purchase the arms that it needed for its defence.[40] However, although the Internationals never wavered from this principle, it was left to the individual national centres to decide their particular response to Non-Intervention.

[37] TUC, Documents 1, Labour Movement Conference, verbatim report, 28 August 1936, p. 42. For Cripps' opposition to Non-Intervention see *Manchester Guardian*, 31 August 1936; *News Chronicle*, 26 August 1936.
[38] TUC, Documents 1, Labour Movement Conference, verbatim report, 28 August 1936, p. 2.
[39] TUC, Documents 1, IFTU/LSI meeting, verbatim report, 28 July 1936, pp. 9–11.
[40] Copy of resolution in TUC, Documents 1.

In the course of the meeting De Brouckère had drawn attention to the need for more information on what was happening in Spain and it was agreed to send a delegation to consult with the Spanish comrades as to the best way in which assistance could be given.[41] A reluctant Citrine[42] was persuaded to represent the IFTU, but by the time that the Spanish representatives in Paris had authorised the mission de los Ríos had other plans for him. Due to the French embargo alternative sources of arms were now being sought, and it was felt that Citrine's presence would be more valuable in London to smooth relations with the British government on this score.[43] He returned there on 4 August while De Brouckère travelled on alone in Spain. The TUC had already been approached by Ramos Oliveira, a Spanish socialist journalist, on this matter and he had been put in touch with certain armaments firms.[44] In December 1936 Citrine was privately to claim that the TUC had actually attempted to purchase aircraft, bombs and other *materiel* for the Spanish government, but had discovered that the manufacturers were booked up with government orders and unwilling to sell their stocks without official permission. This experience led him to believe that even if the embargo were lifted it would be very difficult to supply arms from Britain.[45]

Despite the LSI/IFTU resolution of 28 July the British labour movement had still not defined its own attitude to Non-Intervention, and was in danger of being overtaken by events. Alarmed by the weakness of the Spanish government and fearful that there would be an international conflict, the leadership was drawn almost ineluctably into support for Non-Intervention with barely a glance at any alternative, although not through any absence of them. On 13 August a 'Special European Conference' was held in Paris, ostensibly called by the secretaries of the IFTU and CGT, Schevenels and Jouhaux, with the aim of circulating first-hand information on Spain and discussing how to provide practical assistance. The Amalgamated En-

---

[41] TUC, Documents 1, IFTU/LSI meeting, verbatim report, 28 July 1936, p. 7; TUC, Documents 1, memorandum by Citrine, 11 August 1936, p. 2.

[42] Citrine initially refused to go as 'he had already spent so much time on international work that some resentment might be caused by his presence on the delegation' (*ibid.*, p. 12). He was also keen to take a holiday in Belgium (TUC, Documents 1, memorandum, p. 2).

[43] TUC, Documents 1, memorandum by Citrine, 11 August 1936, p. 4.

[44] *Ibid.* The Special Branch followed Oliveira's activities in Britain and in September 1936 claimed that he had recruited aircrew for the Spanish Government. PRO, FO 371 20577, W11972/9549/41, 19 September 1936, nos. 235–7; W11975/9549/41, 21 September 1936, nos. 257–9.

[45] TUC, Documents 2, 21 December 1936, report of meeting with 'rank and file' delegation, p. 12. See also TUC, Documents 1, NCL, verbatim report, 25 August 1936, pp. 51–2. I have been unable to find any evidence to corroborate Citrine's claim.

gineering Union (AEU) overcame its reservations that Spain should be left to the TUC and Labour Party, and sent its President Jack Little and leading left-winger Jack Tanner to Paris as delegates.[46] The TUC was invited but treated the matter with typical caution. Citrine 'did not feel disposed to attend as the invitation emanated from individuals' rather than institutions, a foretaste of the coolness with which the TUC would treat any unofficial initiative on solidarity with Spain. He was also surprised to see the involvement of Schevenels, who confessed that he had lent his name to the meeting only at Jouhaux's request and felt that he had been 'a little precipitate'. He later reported that the conference had produced little of practical value. The main problem for the European left was that, initially at least, it was reluctant to criticise Blum's actions. The meeting recognised that the French government had 'completely done its duty and could not be expected to do anything more than take up its attitude of neutrality'. This forced it to place all the onus on the British labour movement to change its own government's policy – a point strongly supported at the meeting by Ellen Wilkinson.[47]

This was a challenge that Citrine, for one, was unwilling to accept. He believed that 'the question of arms was quite clearly one which concerned the French more than it concerned the British'.[48] A good example of this came when, a month after the outbreak of the Civil War, Citrine joined with Arthur Greenwood (in the absence of Attlee) and Labour Party officials in two delegations to Foreign Secretary Anthony Eden. These contacts made no effort to change government policy and reflected, instead, the delegates' preoccupation with making Non-Intervention as watertight as possible, in such a way that it could be sold to their members in the forthcoming TUC Congress and Labour Party conference. They were, indeed, severely hampered by the lack of a clear policy towards Non-Intervention and the Labour Party General Secretary James Middleton later confided, with reference to the first meeting, that 'they had been thankful that [Eden] had not asked them what was the [party's] position, because they could not have answered him'.[49]

[46] MRC, Mss 259, AEU Executive Council minutes, 10 August 1936. Little later referred to this meeting in his speech at the TUC Congress, *TUC CR*, 1936, p. 377.

[47] TUC, Correspondence 1, 8 August 1936, circular for the conference. Speakers just returned from Spain included Jean Richard Bloch, Jean Cassou and Conrad Ulrich. 14 and 18 August 1936, Schevenels to Citrine for a report on the conference. TUC, Documents 1, memorandum, p. 5, for Citrine's response.

[48] TUC, Documents 1, NCL, verbatim report, 25 August 1936, pp. 15–16. Citrine was here referring to the 'Secret Clause' in the 1935 Franco-Spanish treaty which he learnt of for the first time at this meeting. This treaty, concluded between two right-wing governments, committed France to supply arms to Spain.   [49] *Ibid.* p. 46.

These meetings were purely consultative, and were unsatisfactory as a means of influencing government. One reason was that the very personal nature of the exchanges could be intimidating. After the second meeting in August, for instance, Citrine, an inveterate note-taker, regretted the delay in producing his report because of his 'embarrassment at taking notes'.[50] Moreover, there was some doubt as to who was more influenced as a result of the interviews – after Eden had expounded his views on the dangers of a Europe divided by the Civil War into ideological 'blocs', Citrine then regurgitated these arguments, as if his own, a few days later.[51] Indeed, at these first meetings there was a marked reluctance to criticise the government and a preference for working with it rather than against it. The somewhat misplaced respect of some labour leaders for the intentions of the British government was later emphasised by Bevin's speech to an international conference in March 1937 when he challenged the view that the British government wanted to help Franco to win: 'I do not think that is true. Not because they have any special love for the legal government of Spain, but there is such a thing as British interest, and a Conservative Government is sometimes influenced by British interests'.[52]

During their first mission (on 19 August 1936) the delegates simply sought information on the embryonic Non-Intervention policy, with one of them reporting the rumour that the French government's initiative on the matter came as the result of British pressure. Eden categorically denied this, the Foreign Office minute noting with some satisfaction that 'the deputation at once seemed to accept this explanation, and it seemed that they had not altogether credited the rumour to which they had given expression'.[53] Citrine's report reinforces this impression as it reveals that Eden had offered to show them the correspondence which had passed between the French and British governments, but they had not taken up the offer as 'they had no reason to doubt the truth of what he said'.[54] The delegation went on to argue that the 'neutrality' policy favoured the Spanish rebels over the elected government. However, their hand was not strengthened when Greenwood blundered into revealing that 'he thought that the outcome of this dispute would be a Communist dictatorship in Spain', a view at once 'vigorously challenged' by his colleagues.[55] Citrine himself was privately

[50] TUC, Documents 2, 27 August 1936, report of interview, p. 1.
[51] TUC, Documents 2, Labour Movement Conference, verbatim of Citrine's speeches, 4 September 1936, p. 13. [52] TUC, International Conference 2, verbatim report, p. 53.
[53] PRO, FO 371 20574, W 9331/62/41, nos. 122–4, 19 August 1936.
[54] TUC, Documents 1, NCL, verbatim report, 25 August 1936, p. 15.
[55] PRO, FO 371 20574, W 9331/62/41, nos. 122–4, 19 August 1936.

sympathetic to this argument, but was clearly unwilling to present Eden with the gift of actually saying so. Citrine also pressed Eden on the danger of war over Spain, and received the reply that – 'We think that the situation is full of danger and we don't want to make Spain the cockpit'.[56]

Reporting on the talks a week later at the NCL Citrine commented that Eden had promised 'general support' to Non-Intervention.[57] In the ensuing debate William Gillies voiced the widespread concern about the position of Portugal which, according to the *News Chronicle*, was still being used by the fascist powers as an arms conduit to the rebels. The Spanish representative in London had visited him urging the labour movement to take action to help bring Portugal fully into the Agreement.[58] This point was developed by Dalton who argued that the Foreign Office should be asked to put pressure on Portugal – 'a state subject to our influence, almost a vassal...for hundreds of years a miserable little country easy to bully if they did wrong'.[59] In a general atmosphere of indecision, the question of Portugal was seized upon as one area where the movement could take definite action and it was agreed to send a further delegation to the Foreign Office.

Meanwhile, further doubts had been shed on the origins of Non-Intervention. At the 28 July LSI/IFTU meeting there had been no suggestion of the British government's culpability in the project. However, in the intervening weeks evidence of overt British pressure on the French government was provided by leading figures in the French labour movement. At an LSI/IFTU meeting on 21 August Jouhaux had reported the claim by Delbos (the French Foreign Minister) that the British government was 'largely responsible' for the French adoption of Non-Intervention, having threatened to remain neutral if the French continued to support the Spanish government and 'any incident arose'.[60] In reply, Citrine reported the British government's stated opinion that the proposals came direct from the French, and that the British found them desirable as a means to limit the conflict – otherwise there was great danger of 'a conflict on an international scale'.[61] According to De Brouckère, however, who had recently spoken to Blum, Delbos had returned from his conversations with Eden in London 'with the impression' that France would stand alone if there was war over Spain. Similar threats had also been made at a meeting between Admirals Darlan and Chatfield, and Vansittart (Permanent Under-Secretary at the British Foreign Office) had warned Blum that there were '200 conservative

[56] TUC, Documents 1, NCL, verbatim report, 25 August 1936, p. 26.
[57] NCL minutes, 25 August 1936.
[58] TUC, Documents 1, NCL, verbatim report, 25 August 1936, p. 19.   [59] *Ibid.* pp. 32–3.
[60] TUC, Documents 1, IFTU/LSI meeting, verbatim report, 21 August 1936, p. 3.
[61] *Ibid.* p. 5.

diehards' who would oppose any support for the Spanish government.[62] When Gillies continued to defend Eden, on the grounds that Delbos had mistaken Eden's warning of prudence for demands for a policy of neutrality, the French socialist Zyromsky made the astonishing claim that Blum had been told that, if the French supplied arms to Spain, 'the British Government would supply arms to the rebels'.[63] Citrine had hurriedly moved the debate away from this uncomfortable area, which he dubbed the 'realm of diplomatic intrigue', towards the 'public facts', most significantly that the French government had declared first for 'neutrality' in spite of its support for arms for Spain.[64]

Citrine and Gillies went directly from this meeting to visit Delbos and, although the interview was conducted by Gillies, Citrine came away with the clear impression that 'nothing Delbos said in my hearing' endorsed the claim that he had been intimidated by the British government. This interpretation was, however, implicitly challenged by Gillies who reported that Spain had been mentioned at Delbos' 23 July meeting with Eden and, therefore, when the French cabinet made their decision 'they believed they were doing what the British Government wished them to do. Delbos did say that'.[65] However, at no stage do the labour leaders appear to have believed that Eden had intimidated the French government, and they were happy not to push Zyromsky's point when they met Eden again. Gillies and Citrine also visited Jouhaux who said that he would not press the French government to supply arms. When Citrine asked him what they should do in Britain he had 'just shrugged his shoulders'.[66]

On 26 August the second delegation pursued the origins of Non-Intervention unenthusiastically. Citrine recorded that when he raised Zyromsky's point concerning British threats, the suggestion was 'laughed out of court'.[67] The delegates then referred to Portugal, and the view was 'strongly put' that Non-Intervention would be worthless 'unless Portugal could be made to come into the agreement at once'. In reply, Eden assured his visitors of the government's efforts to enforce Non-Intervention, especially in respect of Portugal in its 'unique and difficult position'.[68] However, he pointed out that British influence was not as strong there as

---

[62] *Ibid.* p. 6.   [63] *Ibid.* pp. 7–8.   [64] *Ibid.* pp. 8–9.

[65] TUC, Documents 1, NCL, verbatim report, 25 August 1936, pp. 17–18.

[66] *Ibid.* p. 17. Citrine and Gillies went on to visit Hugh Lloyd Thomas, Minister at the British Embassy and reported on the views of Jouhaux and others. Jill Edwards, *The British Government and the Spanish Civil War*, pp. 27–8.

[67] TUC, Documents 1, 27 August 1936, report of meeting, p. 2.

[68] PRO, FO 371 20534, W 9331/62/41, nos. 189–91, 26 August 1936, report of meeting.

some seemed to think. The delegates did not challenge Lord Halifax's revealing comment that 'they were not deluding themselves that they were going to get agreement of 100 per cent'.[69]

Finally, delegates raised the question of humanitarian aid. This part of the discussion is of particular interest because it demonstrates that the delegates were happy to accept an embargo on weapons so long as they could continue to supply the relief which was the mainstay of labour's internationalist assistance.[70] They reminded Eden of the importance of 'coming to no understanding with the other powers which would preclude the supply of foodstuffs and medicines by the Labour organisations to their corresponding organisations in Spain'.[71] According to Citrine they made it plain that there would be 'uproar' if the Italians had their way in excluding humanitarian aid under Non-Intervention.[72] At Citrine's request, Eden undertook to receive a further delegation before any decision was taken on this matter.[73] Although there is no evidence that the British government would have countenanced such restrictions on humanitarian aid, the forcefully expressed views of the labour movement would have strengthened its resolve. However, Eden told the delegates that 'there would have to be no collections except for humanitarian purposes...[and] no organised recruiting [of soldiers]'.[74] Reporting to the 27 August NCL Citrine said that Eden had given assurances both on this point and on the question of Portugal.[75]

Subsequently both sides pondered the meaning of the information that they had gathered. Greenwood and Gillies, for instance, came away with very different assessments of the government's attitude towards Portugal.[76] Similarly, Foreign Office officials were forced to pore over press reports to gauge the attitude of the labour movement. They were particularly taken with a *Manchester Guardian* article which intimated that their visitors had been persuaded that Non-Intervention was the best option, but that 'it looks...as if the representatives of Labour may also be criticised by some of

[69] TUC, Documents 1, 27 August 1936, report of meeting, pp. 4 and 5.
[70] However, the delegates also hoped that the embargo would not be enforced before a shipment of weapons had arrived from Mexico.
[71] PRO, FO 371 20534, W 9331/62/41, nos. 189–91, 26 August 1936, report of meeting.
[72] TUC, Documents 1, 27 August 1936, report of meeting, p. 5. On the Italian demands see Hugh Thomas, *The Spanish Civil War* (1961), p. 257.
[73] PRO, FO 371 20534, W 9331/62/41, nos. 189–91, 26 August 1936, report of meeting.
[74] TUC, Documents 1, Labour Movement Conference, verbatim report, 28 August 1936, p. 42.   [75] NCL minutes, 27 August 1936.
[76] TUC, Documents 1, 27 August 1936, report of meeting, pp. 6–7. Greenwood had been impressed by the limits of British influence over Portugal, whereas Gillies came away thinking that the British government 'are exerting pressure on Portugal and have given them serious warnings'.

their supporters'.[77] They were less happy with a *Daily Herald* report which claimed that Eden had given certain assurances for the future. George Mounsey felt that:

> This is intolerable ... the effect is to make it look as though the Labour Party were able to obtain interviews with the Secretary of State in order to extract from him assurances such as meet their criticisms of his foreign policy. That is entirely unfair and wrong: and I greatly doubt whether it is advisable that these 'delegation' interviews should be continued.[78]

Eden took a more lenient view, preferring to see evidence of 'discussion in the ranks of the opposition' rather than of chicanery. However, he agreed that, with Attlee's return from Russia, contacts should now be on a more limited basis.[79] Some Labour Party politicians were also unhappy – Cripps, for instance, complained that 'it was no use having interviews with the Foreign Secretary ... which were confidential and could not be repeated'.[80] One further consequence of the second delegation was that Mounsey raised with Cambon (Minister at the French Embassy in London), as requested, the question of whether the Non-Intervention agreement was to be confined to Europe or extended worldwide.[81]

This spate of activity cleared the ground for the crucial series of meetings that began on 25 August and guaranteed Citrine and his allies a dominant position in the labour movement response to Non-Intervention. Thus, the parameters of debate had already been established to his satisfaction on a number of vital issues. In fact, there were three propositions which formed the intellectual underpinning of support for Non-Intervention, and all of them required some degree of self-deception.

The first proposition was that Non-Intervention was a purely French initiative. The NCL officers drew up a memorandum for the decisive Labour Movement Conference on 28 August, which explained that the Non-Intervention initiative was an internal French decision in response to French political pressures, and 'inspired by the fear that competition in the supply of arms' might 'precipitate a conflict into which France might be drawn without any guarantee of support'.[82] This position was reiterated by Citrine at the actual meeting where he said that the French government 'not only made the proposals for non-intervention, but at once acted upon it

[77] PRO, FO 371 20534, W 9331/62/41, nos. 203–4, 27 August 1936, FO minute, Warner to Mounsey.   [78] *Ibid.* 27 August 1936, Mounsey to Warner.
[79] *Ibid.* 28 August 1936, note by Eden.
[80] TUC, Documents 1, Labour Movement Conference, verbatim report, p. 43.
[81] TUC, Documents 1, NCL, verbatim report, 25 August 1936, p. 15.
[82] TUC, Documents 1, memorandum prepared for 28 August 1936 Labour Movement Conference.

themselves'.[83] This acceptance of the British government's account of the origins of Non-Intervention persisted in the face of growing French claims to the contrary, and as late as the 26 October 1936 LSI/IFTU meeting Greenwood felt compelled to make a vigorous defence of his own government's case.[84]

Following on from the first proposition, it became vital to establish the internal factors behind Blum's decision, and thus to ascertain that his government would fall if Non-Intervention were challenged. Bevin, in particular, made this argument central to his defence of Non-Intervention.[85] On 25 August, for instance, his view was that they were 'tied up to France to some extent' in their response to Spain,[86] and in October he claimed that 'if Blum...moves one inch from his present position, there is revolution in France'.[87] However, although there was clearly some basis to such a belief, due to the unstable nature of the French coalition government and the presence of an extremist right wing, it reflected a partisan reading of the French situation. On 28 July, for instance, Jean Longuet had said that the French efforts for Spain had run into 'obstacles from the reactionary elements', and this was corroborated by Jouhaux at the 21 August LSI/IFTU meeting when he drew attention to the activities of French fascists near the Spanish border.[88] Citrine's reading of this same information was altogether more loaded, however – 'the French Fascists and reactionaries were becoming a real menace to the Government itself'.[89]

Yet, in fact, the message from the French socialists was far from clear, hardly surprising given the many political currents within the French labour movement. The socialist party contained two distinct left-wing tendencies (led by Zyromsky and Pivert) as well as the two moderate tendencies led by Blum and the General Secretary Paul Faure (whose pacifism later distinguished him from Blum). Moreover, the CGT, derived originally from French Anarcho-syndicalism, was politically independent of the SFIO and, since the unification with the CGTU, was open to communist influence. Its leader Jouhaux was a keen supporter of the Spanish Republic. A final complication were the regular shifts in communist strategy. Until the end of

[83] TUC, Documents 1, Labour Movement Conference, verbatim report, 28 August 1936, p. 13.

[84] TUC, Documents 2, Labour Movement Conference, verbatim report, 28 October 1936, pp. 11 and 16.

[85] *TUC CR*, 1936, p. 386. Bevin quoted at length from Blum's recent speech at Luna Park, Paris.   [86] TUC, Documents 1, NCL, verbatim report, 25 August 1936, p. 24.

[87] TUC, Documents 2, Labour Movement Conference, verbatim report, 28 October 1936, p. 55.

[88] TUC, Documents 1, IFTU/LSI meeting, verbatim report, 28 July 1936, pp. 7–8; TUC, Documents 1, IFTU/LSI meeting, verbatim report, 21 August 1936, p. 3.

[89] TUC, Documents 1, Labour Movement Conference, verbatim report, 28 August 1936, p. 17.

August the French communists had sought to prop up the government by actively restraining strike action. However, in early September there was a sudden change to aggressive opposition to Non-Intervention, backed up by strikes in Parisian metallurgical factories, possibly connected with the Soviet decision to intervene in Spain.[90] Equally suddenly, in October, the communists called off the strikes and returned to a more moderate stance.

Thus, there was no shortage of authoritative voices within French labour questioning Non-Intervention. Alexandre Bracke (editor of *Le Populaire*), for instance, while 'in favour of the non-intervention policy by Governments...thought that the Socialist Movement itself should see that arms were supplied and get their Governments to wink at it' – an attitude which Citrine found repugnant.[91] However, the case of French socialists who opposed Non-Intervention was denied a hearing in Britain, and the opinions of the CGT and left-wing socialists were virtually disqualified on political grounds. After all, the CGT was a united front organisation with the communists, which was running its own fund-raising operation for Spain and was known to be involved in smuggling goods over the Pyrenees.[92] An influential source in Paris told the labour leaders in early September that the CGT was 'now in communist hands', alleging that the communists enjoyed its full support along with that of socialist ministers such as Auriol and Salengro.[93] Soon afterwards the TUC suppressed a resolution passed by the CGT calling on British labour to reconsider Non-Intervention, because it might have rocked the boat at the TUC Congress.[94] Similarly, in November 1936 Citrine refused to meet an unofficial delegation of French socialist deputies who had come to London to discuss Spain under the auspices of the 'International Committee for the Co-ordination of Aid to the Spanish Republic', an organisation linked with the French Front Populaire, who did not class as authorised delegates of the SFIO or the CGT.[95] Subsequently it became official NCL policy that in international matters contacts and action were to be pursued only in official co-operation with the IFTU and LSI and unofficial contacts were discouraged.[96]

---

[90] Julian Jackson, *The Popular Front in France*, pp. 225–6.
[91] TUC, Documents 1, IFTU/LSI meeting, verbatim report, 21 August 1936, p. 6; TUC, Documents 1, NCL, verbatim report, 25 August 1936, pp. 17–18.
[92] TUC, Documents 2, 21 December 1936, report of meeting with 'rank and file' deputation, p. 10. Citrine said that the CGT had spent 'millions of francs on getting vital supplies to the Spanish Government...They can only do that by smuggling.'
[93] TUC, Correspondence 1, 1 September 1936, W.H. Stevenson, (*Daily Herald*) to Citrine, enclosing a 'Confidential Memorandum on the Spanish situation and its repercussions in France', p. 2.   [94] See below pp. 65–6.
[95] TUC, Correspondence 1, 20 November 1936, Belin to Citrine; TUC, Finance and General Purposes Committee minutes, 23 November 1936.
[96] NCL minutes, 24 November 1936; TUC, Correspondence 1, 14 December 1936, Citrine to CGT. Citrine did eventually agree to an informal meeting (TUC, General Council minutes,

Thus, when listening to the voice of French labour, the British labour leaders in fact practised a form of selective deafness: the views of French socialists who opposed Non-Intervention were consistently ignored in favour of Blum's opinions, even though there was no direct British contact with him until early September.[97] Instead, labour leaders came to rely on the confidential despatches of the *Daily Herald*'s Paris correspondent who was thought to have access to 'inner circles' of government, and at both the 25 August and the 4 September meetings lengthy memoranda were read out from him to the effect that Moscow, through the French communists and the CGT, was seeking to manoeuvre France into war with Germany over Spain.[98] Non-Intervention could, therefore, be seen as a means of thwarting this design. Thus, the public commitment of labour leaders to the support of Blum reflected their suspicion of international communism working through the CGT.

The third proposition concerned the nature of Non-Intervention. It was believed that some form of Non-Intervention agreement was in the best interests of the Spanish workers in spite of the repeated assertions from Spanish representatives to the contrary. According to Gillies the mood at the 21 August LSI/IFTU meeting had been that the Spanish government 'didn't really need [arms] very much'.[99] Citrine claimed that the Spanish government was successfully converting factories for arms production in Barcelona and Toledo.[100] Indeed, in debates as late as October 1936 it was being reported from respected sources that it was more than the lack of arms that held back the Spanish socialists – 'it was the inefficiency, the incompetence of the military leaders of the Government...'[101] Bevin chipped in that the Spanish ambassador in Geneva had told him that while the arms situation was improving, the main difficulty was an inability to use them because 'they haven't got the organisation'.[102] Having sown such doubts it was relatively easy for Citrine and his colleagues to assert that free trade in arms would favour the rebels and that their own task was to make the embargo as effective as possible. Moreover, it was felt that it was impossible

---

25 November 1936). *Manchester Guardian*, 25 November 1936 carried an interview with Belin who found Citrine 'fully alive to the danger in Spain'.

[97] TUC, Documents 2, Labour Movement Conference, verbatim report of Citrine's speeches, 4 September 1936, p. 4.

[98] TUC, Documents 1, Labour Movement Conference, verbatim report, 28 August 1936, p. 11; TUC, Documents 2, Labour Movement Conference, verbatim report of Citrine's speeches, 4 September 1936, pp. 4–5. No copies of the memoranda were enclosed with either report, although there are copies of those used on 4 September 1936 in TUC, Correspondence 1, 1 September 1936 and 2 September 1936, Stevenson to Citrine.

[99] TUC, Documents 1, NCL, verbatim report, 25 August 1936, p. 20. [100] *Ibid.* pp. 20–1.

[101] TUC, Documents 2, Labour Movement Conference, verbatim report, 28 October 1936, p. 21. Dallas was reporting the views of the LSI representative in Spain, Pietro Nenni.

[102] *Ibid.* p. 23.

and undesirable to challenge the Non-Intervention policy. As early as 25 August Citrine's position was that 'it was morally impossible now that the agreement had been concluded to say that we wanted [it] broken and let everybody have a free hand'.[103] Concomitant with this belief was an element of defeatism, summed up in Greenwood's remark that 'no resolution [of the NCL] nor motion of the Party would alter the Government's policy'.[104] Citrine believed that if a Labour government were in power it would act in exactly the same way as Baldwin's had done.[105]

The broad agreement on these propositions (only Herbert Morrison dissented from any of them) stemmed directly from the established practice in the labour movement which gave almost total control over information to a limited circle of leaders and officials. This laid the foundations for the ensuing debates to take on a peculiar character. Quite simply, the initial debates over the Spanish Civil War were only tangentially concerned with Spain, and the question of how political assistance could be given to the Spanish workers was eclipsed by more abstract questions such as the danger of war or the future of Blum's government. Instead, the debate over Non-Intervention revolved around a consideration of British national interests to which the interests of the Spanish workers had to be accommodated. On 25 August, for instance, Bevin depicted the Spanish crisis in terms of the danger to the British position in the Mediterranean – 'He had often said that it would be a strange thing that it would fall to the lot of the Labour Party to save the British Empire'.[106] Again, at the 4 September meeting, ostensibly solely devoted to Spain, Hugh Dalton addressed himself purely to the defence situation and 'deliberately abstained' from speaking on Spain at all.[107]

In fact, when discussing Spain the major issue was really the threat of war to Britain, and in many respects the debates were a clear extension of the arguments within the labour movement over international policy and defence which had dominated the decade. Some historians have seized on pacifism as an explanation for the labour movement's passivity in response to Spain.[108] However, expressions of overt pacifism were comparatively rare,[109] although George Lansbury warned his colleagues against the belief that 'only by a very long and bloody struggle' could peace be achieved in

---

[103] TUC, Documents 1, NCL, verbatim report, 25 August 1936, p. 36.   [104] *Ibid.* p. 43.
[105] *Ibid.* p. 45.   [106] *Ibid.* p. 49.
[107] TUC, Documents 2, Labour Movement Conference, verbatim report, 4 September 1936, p. 25.
[108] See D. Cattell, *Soviet Diplomacy and the Spanish Civil War* (University of California, Berkeley, 1957), p. 27.
[109] The speech by the shopworkers' leader Maurice Hann at Plymouth was one example of this, *TUC CR*, 1936, p. 382.

Europe.[110] A more representative position was probably that of the Labour MP David Grenfell who confessed that 'he had seen for a long time that pacifism was not enough'.[111] Much more important than overt pacifism was the question of whether the British people and the labour movement would fight in a war over Spain – as Bevin put it: 'The bulk of the Party had been brought up on the Pacifist attitude and if you are going to tell your people that they will shortly be plunged into war, you ought to know where you stand with your own people'.[112]

The danger of war arising from uncontrolled intervention in Spain was fully apprehended and made a central theme by Bevin at the 25 August NCL meeting. He was particularly worried that the Labour Party, which still voted against the military estimates, was not yet ready to give its support to measures vital to the nation's defence.[113] Citrine added that Britain was not yet able to 'face the challenge' from Germany – 'they wanted this country to take risk after risk, but were not ready to give the backing'.[114] Many of the MPs present, in particular James Walker and Hugh Dalton, happily joined in this criticism of Labour Party defence policy. According to Dalton 'we have played into [Italian and German] hands by the decision to vote against every stick of arms which the Government asked for'.[115] This culminated in a fully blown assault by Bevin on the record and competence of the Labour Party. He felt that the party should decide where it stood before it made any pronouncements on Spain and he threatened that 'they were at the parting of the ways. His own personal view was that the Trade Unions would have to strike out on their own. They were the first people to be destroyed if Fascism came'.[116] The only real challenge came from Herbert Morrison who, although often depicted as an innocent in foreign affairs, had at least taken the trouble to speak with de los Ríos in Paris on the previous day and reiterated his plea for arms. Unlike the other speakers he built his case around the unequivocal right of the Spanish government to arms and made a vain attempt to persuade his colleagues to condemn the embargo as part of 'their elementary duty, both as a matter of international law and of solidarity with those who were fighting for democracy'.[117]

The meeting parted with the agreement that the NCL officers should draw up a statement for the 28 August Labour Movement Conference. This document reinforced the many assumptions that had been made, concluding with the rhetorical question of 'how the movement will be affected if it should decide to oppose the non-intervention policy, having regard to the

[110] TUC, Documents 1, Labour Movement Conference, verbatim report, 28 August 1936, p. 65.   [111] TUC, Documents 1, NCL, verbatim report, 25 August 1936, p. 26.
[112] *Ibid.* p. 25.   [113] *Ibid.* pp. 24–5.   [114] *Ibid.* p. 26.   [115] *Ibid.* p. 33.
[116] *Ibid.* pp. 40–1.   [117] *Ibid.* pp. 22–3.

Party vote on the [military] estimates. Are we free to advocate a policy which seriously increases the risk of war in view of that vote?'[118] On the 28 August Citrine's lengthy exposition of the situation again guided the meeting towards his favoured terrain, asking whether the Germans and Italians could be restrained other than by military and naval action which could escalate into open war. 'Would British public opinion support taking the risk? We did not feel that we could confidently say that they would'.[119] Again the only real challenge came from Morrison, who admitted that the matter 'involved the risk of war' but felt that they should not 'surrender' so readily to such threats. Moreover, they should come to a British decision – 'they were being asked to follow the decision of French Radicalism, and he was not going to do it'. Instead, they should condemn the policy of neutrality outright.[120]

However, a succession of speakers, including Cripps, put the case for accepting Non-Intervention as being in the best interests of all interested parties. In the afternoon session Bevin traversed the draft resolution in detail, defining its contents as neither accepting the policy nor being able to 'take the plunge and throw the agreement over'. Instead he highlighted the areas where they could develop their political attacks, such as the issues of civilian control of the military and Franco's use of Moorish troops.[121] The amended resolution, carried unanimously, reiterated the right of the Spanish government to the supply of arms but accepted that a policy of Non-Intervention was necessary to prevent a European war.[122] However, if Non-Intervention was not 'loyally observed' the conference would be recalled for discussion. One trade union leader captured the mood of relief amongst delegates as the TUC Congress loomed, asserting that the document was 'the best that could be done at the time...the best policy that could be presented to the movement'.[123]

These two debates settled the attitude of the labour movement until the TUC Congress in September 1936. Perhaps the most notable feature had been the abstractness of the discussion, avoiding the practicalities of solidarity action. Indeed, the miners' leader Ebby Edwards struck a deeply incongruous note when he said that, irrespective of the broader issues, 'this meeting should consider the organisation of the Movement behind the Spanish workers. He thought we could do something in the conflict, that

---

[118] TUC, Documents 1, memorandum prepared for 28 August 1936 meeting.
[119] TUC, Documents 1, Labour Movement Conference, verbatim report, 28 August 1936, p. 20. [120] *Ibid.* pp. 26–30.
[121] *Ibid.* pp. 46–54. Bevin followed a similar procedure in his Congress speech, *TUC CR*, 1936, pp. 368–9. [122] See Appendix to *TUC CR*, 1936, p. 488.
[123] TUC, Documents 1, Labour Movement Conference, verbatim report, 28 August 1936, p. 64.

would at least focus people's attention,' advocating the recall of Parliament as the solution. Citrine's response was almost inane – 'he wondered how they were going to get speakers'.[124] Astonishingly, this was almost the only discussion of any form of mobilisation in solidarity with Spain, highlighting the fact that policy was continuing to be made in a vacuum, particularly on the trade union side. Few unions discussed Spain over the summer months other than to make donations for humanitarian relief. When the AEU London District Council suggested to its Executive that it should demand that the government send supplies to Spain, the reply was that 'questions of this kind can best be handled by bodies such as the NCL'.[125] Activism amongst trade unionists was largely restricted to the unofficial rank-and-file movements and easily dismissed by union leaders as a communist manoeuvre. Bevin, for instance, denied that there was any mass feeling for 'intervention'.

> He had a very large union and the only resolutions were from Communist sources and he might say they had a stereotyped resolution from 38 branches and everyone could have said where it had come from.[126]

Such blinkered thinking was finally swept away at the Labour Party's conference in October. In fact union leaders were more frightened by the backlash among Catholic workers, in Bevin's case especially among his Irish members,[127] and tended to take them much more seriously than left-wing rank-and-file opinion.

With the agreement on policy at the 28 August meeting, attention was concentrated on building support for it at the imminent TUC Congress. Accordingly Greenwood and Citrine returned to the Foreign Office on 1 September to visit Under-Secretary of State Lord Cranborne, bearing new press reports of arms shipments, aboard German and British vessels, from Germany to Spain via Portugal. Due to the proximity of Congress they desperately needed information on the progress of the Non-Intervention Agreement to counter possible critics. Citrine told Cranborne that 'their

---

[124] TUC, Documents 1, NCL, verbatim report, 25 August 1936, pp. 37–8.
[125] MRC, Mss 259, AEU Executive Council minutes, 12 August 1936, pp. 37–8. There were two notable exceptions to the general reluctance by trade unions to advocate political action. The Durham miners wrote to the NCL calling for a one-day solidarity strike for Spain, and the South Wales miners called for a 'National Conference of all Labour Forces' to compel the government to assist the Republic. Both initiatives were dismissed without discussion. (See TUC, Documents 1, NCL, verbatim report, 25 August 1936, p. 53; TUC, Correspondence 1, 2 September 1936, Harris to Citrine.)
[126] TUC, Documents 2, Labour Movement Conference, verbatim report, 4 September 1936, p. 15. See also James Middleton's comments at the 25 August NCL meeting: 'he had to deal with the letters, telegrams etc. that have been coming into the Party. There was a campaign being run by the Left of all sections against the decision of the French Government' (TUC, Documents 2, verbatim report, p. 45).   [127] See below pp. 192–4.

people were reluctant to support the agreement' so long as it appeared to favour the fascists, and he almost begged him – 'couldn't they give him a date? Could they not say when the Committee would meet?' However, the response was unhelpful. The minister pointed out that the agreement could not 'be regarded as a watertight thing. There were bound to be evasions.' However, he promised to investigate the specific cases of violation raised by Citrine, and would forward any relevant information so that 'they would be in a better position for Congress'.[128] A telegram was duly sent on 4 September, which Bevin read out to Congress, although all that the Foreign Office had been able to glean was that the British vessel allegedly running guns to the rebels was, in fact, loading an innocuous cargo in Australia.[129]

Nonetheless, the mission did have some impact on the Foreign Office. Mounsey was moved to record that if there was much more delay: 'The extreme elements both here and in France will at once make this a pretext for forcing the French Government and H.M. Govt [sic] to give up the whole idea of non-intervention'. The ambassador in Berlin was informed of the 'most unfortunate results on public opinion here' if Germany failed to join the initiative.[130]

At the 4 September Labour Movement Conference the manoeuvres required to present a convincing policy to Congress formed the main consideration. The meeting decided, on Bevin's suggestion, that pressure should be placed on the government at the delay in drawing up an international agreement.[131] However, the idea that this should be accompanied with a reaffirmation of support for Non-Intervention was abandoned after opposition from the railwaymen's leader John Marchbank who argued that, unless the government could give an assurance that genuine steps would be taken towards an agreement, then 'he was with those who were definitely opposed to the continuance of the neutrality policy'.[132] Accordingly a telegram was sent to Eden expressing grave concern at the delay in concluding an effective agreement in the light of continuing reports of violations. Citrine had felt that 'the mere fact of their writing might have some influence upon getting the agreement concluded'.[133] Subsequently Lord Cranborne informed him that the international (Non-Intervention) Committee was due to meet on 9 September, and assured him of the government's commitment to 'the rigid enforcement' of any measures

---

[128] TUC, Documents 2, Labour Movement Conference, verbatim report, 4 September 1936, pp. 2–3.   [129] *TUC CR, 1936*, p. 387.
[130] PRO, FO 371 20574, W 10289/9549/41, 1 September 1936, report of meeting by Mounsey.
[131] TUC, Documents 2, Labour Movement Conference, verbatim report, 4 September 1936, p. 15.   [132] *Ibid.* p. 20.
[133] PRO, FO 371 20576, W 10939/9549/41, nos. 63–6, 4 September 1936; TUC, Documents 2, Labour Movement Conference, verbatim report, 4 September 1936, p. 24.

that it might recommend.[134] At the TUC Congress Bevin claimed a degree of credit for these developments: 'the constant pressure of the National Council of Labour on the Government resulted in a speedy meeting of that Committee. We have represented a great body of public opinion in this country.'[135] Needless to say, when that body of opinion was later deployed in opposition to government policy it became far less easy to claim such success.

It was further decided on 4 September to send delegates to Paris to ascertain the situation there and Hicks, Dalton and Dallas, along with Gillies, were sent to represent the General Council, NEC and PLP. Hicks denied press speculation that he had gone to consult with Blum about Spain: 'How could the Prime Minister of a country agree to meet in an official capacity a representative of Trade Unionism or Socialism from a foreign country to discuss with him, or they [sic], the foreign policy of its Government towards a third country?'[136] While in Paris, however, the delegates met a wide range of figures including Blum, Jouhaux, representatives of both Internationals, de los Ríos and the Paris correspondents of the *Manchester Guardian* and *Daily Herald*.[137] Their report concluded that there was no reason to modify labour's attitude towards Non-Intervention. To call for an end to Non-Intervention would embarrass the French government and 'play the game of the French communists. We should not be helping the Spanish government'.[138] However, their conclusion that French labour was not divided on the issue was hardly truthful to their observations and again reflected the official hostility and suspicion towards the CGT. Indeed, their report had paid particular attention to the communist opposition to Non-Intervention acting through the CGT, and in supplementary comments Hicks said that Jouhaux 'seemed to be a good deal under communist influence'.[139]

The delegation to Paris had unhappily coincided with the shift in communist and CGT strategy to agitation against the Blum government over Non-Intervention. On their last day in Paris the CGT Administrative Committee had addressed a resolution to the TUC, according to which the CGT considered it

---

[134] PRO, FO 371 20576, W 10939/9549/41, nos. 27–8, 7 September 1936, Cranborne to Citrine.   [135] *TUC CR*, 1936, p. 387.

[136] TUC, Correspondence 1, 6 August 1936, Hicks to Citrine. Although dated 6 August the letter should be dated 6 September: Citrine's comments at the TUC Congress confirm this correction (*TUC CR*, p. 366).

[137] TUC, Documents 2, Hicks' report for 9 September 1936 Labour Movement Conference.

[138] *Ibid.* p. 6.

[139] TUC, Documents 2, Labour Movement Conference, verbatim report, 9 September 1936, p. 1.

to be its duty to ask the French Government to reconsider in agreement with the British Government and other democratic Governments the policy of neutrality...and asks [the TUC] to take the same actions with the same aims as far as their Government is concerned.[140]

Citrine read out this resolution to the Labour Movement Conference on 9 September and delegates were afraid that if Blum's policy were forcibly changed they would be embarrassed at Congress. Citrine, however, remained confident that the CGT would not press its demands in a 'show down' with Blum if this would mean the defeat of his government.[141]

No mention was made of the CGT resolution in the Congress speeches and this sparked accusations in the left-wing press that vital information concerning the attitude of the CGT had been suppressed. Although Citrine hotly denied this allegation, his arguments were deceptive[142] and obscured the fact that instead of revealing pertinent information concerning the attitude of the CGT, he had used the opportunity to score points against the 'irresponsibility' of the French communists (who were ready to criticise Blum's government yet unwilling to leave the Front Populaire or to question the Soviet Union's acceptance of Non-Intervention).[143] The suppression of the information related directly to suspicion felt by labour leaders towards the CGT, summed up in Bevin's comments that the TUC should not be manoeuvred by the CGT into passing a resolution that would bring Blum down.[144] Attlee, too, thought that the CGT message was a 'communist manoeuvre' and could not be taken as representative of the views of 'responsible members'. Philip Noel-Baker warned him that if they disregarded official communications from the representatives of the French workers 'how are we ever going to get international working class unity or

---

[140] Typescript copy of resolution, undated but between 1 and 21 September 1936, TUC, Documents 2.

[141] TUC, Documents 2, Labour Movement Conference, verbatim report, 9 September 1936, p. 5.

[142] For proof that the resolution was discussed see General Council minutes, 9 September 1936 and TUC, Documents 2, Labour Movement Conference, verbatim report, 9 September 1936, p. 1. This story was reported in the *News Chronicle* 10 September 1936 and allegations of the suppression of information were made by its 'Covenanter' column on 30 September. The story was belatedly taken up by the *New Statesman and Nation* (3 October 1936) and the *New Leader* (9 October 1936). Citrine's claim that this latter story was 'definitely libellous' and that 'There is not the slightest truth that either a telegram, message or communication of any kind came to the General Council from the French Trade Union organisation' is not concordant with the facts of the case (TUC, Correspondence 1, 24 December 1936, Citrine to Stapleford and District Labour Party and Trades Council).

[143] *TUC CR*, p. 366.

[144] TUC, Documents 2, Labour Movement Conference, verbatim report, 9 September 1936, p. 6.

co-operation'.[145] Nor was this the only example of the suppression of potentially damaging information at the 1936 Congress. Citrine made no mention of a message sent to the General Council from Viscount Churchill in Barcelona claiming to supply proof of Italian and German military aid to the rebels.[146]

At the last Labour Movement Conference prior to Congress the mood was anxious. Marchbank feared that there would be a split in the trade union movement and that 75 per cent of the delegates would 'definitely oppose' the official policy because none of them would be aware of all the confidential information on which it had been decided. Citrine's comment that 'if they had a case they believed in, then he was not in the least nervous' failed to reassure Will Lawther whose miners' delegation was awaiting the outcome of the meeting before deciding its own policy for Congress. He felt that if the full facts were placed before Congress 'there would be nothing to fear', but that if they were not frank with delegates 'the results might be unfavourable'.[147]

Such fears proved unjustified, however, when the TUC debated Spain on the following day. Citrine gave a reasonably full account of the formulation of policy, basing his justification of Non-Intervention on the well-rehearsed arguments that an Agreement would serve the best interests of the Spanish government, prevent international conflict and protect the Blum government.[148] Bevin then moved a resolution which endorsed the 28 August statement and gave guarded approval to the recent international agreements, though warning that they should not be used to injure the Spanish government.[149] The General Council received valuable backing from Lawther who seconded the motion on behalf of the miners, contending that the alternative to this policy would undoubtedly be war.[150]

However, the official policy came under attack from Bill Zak of the left-wing union NAFTA who proposed an amendment which deplored 'so-called neutrality' as a hindrance to the Spanish government and called on the General Council to request the Internationals to launch a campaign against it, enabling the Spanish to receive arms. In his speech he challenged those who claimed that the only alternative to an embargo was 'intervention' – in fact, they only sought 'normal commercial relations' for

---

[145] Churchill College, Cambridge, Philip Noel-Baker papers, 'Spain' Correspondence, vol. 1, NBKR 4/656, 26 September 1936, Noel-Baker to Attlee.
[146] TUC, General Council minutes, 9 September 1936. The telegram was forwarded to the TUC by Viscountess Hastings (TUC, Correspondence 1, 8 September 1936).
[147] TUC, Documents 2, Labour Movement Conference, verbatim report, 9 September 1936, pp. 4–6.   [148] TUC CR, pp. 359–67.   [149] *Ibid.* pp. 367–70.   [150] *Ibid.* pp. 370–1.

the Spanish government.[151] Another NAFTA member, A.G. Tomkins, asserted that working-class solidarity should dictate their policy and 'International law is of secondary importance when dealing with working class policy'.[152] In debate supporters of the amendment outnumbered those for the resolution. Indeed, the engineers' president, Jack Little, while supporting the resolution did so 'with all my inclinations in favour of the amendment'.[153] Yet most of these speakers expressed a personal view and could not bring their delegation's votes with them. Bevin then concluded the debate. His theme was that the policy had been decided by reason rather than emotion in a dangerous international situation. 'The choice before us was whether or not we would take a step which in our view would lead to war'.[154] On a card vote the big battalions carried the policy by an overwhelming 3,029,000 to 51,000.

However, the Plymouth decision, although a remarkable victory, was short-lived for two reasons. First, it could not purport to establish a permanent policy because it was intimately related to the evolution of the Spanish and international situation, and a mounting weight of accusation suggested that Non-Intervention was far from being 'loyally observed' by the fascist powers. Moreover, many independent contacts were being made with Spain and this began to puncture the earlier tight control of information. On 24 September, for instance, the Labour MPs William Dobbie and Seymour Cocks reported to the TUC and Labour Party International Departments that, following their recent visit to Spain, they believed that the embargo should be lifted whatever the price.[155] Secondly, Non-Intervention was soon due to come under further intense scrutiny, this time at the Labour Party Edinburgh conference where support was far less reliable than at Plymouth.

In the interim the Internationals met again in Paris on 28 September at the request of the UGT, with Hicks deputising for Citrine while he was visiting the USA with Schevenels. The UGT Secretary Pascual Tomás stated clearly that arms were needed above all else, and appealed specifically to the British to put pressure on their government to abandon Non-Intervention. Otherwise he 'would call on the British workers to do their duty by their class and send arms to their Spanish brothers who are fighting for them'.[156]

---

[151] *Ibid.* pp. 371–4.   [152] *Ibid.* p. 375.   [153] *Ibid.* p. 377.   [154] *Ibid.* p. 388.
[155] TUC, Documents 2, report of interview, 24 September 1936. They had visited Spain in a delegation with Lord Hastings and the communist Isabel Brown (for an account see Imperial War Museum, Department of Sound Records, Acc No 000844/08, transcript of interview with Isabel Brown, pp. 28–31).
[156] TUC, Documents 2, IFTU/LSI meeting, report, 28 September 1936, p. 3.

Both Tomás and Jiménez de Asúa (PSOE), again addressing themselves to the British, went out of their way to redress the bad impression created by earlier delegates and minimised the danger posed by anarchism, stressing that it would only become a threat if the Spanish people felt deserted by the democracies.[157] Further pressure came from Zyromsky and Jouhaux who drew attention to the CGT's demand for reconsideration of Non-Intervention.[158] Hicks, however, remained non-committal, claiming that the British labour movement had never been happy with the policy 'which favoured the rebels'. Yet to have any chance of changing their government's policy they had to be in possession of new and accurate information concerning violations of the embargo.[159] Although the meeting reaffirmed the existing policy, the resolution demanded that the British and French governments should examine Spanish Foreign Minister Álvarez del Vayo's recent allegations of violations made in Geneva,[160] and on Hicks' return a telegram was sent to Eden on these lines.[161] Hicks emphasised this point when speaking at a CGT rally in Paris where he said that if fascist intervention continued then 'even at the risk of international conflagration, the international working class of the Socialist democracy of Europe must assume the offensive'.[162]

However, any hopes of maintaining the 28 August policy were shattered by the dramatic events at the Labour Party's Edinburgh conference. Spain was debated on 5 October and Greenwood moved the endorsement of the most recent International and NCL resolutions. In a distinctly unenthusiastic address he characterised Non-Intervention as 'a very, very bad second best' that was, however, 'the real way out of a grave situation'.[163] He confessed the need for constant monitoring of the situation, but felt that the alternative would be free trade in arms leading inevitably to war and the defeat of Blum. After seconding from Grenfell the motion received support mainly from trade union leaders including Bevin, Hicks and Charles Dukes. The latter argued, improbably, that Non-Intervention was working – 'we cannot discover a single instance of munitions being despatched subsequent to the signing of that Agreement'.[164] The resolution was carried comfortably with the trade union block votes although Aneurin Bevin called on the leaders to consider whether they were truly expressing the opinion of their rank-and-

---

[157] Ibid. pp. 5–7.   [158] Ibid. pp. 7 and 8.   [159] Ibid. p. 8.   [160] Ibid. p. 9.
[161] NCL minutes, 30 September 1936; PRO, FO 371 20579, W12807/9549/41, 1 October 1936, pp. 83–6 for copies of the telegram and reply.
[162] Manchester Guardian, 29 September 1936.   [163] LPCR, 1936, p. 169.
[164] Ibid. p. 176. Dukes was General Secretary of the National Union of General and Municipal Workers. On 25 September the Daily Herald had sent the TUC a secret report from a 'Special envoy' in Portugal which indicated that large-scale movements of war material through Portugal had ceased (TUC, Documents 2).

file members.[165] Yet these proceedings were transformed two days later by the intervention of the fraternal delegates from Spain, Jiménez de Asúa and Isabel de Palencia, who made rousing speeches[166] and swept the mass of delegates towards a renunciation of Non-Intervention. Attlee and Greenwood were despatched to London to confer with Neville Chamberlain (temporarily in charge of the government) and on their return a new resolution was passed which urged investigation into alleged breaches of the agreement. If it were proven that the agreement was ineffective then the British and French governments should restore the right to buy arms to the Spanish government. With a melodramatic flourish which he must later have regretted, Bevin promised that 'from the moment we leave this conference, our officers will be on the [government's] doorstep, not in a week but every day, putting pressure on to get results'.[167]

Many senior Labour Party figures were privately appalled by the turn of events in Edinburgh. One alleged that the conference had acted under the influence of paid agitators and another said that the fraternal delegates had added no new information but had created an atmosphere that 'carried the majority of the delegates off their feet by the emotion of their appeals'.[168] In spite of this bitterness, however, they now had no choice but to adjust to the new terrain. On 21 October the NCL met to review the situation and the majority opinion was that 'it was quite impossible in the state of mind in which our movement was to take any continued responsibility for the Non-Intervention Agreement'. Although the charges of violation were not proven, they were held to be 'substantially true'. In spite of some dissent the meeting decided that Non-Intervention could no longer be supported and that the Spanish government should be given the right to purchase arms. However, such a decision was deemed beyond the ambit of the NCL alone and a new sequence of meetings began. At the British request a meeting of the Internationals was called for 26 October and it was agreed that the British and French should send enlarged delegations.[169] This practice marked a deterioration in the mechanism of international policy-making as it implicitly recognised that the issue of Non-Intervention was too important

---

[165] *LPCR*, p. 178.
[166] The attendance of the fraternal delegates was arranged at such short notice that Bevin believed that they were deliberately sent to overturn the vote taken on 5 October. In fact, however, they would have arrived in time for that debate had they not been delayed by Home Office officials at Hendon airport (TUC, Documents 2, Labour Movement Conference, verbatim report, 28 October 1936, p. 24).
[167] *LPCR*, 1936, p. 261. See below p. 204.
[168] TUC, Documents 2, Labour Movement Conference, verbatim report, 28 October 1936, p. 22 and 26. The speakers were Mr W.A. Robinson (Political General Secretary of NUDAW), who suspected that the Russian government had financed the agitation, and Mr Brothers (United Textile Factory Workers' Association).   [169] *Ibid.* pp. 3–5.

to be left to the Internationals and would effectively be decided between the British and French. The British delegation was sent without formal instructions beyond transmitting the new attitude of the labour movement.[170]

At the 26 October meeting roles were somewhat reversed from previous encounters, with the British aggressively pushing the French to define their policy clearly. Citrine, explicitly distancing himself from his brief and merely speaking 'as the voice of our Movement'[171] said that if Non-Intervention were abandoned it had to be replaced with something which would benefit Spain. This made the French attitude highly important and he pushed them as to whether they were 'ready to press the French Government on this matter even if it might lead to a break up of the Government of the united front'.[172] The French refused to give a clear answer and Solomon Grumbach (SFIO), with some justification, argued that it was up to each national section to decide its own policy and wrong for the British to put the onus on the French.[173] However, Citrine replied that it would be 'an impossible situation' for divergent policies to be adopted.[174] Both Citrine and Greenwood came away with the firm belief that even if the French challenged their government they would not do so with any degree of conviction, in the knowledge that the French people did not wish to fight a war.[175]

After consultation amongst the French delegates, however, Bracke stated their readiness to seek a reversal in policy, while stressing that this could not be taken in isolation from a similar commitment from the British government.[176] The British accepted the French draft in principle and a joint committee formulated a final version which acknowledged the failure of Non-Intervention and called for the working class 'to secure by their influence upon public opinion and upon their respective Governments the conclusion of an international agreement' to restore commercial liberty to Republican Spain. A further paragraph, inserted on the insistence of Jouhaux, called for the co-ordination of activities to prevent supplies reaching the Spanish rebels and heralded a new stage in the debate.[177] Citrine, who, along with Greenwood and Gillies, opposed this policy although voting in favour of it, was convinced that it implied 'a wiping out of the present [Non-Intervention] agreement'.[178]

---

[170] *Ibid.* p. 48.   [171] *Ibid.* p. 53.
[172] There is an abbreviated account of this meeting in TUC, Documents 2. The best account is in TUC, Documents 2, Labour Movement Conference, verbatim report, 28 October 1936, pp. 6–15.   [173] *Ibid.* p. 12.   [174] *Ibid.* p. 13.   [175] *Ibid.* p. 17.   [176] *Ibid.* pp. 13–14.
[177] *Ibid.* pp. 14–15. The controversy concerning this clause is dealt with below, pp. 80–1.
[178] *Ibid.* p. 53 and 15.

The new policy was discussed at a Labour Movement Conference on 28 October, an occasion given added urgency because Parliament was due to debate Spain on the following day, and initially encountered considerable opposition from those delegates still smarting from the Edinburgh debacle. There was particular scepticism about the alleged violations of the embargo. James Walker MP, for instance, refused to accept 'any cock and bull story that comes along without at least getting some evidence'.[179] When challenged on this point Citrine conceded that there was 'not one shred of evidence' for these charges other than 'the usual story about 200 tanks and so many flame throwers'.[180] However, despite his personal belief that labour's mood was based on unproven assumptions, Citrine argued tenaciously for the acceptance of the new policy on the grounds that those assumptions, unchallenged at the recent NCL, had formed the basis of their case at the International meeting. Having now persuaded the French to accept a particular course of action they had to trust them to follow it. If the policy were rejected in Britain then: 'What position are we going to be in internationally? What will our comrades think?'[181] Moreover, the only alternative on offer was Morrison's motion that, given the breakdown of Non-Intervention, the British government should 'permit and facilitate' the supply of arms to the Spanish government.[182] This was forcibly opposed by Bevin who felt that such a proposal would be counter to the whole thrust of collective security – 'It is isolation…it is asking the Trade Union Movement to reverse everything it has asked for in the last 5 years'.[183] Morrison's motion was not put to the vote. After separate consultations Citrine's draft resolution was accepted which called on the British government to act jointly with the French to take the initiative in an international agreement that would restore the Spanish government's right to the arms it needed for its defence.[184] On paper, at least, Non-Intervention had been repudiated.

The debate over Non-Intervention had, in this phase, been successfully divorced from the question of solidarity with the Spanish workers. Citrine, the pivotal figure, had skilfully manipulated the structure of internationalism to denude the debate of internationalist content. However, his success was mainly due to a unique combination of factors which was not to be repeated. In particular, there had been a general bewilderment and quiescence among the rank and file. Isabel de Palencia's achievement had been to cut through Citrine's obfuscations and pose a stark question: do you support Spain against fascism or not? Now, the stirrings of mobilisation

[179] *Ibid.* p. 43.   [180] *Ibid.* pp. 20–1.   [181] *Ibid.* p. 49.   [182] *Ibid.* p. 40.   [183] *Ibid.* p. 54.
[184] *Ibid.* p. 57.

around Spain, both on the far left and within the labour movement, ensured that labour leaders would be more answerable to their affiliates and their members as to the actions taken in their names, and the growth of direct contacts with Spain meant that internationalism could not be compartmentalised so neatly in future.

2

BREAKING WITH NON-INTERVENTION:
OCTOBER 1936–OCTOBER 1937

In the autumn conferences of 1937 the British labour movement united in its rejection of Non-Intervention. The TUC Congress supported the Spanish government in its appeal to the Council of the League of Nations, with the hope that the Council would propose measures which would 'enable the Spanish people to recover their political and territorial independence'.[1] A month later the Labour Party conference went even further than this in instructing the NEC to launch a nation-wide campaign to compel the government to abandon Non-Intervention and to restore to the Spanish government its right both to purchase arms and to establish law and order within its borders.[2] In a clear display of unity the TUC resolution was moved by Citrine and seconded by his erstwhile adversary from the 1936 Congress Bill Zak; the Labour Party resolution was moved by Sir Charles Trevelyan, one of the harshest opponents of official policy in Edinburgh. Yet the basis for such unity was in fact very shallow. Chapter 3 will show that these resolutions did not represent a united policy on how to proceed against Non-Intervention, while the current chapter argues that the path towards even this limited unity was much more tortuous than was admitted at the time.

Citrine had disingenuously presented the new position as a natural evolution from that adopted a year before – after all, he claimed, 'we have never accepted the position of neutrality'. The British labour movement, he said, had decided to accept the new policy, which was based on proposals submitted by the Spanish affiliates in June 1937, due to the 'demonstrable fact' that the Non-Intervention Agreement had 'broken down completely' and in full knowledge of the risks that it might involve.[3] In fact, however, the transition of policies had been far from smooth, nor had it been in direct

---

[1] *TUC CR*, 1937, p. 266. For the outcome of this initiative see below p. 94.
[2] *LPCR*, 1937, p. 212.   [3] *Ibid.* pp. 260 and 263.

response to the factors outlined by Citrine: it had been a 'demonstrable fact' that Non-Intervention was being flouted as long ago as a year before. The reason for this was that the declaration of 28 October 1936 did not constitute an unequivocal rejection of Non-Intervention, but rather evoked the distant prospect of joint intervention by the British and French governments. In the absence of such an initiative the labour leaders felt justified in advocating the stricter application of the Agreement, and as late as March 1937 they were convinced that a chimerical 'real' Non-Intervention (loyally observed by all parties) was the correct objective. Ironically, they were assisted in this by the very success of the Spanish Republic in surviving, buoyed up by Soviet arms, which suggested that even an incomplete system of Non-Intervention was better than none.

Thus, in this second phase of the war the labour movement, with the trade union leaders again leading the way, stubbornly clung to Non-Intervention rather than facing the inevitable conflict with government which would accompany any campaign against it. This chapter examines the process by which the change was enforced, and emphasises the growing isolation of the labour leadership both internationally and in relation to their own members. In particular it identifies the impact of three factors which had not affected the earlier debates – the demands for industrial action on an international level; international pressure from the Spanish labour movement and its allies in the IFTU and LSI; and internal pressure from the British labour movement. It concludes with an examination of labour's attempts to provide practical assistance to the Republican enclave on the north coast of Spain.

During this period the context of decision-making changed in a number of important respects. Firstly, active solidarity with the Spanish Republic became widespread in Britain, involving all classes to some degree. Unlike the summer of 1936 when concerned individuals had left the matter to their political party or trade union, by the end of that year organised solidarity with Spain, independent of the official labour movement, had spread throughout Britain. The founding of Spanish Medical Aid in August 1936 had stimulated a network of local 'Spanish Aid' committees. These came together with other humanitarian and campaigning groups in the National Joint Committee for Spanish Relief (NJCSR) founded in January 1937, headed by the cross-party *troika* of the Tory Duchess of Atholl, the Liberal MP Wilfred Roberts and the communist Isabel Brown. A further focus of British interest was provided by the formation of the British Battalion of the International Brigades in late 1936 which played an important role in checking Franco's attempt to encircle Madrid at the battle of the Jarama in

February 1937. Subsequently a fund-raising campaign was established to care for the Brigade's wounded and dependents. While the labour movement eschewed any formal relationship with most of these organisations, they undoubtedly had a major impact in sensitising the labour rank and file to the importance of Spain, and impelling them to question what their leaders were actually doing about it.[4]

Equally importantly, in Spain itself the situation seemed much more hopeful. The revolutionary chaos of the first months of the war gave way to increasingly stable government in the Republican zone. The government of Largo Caballero, until May 1937, and the government of Juan Negrín thereafter, practised a policy of political stabilisation which sought to extend control over the whole of Republican territory, especially the anarchist stronghold of Catalonia. The strengthening of the army was central to this process, and militias relying on enthusiasm alone gave way to a reasonably disciplined and equipped People's Army which scored its major success of the war over Mussolini's Italian 'volunteers' at Guadalajara in March 1937. The Brunete offensive to the north of Madrid in July, although inconclusive, showed that the Republic was capable of mounting sophisticated military operations. By the summer of 1937 there was stalemate on the war's main front, although the Nationalists continued to make inroads into the surviving Republican territories on the northern coast of Spain.

Yet the British labour movement remained lamentably ill-informed, and dependent on outside sources of information, concerning the equally crucial political developments within the Republican zone. The superior discipline of the Spanish communists, combined with the arrival of Soviet military aid and of the International Brigades, meant that they exercised increasing influence within the government. Their overriding objective was to reverse the social revolution of the first months of the war and crush the anarchists and POUM socialists in Catalonia who had propagated it. The independently minded Caballero – the 'Spanish Lenin' of 1936 – bridled at this and was removed from power in May 1937.[5] Yet, ironically, the British leaders paid little heed to the communist advance. Indeed, Citrine and Bevin would consistently lecture their Spanish comrades on the virtues of 'unity' as the best way to defeat fascism in Spain, while resisting all invitations to form a united front with the communists either internationally or in Britain. Clearly their conception of 'unity' involved the restoration of internal order at the anarchists' expense rather than a united front with the communists. However, their rather simplistic approach created tensions with inter-

---

[4] See below pp. 137–40.   [5] See below p. 113.

national labour leaders who were more worried by the threat that the growth of Soviet/communist influence in Spain posed to the future of the LSI and IFTU.

In February 1937 Schevenels visited Spain and returned with a very bleak picture of the situation there, fearing that the Spanish labour movement would be totally lost to communist influence.[6] However, in April, when he and his deputy Stolz made another visit, they felt that there had been a 'definite change of mind on the part of the Trade Union Officials and Socialists there' who seemed more willing to assert their presence on bodies such as the Madrid City Council. They reported that there was considerable tension between Caballero, who saw a 'very great danger of Communist domination in future' and the other socialist leader, Prieto, who favoured collaboration with the 'more reasonable' communists and was alarmed by the anarchists and POUM in Catalonia. The IFTU leaders were more sympathetic to the latter view and reported that between fifteen and twenty of their 'comrades' had been assassinated in the course of the anarchists' violent campaign to take over the UGT dockers' union in Barcelona. However, the report concluded on an optimistic note – the IFTU now 'had every opportunity of holding and retaining' its membership outside Catalonia, and this 'altered the general feeling of one time that we had lost Spain definitely'.[7] This satisfaction was not shared by Adler and De Brouckère in the LSI, and their fear that the Spanish socialists might leave the LSI helped to precipitate the change of policy in June 1937.[8]

Still influenced by their hostility towards Caballero, dating from the previous summer when he had been seen as a dangerously unstable leader, the British labour leaders did not feel personally committed to him. Thus, when mounting tensions in Barcelona, culminating in the week of street fighting between government forces and the POUM and anarchists so vividly captured by George Orwell in *Homage to Catalonia*, precipitated Caballero's fall from power, they showed little sympathy. Indeed, as early as 9 March Citrine had been tipped off by Pietro Nenni, the LSI representative in Spain, that 'it might be necessary for Caballero to resign because of internal dissensions'.[9] In May the *Daily Herald* characterised the Barcelona events as an 'Anarchist–Trotskyist rising supported by Monarchists',[10] and, after Caballero's fall, greeted Negrín's government as 'more democratic' than that of his predecessor who had purchased anarchist

[6] See below, pp. 148–9.
[7] TUC, Documents 2, 29 April 1937, IFTU Executive, report, pp. 6–9.
[8] See below pp. 91–3.
[9] TUC, Documents 3, 9 March 1937, report of Joint Meeting, p. 4.
[10] *Daily Herald*, 7 May 1937.

support 'at the price of military inefficiency and civil disorder'.[11] Victor Schiff wrote of the new Negrín–Prieto leadership that 'This Partnership may Save Spain', adding that the communists found Caballero 'too much of a doctrinaire'.[12] However, the communist vendetta against POUM leaders later forced Citrine to speak out against their execution – 'nothing would revolt British Labour more than shooting Socialists'.[13]

The only chink in the otherwise unconditional support for the Spanish government came in February 1937 when Nathans, the Assistant Secretary of the International Transport Workers Federation (ITF), confided to Bevin that informed sources in Spain had told him that the Spanish government 'would probably not be disinclined to consider proposals for a settlement from outside sources, provided the terms were reasonable'. He asked Bevin to investigate whether the British government might take such an initiative and whether there were 'any means of inducing them to do so'.[14] Bevin was 'very interested' in the suggestions, and wondered if the Spanish authorities could 'find a discreet way to indicate this'.[15] However, at this point Edo Fimmen, the ITF Secretary, stepped in to say that, while Nathans' information was reliable, the Spanish government could not admit to it, and the matter was dropped.[16] In May the question of mediation was again raised at an LSI/IFTU meeting during discussion of a rumoured plan to install the Spanish academic Madariaga as head of an interim government. This was, however, ridiculed by both Schevenels and Gillies, who said that 'if the British Foreign Office were suggesting a Madariaga Government to replace the other two it was impossible'.[17]

The main complication that distinguished this period was the arrival in Spain of large numbers of foreign 'volunteers' on both sides and a heightened awareness of foreign intervention in the conflict. The Comintern began to organise the International Brigades in the autumn of 1936, in time for them to play a decisive role in the defence of Madrid in December. Correspondingly, Mussolini threw large numbers of Italian soldiers into the war, and these were complemented particularly effectively by the German Condor Legion, including the bomber planes that were to demolish Guernica in April 1937. The Brigades posed a problem for the Labour Party

[11] *Daily Herald*, 19 May 1937.   [12] *Ibid.*   [13] *Daily Herald*, 3 July 1937.
[14] MRC, ITF records, 159/3/c/6/3, 22 February 1937, Nathans to Bevin.
[15] MRC, ITF records, 159/3/c/6/3, 1 March 1937, Bevin to Nathans.
[16] MRC, ITF records, 159/3/c/6/3, 3 March 1937, Fimmen to Bevin. There is also a copy of this correspondence in TUC, Correspondence 2, 1 March 1937 and 3 March 1937 with a covering note from Bevin to Citrine.
[17] TUC, Documents 3, 25 May 1937, Joint LSI/IFTU, report, pp. 1 and 3. On the scheme involving Madariaga see Hugh Thomas, *The Spanish Civil War* (1961), p. 334.

because, while it could claim no credit for their organisation, it could not repudiate such a popular initiative in which many party members were serving. At the 1937 conference G.T. Garratt went as far as to say that 'I believe that ten years hence, history will record that all unwittingly the Communists saved the British Empire and modern democracy in March of this year [by organising the Brigades]'.[18] Citrine too was willing to pay fulsome tribute to the International Brigaders in public,[19] but privately was sceptical about their significance. In December 1936 he said that, while he would not wish to minimise the 'psychological importance' of individuals going to fight in Spain, during his numerous meetings with Spanish leaders he had 'not yet heard the suggestion that what they need are volunteers from other countries'. Manpower was not a problem, he argued, while Franco's army of 25,000 soldiers besieged Madrid – a city of 1 million people. Also, he doubted whether the experience of many of the volunteers would be of any real value – 'Modern mechanised warfare is not something that anyone who fought in 1914 can pick up again'.[20]

Moreover, the TUC was keen to dissociate itself from helping volunteers even prior to the Home Office decision, in January 1937, to employ the Foreign Enlistment Act of 1870 against them. On 30 December a certain Captain R.F. Browne, who was recruiting aircrew for the Spanish government and wanted help with their travel expenses, received short shrift from the TUC International Secretary W. Bolton. When Browne said that volunteers had claimed to have been sent by the TUC, Bolton replied 'that this was all news to me'.[21] Subsequently the TUC refused even to involve itself with fund-raising on behalf of the dependants of volunteers.[22] Apart from the dubious legal status of the venture, Citrine was also worried by the communist domination of the Brigades, although in April 1937 Schevenels told him that the socialists were becoming more prominent in the organisation.[23] Thus, the British labour leaders felt sufficiently detached from the Brigades to look at them as part of the broader problem of ending the war, particularly as they were convinced that many more 'volunteers'

[18] *LPCR*, 1937, p. 214. G.T. Garrett was an author and journalist as well as a Labour Party candidate. In 1937 he was honorary administrator for the National Joint Committee for Spanish Relief and spent much of that year in Republican Spain.
[19] *TUC CR*, 1937, p. 261.
[20] TUC, Documents 2, 21 December 1936, verbatim report of meeting with rank-and-file delegation, p. 11.
[21] TUC, Documents 2, 30 December 1936, Bolton to Citrine. The Foreign Office were at this time monitoring the activities of an F.K. Browne (alias Mr Macarthy) who they believed to be recruiting airmen: PRO, FO 371, 20588, W 17769/9549/41, 9 December 1936.
[22] See below pp. 159–61.
[23] TUC, Documents 2, 29 April 1937, IFTU Executive, report, pp. 6–7.

were arriving to aid the rebel side than the government.[24] Accordingly, they supported a withdrawal of all foreigners from Spain as the prelude to a general settlement and, in this, they were at variance with the Spanish socialists whose delegate to the 9 March LSI/IFTU meeting distinguished between 'men who had gone voluntarily without Government assistance or encouragement, and those who had been sent as conscripts, in effect, from Germany and Italy'.[25]

The volunteer question was just one of the concerns of the Non-Intervention Committee which continued on its slow and stately progress. In March 1937 consensus was reached on a system of control to impose the Agreement, at the core of which was a naval patrol of zones of the Spanish coast by the British, French, Italian and German navies. The Labour Party was much less keen on this development than its French counterparts – in January 1937 Arthur Greenwood had told them that 'he or his colleagues could not get up in the House of Commons to ask for the British fleet to act as the "policeman" of the world'.[26] However, the control scheme was short-lived in its original form, and began to disintegrate after Republican air attacks on German and Italian warships. From this point onwards continued adherence to the Agreement was largely formalistic – indeed, Jill Edwards concludes that by July 1937 'non-intervention in any practical sense may be said to have ceased...'.[27] By the summer of 1937 a more pressing problem was the spate of attacks on ships proceeding to Republican Spain by 'pirate' submarines (in practice Italian warships). Eden, whose patience with the Italians was wearing thin, rallied the democracies for a surprisingly resolute response at the Nyon conference (10–14 September 1937) which divided the Mediterranean into British and French areas of patrol, with orders to engage the pirates. However, this show of resolve soon faltered – Italy was allowed into the patrol scheme, and the more conciliatory posture of the new Prime Minister Neville Chamberlain marginalised Eden, propelling him towards his eventual resignation.

A final international variable was provided by the changing political situation in France. Blum resigned in June 1937 following his defeat in the Senate, although remaining as vice-premier in the new cabinet. He had, however, gone a long way towards fulfilling many of the original objectives of his government, by averting the threat to democracy from within France.

---

[24] TUC, Documents 3, 9 March 1937, Labour Movement Conference, verbatim report, p. 10, where Citrine estimated the strength of the International Brigades at between 8–20,000 and the number of 'volunteers' on the other side at 40–60,000; *TUC CR*, 1937, p. 261.

[25] TUC, Documents 3, 9 March 1937, Labour Movement Conference, verbatim report, p. 3.

[26] TUC, Documents 2, 14 January 1937, IFTU/LSI meeting, verbatim report, p. 4.

[27] Jill Edwards, *The British Government and the Spanish Civil War*, p. 63.

Thus, although he was replaced as premier from within the Front Populaire by the Radical Chautemps, this inevitably undermined the argument that Non-Intervention was vital to French stability. Indeed, freed from the cares of the premiership Blum himself began to question the policy. When Dalton visited Blum's country house in September 1937 Blum had admitted that, whereas a year before he had been 'paralysed by Radical opinion', British labour would not now 'embarrass' him by denouncing Non-Intervention.[28]

At the 28 October 1936 Labour Movement Conference the paragraph of the resolution from the recent International calling for co-ordinated action to prevent the dispatch of supplies to the rebels[29] caused considerable controversy. Indeed, Citrine was later to recount how 'he had been repudiated by Bevin when he reported that the British delegates at a previous meeting had voted for a blockade of ships destined for the rebels'.[30] Bevin, who was chairing the meeting, rejected the clause on industrial grounds as

> I would split my union from top to bottom...It would mean that I would break my agreements and hold up ships. Whatever happens we are not going to do it. It would mean risking wages and lock-outs...It would involve us immediately with the Port of London Authorities.[31]

This stand was supported by Stott, the railway clerks' leader, and Joseph Toole who felt that if the resolution were passed then 'the Transport workers will have a most difficult situation'.[32] Dalton hoped that during the following day's Commons debate no one on the Front Bench would cause embarrassment by calling for action from particular unions.[33] James Walker, the steel workers' leader feared that the unions would be drawn into industrial action on an erroneous basis as 'in 99 cases out of 100 [they would be] expected to act without evidence, merely on statements by irresponsible individuals, who if they saw a box of rifles would immediately call a meeting and say they were going to the Spanish rebels'.[34] With the exception of Morrison[35] no speaker saw anything good in the proposal,

[28] BLPES, Dalton Papers, Diary 1/18, entry for 14 September 1937. Dalton makes no reference to this incident in his memoirs, although he refers to a meeting in 1938 when Blum had said, with reference to Non-Intervention, that 'he still thought that he had been right to make that proposal at that time' (*The Fateful Years*, pp. 252–3).

[29] TUC, Documents 2, 28 October 1936, Labour Movement Conference, verbatim report, p. 15.   [30] MRC, ITF records, 159/3/c/6, 16 December 1936, Fimmen to Henson.

[31] TUC, Documents 2, 28 October 1936, Joint Meeting, verbatim report, pp. 19 and 20.

[32] *Ibid.* pp. 20 and 23. Toole was a former Labour MP and a constituency member of the NEC. He lost his place when the rules of election to the NEC were changed in October 1937 and trade union influence reduced. Although a Catholic he was opposed to Franco. He helped to care for Basque refugee children during the Civil War. See *Dictionary of Labour Biography*, Vol. 7, (1984), p. 234; Ben Pimlott, *Labour and the Left*, p. 138.

[33] *Ibid.* p. 35.   [34] *Ibid.* p. 45.   [35] *Ibid.* p. 40.

although Citrine felt that they were exaggerating 'the danger' it posed because the British government's effective embargo prevented any such responsibility falling upon the unions.[36] After consultation a final draft was approved which struck out any reference to the contested clause.

However, the British trade unions were not able to insulate themselves so completely from international pressures. Already, within days of the military rising both the ITF and the IFTU had appealed to their affiliates to take action against any movements of war materials to the rebels, an action made redundant by the imposition of the arms embargo in countries with free trade unions.[37] In late 1936, however, the ITF, one of the Trade Secretariats which organised workers internationally by trade, began to promote a blockade on all trade with rebel Spain, prompted by its Scandinavian member unions. At the 4 and 5 December LSI/IFTU meeting, Jouhaux drew attention to the Swedish seamen's action and argued that the Internationals should now call on the unions to boycott all trade with the rebels.[38] On the next day Fimmen announced that the ITF would try to initiate a boycott and had circulated its affiliates, but had elicited no response from the British. However, the project would continue and 'he regretted that his declaration did not cover the British Transport workers'.[39] Fimmen later wrote that he was 'appalled' by the legalistic opposition coming from the British delegates – 'it was just as if they were representing their own Government'.[40] A resolution from the meeting was subsequently issued as an IFTU circular urging all affiliates 'to do their utmost in boycotting any transport of whatever goods there may be despatched or suspected to be despatched to the Spanish rebels'.[41]

Fimmen's comments worsened his relations with Bevin, who had not been at the meeting and felt that his own union had been singled out for attack when, in fact, 'the British Movement, not only ourselves but all the Trade Unions, will not use their unions for a political purpose as you suggest'.[42] When Fimmen indicated that he had not singled out the T&GWU[43] Citrine acknowledged that the British transport workers rejected any 'special obligations' in this matter, but stressed that they were no less sympathetic

[36] *Ibid.* p. 52.
[37] MRC, ITF records, 159/3/c/6/20, 16 December 1936, Fimmen to Wallari, Secretary of the Finnish Seamen's union, gives an account of ITF activities in this period; IISG, Amsterdam, IFTU records, no. 173, 5 August 1936, IFTU circular.
[38] TUC, Documents 2, 4 and 5 December 1936, report of LSI/IFTU meeting, p. 3.
[39] *Ibid.* pp. 5–6.
[40] MRC, ITF records, 159/3/c/6/17, 16 December 1936, Fimmen to Henson.
[41] IISG Amsterdam, IFTU archives, no. 173, circulars, 28 December 1936.
[42] TUC, Correspondence 1, 4 January 1936, Bevin to Fimmen.
[43] TUC, Correspondence 1, 11 January 1937, Fimmen to Citrine.

to the Spanish cause than workers elsewhere.[44] Fimmen apologised for giving the wrong impression on this point, but concluded that it was 'impossible to give an undertaking on behalf of the ITF without mentioning that it did not bind them [the British unions]'.[45]

On 16 December Fimmen issued his circular calling for shipping to the rebels to be blacked, although deliberately not contacting the British unions because he was 'more than doubtful as to their willingness to help'.[46] Instead, he sought the assistance of the ITF's officer in Cardiff, Jim Henson, to facilitate action against the trade from South Wales. Henson agreed with his decision to bypass the British unions – 'I regret to state that I think it would be useless for you to ask any assistance officially in the fight from the NUS or TGWU'. Moreover, he was doubtful whether the rank and file, though sympathetic to the Spanish government, would take action without sanction from their executives.[47] Henson soon became heavily involved when the Scandinavian seamen voted to black all vessels proceeding towards rebel Spain. Alongside the local Spanish consul and the Norwegian seamen's union representative he succeeded in preventing the departure of a number of ships and the recruitment of blackleg crews from South Wales. Even greater success was achieved in ports such as Newcastle.[48] Fimmen, however, was placed in a difficult position, trying to support these actions while

> at the same time being faced with the fact that the British unions not only do not join in the action, but indirectly try to hinder it by allowing their own people to load ships for the rebels and man them so long as the seamen get their 50% bonus, and even – as I gather from reports in the Dutch press – are even prepared to let their men take the place of the Scandinavian seamen who stood up for their principles and obeyed the orders of their unions. Heaven only knows what will be the final outcome of this situation.[49]

Matters within the ITF came to a head when the Scandinavian unions called a special meeting of the federation's 'seamens' and dockers' section' for 28 January 1937, to co-ordinate further actions. This incensed the British leaders, especially Bevin who challenged the very convening of such a

[44] TUC, Correspondence 1, 13 January 1937, Citrine to Fimmen.
[45] TUC, Correspondence 1, 14 January 1937, Fimmen to Citrine.
[46] MRC, ITF records, 159/3/c/6/20, 5 December 1936, Fimmen to Wallari, for copy of circular.
[47] MRC, ITF records, 159/3/c/6/17, 22 December 1936, Henson to Fimmen.
[48] MRC, ITF records, 159/3/c/6/3, 23 January 1937, Henson to Fimmen; 159/5/3/202, 23 January 1937 for copy of circular from Newcastle Trades Council on implementation of the Scandinavian blockade.
[49] MRC, ITF records, 159/3/c/6/3, 26 December 1936, Fimmen to Henson. The NUS won the first of a number of bonuses for its members sailing to Spain in January 1937.

meeting and threatened to consider pulling his union out of the ITF. He was supported by Spence of the National Union of Seamen (NUS), who was due to have chaired the meeting and who saw 'no useful purpose' in his attendance, and Marchbank of the NUR, an ITF Vice-President. Fimmen had intended to invite Henson to the meeting, to improve liaison with Scandinavia, but in the aftermath of the row with Bevin thought better of it. He confided that: 'The fact is that the British unions, this between you and me, do not play their part and try to excuse it by blaming those who stand by the Resolutions adopted [by the ITF and IFTU].' He feared that much criticism would be directed at the British attitude towards solidarity with Spain at the coming meeting.[50]

However, the situation was defused when Spence made a last-minute decision to chair the meeting and was able 'by giving a frank and open explanation of the situation, to dissipate a good deal of misunderstanding and at least to prevent an intensification of the feeling against the British Labour movement which exists in some quarters'.[51] The very weakness of the ensuing resolution demonstrated the inability of the ITF to impose decisions upon unwilling affiliates, especially those as powerful as the British unions.[52] Thus, the attitude of the British leaders had effectively killed off any prospects for industrial solidarity action, and the ramifications became clear later in the year when the Scandinavian unions met to discuss similar action against Japan in the light of its aggression against China. Fimmen confided that the Scandinavians were not 'willing to take any action unless they were sure that the Britishers were prepared to play their part, [and] that means in all probability that they will do nothing since in all probability Bevin and those who follow him will not change their passive attitude'.[53]

The British labour movement's obduracy on this issue was repeated on the more important question of how to treat Non-Intervention. Increasingly this was bound up with the continuing attempt by the Spanish labour movement to draw the IFTU and LSI into united action with the Comintern over Spain, primarily through an 'all-in' conference of interested organisations.[54] Despite the dictates of anti-communism, it was apparent to many European labour leaders and this proposal would become progressively harder to resist so long as the credibility of the LSI depended on its ability to offer positive aid to Spain. The failure to end Non-Intervention, as stated

[50] *Ibid.* 27 December 1937, Fimmen to Henson.
[51] MRC, ITF records, 159/3/c/6/17, 18 February 1937, Fimmen to Henson.
[52] IISG Amsterdam, INT 3051/41, ITF *Report for 1935–37*, p. 104.
[53] MRC, ITF records, 159/3/c/6/13, 21 December 1937, Fimmen to Wallari.
[54] This proposition had already been rejected at the 28 July International meeting, TUC, Documents 1, 28 July 1936, IFTU/LSI meeting, verbatim report, p. 3.

baldly by Pascual Tomás at the 4 December 1936 LSI/IFTU meeting, 'was making it very difficult for the Socialists and Trades Unionists in Spain to maintain their Socialist principles'[55] and, out of gratitude to the Soviet Union, Spanish labour could gravitate towards communism.[56]

However, Citrine's comments at the same meeting underlined the shallowness of the rejection of Non-Intervention on 28 October. He claimed that since then the Labour Party had gone further than any other LSI-affiliate in staging a parliamentary debate on Spain, in the face of a formidable government majority. However, he reminded delegates that none of them would go so far as to call for the 'abrogation' of Non-Intervention for the simple reason that, in Britain, 'no Government would be able to secure public support for any action which the people believed would lead to war'. Accordingly, there were clear limits to British support for Spain – 'the British Labour Movement could give the Spanish comrades help of any other kind, but it was impossible to secure arms'.[57] This was unsatisfactory to Tomás who felt that the British people could be roused to action in view of their 'long democratic traditions', as they had been in 1914 in the case of Belgium.[58] Soon afterwards Citrine restated his position, arguing that whereas Non-Intervention had recommended itself to Congress on the grounds of 'expediency', the subsequent violation of the Agreement meant that 'we are now driven to the question of finding arms for Spain, but we do so with our eyes open'. However, he was convinced that if the embargo were ended it would work to the detriment of the Spanish government and, moreover, that the British and French governments were unlikely to change their stance and were impervious to pressures on them to do so.[59]

Similar ambivalence underlay the Labour Party's debating position in the House of Commons. Indeed, by March 1937 Citrine felt that the parliamentary debates showed that the arguments over Spain were finely balanced and the government had 'the most effective retorts' to many of their statements.[60] On 29 October 1936 Attlee, Noel-Baker and Greenwood had put Labour's new case for the restoration of rights to the Spanish government (the latter in the teeth of repeated quotations from his own speech supporting Non-Intervention in Edinburgh).[61] However, this debate

[55] TUC, Documents 2, 4 and 5 December 1936, LSI/IFTU meeting, verbatim report, p. 2.
[56] IISG Amsterdam, IFTU records, no. 173, report of 4 and 5 December 1936 meeting, p. 2.
[57] TUC, Documents 2, 4 and 5 December 1936, LSI/IFTU meeting, verbatim report, pp. 3–4.
[58] IISG Amsterdam, IFTU records, no. 173, report of 4 and 5 December 1936 meeting, p. 4; TUC, Documents 2, 4 and 5 December 1936, LSI/IFTU meeting, verbatim report, p. 6.
[59] TUC, Documents 2, 21 December 1936, verbatim report of meeting with rank-and-file delegation, pp. 11–12.
[60] TUC, Documents 3, 9 March 1937, Labour Movement Conference, verbatim report, p. 11.
[61] *Hansard*, 5th series, vol. 316, columns 51–142.

did not, as Naylor states, 'draw the parliamentary lines for the rest of the Civil War'.[62] In fact, in subsequent debates this clarity was lost, and by the spring of 1937 had given way to calls for the application of 'real' Non-Intervention. On 6 May Noel-Baker offered as the 'majority' view within his party that

> we hope that...having accepted the policy of non-intervention, it will be loyally carried out, and that, if it is, it will rapidly bring the civil war to an end. We protest with all our power against the sham, the hypocritical sham, that it now appears to be.[63]

Such prevarication encouraged the Spanish and their allies to step up their campaign. On 14 January 1937, when the Internationals met again, Jouhaux unveiled his plan for an LSI and IFTU conference extended to include 'all bodies that favoured peace' (including communists), arguing that such action would prevent the initiative passing to other organisations.[64] Citrine immediately rejected any idea of co-operation with the communists:

> the matter could be dismissed from consideration as far as the British Labour Movement was concerned. Our position was quite definite. They would not act [in] association with communists. It would mean only division and weakness; it would be no help to the cause of peace for the workers.

Moreover, there was no question of losing the initiative because 'the Trade Unions knew what they were about and could and would determine their own policy'. Jouhaux recognised that no progress was possible without British co-operation, but was convinced that some form of conference was essential.[65]

Soon afterwards Schevenels visited Spain to interview the Spanish leaders. On his return he candidly told Citrine that there were problems with the UGT due to the degree of Soviet influence and that, even after the war, it might be difficult to restore relations 'unless under the plain conditions that the IFTU comes to terms with Moscow'. However, in spite of this he felt that it was their duty to continue to help the Spanish unions because 'our own membership would not understand otherwise'.[66] This assessment matched that of the Belgian socialist Camille Huysmans who, while on a brief visit to London, told the TUC that IFTU and LSI influence in Spain was 'nil'. Indeed, he had verbally committed the Internationals to the

[62] Naylor, *Labour's International Policy*, p. 184.
[63] *Hansard*, 5th series, vol. 323, columns 1380–1.
[64] TUC, Documents 2, 14 January 1937, report of Joint IFTU/LSI, p. 4. [65] *Ibid.* p. 5.
[66] IISG Amsterdam, IFTU records, no. 174, Schevenel's report, dated 6 February 1937; TUC, Documents 3, 8 February 1937, report of interview.

construction of a large base hospital as a way to revive their fortunes.[67] Schevenels had met the Spanish leaders Caballero and Tomás, both of whom were convinced that the organisation of an all-in conference of anti-fascists, including the communists, was the best service that the international labour movement could perform for them. Both felt that the LSI and IFTU 'were not doing as much as they might to assist the Spanish Government, either through the Non-Intervention Committee or through [the League of Nations at] Geneva'.[68] Unlike Caballero, Tomás accepted Schevenel's arguments against such a conference. However, when he appealed for a special conference of the Internationals in its place, Schevenels felt 'bound to accept' the idea.[69]

At the 17 February LSI/IFTU meeting only the French backed the idea of an all-in conference. Citrine opposed any form of conference on the basis that 'if the "mountain produced a mouse" he did not think it would redound to the credit of the Internationals'. However, if a conference were considered necessary he argued that it should be held in London so that the Spanish accusation that British representatives had not previously reflected the views of their members could be repudiated.[70] Thus, it was agreed to call a conference for 10–11 March in London, and great emphasis was placed on the need for large numbers of socialist MPs to attend.[71]

Citrine took considerable care to ensure that the outcome of the conference was not a radical departure from previous policy. The meeting was closed to journalists, ostensibly so that delegates could speak freely, and a public rally was arranged for the evening of 10 March to compensate for this. After consultation with the Home Office, permission was granted on the condition that speakers would only address themselves to humanitarian fund-raising and refrain from 'propaganda'.[72] Later, labour leaders used the allegedly poor attendance at the rally as an argument against mounting a more vigorous campaign in Britain. The rally was, however, also an unhappy experience for Citrine who chaired the meeting in the face of continuous heckling from the floor.[73]

On 8 March the LSI met in London, and De Brouckère reported to a meeting of both Internationals on the morning of 9 March that they had

[67] TUC, Documents 3, 4 February 1937, report of Huysman's interview with Gillies and Miss McDonald, Citrine's secretary. See below, p. 145.
[68] TUC, Documents 3, 17 February 1937, LSI/IFTU meeting, verbatim report, p. 1.
[69] TUC, Documents 2, 14 January 1937, LSI/IFTU meeting, verbatim report, p. 5.
[70] TUC, Documents 3, 17 February 1937, LSI/IFTU meeting, verbatim report, pp. 3–4.
[71] *Ibid.* p. 5.   [72] IISG Amsterdam, IFTU report, no. 174, circular dated 2 March 1937.
[73] NCL minutes, 23 March 1937; University College Dublin (UCD) TU7/149, NUBSO *Monthly Record*, 1937, report of 1937 conference, p. 198; TUC, International Conference 2, account of rally.

decided that 'they would unanimously support Non-Intervention' at the conference, on the grounds that 'control was better than no control'. Citrine argued that the conference should not be held on the basis of any recommendation from the executives, as the idea was for a 'free and unfettered discussion'. However, he was convinced that a 'policy of non-intervention will emanate from these discussions but, of course, it will be necessary to see that it is not operated in such a way that it aids the rebels at the expense of the Government'. Serious doubts were expressed at the practicality of any scheme to withdraw 'volunteers', and these were amplified by a Spanish delegate who argued that while a withdrawal would numerically favour the government side, the duplicity of the fascists would undermine any such advantage.[74]

When this information was discussed by the British Labour Movement Conference on the same afternoon there was general support for the continuation of Non-Intervention so long as it could be made more effective. This was the attitude of Attlee, Grenfell and Noel-Baker, another leading critic at Edinburgh, who argued that Non-Intervention was 'the right policy provided it was equally applied'.[75] Citrine said that there was no alternative to Non-Intervention that could 'really materialise for the benefit of the Spanish people'. He perceived the question of 'volunteers' as one area where Non-Intervention had not been applied and had worked, at least in numerical terms, against the Spanish government. Finally, he believed that they should not create the false impression at the conference that they had the potential to supply British arms to Spain – under no circumstances could they 'get the people of this country to go to war about Spain'. Therefore, all of their efforts should concentrate on making Non-Intervention 'as complete and strong as possible'.[76] Bevin continued in this vein, arguing that they had to tell the Spanish 'the truth about our position here and [tell them] their only salvation was to get absolute unity to face Franco in Spain'. He also suggested that the Labour Party should concentrate its future attacks on the German threat to British financial interests in the Rio Tinto mines. He concluded with a four-point programme which was duly accepted as British policy for the conference.

1   We should tell the Spanish people from the arms point of view it was impossible to help.
2   We should urge that they should get unity over there.

---

[74] The only apparent record of this meeting is contained in TUC, Documents 3, 9 March 1937, Labour Movement Conference, verbatim report. This reference pp. 2–4. The Spanish delegate was probably Manuel Cordero of PSOE.   [75] *Ibid.* p. 7.   [76] *Ibid.* pp. 9–11.

3 If we can try to induce them to pay more attention to the food problem it would help.

4 If the Party could begin an insistent hammering of the Government on British industries [i.e. raise the question of the British industries in Spain] that would make an approach which might, in its effect, have a helpful value [for] the Spanish Government.[77]

Developing these themes Bevin made by far the most significant contribution to the subsequent conference, later to become highly controversial on the basis of extracts published in the *Daily Worker*,[78] following speeches from two Spanish delegates. Pascual Tomás defended the idea of an all-in conference and appealed to socialist MPs to bring about an end to Non-Intervention. Then, directly addressing himself to trade unionists, he asked how many national centres had implemented the embargo on the movement of troops and arms, and called on them to threaten a one-day stoppage against government policies towards Spain.[79] Manuel Cordero (PSOE) dismissed the alleged problems of communism and anarchism in Spain – in particular, the Communist Party had 'adapted itself to the realities of the situation in Spain' and was not fighting to install communism.[80]

In this context, Bevin clearly saw his first task as rebutting any co-operation with the communists. 'Sometimes I wonder,' he began 'whether we are being asked to help Spain, or to promote the United Front.'[81] He denied that British delegates had, in the past, not expressed the true feelings of their members. In Britain the labour movement presented its own united front and 'we do not propose to allow the Communists or anybody else to disrupt us'. Later he was to 'beg of our friends abroad not to play with factions in this country'.[82] Having established this point he went on to outline the factors which had influenced British labour to adopt its specific response to Spain, drawing attention to the internal problems with Catholic members. The attitude to Non-Intervention had been defined in the knowledge that 'public opinion in this country, even in our own Movement, was not ripe to face a struggle with Hitler over Spain'.[83] Turning to the conference he proposed that no one had yet addressed the problem of how to replace the policy of Non-Intervention, even though there was 'no half way house. It is either Intervention or Non-Intervention, one thing or the other has got to be done.'[84]

[77] *Ibid*. pp. 12–14.   [78] See below, pp. 94–5.
[79] TUC, International Conference 2, verbatim report, pp. 13–14.   [80] *Ibid*. pp. 23–4.
[81] *Ibid*. p. 50.   [82] *Ibid*. p. 51 and 59.   [83] *Ibid*. p. 55.   [84] *Ibid*. p. 56.

The one subject on which Bevin was more positive was the withdrawal of foreign 'volunteers', judging that this would be a popular political cause because in Britain there was a traditional 'antipathy against foreigners involved in the domestic quarrels of another country'.[85] Yet, even on this matter, he refused to adopt the distinction which others had drawn between genuine volunteers and those sent to Spain as serving soldiers – the British movement would only accept a simultaneous withdrawal from both sides. Moreover, care must be taken to prevent such discussions being abused in order to engineer the recognition of Franco.[86] He promised British support on only two subjects, volunteers and the supplies of raw materials to Germany from British mines, with which Franco was believed to be financing his war effort. However, he again assured delegates that, if there was the 'slightest evidence of violation or ineffectiveness' in Non-Intervention, the TUC and Labour Party would 'bombard our Government...to make them carry out the scheme as reported to Parliament'.[87]

Bevin's speech had a sobering effect on the other delegates. For Vandervelde, the Belgian leader, it 'had the effect of a stream of cold water on our deliberations'. He acknowledged the British delegates' concern for the growth of communism – 'that is natural and they are not alone in their feelings' – yet Spain was by no means a communist country.[88] Although Attlee, in a concluding speech, again stressed that 'we have got to try and make this Agreement work',[89] the conference resolution expressed little confidence in the ability of Non-Intervention to prevent fascist support for the rebels but merely promised to take action if experience should prove 'in a few weeks' that this was, indeed, the case. It also called for the simultaneous withdrawal of all foreigners fighting in Spain.[90]

In many respects the International Conference represented the apogee of the British trade union leaders' influence over policy towards Spain. An indecisive opposition had been trounced and trade union authority asserted not only nationally but internationally – the unions had used the conference to claim primacy over the Labour Party as the voice of the labour movement. This much was evident in the delivery of the conference resolution to the Foreign Office, for within two weeks a solely trade union delegation had left the government with a highly congenial view of the movement's attitude over Spain. The arrangements for this delegation were in themselves revealing: Citrine told the Labour Party that the General Council preferred to meet Eden on its own as this would leave the PLP 'free to have at it in Parliament without feeling that they were tied by any talk

[85] *Ibid.* p. 57.   [86] *Ibid.* p. 58.   [87] *Ibid.* p. 60.   [88] *Ibid.* p. 63.   [89] *Ibid.* p. 86.
[90] TUC CR, 1937, p. 176.

that they had had with the Minister'. Attlee tamely agreed that this was 'a very good idea...it was the [PLP's] job to see to the matter in the House'.[91] Citrine then told the Foreign Office that 'they would not come in a political aspect, but simply as T.U.C. [*sic*]'.[92]

When the deputation met Eden on 22 March, Bevin stated that it was now imperative for the government to see that Non-Intervention was properly enforced. Moreover, the presence of foreign troops in Spain meant that there was now a good case for involving the League of Nations in resolving the problem. He also returned to the theme of the danger posed by Franco to British mineral assets – 'Why was Franco allowed to use British property to pay for his help from Germany, thus allowing that country to get its copper...from the Rio Tinto mines? Insistence should be made on British rights.'[93] Citrine chose to concentrate on the presence of Italian troops in Spain and the need to arrange for their removal. In his estimation 'the view of the Labour movement was that the interests of the British people were being gravely menaced and it was absolutely necessary that the British Government, like the French, should now take clear, decisive and energetic action'.[94]

In reply, Eden stressed the need for a supervision scheme for Non-Intervention and said that the government would do all that it could to address the question of foreign nationals in Spain.[95] In a disarming aside, however, he mentioned that British consuls were constantly being approached by British deserters from the International Brigade who had alleged ill-treatment. Nor did he choose to consider the Italians in Spain as regular soldiers. He reminded the delegates that the Italians would not receive any thanks from the 'very proud' Spanish people, and Mussolini should not think that he would have any permanent power there as 'Napoleon himself could not do it'. Under questioning Eden expressed the belief that the Spanish government had more arms than was commonly believed.[96] Eden later declared himself pleased with the meeting, reporting to the Cabinet that the trade unionists'

---

[91] TUC, Documents 3, 18 March 1937, report of telephone conversation between Citrine's and Attlee's secretaries.

[92] PRO, FO 371, 21328, W 5965/7/41, no. 108, 18 March 1937, F.O. Minute, Harvey to Eden.

[93] TUC, Documents 3, 22 March 1937, report of deputation to Foreign Office, pp. 1–2.

[94] *Ibid.* pp. 3–4.

[95] PRO, FO 371, 21328, W 5965/7/41, no. 109, 22 March 1937, text of communiqué from meeting.

[96] TUC, Documents 3, 22 March 1937, report of meeting, pp. 6–7. This was a widespread view at the time. Dalton records in his diary (24 June 1937, pp. 14–18) that he was assured of this by both Vansittart and the Russian Ambassador Maisky. Moreover, according to Gillies, a month earlier del Vayo had told Schevenels that 'the Spanish Government are getting all the arms they need'.

attitude had been very reasonable, and on the day following the meeting the *Daily Herald* had published a very satisfactory leading article supporting non-intervention. The members of the [General] Council, however, had admitted that they were rather worried at the present position.[97]

Such appearances were, however, deceptive and a combination of internal and external factors soon combined to force the movement's leaders to temper their policy and adopt a more hostile attitude towards Non-Intervention and the government which defended it. The first of these was the threat of the total decomposition of the LSI if stronger action were not taken over Spain. This was directly related to the worsening military situation in Spain with the collapse of the government's northern front around the Basque capital of Bilbao. Following the German shelling of the Republican port of Almería on 31 May 1937, after a German vessel on Non-Intervention patrol had been attacked by a government aircraft, the Spanish labour organisations called for 'common action' by the Second and Third Internationals on behalf of Spain, and the Comintern's leader Dmitrov took the opportunity to propose that a co-ordinating committee should be set up as the basis for such activity with the LSI. De Brouckère, although initially reticent, agreed to a preliminary meeting at Annemasse on 21 June. The LSI leaders were motivated by the fear that the PSOE might leave the LSI altogether,[98] and De Brouckère expressed his willingness to meet with the Comintern so long as the discussion was limited to joint action rather than a united front. Prior to this a meeting of the Internationals was called at very short notice in Geneva, at the request of the Spanish affiliates. Citrine was unable to attend and sent detailed instructions on the policy to pursue to his deputy, Arthur Hayday (who was already in Geneva), the crux of which was simply that 'the General Council is determined not to be dragged into consultations with the Communists'. Nor did Citrine see any value in another conference unless specific proposals were tabled for it, especially as he and his colleagues still felt 'very sore' at the recriminations directed at British labour at recent conferences.[99]

At the 16 June meeting Azorín, for PSOE, said that the position in Spain, in the light of the impending fall of Bilbao and the Almería incident, was

---

[97] PRO, FO 371, 21328, W 6317/7/41, 25 March 1937, extract from Cabinet conclusions, 12 (31) no. 2. The *Daily Herald*, 23 March 1937, had used Mussolini's recent humiliation at the battle of Guadalajara as a sign for the need to 'press resolutely ahead with Non-Intervention' while making it as effective as possible.

[98] E.H. Carr, *The Comintern and the Spanish Civil War* (1984), pp. 48–9. See also the reprinted excerpts from Togliatti's reports to the Comintern concerning the affair, p. 89.

[99] TUC, Correspondence 2, 14 June 1937, Citrine to Hayday.

now such that they needed 'something more than a platonic declaration'.[100] The Spanish suggested a number of proposals which included pressure on the League of Nations to take action over Spain in accordance with its Covenant, international action to enforce a return to commercial liberty for Spain, and a declaration to make 'unquestioned obligations of solidarity' with Spain incumbent on organisations affiliated to the two Internationals.[101] The discussion soon moved on to the subject of united action. Jouhaux argued in favour of it embracing not only the communists but all those who opposed Non-Intervention, although he envisaged it as a measure for the LSI rather than for the IFTU.[102] Hayday then repeated Citrine's injunction against any co-operation with communists. All that he could offer the Spanish was the chance of submitting proposals for action to the forthcoming General Council of the IFTU in Warsaw.[103] This did not satisfy Tomás who asked for the Executives of the Internationals to be called together at once to consider Dmitrov's proposal.[104] In the absence of Citrine, the standard of anti-communism was taken up by Gillies who said that the Labour Party was unwilling to discuss united action any longer within the LSI. He proceeded to sum up the ideological misgivings of the British labour movement concerning its prospective allies.

> They did not regard the Communists as democrats. They had no confidence in their professions of faith in favour of bourgeois democracy. They had no confidence in their organisational basis, which was that of a series of national groups accepting orders from a centralised authoritarian executive which, in fact, is guided, controlled and subsidised by the Russian Government...[the communists were] a paid agent of a foreign Government.

Moreover, he failed to see how a united front with the communists could benefit Spain – after all, if the British movement became embroiled in such an exercise it would merely be discredited before British public opinion.[105] In spite of this opposition, however, a resolution was carried which recognised the need to take action against Non-Intervention, as had been envisaged at the International Conference in March. A further meeting was arranged for 24 June.[106]

With their political initiative apparently repudiated, De Brouckère and Adler promptly resigned in the wake of their 21 June meeting with the

---

[100] TUC, Documents 3, 16 and 17 June 1937, LSI/IFTU meeting, verbatim report, p. 1.
[101] NCL minutes, 22 June 1937. Citrine later said of these proposals that 'the words may appear to be moderate, but the action that they contemplate is very grave indeed'. The invocation of the League Covenant would result in an escalating series of sanctions; *TUC CR*, 1937, p. 263.
[102] TUC, Documents 3, 16 and 17 June 1937, LSI/IFTU meeting, verbatim report, p. 2.
[103] *Ibid.* p. 2.   [104] *Ibid.* p. 2.   [105] *Ibid.* p. 3.   [106] *Daily Worker*, 19 June 1937.

Comintern, and were later joined by the LSI's Treasurer. Thus, when the NCL discussed the situation on 22 June it did so in an atmosphere of crisis and, while endorsing the actions of the delegates in Geneva, it also agreed to support the Spanish proposals.[107] On the following day the General Council and the NEC met separately. Bevin repeated his opposition to the united front, but conceded that the Spanish proposals were, in fact, little different from what the British movement had already declared.[108] Citrine rather scorned the idea of looking to the League for help as it was now, without Germany or Italy, weaker even than the Non-Intervention Committee. He then informed the NEC that the General Council still could not endorse the Spanish proposals and would seek a new interview with Eden for information.[109]

Accordingly he and Bevin visited the Foreign Office that afternoon. They reported to the Labour Movement Conference that an attempt had been made to persuade them that Republican Spain was receiving plentiful supplies of arms from Russia, Mexico and even France. This was overwhelmingly rejected by the delegates who decided that while their opposition to the united front was unstinting, they would now accept the Spanish proposals,[110] and this was adopted when the executives of the Internationals met on 24 June.[111] This declaration represented the most significant break yet with Non-Intervention, and was the price for preventing the collapse of the LSI.[112] Yet, Citrine almost immediately gave notice that little had really changed. Two weeks later the IFTU General Council in Warsaw had passed a similar resolution which Citrine interpreted as a commitment to stand by the League Covenant in order to restrain Germany and Italy 'whether it meant war or not'. However, he immediately qualified this by pointing out that they were hindered in Britain by a lack of 'complete unanimity' in public opinion towards the conflict in Spain and, secondly, that the British labour movement still bitterly opposed any attempt to use Spain to 'engineer' a united front.[113]

---

[107] NCL minutes, 22 June 1937.
[108] TUC, Documents 3, 23 June 1937, General Council meeting, report, p. 1.
[109] *Ibid.* p. 2.
[110] There is no record of what transpired at the Foreign Office meeting with Lord Cranborne in either the TUC or PRO archives. The only mention comes in Hugh Dalton's diary, BLPES, 1/18, 24 June 1937, pp. 13 and 14. On the decisions taken subsequently see TUC, Documents 3, 23 June 1937, Labour Movement Conference, report; TUC, General Council minutes, 23 June 1937; BLPES, Dalton Diaries 24 June 1937, pp. 13 and 14.
[111] TUC, Documents 3, 24 June 1937, IFTU/LSI meeting, report.
[112] The LSI officers withdrew their resignations and held a second meeting with the Comintern on 9 July 1937 which produced no practical conclusions.
[113] TUC, Documents 3, 30 June–3 July 1937, IFTU General Council report, pp. 6–7; *Daily Herald*, 3 July 1937.

The limited scope of this new departure was soon made clear. Backed with the authority of the TUC Congress, the Internationals met again between 13–16 September 1937, although the proceedings were somewhat overshadowed by the widening split within the Spanish labour movement.[114] Caballero's demand that they should now call for Italy and Germany to be branded as aggressors under Article 16 of the League's Covenant was resisted by the International leaders. Citrine openly pondered whether he 'would be justified in committing the British Trade Union movement to the application of extreme measures'.[115] The resolution finally adopted called for the suppression of 'piracy' in the Mediterranean, the withdrawal of invading armies from Spain and for the restoration to the Spanish government of its right to purchase arms. Citrine, De Brouckère, Longuet and Jouhaux were sent to Geneva to urge such action upon the democratic governments and, subsequently, the NCL sent a deputation to the Foreign Secretary to recommend that the British government should support the French in re-opening the Franco-Spanish border.[116] However, these actions did not represent the beginning of a campaign of pressure on the government, but rather a plateau of activity upon which the labour movement would be lodged until the end of the war.

The second major development tending towards a more decisive break with Non-Intervention was the adoption of a more critical attitude within the labour movement by local Labour parties and the trade unions. At the International Conference Bevin had claimed to speak on behalf of the British labour movement, yet when an account of his speech was published in the *Daily Worker* there was widespread condemnation. Most significantly the discontent arose from branch level, and a number of union conferences passed resolutions calling for publication of the speeches and condemning the secrecy surrounding labour movement policy towards Spain.[117] In practice the criticism was quite easily resisted by the TUC, the main line of defence being that Bevin, and Attlee, had spoken 'at the request and on behalf of the British delegation' and Bevin's remarks had been mis-

[114] BLPES, Dalton Diary, 13 September 1937; see below p. 114.
[115] TUC, Documents 3, 13–16 September 1937, IFTU/LSI meeting, verbatim report, p. 9.
[116] NCL minutes, 21, 22 and 29 September 1937. I have been unable to locate any other sources for these meetings, although the *Daily Worker*, 21 September 1937, carries a report of Citrine being 'snubbed' by Eden in Geneva. This was based on a leak to Pitcairn, TUC, Documents 3, 12 October 1937, report of meeting with del Vayo. The *Manchester Guardian* reported that Eden had arranged to meet the delegates in Geneva, but then withdrew 'no doubt on instructions from London. Mr Eden is understood to have said to Sir Walter Citrine that the opening of the French frontier would not be to the advantage of the Spanish Government' (21 September 1937).
[117] MRC, UCATT records, Mss 78/AU/1/2/10, AUBTW Conference, 27 July 1937, pp. 81–3; USDAW records, NAUSA AGM report, 28 and 29 March 1937, p. 65.

represented in the press.[118] However, the affair caused considerable embarrassment and Citrine forced Schevenels to investigate the origins of the leak. It transpired that the article was the work of the maverick communist journalist Frank Pitcairn (the pseudonym of Claud Cockburn) who had gained access to the conference as a translator with the Spanish delegation.[119]

Pitcairn's report was, in fact, a relatively fair rendition of Bevin's comments, although it is impossible to corroborate his claim that Bevin had said that 'the fact of the war must not be allowed at any cost to influence the decisions and the policy of the British Labour leaders in this country'.[120] However, the textual accuracy of the report was not the main issue. Of much greater importance was the question of secrecy and the manner in which the policy towards Spain was conducted – indeed, the very secrecy surrounding the conference now made it much more difficult to prove conclusively that there was no basis for the discontent. The affair represented a degree of poetic justice for the manner in which the labour leaders had conducted their response to Spain. Citrine and his colleagues were still operating as if conditions were unchanged from the first months of the war when the formulation of policy had been left to the official bodies such as the NCL. Trade unions which did make pronouncements in the earlier period tended merely to affirm their support for the Spanish workers without commenting on the more sensitive issues such as Non-Intervention. From late 1936, however, this attitude started to change significantly so that union executives and conferences began to debate Spain and suggest changes in policy. Although there was still no coherent campaign for such changes and, indeed, most unions remained very tentative on this subject, it was clear that dissatisfaction with Non-Intervention was being transmitted upwards from the rank-and-file members to the discomfort of their leaders.

This more critical mood was even more evident among the rank and file of the Labour Party, which had been only temporarily satisfied by the outcome of the Edinburgh conference. Significantly, the campaign for Spain in 1937 developed symbiotically with the successful struggle by the Constituency Labour parties for greater influence which came to fruition at the 1937 conference. The Home Counties' Labour Association (HCLA) had been set up in 1934 under the leadership of Ben Greene and it was at a conference called by this body on 13 March 1937, to express dissatisfaction

[118] TUC, International Conference, 2, 22 April 1937, Tewson to Hann.
[119] TUC, International Conference 1, 24 March 1937, Citrine to Schevenels; *ibid.* 30 March 1937 and 26 April 1937, Schevenels to Citrine.
[120] *Daily Worker*, 12 March 1937. Quoted by Fyrth, *The Signal Was Spain*, p. 281.

at the record of the Labour Party NEC over Spain, that the Labour Spain Committee (LSC) emerged.[121] The LSC, run by its secretary Joseph Pole, was deliberately intended to mobilise rank-and-file discontent with official policy over Spain rather than to act as a fund-raising body. It enjoyed initial success, with conferences on Spain rippling out from the South East of England alongside the movement for constituency organisation, and held a further London conference on 29 May 1937. However, although giving voice to the feelings of many in the Labour Party, the committee was ignored by the NEC on the grounds that the HCLA was an 'unofficial' body and not recognised. Thus, all appeals for meetings with the NEC were refused. Even so, the existence of the LSC clearly influenced the NEC's formation of its own Spain Campaign Committee in late 1937. Pole had to content himself with ridiculing the intellectual justification for Non-Intervention in an invigorating correspondence with James Middleton.[122]

But although the LSC could be ignored, the political fact it represented, that the Labour Party leadership was out of step with the mass of its members, could not be. Constituency parties simply could not understand how, given the decisions reached in Edinburgh, and the proven violations of the Agreement since then, the party could still be associated with Non-Intervention. As Konni Zilliacus put it in April 1937, 'the Labour Party's continual fiddling with Non-Intervention is getting beyond a joke', and as long as it continued to support it the party would have 'some of the Spanish workers' blood on its hands'.[123] Indeed, so low had the leadership's credibility sunk that a rumour was rife in the Birmingham Labour Party that the NEC had sent out instructions to all party agents that nothing should be done which would embarrass the government over Spain.[124] Increasingly dissatisfaction with Labour Party policy over Spain was manifested in hostility to the influence of the trade union leaders.

Amongst the trade unions one of the first signs of independent pressure came in January 1937 when the Executive Council of the Amalgamated Engineering Union (AEU) debated a motion submitted by leading left-winger Jack Tanner, taking his cue from branch resolutions and letters.

---

[121] On Ben Greene and the HCLA see Ben Pimlott, *Labour and the Left*, p. 111 and ff. On the LSC see C. Fleay and M.L. Sanders, 'The Labour Spain Committee: Labour Party Policy and the Spanish Civil War', *The Historical Journal*, 28, 1 (1985), 187–97.

[122] Churchill College, Cambridge, Labour Spain Committee papers, LSPC 1/2, 13 May 1937, Pole to Middleton; 14 May 1937 Middleton to Pole.

[123] Churchill College, Cambridge, Noel-Baker papers, 4/660, 9 April 1937, Zilliacus to Noel-Baker.

[124] Ruskin College, Oxford, James Middleton papers, MID 59, 17 February 1937, Tom Baxter to Middleton; Middleton replied (20 February 1937) that this was 'as downright a lie as has even been uttered'.

Although not explicitly condemning Non-Intervention, the motion heavily criticised German and Italian intervention in Spain and called on the TUC to convene a national conference of the representatives of affiliated unions alongside those from the Labour Party. One speaker felt that they should continue to 'stand behind' the TUC and Labour Party and not 'in any way offer opposition to their efforts to find a solution', but others believed that they must reserve the right to voice their own opinions. Eventually, although heavily amended so as to 'endorse and fully appreciate' the steps already taken over Spain, the final resolution called for a national conference to bring pressure on the British government and demonstrate trade union solidarity with Spain.[125] The response of the General Council's Finance and General Purposes' Committee, which saw 'no good purpose' in a conference,[126] failed to satisfy the AEU Executive which conveyed its regrets at the decision, emphasising that its intention was nothing less than 'compelling the Government to reverse their present policy'.[127]

However, this episode was somewhat anomalous as it dealt with the question of how to set about overturning Non-Intervention, and in this gave a foretaste of the struggles to come in 1938. Yet, as the debates at union conferences in the spring of 1937 showed, the real problem at this time was how to interpret the official attitude of the labour movement towards Non-Intervention at all. At the Congress of the Scottish TUC (STUC) in April a motion was adopted that called for an 'intensified effort' by the Scottish labour movement against Non-Intervention.[128] However, this only reached the floor after prolonged discussion by the Standing Orders Committee and on the understanding that the resolution was 'not to be interpreted as a declaration for intervention but as a declaration against the non-intervention policy as practised by the National Government' (and hence not a criticism of the Labour Party).[129] In the ensuing debate a further distinction was drawn – the motion did not condemn the 'principle' of Non-Intervention, but rather the 'policy' as practised by the British and other governments to the disadvantage of Spain.[130]

Union leaders often had to go to considerable lengths to stave off calls for stronger action. At the conference of the Boot and Shoe Operatives (NUBSO) in mid-May, for instance, a motion called upon the NCL to mount an 'intensified campaign' for the abandonment of Non-

---

[125] MRC, Mss 259, AEU EC minutes, 13 January 1937, pp. 79–81, 14 January 1937, p. 84.
[126] *Ibid.* 4 February 1937.   [127] *Ibid.* 4 February 1937.
[128] STUC *1937 Annual Report*, p. 144.
[129] National Library of Scotland (NLS), Edinburgh, Mf Mss 140, STUC General Council Minutes, 29 April 1937, minute 195.   [130] STUC, 1937, *Annual Report*, p. 146.

Intervention.[131] Opposing it, the union's National Organiser Alfred Dobbs (a member of the Labour Party NEC) challenged the assumption that the NCL was not doing all it could 'to assist the people in Spain'. He then defended Non-Intervention with some spirit, basing his argument on the dangers inherent in abandoning it. Firstly, he argued, it was a 'debatable point' whether the abolition of Non-Intervention would help or harm the Spanish people. This point was reinforced by the President, Townley, who stated that 'I don't think the Spanish people would like to see the British Government abandon the policy of Non-Intervention at this particular stage', due to the 'disastrous effects' that this would have. Secondly, according to Dobbs, the alternative to Non-Intervention would be 'for England to *declare* that they are going to be the saviours of all countries where Fascism raises its head', a policy that could easily lead to war.

Finally, and here Dobbs claimed that he was 'speaking with inside knowledge that some of you do not possess', and that France would not back Britain in ending the embargo fearing a 'second Spain within France'. The leaders then proceeded, quite blatantly, to bamboozle their members as to what the NCL was actually doing for Spain. Dobbs said that one of the main problems in Spain was not the lack of arms but poor military knowledge and the NCL 'has played a part in helping them to get over it in every sense of the word, and I don't want to say any more about that because of the interpretations that might be placed upon it'. Equally cryptically, Townley appealed for the motion's withdrawal because 'it is extremely difficult to impart all the information that there is on the question. If the history of it was written up it would be startling to know what has been done, but cannot be published at this stage.' The motion was withdrawn.[132]

However, appeals to authority did not always succeed. In late March the conferences of both the distributive workers (NUDAW) and the shop assistants (NAUSA) passed resolutions condemning Non-Intervention, despite opposition at the latter on the grounds that the union should 'have confidence in the Labour Party correctly interpreting the mind of the Trade Union and Labour Movement'.[133]

The decision to change policy on 24 June 1937 came in the middle of the unions' conference season, yet many of the ambiguities of the earlier period

[131] UCD, TU7/149, NUBSO *Monthly Record*, 1937, Conference report, 17–19 July, 1937, p. 55. The resolution came from Kilmarnock Branch.
[132] *Ibid.* pp. 196–9. Alfred Dobbs was tragically killed in a car accident on the day after his General Election triumph at Smethwick in 1945.
[133] USDAW archives, NAUSA AGM report, 28 and 29 March 1937, p. 43; NUDAW AGM Minutes, 28 and 29 March 1937, p. 52. This resolution regretted 'the confusion caused within the Labour Party by the Spanish Non-Intervention Pact'.

were carried forward into the later debates. Perhaps the best example of this came at the mental health workers' conference in mid-July where the General Secretary George Gibson spoke with some passion in support of a resolution that called for the British government to raise the matter of Spain at the League of Nations 'with a view to organised intervention (on behalf of the legitimate Spanish Government)'.[134] Gibson claimed to speak on behalf of the 'decent people' of Britain against the horrors of German and Italian intervention and the resolution was carried unanimously. Yet, almost immediately afterwards, speaking this time against the motion advocating support for the communist-backed Unity campaign in Britain, Gibson defended Non-Intervention as if there were no contradiction with his support for the earlier resolution:

> intervention would have meant war. I want to put to you this question … Do you think that our members, that the working people of this country would go to war for Spain. (Mr Farmer – 'Yes') … Well, it is a different thing if you have the lives of millions of your class on your shoulders. I refuse to stand for a policy that would put millions of our class under the sod – dead – fighting for a cause that the people of Spain are not agreed on! The problem is not merely … trying to help the Spanish Government – we all want to do that; all of us *have* helped; but when you say intervention you must consider all the consequences.[135]

However, the change in policy did begin to filter through and was expressed by a greater sense of confidence among the rank and file. At the railwaymen's conference in mid-July, for instance, a resolution calling for the restoration of 'complete commercial liberty' to the Spanish government which would, until recently, have been thought radical, was now roundly condemned from the floor as inadequate, much to the surprise of the leaders. Speakers felt that it failed either to stress the need for the supply of arms to Spain or the need to organise the labour movement to enforce the new policy.[136] Thus, the adoption of a policy acceptable to the mass of the labour movement merely heralded the debate over how the intention of that policy could be put into practice.

Although the labour movement had been slow to respond to pressures from below, its record of activity on behalf of the Spanish Republic during this period is perhaps better than has been credited. It was central to Citrine's concept of political action that, acting on behalf of the labour

---

[134] MRC, Mss 229/NA/1/1/5, Annual Conference minutes, 14 and 15 July 1937, p. 15. The part of the resolution in brackets was adopted as an amendment.   [135] *Ibid.* p. 39.
[136] *Railway Review*, 16 July 1937, pp. 2–3.

movement, he could exercise a beneficial influence on the government even if it would not abandon Non-Intervention. In this case the communist allegation that Citrine was selling out labour's interests in the craven pursuit of accommodation with the government[137] was wide of the mark. Instead, Citrine was carrying his usual style of leadership by (unaccountable) negotiation into the realms of international politics. The situation in northern Spain between April and October 1937 provides an ideal test case for the validity of his approach. He was dealing with a Foreign Office that was far from unsympathetic to his objectives – he was on good terms with Eden and the Permanent Under-Secretary Vansittart.[138] Moreover, it was much easier to act on behalf of the Basques than the Spanish in general. Especially after the atrocity of the bombing of Guernica on 26 April 1937 the Basques were widely perceived in Britain as decent, Catholic people, martyred to fascism.[139] The TUC enjoyed close relations with the London representatives of the autonomous Basque government and Citrine was a favourite channel of communication for the Basques, not only to the government but also to the Labour Party.

In April 1937 the Basque country was threatened with starvation following a largely fictitious Nationalist blockade of the port of Bilbao in which the British government had colluded by warning ships not to proceed to their destination. On 14 April Attlee had moved an effective, though unsuccessful, motion of censure on the government for its failure to protect merchant shipping and there was a further chance to debate the issue on the adjournment of the House on 20 April. On 15 April Citrine told Schevenels that the TUC had a vessel, the *Backworth*, ready to sail with a cargo of food, but that the British government, which had ships on patrol in the area, refused to offer protection. He suggested that pressure could be brought to bear on Blum through the French trade union movement to offer protection to ships on humanitarian business. This, in turn, would strengthen the TUC's hand with the government at a time when popular feeling was 'rising rapidly' against government policy. However, by the time that word came that Blum had promised to give his 'greatest attention' to the matter, the *Backworth* had sailed. Jouhaux later recalled how he had immediately

---

[137] *Daily Worker*, 21 September 1937; *The Week*, 17 March 1937.
[138] Since 1933 Citrine had been engaged in supplying Vansittart with information from inside Germany (Citrine, *Men and Work*, p. 347), and during the Civil War he regularly provided information on German arms shipments to the rebels, see TUC, Box 434, File 946/526, 'Spanish Rebellion – ITF, Shipping to Germany'.
[139] According to David Grenfell, the Basques were 'kindly and religious people, and they cannot be described in terms frequently used in this House regarding a section of the Spanish people'; *Hansard*, 5th series, vol. 322, 20 April 1937, col. 1712. See also Tom Buchanan, 'The Basque Children's Committee', pp. 164–5.

contacted Blum and Delbos 'and asked [Delbos] to get in touch with the British government to change its policy'.[140]

Soon afterwards Citrine met Sr. Aznar, the Basque government's Minister of Commerce and Industry, who wanted him to ask Attlee not to press the matter of the blockade too hard in debate, fearing that this might 'drive [the government] into obstinacy and that would bolt and bar the door, so that a change for the better would not be possible'. Although the Labour Party might sacrifice some political advantage, the Basques were keen to allow the government to make 'a conciliatory reply'.[141] When Citrine saw Attlee and A.V. Alexander in the Commons he found them unsympathetic to the proposal – the blockade of Bilbao was one of the few occasions when the PLP succeeded in seriously embarrassing the government over Spain – although they appreciated the need not to damage the Basque government's interests. They felt that the Basques did not understand the 'method by which we proceeded in this country'.[142] This was not the first occasion on which the Basques were to voice their opposition to becoming drawn into party politics in Britain.[143] Nor is it apparent that the Labour Party front bench changed its approach to the debate – Alexander launched a ferocious assault on the government's derogation of duty which a Tory member quite justifiably called an 'orgy of emotional jingoism'.[144]

Prior to the debate Citrine visited Eden claiming that the TUC was coming under pressure from areas such as South Wales due to the blockade's adverse effect on trade with northern Spain. Citrine reminded Eden of his earlier promise 'that no impediment would be put in the way of supplying the humanitarian needs of Spain', yet now, due to the government's warning, traders were unwilling to carry a cargo on the *Backworth*. Eden, who said that he felt 'personally very sympathetic towards the Basques', stressed that there were very real dangers facing shipping but promised to speak in the debate 'and would endeavour to say something conciliatory'. Citrine added that the labour movement felt 'considerable disquiet' that Sir Samuel Hoare (First Lord of the Admiralty and Foreign Secretary at the time of the infamous Hoare–Laval Pact in 1935) was due to speak for the government. Eden said that he 'would get into the debate of he could...'[145]

---

[140] TUC, Fund 2, 15 and 19 April 1937, Citrine to Schevenels, and 19 and 23 April 1937, Stolz to Citrine; TUC, Documents 3, 29 April 1937, report of IFTU Executive meeting, p. 4; NCL minutes, 27 April 1937.

[141] TUC, Documents 3, 20 April 1937, report of meeting, p. 1.

[142] *Ibid.* 5.30 p.m., House of Commons, p. 2.

[143] TUC, Basque Children 2, 3 June 1937, Tewson to Parker.

[144] *Hansard*, 5th series, vol. 322, 20 April 1937, col. 1700 (Sir Adrian Baillie).

[145] TUC, Documents 3, 20 April 1937, 5.45 p.m., pp. 2–3. The Hoare–Laval Pact was an unsuccessful Anglo-French plan to dismember Abyssinia in order to prevent its complete

On the following day Citrine met Vansittart and told him that the government was wrong to attempt to restrain British shipowners if they were willing to take the risks involved. Moreover, the Royal Navy should escort them to the Spanish three-mile limit. Vansittart replied that the government was keen to avoid an 'international difficulty' on the matter, but added that Franco had made 'a profound mistake' in attacking the Basques as 'this autonomous government had behaved in the most exemplary fashion, and that all they wanted was to be left alone'. He promised to pass on Citrine's comments to Eden.[146] Five days later Citrine was gratified to receive a visit from the Basque representative in London, Sr. Lizaso, and two colleagues who thanked him for his intervention, saying that 'my action had undoubtedly improved the position, and the food situation, which was crucial, had now become considerably eased'.[147] Within a week this co-operation was revived on a much larger scale when the labour movement became involved with the care of Basque children evacuated to Britain from Bilbao.[148]

On 19 June, when Bilbao fell, Citrine, prompted by Lizaso, telephoned Eden to complain that the British battleship *Resolution* had refused to escort refugee ships from the port. Eden was at this stage in the middle of negotiations over refugees with the French ambassador who was apprehensive at the prospect of another large influx from northern Spain. However, despite his sympathy, Citrine's position was weakened by his unwillingness to commit the labour movement to caring for any more refugees on top of the newly arrived children – 'any question of our taking refugees into Great Britain and of giving financial assistance would necessarily take some little time to solve'. Thus, Eden was unable to give any assurance of protection to the refugee ships until he was certain that France would receive them. Citrine told Lizaso to 'direct all possible pressure upon the French government'.[149]

Interest in the northern front was maintained even after the defeated Basques had retreated west to Santander and in September 1937 the TUC General Council sent a telegram to Chamberlain voicing its dismay at reported claims that 5,000 Basque militia, civil servants, councillors and priests faced execution in the captured city. They reminded the Prime Minister of the humane behaviour of the Basque government when it had

---

conquest by Mussolini in 1935, strongly opposed by British public opinion. For Eden's 'promise' on humanitarian assistance see above p. 54.
[146] TUC, Documents 3, 21 April 1937, report of interview, 10.45 a.m.
[147] TUC, Documents 3, 26 April 1937, report of meeting. Citrine promised to introduce Lizaso to Vansittart to discuss some other matters of concern.   [148] See below pp. 163–4.
[149] TUC, Documents 3, 19 June 1937, report of telephone conversations, 10.30 and 12.30 a.m.

been in power in Bilbao, and appealed to the government to ensure that the executions 'be discontinued and prevented by the League of Nations'. The Prime Minister's office replied, incredibly, that it could see no evidence that 'severe measures are, in fact, contemplated'.[150]

However, the most notable attempt to influence the government for humanitarian ends came in October 1937 when there were fears that a Nationalist victory in Asturias would result in a bloody massacre. Asturias was the final Republican stronghold on the northern front and enjoyed particular links with the British labour movement due to the long-established trade unionism of its mineworkers. On 15 September the Nationalists began a major offensive, although progress was slow until 14 October when resistance began to collapse. On 11 October Citrine met the Spanish Foreign Minister Álvarez del Vayo who sought his help in putting pressure on the British government to facilitate the evacuation to Spanish government territory of 50–60,000 Asturians, having already gained Blum's support for the enterprise. Citrine pointed out that this meant, in practice, that 'the British government would be asked to send reinforcements to the Republican Army', but still undertook to contact the Foreign Office.[151]

Some hours later Citrine visited Lord Cranborne, conveying del Vayo's story that the Asturian miners and their families were gathered in Gijón and could be massacred if it fell. There were particular grounds for fear in that 'the miners had always been an extremist element and considerable excesses had taken place in the neighbourhood of Gijón in the early part of the Civil War'. Cranborne said that this matter had already been raised in Geneva by Delbos (the French Foreign Minister) who had wanted these men evacuated by France and Britain to Catalonia. This, however, could only apply to non-combatants. Citrine then raised two more points: firstly, whether, failing an evacuation, the government would still protect refugee ships, and secondly, whether an official appeal could be sent to Franco concerning the men of fighting age – after all, 'there were among them many leaders of trades unions who were personal friends of his own and not of extremist character'. Cranborne promised to raise both points with Eden.[152] According to Citrine's account, Cranborne revealed that, after meeting Delbos in Geneva, the idea of an exchange of hostages for an evacuation had been broached to Franco 'indirectly', but he

[150] PRO, FO 371, 21375, W 17259/37/41, nos. 212–13, 15 September 1937, telegram from labour movement leaders, headed by Bevin, to Chamberlain; TUC, Correspondence 2, 14 September 1937, Prime Minister to Bevin.
[151] TUC, Documents 3, 11 October 1937, 3.15 p.m., report of meeting.
[152] PRO, FO 371, 21377, W 9114/37/41, nos. 121–3, 12 October 1937, F.O. Minute, Lord Cranborne.

did not seem very concerned about these hostages. The excesses at Gijon in the early days of the war had been so great that Franco thought that the hostages now held by the Republican forces were of little consequence to him, as all his best allies had already been killed.

Moreover, Franco was ill-disposed towards the British government, which refused to grant him recognition, and he blamed it for prolonging the war by allowing food ships to reach Bilbao.[153]

However, it was not until 20 October that Eden replied, saying that the government concurred with the French government's view that an evacuation of the civil population would be impossible 'in the teeth of General Franco's opposition'. The best remaining hope was to attempt to mediate between the two sides on the fate of the 2,000 prisoners in government hands in Gijón, and the governments were making joint representations to Franco on behalf of the non-combatants. He saw no possibility of an evacuation involving men of fighting age.[154]

In spite of the lack of government interest, the initiative was revived by the intervention of the British mineworkers' federation (MFGB). On 13 October 1937 Citrine attended a dinner at the Spanish embassy in honour of del Vayo, who informed him of his recent discussion with the MFGB Secretary Ebby Edwards concerning a miners' delegation to Gijón to protect their comrades there. Citrine initially approved the idea, although typically suggesting that the delegation would have more credibility if bolstered by 'persons not connected with the Labour Movement', especially representatives of the church and the legal profession, as well as 'a public man or so'.[155] Citrine transmitted these suggestions to Edwards, together with some information on his own recent dealings with the Foreign Office which, he felt, implied that it would now be very difficult to send any help to Asturias.[156] After lengthy discussion on 15 October the miners' Executive decided that they were prepared to support any action that the TUC might take, and in the event of a Commission of Inquiry being set up to visit Spain would be willing to 'support and assist' the members of the Commission

---

[153] TUC, Documents 3, 11 October 1937, 5.15 p.m., report of meeting.

[154] PRO, FO 371, 21377, W 9114/37/41, nos. 124–5, 20 October 1937, Eden to Citrine. Strangely, on the same day as Citrine's visit, Attlee had been to see Eden on the same subject, postulating 40,000 potential victims, although the two initiatives were not, apparently, co-ordinated (PRO, FO 371, 21377, W 19345/37/41, nos. 156–7, 12 October 1937, F.O. Minute (Eden)); Citrine met del Vayo again on 12 October, who told him that he had seen Attlee and was now going to make representations to the French government, TUC, Documents 3, 12 October 1937, 10.30 a.m., report of meeting.

[155] TUC, Documents 3, 13 October 1937, memorandum. Also at the dinner were Attlee, Noel-Baker, Commander Fletcher, Lord Listowel, Ellen Wilkinson, Victor Gollancz and Ramos Oliveira.   [156] TUC, Correspondence 2, 15 October 1937, Citrine to Edwards.

with some of their own members.[157] On 18 October Edwards met Citrine and placed the matter entirely in his hands.[158]

Citrine contacted Vansittart at the Foreign Office, who felt that a Miners' Commission would not be able to restrain Franco, would place its own members in peril and would anyway find it difficult to reach Gijón. He proposed instead that the Spanish government should release its prisoners to mollify Franco, a view shared by Eden who thought that a delegation would be in a 'humiliating position' even if it reached Gijón, as Franco 'would in all probability have no dealings with it'.[159] Citrine also contacted Schevenels who 'didn't see the use' of a commission. He thought that unless it was composed of very high-ranking people (such as Adler or De Brouckère of the LSI) it would find itself in danger – 'if a Trade Union Secretary or Left wing leader went Schevenels would not give a penny for his life – he would be thrown in prison'. However, although he doubted whether such a party could even reach Asturias, Schevenels promised to canvass the leaders of the Internationals to see if they would join the venture.[160] He later contacted the Spanish ambassador in Paris and the Paris representative of the Asturian miners who were 'greatly divided' as to the wisdom of sending a delegation to Gijón.[161]

On the following day Citrine referred these opinions to the Spanish ambassador who said that the Commission project had now been abandoned and felt that an exchange was the most that could now be achieved.[162] Subsequently he submitted a memorandum to Citrine suggesting that Asturian soldiers could be allowed to be interned on British ships as if they had crossed a land border.[163] The ambassador also regretted the publication in the *News Chronicle* of a statement by Oliver Harris, the South Wales miners' leader, calling on the British government to evacuate the Asturian miners – similar requests had also been sent to the TUC and the Foreign Office.[164] The plight of the miners clearly struck a deep chord with their British counterparts. Edwards told Citrine that 'as nearly all my E.C. have volunteered to go to Gijon if necessary, I am also having letters as if all one

[157] MFGB *Annual Proceedings*, Executive Council minutes, 15 October 1937.
[158] TUC, Documents 3, 18 October 1937, 11.00 a.m., report of meeting.
[159] TUC, Documents 3, 18 October 1937, 3.30 p.m., report of meeting. Citrine did not tell Eden that he had seen Vansittart.
[160] TUC, Documents 3, 18 October 1937, 12.43–12.55 a.m., report of telephone conversation between Schevenels and A.E. Carthy (International Department).
[161] TUC, Documents 3, 19 October 1937, report of meeting with Spanish ambassador, p. 2.
[162] TUC, Documents 3, 19 October 1937, 11.30 a.m., report of meeting.
[163] TUC, Correspondence 2, 20 October 1937, text of memorandum.
[164] TUC, Documents 3, 19 October 1937, 11.30 a.m., report of meeting. PRO, FO 371, 21377, W 19444/37/41, 20 October 1937, no. 160, Harris to Eden; TUC, Correspondence 2, 20 October 1937, Harris to Citrine.

had to do in such a case was to get tickets for a WTA [Workers' Travel Association] cruise'.[165] Later Arthur Horner was to pay tribute to 'the elderly members of the Executive Council who, at the risk of physical inconvenience, and at the risk of their lives, were ready to...render whatever help they could'.[166]

In spite of such enthusiasm, however, the fall of Gijón on 21 October served to underline the powerlessness of the labour movement to intervene directly in Spain in the face of government obstinacy.[167] The government had resisted Citrine's powers of negotiation and it was clear that, beyond the sending of humanitarian relief, he could not establish the special interests of British labour in relation to the Spanish conflict. In the final year and a half of the war Citrine's position, ground between a government more committed than ever to Non-Intervention and a labour movement ostensibly committed to its overthrow, would become increasingly difficult to defend, especially as the Republic's situation began to deteriorate rapidly.

[165] TUC, Correspondence 2, 22 October 1937, Edwards to Citrine.
[166] MFBG *Annual Proceedings*, Executive Council minutes, 28 April 1938, report of special conference on the Spanish situation, p. 53.
[167] However, the British Government later admitted that in the chaos following the fall of Gijón, some 2,598 men of military age, approximately a half of them wounded, had been evacuated on British merchant ships and landed in France (*Hansard*, 5th series, vol. 329, 29 November 1937, cols. 1663–4, Parliamentary answer by Viscount Cranborne).

3

THE FAILURE OF THE LEFT: OCTOBER 1937–APRIL 1939

During the final phase of the war the Spanish Republic's stubborn resistance was regularly punctuated by military and diplomatic defeats which denied it the hope of eventual success. Yet while the British public, perhaps predictably, sympathised with the Republic in its death agonies as never before,[1] and rank-and-file solidarity in the labour movement reached ever higher levels, Spain's fate was less and less central to the attention of the leaders of British labour. This disjuncture led, in 1938, to sustained attempts to force both the Labour Party and the trade unions to take action to overturn Non-Intervention. The criticism of labour's policy which had previously been somewhat restrained, now became widespread within the movement.

Ironically, 1937 had ended on a note of optimism. Large Republican offensives were mounted in Aragon to deter Franco from attacking Madrid and the strategic city of Teruel was taken. Yet the celebrations were short-lived. Franco was not a general who lightly ceded territory and after bitter winter fighting all the Republican gains were lost. In lightning counter-offensives in the spring the rebel air supremacy was used to great effect in routing the People's Army. Franco's forces reached the sea at Vinaroz on 15 April 1938 and the Republic was split into two separate zones; Catalonia, now the seat of government, and a central zone inaccessible other than by increasingly hazardous sea routes. Defeat was staved off by the temporary reopening of the French border by Blum's short-lived second administration, and the Republic was able to mount one further offensive when its forces

---

[1] A series of early opinion polls in 1937–8 showed the mass of British opinion to be sympathetic to the Republic, while support for Franco was usually below 10 per cent of those polled. However, it proved very difficult to transmute such broad expressions of sympathy into meaningful political action (Hugh Thomas, *The Spanish Civil War*, p. 574, fn 3).

crossed the river Ebro and briefly threatened Franco's salient in August 1938. However, this turned into yet another battle of attrition which it was ill-equipped to win and the withdrawal across the Ebro was soon followed by the triumphant Nationalist offensive against Catalonia in January 1939.

For the British government Spain had become an embarassment to its diplomacy that stood as an obstacle to more important business. Prime Minister Neville Chamberlain was increasingly suspicious of Hitler's intentions but hoped for a *rapprochement* with Mussolini that would prevent a fascist alliance threatening Britain's position in the Mediterranean. Chamberlain's private diplomacy, pursued behind his Foreign Secretary's back, led to Eden's resignation and his replacement with the more malleable Lord Halifax in February 1938. This opened the way for the signing of an Anglo-Italian pact on 16 April, whereby Britain accepted Italy's conquest of Abyssinia and Italy agreed to withdraw its troops from Spain once the Civil War was over. The agreement could not, however, be ratified until December when Chamberlain felt satisfied that 'the Spanish question is no longer a menace to the peace of Europe'.[2] In a vain attempt to create diplomatic space the Spanish premier, Negrín, published on 1 May his war aims in the form of '13 points' which, he hoped, could form the basis of a mediated settlement in Spain. In November he unilaterally withdrew the International Brigades in the hope of inviting reciprocal action. Yet in the absence of any such response the Republic's last chance lay in the outbreak of a European war in which it could pose as the ally of the democratic powers. Thus, the failure of Britain and France to resist the German *Anschluss* with Austria in March 1938 and, in particular, the abandonment of Czechoslovakia at Munich in October sounded a death knell for Spanish democracy. Britain and France, it seemed, were not going to stand up to the dictators.

Government policy was made abundantly clear to TUC leaders in April 1938 when they responded to an appeal from the UGT to urge 'decisive actions' against the arms embargo.[3] The TUC's promise to 'do everything to exert pressure on the Government' resulted in the visit of a delegation on 6 April from the Finance and General Purposes' Committee to Lord Halifax.[4] The delegates put the case for the British government to give facilities for the purchase of arms to the Spanish government. Citrine particularly criticised the forthcoming Anglo-Italian agreement, fearing that

[2] *Hansard*, vol. 340, 2 November 1938, col. 210. See also Jill Edwards, *The British Government and the Spanish Civil War*, p. 168.
[3] TUC, Correspondence 3, 30 March 1938, UGT to TUC.
[4] *Ibid.* 1 April 1938, reply. The delegation consisted of Citrine, Elvin, Edwards, Holmes, Marchbank, Kean, Conley and Woolstencraft.

the government would sign it 'whether Mussolini withdrew the volunteers [from Spain] or not. Indeed, the government seemed indifferent even if [Mussolini] waited until Franco had won before the Italian troops were withdrawn.' Halifax replied that the government would not change its policy on Spain. He conceded that Non-Intervention was being broken, but believed that Mussolini had not sent any more troops to Spain (although admitting that it was difficult to monitor movements of aeroplanes). Halifax was reduced to attempting to justify his pro-Italian policy by addressing the delegates as 'responsible leaders of men'. He told them that Britain was now 'in a strategic position which no statesmanship could endure. Real points of danger had been created which must be removed at all costs.' Thus, Britain must attempt to exploit any divisions between Mussolini and 'big brother' Hitler.[5]

Shaken by the Munich agreement, followed in January 1939 by the fall of Catalonia, and facing chronic food shortages, the Republican resistance soon began to unravel. Long-suppressed animosities flared up, in particular resentment against the communists and the Negrín government which was thought to be in thrall to them. In March Colonel Casado, the military commander in Madrid, launched a coup against Negrín in the hope of negotiating a settlement with Franco. Thus, the war ended with street-fighting between the communists and their adversaries in Madrid, with the consequence that Franco marched unopposed into his new capital on 27 March 1939.

The pervasive sense of international crisis and the proximity of war in 1938 transformed the position of Spain within British political discourse. The leaders of the labour movement never ceased to promote the interests of the Spanish government, but it is clear that for them, unlike for the left, Spain was no longer a leading priority. Thus, in 1938, the gulf that separated the leaders and their left-wing critics over Spain was wider than at any point in the Civil War, because the argument was no longer just over how Spain could best be helped, but also about the degree to which the Spanish conflict should be allowed to intrude into British politics. Indeed, Spain had come to symbolise such different political truths that the two sides had largely ceased to be able to communicate, and this had very damaging implications for practical solidarity with Spain. The left saw the Civil War as the central drama in the struggle between fascism and democracy which, at the same time, could provide the mobilising focus for a campaign that would defeat

---

[5] TUC, Documents 4, 7 April 1938, report of meeting. There is no record of this meeting in the PRO archives FO 371 series.

the British government and save the peace of Europe. Yet although the leadership continued to regard Spain as a clear example of the failure of the government's foreign policy, it rejected the idea that extra-parliamentary pressure should be brought to bear on the government in order to remedy it, recognising that this would destabilise the labour movement quite as much as the government.

A good example of this divergence came in the debate over rearmament. In March 1938 the British government had announced an acceleration in its rearmament programme and sought the TUC's goodwill in the project. The left, ambivalent towards such a programme on political and moral grounds, saw this as a sign of government weakness and sought to inspire the engineering workers to drive a hard bargain for their co-operation, in particular to force the government to abandon Non-Intervention. The left were heartened when the Amalgamated Engineering Union (AEU), the main union organising skilled workers, publicly rejected the government's advances in April 1938. Yet the labour leadership, which had accepted the merits of rearmament, adopted a very different attitude. While it, too, was willing to threaten the government with non-co-operation, it did so with the intention of building a greater basis of support for rearmament through the abandonment of unpopular foreign policies, while at the same time reducing agitation amongst its own members.[6]

Hence, the leaders saw the labour movement's policy towards Spain as settled; Non-Intervention had been condemned, but there was little that could be done to dismantle it while Chamberlain's government was in power. In particular, they refused to make the transition which the left demanded from a rejection of Non-Intervention to a positive demand for 'Arms for Spain'.[7] Thus, in practice, labour policy was restricted to three main aims; firstly, continued pressure on the government to end Non-Intervention by legitimate means such as Parliamentary debate, demonstrations and personal conversations with ministers; secondly, the raising of funds for humanitarian relief; and thirdly, assistance in the preservation of labour movement unity in Spain. Although some of the labour leaders (for instance, Greenwood and Attlee) were to become more responsive to the plight of the Spanish Republic than others, their concept of political action

---

[6] See below pp. 116–17.
[7] Labour's priorities were clear in the approved wording of banners for a large demonstration on Spain held by the London Labour Party in February 1939: 'British Democracy condemns betrayal of Spanish Democracy'; 'For Freedom and Democracy in Spain – and Everywhere!'; 'Away with the Government that betrays British Security – Let's have a Labour Government' (TUC, Correspondence 3, 20 February 1939, London Labour Party to Tewson).

still fell within this framework.[8] Accordingly, after September 1937 meetings of the Internationals lost any aspiration of winning the initiative and became exercises in futility, dwarfed by the power of national governments. Indeed, British leaders who attended them appeared already to have one eye on posterity – in November 1938 George Hicks announced that he and his colleagues had always done their best for Spain but had been restrained by 'a large unemployment problem and an unsympathetic government'.[9]

A useful indication of labour's attitude came in April 1938 when Julius Deutsch, formerly a leader of the Austrian socialists and now a roving ambassador for the Spanish government, visited Transport House to ascertain exactly what help British labour could give to Spain. Citrine, accompanied by Middleton and Gillies for the Labour Party, went out of his way to 'disillusion' their visitor. He felt that the British government had won the argument by convincing the majority of the people that the alternative to Non-Intervention was war. The government was quite secure and would win any forthcoming election. When Deutsch inquired about the possibility of strikes to bring down the government, Citrine replied that the 1927 Act would prevent such action from being successful. Moreover, they would have against them many of the British people: 'It had to be confessed that not all the people in this country saw the evil consequences of Franco establishing a military regime.'

Then Deutsch raised the possibility of an armistice, although it is not clear whether he was acting on Negrín's authority or on his own initiative. Although on this occasion his hosts felt unable to act on his proposal,[10] this did not prevent him from returning to the subject immediately afterwards when he met senior Labour Party politicians over lunch. Dalton has left a vivid picture of this meeting and was appalled that all Deutsch could initially advocate were further resolutions from the Internationals – 'what pathetic drivel and self-delusion this is' he wrote, 'It nearly makes me sick.' Dalton was even more horrified, however, when Deutsch again volunteered the

---

[8] Ruskin College, Oxford, James Middleton papers, MID 60, 7 August 1938, Greenwood to Middleton, records Greenwood's conversation with the Russian Ambassador Maisky who convinced him of the gravity of the situation in Spain. However, Greenwood told him that a 'raging campaign' on the issue was 'hopeless in August'. Instead, he thought that the Labour Party should issue a declaration stating that Non-Intervention was now 'completely *dead*', and that if the French border were opened 'the situation might be saved'. This spurred Attlee to call for a meeting of the NCL when the TUC met in Blackpool (24 August 1938, Attlee to Middleton). The sense of urgency that this correspondence suggests was immediately negated, however, by the Munich crisis.

[9] TUC, International Committee minutes, 25 January 1939, a report of the IFTU Executive and extraordinary General Council meeting, 9–10 November 1938.

[10] TUC, Documents 4, 12 April 1938, memorandum.

need for mediation in Spain only to be rebuffed by his colleagues. Attlee went 'into his shell' and felt that they could not act without authorisation from Madrid. Noel-Baker who had 'transferred all his eager enthusiasm and credulous optimism from Geneva to the Spanish Front' was reduced to sloganeering on the lines that Barcelona could yet become another Madrid.[11] Although Dalton and A.V. Alexander thought the matter should be pursued, at a subsequent LSI/IFTU meeting the subject was not raised, and the meeting degenerated into bitter recriminations between the British and French delegates as to who had done most, or least, for Spain.[12]

This episode has to be seen in terms of the continuing debate within the Spanish government parties over how the war was to be concluded,[13] with the communists most firmly opposed to any mediation. In June 1938 the UGT alleged that certain persons in the international labour movement, and in particular newspapers of the British Labour Party, had been influenced by a reactionary campaign to end the war through a mediation which would amount, in fact, to a total surrender.[14] At the same time four Labour councillors serving in the International Brigades wrote to the Labour Party urging it not to support any such initiative.[15] The NCL refuted these allegations. Citrine told the UGT that every action of the labour movement was taken in harmony with the 'express policy and desires' of the Spanish government and of the UGT, adding that all labour's official journals had 'steadfastly insisted upon the termination of the Non-Intervention agreement...'.[16] James Middleton, replying to the Labour councillors was even more cavalier with the truth when he told them that an armistice had not been discussed prior to the UGT allegation: yet an armistice in Spain had definitely been on the agenda at the previous month's NCL meeting.[17]

Nor was this the first time that factional conflict within Spain had made an impact far beyond its borders. For, under the government of Juan Negrín, Spain had achieved a degree of political unity only at the expense of

---

[11] BLPES, Dalton Diary, 12 April 1938.

[12] TUC, Documents 4, 14 April 1938, report of meeting.

[13] See Helen Graham, 'The Spanish Socialist Party in Power and the Government of Juan Negrín, 1937–9', *European History Quarterly*, vol. 18, 2, April 1988, pp. 189–90.

[14] MRC, ITF records, 159/3/c/6/14, 29 June 1938. According to the UGT *Bulletin*: 'we observe with sadness how certain personalities of the international workers' movement and newspapers of the great British Labour Party are influenced by a reactionary campaign which aims to liquidate the Spanish conflict. This has been termed a "mediation" but is, in fact, no more than a capitulation and a surrender' (my translation).

[15] Labour Party archives, LP/SCW/7/3, 9 July 1938, letter from councillors J.L. Jones (Liverpool), Thomas Murray (Edinburgh), C. Broadbent (Dewsbury) and L. Clive (Kensington) to James Middleton.

[16] NCL minutes, 26 July 1938; TUC, Correspondence 3, 16 July 1938, Citrine to UGT.

[17] Labour Party archives, LP/SCW/7/4, 11 August 1938, Middleton to Jones; the NCL on 21 June 1938 discussed the political situation in Spain and the possibility of an armistice.

Caballero and his followers in the UGT who now presented themselves as the victims of communist machinations. The response to the power struggle within Spain again demonstrates the extent to which British labour followed a non-doctrinaire approach to Spain and was willing to accept the communist line that political objectives should be made secondary to winning the war. At the time of his fall in May 1937 Caballero was attempting to resist communist interference in the army for which he was responsible as War Minister. In response to communist pressure for political unity with the PSOE, Caballero sought trade union unity between the UGT and the anarchist CNT, and was thus even less disposed to take strong action against the anarchists. After the May events in Barcelona the communists and Caballero's old rival Prieto on the socialist right took the opportunity to remove him from office. However, Caballero retained his position as leader of the UGT which refused to enter the new government. Moreover, he was willing to speak out publicly against government policy. In October 1937 the UGT split and an alternative leadership was formed, composed of Ramon Gonzáles Peña as President and José Rodríguez Vega as Secretary.[18]

Given this situation it would have been conceivable, even rational, for British labour to side with Caballero against the alleged communist usurpers. Certainly Citrine was influenced in this direction by Caballero's friends in the international socialist community.[19] However, this tendency was restrained by a lingering distrust of Caballero and by advice from the leaders of the IFTU who were much more closely involved with the dispute. The IFTU was under no illusions that the Spanish communists were making deep inroads into the PSOE but felt that this should not colour their relations with the UGT. Schevenels wrote to Citrine that Peña and his colleagues were

> one hundred per cent reliable Socialists and Trade Unionists, beyond any shadow of doubt, and certainly not less so than Caballero. In their attempt to resist the rebellion and to lead Republican Spain to final victory in the civil war, they may be using methods which, in our opinion, are the wrong ones, but then this applies at least as much to Caballero – both when he was Prime Minister and later – as it does to Peña.

[18] See the briefing papers sent by Stolz to Citrine, TUC, Correspondence 2, 30 August, 31 August and 3 September 1937.

[19] TUC, Correspondence 2, 26 August 1937, Citrine to Schevenels, voiced suspicions of 'intrigues' within the UGT. Citrine was initially influenced by information that he received from Mme Lily Krier-Becker, a socialist from Luxembourg, who sympathised with the 'old and authentic UGT' and believed that Caballero and his followers were being persecuted because he 'would not let go the UGT to the Communists' (TUC, Correspondence 2, 13 November 1937, Krier-Becker to Citrine).

In his view both Caballero and his successors in government had mistakenly based themselves on communist support and must realise that they would be expendable when their interests conflicted with those of their backers. But he concluded that 'it is absolutely out of the question to accuse Peña...of making a Communist manoeuvre or of being used for Communist ends'.[20]

Thus, Citrine supported the IFTU in seeking to play honest broker to the divided UGT, despite Caballero's hopes for partisan support. Some kind of arbitration was desirable not only because of the pressing situation in Spain, but also because of the disruptive effect of the split on international labour – Dalton had characteristically described the scene at the 13 September 1937 LSI/IFTU meeting as 'Six Spaniards present glaring at each other. A Spanish bull fight is expected when they get going.'[21] In early December the IFTU Executive hosted delegations from both factions. Caballero presented himself as the victim of a communist plot, ousted because he had not wanted 'to become merely an agent of Moscow'. Yet his rival Peña said quite frankly that the government crisis in May had arisen due to Caballero's tolerance of the anarchists – 'the communists were quite right in saying that the Anarchists must be punished and the revolt put down', and he favoured working with the communists to win the war.[22] Soon afterwards Léon Jouhaux was despatched to Spain to arbitrate the dispute and devised an acceptable settlement whereby Peña's supporters held a majority in a reunited UGT Executive. Caballero was marginalised and felt great bitterness against Jouhaux who, he believed, had not attempted to ascertain the facts but had simply fallen in with the wishes of the Spanish government.[23] It was apparent that the niceties of international trade unionism, and even the imperative of anti-communism, could be sacrificed to the winning of the war.

---

[20] TUC, Correspondence 2, Schevenels to Citrine, 8 November 1937. In 1940, when Vega was facing a court martial in Spain, Schevenels sent Citrine a glowing testimonial on his behalf: 'Apart from Comrade Vega's political attitude in the earlier days of the Civil War in Spain, I must say that, from 1937 onwards, this comrade took a very courageous stand and defended unreservedly the IFTU and its activities in the Spanish affair' (TUC, 'Aftermath', 24 February 1940).   [21] BLPES, Dalton Diary, 13 September 1937.

[22] TUC, Documents 3, 7/8 December 1937, report of meeting.

[23] TUC, Documents 4, statement by Caballero for IFTU Executive 17/18 March 1938; dated 7 March 1938. He complained that Jouhaux only learnt the views of the Spanish government, with whom he had lunch, and the new Executive, with whom he dined. Caballero's former friend and now pro-communist Ogier Preteceille had not left Jouhaux's side during the entire visit. Citrine was invited to accompany Jouhaux, but claimed that he would not be available until the New Year (TUC, Correspondence 2, 10 December 1937, TUC to IFTU).

Right up until the end of the conflict British labour retained this posture of largely uncritical support for Spanish labour and for the government of which it formed a crucial part. In September 1938, for instance, Sr. Batista i Roca visited Vincent Tewson, Citrine's Deputy, as representative of a recently formed Left Republican Union in Spain which included such important regional parties as the Basque Nationalists and the Catalan Left Republicans. He added that Prieto (sacked as Defence Minister in April 1938) was 'very sympathetic' to the venture, and presented the new party as being at odds with a communist-influenced Negrín government. He had hoped that Citrine could secure support from the UGT: this was something that Tewson was unwilling to contemplate and he told Batista i Roca that 'we did not desire to interfere too much in the internal affairs of Spain'.[24] However, mild criticisms were made when the Spanish government was perceived to be undermining its own international support. After the May events in Barcelona the communist-dominated security police had led a brutal purge against the POUM opposition, and the fate of their comrades in Spain came to preoccupy the British ILP. In 1938 the ILP leader Fenner Brockway urged the TUC to put pressure on the Negrín government to ensure a fair trial and on 10 October Tewson and Middleton visited the Spanish ambassador to this effect. They made clear their support for the Spanish government, but they felt that there had to be an open and fair trial to ensure that 'nothing untoward would arise to cause dissension' amongst British supporters.[25]

The attitude of the labour movement in this final phase of the war thus provides a further corrective to any simplistic use of the term 'anti-communist'. It was bitterly opposed to any side-effect of the war which would bolster the united front internationally, but was happy to tolerate the Spanish communists fighting to defend their Republic. For instance, when a local organisation in Barcelona invited the General Council to send a delegation of British women to witness the Spanish 'tragedy' at first hand, Schevenels warned Citrine that 'delegations have been exploited by those bodies in Spain which are under very strong communist influence and used to support communist propaganda for the international unity slogan'.[26] Yet

[24] TUC, Documents 4, report of interview dated simply 'September' 1938.
[25] NCL minutes, 25 October 1938; see also the material in TUC archives, Box 434, File 946/527, 'Spanish Rebellion – 1938: POUM Leaders on Trial', especially 10 October 1938, report of visit to Spanish ambassador.
[26] TUC, Correspondence 3, 17 September 1938, Schevenels to Citrine. The invitation, dated 16 July 1938, came from the 'Committee of Liaison of the Local Federations of Barcelona (CNT/UGT)'.

in March 1939, as the factions fought in the ruins of the Republic, the *Daily Herald* of all papers paid due tribute to the gallantry of 'a handful of communists' in Madrid who 'fight desperately for the right to go on fighting'.[27]

With the establishment of a settled policy on Spain, the performance of the Labour Party in Parliament markedly improved. Although spokesmen were still not specific about what should replace Non-Intervention, the agreement itself was now regularly denounced as a 'sham' and a 'rotting corpse'.[28] The opposition was particularly successful in attacking those aspects of government policy which ran visibly counter to national interest and prestige, for instance the bombing of defenceless British merchant shipping in Spanish government ports[29] and the Anglo-Italian agreement. However, despite the ferocity and extent of the party's efforts – in April 1938 British delegates boasted to their IFTU and LSI comrades that the PLP had initiated fourteen debates and tabled over 200 questions during the nine weeks of the recent session[30] – they were never able to do more than embarrass a government safe behind its parliamentary majority.

Outside Parliament, pressure on the government continued to be exercised in the form of deputations to ministers. The objective of such initiatives, however, was often far from clear. A good example of this came during Citrine's negotiations with the Foreign Office over the fate of the Asturian miners in October 1937. Citrine had a private meeting with Lords Cranbourne and Plymouth at which he asked whether, in the case of Italy sending yet more troops to Spain, Britain would support the French government in reopening its border with Spain. Cranbourne dismissed this as a 'gesture' which could lead to war, but Citrine was particularly incensed by Lord Plymouth's claim that there was no clear evidence of Italian troop movements. They had checked the Italian claim that 800 men recently arrived at Cádiz were 'medical men' and had 'found that this was true'![31] This was too much for Citrine who pointed out that

---

[27] *Daily Herald*, 10 March 1938.
[28] *Hansard*, vol. 333, 16 March 1938, p. 490, (Attlee); *Ibid.* p. 527 (Greenwood).
[29] The National Union of Seamen worked closely with a Committee of British Shipowners Trading With Spain on this issue. They jointly sponsored a film ('England Expects') which was heavily cut by the Board of Film Censors (*The Seaman*, 21 December 1938). However, the attitude of the NUS leaders was at heart jingoistic – in June 1938 General Secretary William Spence commented that his members were saying 'Oh for a Salisbury, or Gladstone, or even Lloyd George' in whose day drastic action would have followed the death of British seamen. Spence believed that many of his members would approve of the Royal Navy shelling the rebel port of Cádiz the next time that a British vessel was attacked (*The Seaman*, 22 June 1938). See Jim Fyrth, *The Signal Was Spain*, pp. 255–6, on the work of the committee.   [30] NCL minutes, 26 April 1938.
[31] TUC, Documents 3, 11 October 1937, report of meeting.

the support of the Trade Union Movement for the foreign policy of the Government during the next few years would be of paramount importance, in view of the necessity of securing their whole-hearted co-operation in the work of rearmament. He hoped therefore that nothing would be done which gave an impression that the policy of the government was inspired by pro-fascist or anti-democratic sentiment. He himself was constantly being told [at International meetings] that the French Government led the van for democracy and was being constantly held back by HMG! He knew that this was not true, but he was seldom in a position to refute it, and he hoped that in any action that was taken in the near future HMG would make their own attitude clear to the general public...[32]

A similar attitude was taken during the TUC delegation to the new Foreign Secretary Lord Halifax in April 1938. Citrine had assured Halifax that

> there was indeed a very deep feeling of suspicion in the minds of the organised workers of this country that he, Lord Halifax, and his colleagues favoured the Nazi regime, giving the impression that they were not too anxious as to Franco's winning, although his victory meant undoubtedly additional strength to the forces of Hitler and Mussolini...

He referred to the TUC's recent negotiations with Sir Thomas Inskip (newly created Minister for the Co-ordination of Defence) where it was pointed out to the government that arms were being exported from Britain, but not to Spain (Halifax admitted that arms were going to Japan in fulfilment of 'an old contract'). Thus, there was a 'growing feeling' that British workers would not manufacture arms unless they would definitely be used to defend democracy. Citrine concluded with an ominous reference to the agitation in the labour movement against Non-Intervention: 'Requests had been received from many parts of the country for a National Conference to be called to deal with the matter and to take drastic action. Some were even thinking of declaring a "general strike".'[33]

Citrine's strong language had the desired effect in at least impressing other members of his delegation. Miners' leader Ebby Edwards told a special conference of his federation that

> I do not think that any man could have told Halifax straighter than he was told on that occasion by Citrine, that there was a feeling in the whole country, that the Prime Minister, and especially Halifax himself, was a believer in the Fascist philosophy.

[32] PRO, FO 371, 21377, W9114/37/41, 12 October 1937, report of meeting.
[33] TUC, Documents 4, report dated 7 April 1938. Citrine had introduced the deputation with the comment that they came as representatives of the trade unions and should be considered as making representations 'apart from the political side of the Labour Movement'.

Halifax had been forced to reply that 'I can understand nothing as bad as Fascist philosophy, it would be hell.'[34] However, it is clear that here Citrine was adopting his favourite bargaining position, as the moderate leader who could contain his more militant members in return for a more defensible foreign policy. Yet, as subsequent events were to show, this position was in fact fatally flawed – Citrine was just as opposed to industrial action as the government and it did not have to offer him any concessions in order to induce him to confront his left wing.

The one area in which action was justifiably expected from the Labour Party was campaigning – after all, a Spain Campaign Committee had been established in the wake of the Bournemouth conference for this very purpose and the presence of such vigorous supporters of Republican Spain as Stafford Cripps and Ellen Wilkinson on the committee suggested that it would not be ineffectual. Yet the SCC failed to live up to these hopes. After a strikingly successful series of demonstrations, culminating in a rally at the Albert Hall on 19 December, the committee's work tailed off. Indeed, to the communists the SCC seemed more like a spoiling operation. Harry Pollitt told Cripps that in South Wales the local Labour Party was setting up new committees as a way of liquidating cross-party 'Aid Spain' committees established since the beginning of the war.[35] Despite a further burst of activity centred on May Day 1938, the SCC was rapidly losing its political orientation[36] and lapsing into humanitarian fund-raising. Sybil Wingate resigned from the SCC because she felt that it had broken its 'pledge' to the Labour Party conference to campaign for arms for Spain;[37] yet the root of the problem was an inherent lack of definition as to what the committee was intended to achieve.

In this the SCC was just one of many initiatives which was skewered on the dilemma of whether to concentrate on political or humanitarian campaigning. Was it better to demonstrate against Non-Intervention, in the hope that arms might eventually be sent, or to supply Republican Spain with the basic provisions that it needed to continue the fight? Of course, political campaigning and fund-raising can complement each other rather than stand as alternatives, and an organisation such as Spanish Medical Aid combined the two very effectively. Yet it was hard to replicate this success within a labour movement in which the leadership was bent on preventing political mobilisation. For instance, the SCC's Milk for Spain scheme, aimed at the

---

[34] MFGB *Annual Proceedings*, 1938, p. 49.
[35] Nuffield College, Oxford, Cripps papers, 776/521, 25 November 1937 Pollitt to Cripps, 27 November 1937, Cripps to Ellen Wilkinson.
[36] Nuffield College, Oxford, Cripps papers, 776/521, Cripps to Gillies, 12 December 1937.
[37] *New Statesman*, 12 March 1938.

Labour Party and Co-operative movement rank and file, was a great financial success; yet it was candidly presented as a means of depoliticising the campaign. As the *Daily Herald* put it, in comparison with the 'big task' of changing government policy, the relief of famine in Spain presented 'a menace which all British people who love justice and democracy can remove from the Republican cause by their own direct immediate action'.[38] Moreover, even Cripps was aware that Spain was just one campaign among many for the Labour Party,[39] and he himself was increasingly preoccupied with building a Popular Frontist 'Peace Alliance'.

Given that labour movement policy was virtually static after October 1937, the main dynamic in this period came from the attempts by the 'left' to change it, or at least to enforce the more aggressive policy against Non-Intervention which the left believed had been prescribed at Bournemouth. In 1938 there was a very strong campaign to achieve this and at one point, as support snowballed amongst constituency Labour parties and trade unions, it seemed barely conceivable that it would fail. The explanation for its failure has traditionally been provided in terms of the obduracy and weakness of the labour movement leadership. Writing in 1966, Joseph Pole of the Labour Spain Committee blamed the 'stolid caution' of Bevin and Attlee, backed up by 'the bulk of trade union support on the NEC'. The British labour movement would have had a prouder record on Spain had such leaders shown 'stronger leadership, more courage and will'.[40] Certainly during 1938 both the Labour Party and the trade union leaders entrenched themselves against any further changes in policy. The NEC, sheltering behind the absence of any party conference that autumn, spent the summer thwarting demands for a special conference to discuss Spain. The TUC did hold a Congress and actually passed a resolution calling for 'Arms for Spain': however, this was smothered by bureaucratic inaction.[41]

Yet it is too simple to present the leadership as purely negative in its attitude. As has been shown above, it was following a rational policy towards Spain, however inappropriate its critics might find it. Moreover, although deeply frustrating to activists, it was exercising its prerogative in refusing to change course. If change was to come then the onus was very clearly on the left to force it. Thus, it is also important to ask searching questions of the left: How coherent was it, what means did it employ to challenge existing policy, and what alternative did it promote?

---

[38] *Daily Herald*, 13 and 18 November 1937; see below pp. 156.
[39] Nuffield College, Oxford, Cripps papers, 776/521, 18 February 1938, Cripps to Pollitt.
[40] Churchill College, Cambridge, LSC papers, LSPC 1/1, historical note by Joseph Pole.
[41] See below, pp. 131–2.

The left, as defined below, continued to be characterised mainly by its political and institutional divisions. The political left included the Communist Party, leading figures in the Labour Party such as Cripps and Laski with the support of up to a third of the NEC,[42] intellectuals such as G.D.H. Cole, and many activists in the constituencies. In the trade unions one can identify individual leaders such as Jack Tanner in the engineers and Arthur Horner in the miners who consistently adopted left positions on Spain. Certain unions such as the furniture workers (NAFTA) and the South Wales miners (SWMF) had long radical traditions and gave a lead in campaigning on Spain. Yet, despite the strong personal links between individuals on the left, it proved unable to articulate a clear alternative policy over Spain around which the labour movement could unite, and in this sense the one strategy on which the left could agree, namely the need for unity against fascism through the united or Popular Front, was at least as much of a hindrance as an advantage.

1938 saw the most sustained campaign for a Popular Front in Britain, which became increasingly synonymous with the left's advocacy of the Spanish cause. In Jim Fyrth's view 'the political campaign for Spain was implicitly related to that for unity against fascism'.[43] In the spring of 1937 the Unity campaign had foundered when the repression of the POUM in Spain soured relations between the ILP and the British communists,[44] compounding the damage caused by the disbandment of the Socialist League. A year later, however, the left's net was cast much wider than the working-class movements alone, so that the goal was the unity of all opponents of the government from communists to dissident Tories. The first vehicle employed was the United Peace Alliance initiated by Sydney Elliott, the proprietor of *Reynolds' News*, a journal influential with the Co-operative movement. After initial successes, however, the campaign failed to win the support of the NEC and faded away in the summer after a series of defeats in trade union and co-operative conferences.[45]

However, the Popular Front agitation was revived by the Munich agreement and two notorious by-elections. At Oxford in October 1938 the Labour Party candidate was forced to make way for the Master of Balliol standing, unsuccessfully, as a Progressive in a campaign that was deliberately

---

[42] NEC minutes, 5 May 1938. A motion moved by Cripps and Swan calling for a Special Conference on the International Situation was defeated on the Chairman's vote after a 9–9 split, in the absence of nine other NEC members.

[43] Jim Fyrth, *The Signal Was Spain*, p. 284.

[44] The split between the ILP and the CPGB was not resolved. The ILP MP John McGovern visited Spain for a second time in 1938 and wrote a pamphlet entitled *Terror in Spain*, which depicted the Republic as being in the grip of the Cheka. See also *Forward*, 16 July 1938 and following editions.   [45] See Ben Pimlott, *Labour and the Left*, p. 153.

presented as a referendum on government foreign policy. In November the *News Chronicle* journalist Vernon Bartlett succeeded in winning Bridgewater on a Progressive ticket. However, whatever the value of the Popular Front, either in electoral terms or in the sense of a broader political mobilisation,[46] the argument presented below is that, at least in terms of helping Spain, its significance has been consistently overrated both by politicians at the time and by historians since.

The problem was threefold. First, the adoption of the Popular Front strategy in Britain was essentially a sign of the weakness of the left and of its failure to win over the labour movement. It was an attempt to bypass the powerful institutions of the labour movement, as well as to ignore the paralysing divisions within the left itself on political and institutional lines. Crucially, unlike in France, the Popular Front was not accompanied by mass workplace mobilisation and a challenge to the existing trade union structures, and while many trade unions were sympathetic to it they were unwilling to allow it to dictate their industrial strategy.

Secondly, the Popular Front's lack of penetration into the labour movement made it politically divisive. While there were undoubtedly many cases where local popular front activity for Spain surpassed what the labour movement could have achieved,[47] as a national political tactic it was less desirable. Many keen supporters of the Spanish Republic rejected the Popular Front as a basis for their solidarity. David Grenfell refused to be involved with the Labour Spain Committee because he felt that many who denounced the Labour Party most loudly had 'neglected their opportunities for local propaganda and appeal for Spain. I am convinced that we are weakened not strengthened by pretended unity with political opponents.'[48] Even Ellen Wilkinson was 'dismayed' to find that a meeting which she had agreed to address on a 'humanitarian basis' was advertised in the *Daily Worker* as an 'all-party' affair and pulled out of it.[49] She was also exasperated by the constant sniping criticism which she felt was directed at the labour movement as a whole, when it was only applicable to the movement's leadership.[50] The London Labour Party's demonstration for

---

[46] See Roger Eatwell, 'Munich, Public Opinion and the Popular Front', *Journal of Contemporary History*, 1971.   [47] See below p. 166.

[48] Churchill College, Cambridge, LSC papers, LSPC 1/5, 25 August 1938, Grenfell to Pole.

[49] Labour Party archives, LP/SCW, 1/29, 26 March 1938, Wilkinson to Middleton.

[50] She reacted strongly to criticism of the Labour Party while speaking on a Spanish Medical Aid platform in November 1936: 'If you expect me to come here as the national official of a very large trade union, and to do down those magnificent organised workers because of the leaders of that movement, whom I fight inside the movement as hard as I can, then you cannot talk about a united front even as a phrase.' She later wrote that 'I admit I was very angry and told both the audience and Mr Pollitt afterwards that if they did not want Labour

Spain in February 1939 was marred by squabbling between supporters of the Popular Front and its opponents.[51]

Finally, the Popular Front was an essentially electoral strategy, dependent for success on a General Election (which was not due until 1940) or on by-elections. This left its advocates dangerously reliant on the trade unions for more immediate political pressure on the government. As Cripps put it in May 1938, 'any decisive help [for Spain] has got to come through agitation by the unions rather than the [Labour] party'.[52] Yet the political left enjoyed no real influence over the trade unions.

The relationship with the unions was the left's achilles heel. Cripps had not specified what form of agitation the unions could adopt, and nor was the left united on this question. The Communist Party did not support industrial action for Spain which would run counter to the appeal to the middle classes inherent in the Popular Front strategy. Horner made rhetorical allusion to industrial action,[53] but recognised that such action by his own members could only be ultra-leftist, and he preferred to build broader political initiatives.[54] In fact, Cripps and others were suggesting that the unions, especially the engineers, should bargain with the government on the basis of an end to Non-Intervention in return for co-operation with rearmament. Yet this tactic was dependent on the unions acting on a purely 'political' basis and, in practice, no matter how left-wing the unions, they consistently put their members' industrial interests first. An excellent example of this was the AEU, on which so many of the left's hopes rested yet which never allowed political interests to come before industrial ones.[55] The miners were also lionised by the left. The MFGB more than made up for its support of Non-Intervention at the 1936 TUC Congress by becoming the most outspoken opponent of it in 1938. The miners went further than any other union in putting their whole weight behind political and humanitarian support for the Spanish Republic, and this led Robin Page Arnot to conclude that 'throughout the whole Spanish tragedy the [Miners'] Federation had been acting like a political party and in some ways with greater insight and vigour

Party people they should not ask them.' BLPES, Citrine papers, Citrine III/2/2, 12 November 1936, Citrine to Wilkinson (quoting from *The Shields Gazette*, 7 November 1936); 25 November 1936, Wilkinson to Citrine.

[51] *Daily Herald*, 27 February and 1 March 1939; *New Statesman*, 4, 11 and 18 March 1939.
[52] Nuffield College, Oxford, Cripps papers, Box 773, File 537, 30 May 1938, Cripps to Brailsford; see also Cripps' speech in Hyde Park on 10 April, reported in the *Manchester Guardian*, 11 April 1938.
[53] MFGB *Annual Report*, Conference report, 1938, pp. 365–6.
[54] Hywel Francis, *Miners Against Fascism*, p. 171.
[55] See Tom Buchanan, 'The Politics of Internationalism: The Amalgamated Engineering Union and the Spanish Civil War', *Bulletin of the Society for the Study of Labour History*, vol. 53, 3, 1988.

than the broad political party of which they were an important constituent'.[56] Yet the problem for Cripps, and for Pollitt, was precisely that the MFGB was a trade union situated loyally within the labour movement and all of its political initiatives were mediated through the limitations that this imposed.

Thus, although leaders of the left sought to show that they had assembled an irresistible coalition of forces, in practice a number of different battles were being fought on very different fields. However, for a brief period the coincidence of international crisis – the *Anschluss* and the collapse of the Republican front in Spain – with the opportunities for the labour movement presented by rearmament conspired to give the left a seductive image of unity and power. In April 1938 two conferences were held which appeared to show a coalescence of political and industrial forces demanding an alternative policy over Spain. The *Daily Worker* seized upon them as evidence of what the labour movement really wanted and alleged that the NEC was trying to 'hold back the tide of history' by resisting their demand for unity and the Popular Front.[57]

On 23 April, a 'National Emergency Conference' was convened at the Queen's Hall, London, under the auspices of an all-party group of MPs and the slogan of 'Save Spain – Save Peace'. Although treated with suspicion by the Labour Party as a Popular Front exercise with the communists,[58] the 1,800 delegates included representatives from a range of trade union executives alongside those from trades councils, and Labour Party and trade union branches.[59] Speakers included such luminaries as the Duchess of Atholl, Sir Peter Chalmers-Mitchell and Dr Gilbert Murray. However, in an atmosphere enthused by the engineers' recent defiance over rearmament, the main emphasis was on what the industrial strength of the movement could

[56] Robin Page Arnot, *The Miners – In Crisis and War* (1961), p. 271.
[57] *Daily Worker*, 29 April 1938.
[58] On 12 April 1938 the Labour NEC held a special meeting to discuss the conference, voting by 17–4 to leave the question of attendance up to local parties as Transport House had 'no official connection' with it. General Secretary Middleton wrote on 9 April 1938 about the conference that: 'Head Office has had no information about it whatever, and it has every appearance of some sections of the party being rushed into the "Popular Front" as there is clear evidence that Gollancz and Elliott with some of the members of our own EC having been in collusion' (Labour Party Archives, LP/SCW/1/17).
[59] See the published report of delegates from the London Trades Council, copy in TUC, Documents 4. Amongst the sponsors were the Liberal MPs Richard Acland, Megan Lloyd George and Wilfred Roberts, the Independent Eleanor Rathbone, Labour MPs David Grenfell, Geoffrey Mander, Philip Noel-Baker and Ellen Wilkinson, and the National Labour MP Harold Nicholson. Attlee and Elvin (chairman of the General Council) had initially given their approval but pulled out when they realised the Popular Frontist nature of the meeting (*The Times*, 7 and 26 April 1938).

achieve for Spain. Indeed, representatives of the South Wales and Durham miners called for a General Strike to secure for Spain the right to purchase arms[60] and James Griffiths MP appealed to trade unionists to 'go back to their Districts and consider using their industrial might'.[61] A delegate from the (unofficial) Aircraft Shop Stewards National Council stated that in order to end Non-Intervention and defeat the government they should be prepared 'to agitate for demonstration strikes'.[62]

Stafford Cripps, the main Labour Party speaker, while keen not to appear to lecture to the unions, said that the turning point would come when British workers showed the government that they were 'not prepared to enter into any bargains or make any concessions for a foreign policy which was sacrificing their brothers and sisters in Spain'.[63] Resolutions were carried which called for public opinion to be mobilised, for material help to be given to Spain and to 'support any political, economic and industrial action which may be taken in support of these objects'.[64] Over lunch the trade union delegates conferred, with Horner in the chair, and a deputation was appointed to visit the TUC and demand a meeting to discuss 'coercive measures' to bring pressure on the government. However, Citrine refused to meet an 'unofficial body' and advised the deputation to submit their proposals to the General Council.[65]

Five days later the miners' federation (MFGB) held an emergency conference in the Conway Hall specifically to discuss the situation in Spain.[66] Arthur Horner moved the resolution which called on the government to abandon Non-Intervention and to give Spain the right to buy arms, and called on the TUC to convene a meeting of executive committees to examine how to achieve this. Horner said that he was satisfied with the efforts of Labour MPs over Spain but, given the government's intransigence, some other form of pressure was necessary so that their efforts could be supplemented by 'what may be done from the outside'. The intended conference would have to devise a method of 'coercion' against government policy – they needed 'to initiate a movement to give assistance to Spain in a practical way altogether beyond anything we have thought of up to now'.

[60] *New Statesman*, 30 April 1938.   [61] *Daily Herald*, 25 April 1938.
[62] *New Propellor*, May 1938.   [63] *The Times*, 25 April 1938.
[64] *Daily Herald*, 25 April 1938.   [65] *Ibid.*
[66] This conference was called in response to the General Council's refusal to comply with a resolution of the MFGB Executive (10 March 1938) demanding a special conference of trade unions and 'allied bodies' to discuss the international situation. The miners' districts voted by 360–190 in favour of holding their own conference, with South Wales, Durham, the Midlands, Northumberland and Scotland leading those in favour, and Yorkshire, Lancashire and the newly reintegrated Nottinghamshire forming the main opposition (MFGB *Annual Proceedings*, 1938, 28 April 1938, pp. 70–1).

However, in spite of his use of words like coercion, anathema to Citrine, there was an ambiguity at the heart of Horner's speech which suggested that conflict could yet be avoided. For when it came to defining what a conference might achieve, all he had to offer was that it might raise 'scores of thousands of pounds' from the trade union movement.[67] Thus, in practice, Horner was acknowledging that it was more realistic to expect strenuous fund-raising from the trade unions rather than a challenge to the government.

In the ensuing discussion a number of different views were expressed. The leader of the Scottish miners feared that the resolution would be understood as a criticism of official TUC and Labour Party policy towards Spain, and volunteered his 'unbounded confidence' in their leadership.[68] However, a speaker from South Wales asserted that the resolution did not go far enough – the proposed conference should discuss a 'down tool' policy for Spain.[69] Yet others alluded to the overriding weakness of the labour movement *vis-à-vis* the government, because it was 'not able to do much except speak at the present time'[70] As the meeting drew to a close Mr J. Swan spoke from an unenviable position as both a Durham delegate and a member of Labour's NEC. Struggling to give the Labour Party's line against a conference (that it would waste time and energy), he was challenged 'Are you for or against the Resolution?', to which a wag retorted: 'Both sides.' Swan concluded, however, by expressing the ambitions of the Durham Executive for the conference: 'My county believe by democratic action we might supply munitions and at the same time use our forces to get a change of Government, and our people take charge of the international situation'.[71] The resolution was carried unanimously.

Soon afterwards a group of trade union leaders visited Spain, having been invited by the Spanish ambassador, on behalf of the UGT, to refute with their own eyes the 'widespread propaganda' to the effect that the war was almost over and the Spanish government defeated.[72] Joseph Jones (MFGB), Jack Little (AEU) and William Squance (ASLEF) set off for Spain on 11 May. In the course of their week-long stay in Barcelona they experienced Nationalist air raids and met the UGT General Secretary and, later, the Joint

[67] MFGB *Annual Proceedings*, 1938, 28 April 1938, pp. 53–7.   [68] *Ibid.* pp. 58–9.
[69] *Ibid.* p. 64.   [70] *Ibid.* p. 63.   [71] *Ibid.* p. 67.
[72] See Nuffield College, Oxford, Cripps Papers, File 773/537, Azcárate to Cripps. Those initially invited were Bevin, Marchbank (NUR), Walker (ISTC), Dukes (NUGMW), in addition to the three who made the journey. The T&GWU Executive decided that Bevin was unable to go 'in view of the heavy calls upon our time at the present moment in connection with the problems affecting our membership' (MRC, Mss 126/T & G/1/1/16, GEC Minutes, 6 May 1938, p. 134).

Executives of the UGT, CNT and the PSOE.[73] They returned deeply moved by their visit and were to provide a focus, both in their own unions and in the movement at large, for increased activity for Spain.

Thus there can be no doubt that there was a tremendous wave of opposition to the policy pursued by the NCL in April and May of 1938, that united not only the left within the Labour Party, but also included the Communist Party, and some of the leading trade unions. However, it was an illusion induced by the left to believe that all of these forces shared a common objective, let alone common tactics on how to achieve it. Instead, as is argued below, the campaigns of 1938 were at best running parallel to each other touching at individual, but never at institutional, levels. The failure to break down the compartments between trade union and political action doomed this opposition to impotence. Indeed, by the autumn of 1938 it had at all levels been turned away from political objectives and towards the much more limited goal of supplying humanitarian relief.

The experience of the Labour Spain Committee (LSC) in 1938 illustrates this point very well. The LSC was initially eclipsed by the success of the Labour Party's Bournemouth conference and the formation of the 'official' Spain Campaign Committee of the NEC (SCC). For the while the LSC was content with a more auxiliary role, helping, for instance, to build the SCC's Albert Hall rally on 19 December (although even this was resented by party officials).[74] However, it drew new strength in the spring of 1938 when it became apparent that the party was not taking its new commitment to Spain seriously, and coinciding with the apparent crisis in the fortunes of the Spanish Republic. Accordingly an emergency conference of trades councils and local Labour parties was held on 9 April which urged a very public defiance of Non-Intervention – the Labour Party should openly recruit for the International Brigades and purchase weapons such as anti-aircraft guns.[75] A particular target was provided by the decision taken at Bournemouth not to hold a Labour Party conference at all in 1938 – instead, it would be moved to Whitsun with the first meeting in 1939. Thus, the LSC made a priority of persuading the NEC to call an emergency conference to discuss Spain. This was consistently rejected, although supported by some NEC members such as Harold Laski.[76] By June 1938 the LSC was

[73] *Locomotive Journal* (ASLEF), June 1938, pp. 313–15, 'Spain Visited' by W. Squance. July 1938, pp. 388–9 gives the text of the message given to the deputation by the National Co-ordinating Committee of the UGT–CNT.
[74] Churchill College, Cambridge, LSC papers, LSPC 1/3, 7 December and 8 December 1938, Sybil Wingate to Pole.
[75] Churchill College, Cambridge, LSC papers, LSPC 1/4, drafts for conference.
[76] Churchill College, Cambridge, LSC papers, LSPC 1/4, 28 April 1938, LSC circular.

threatening to call a substitute conference if the NEC would not oblige, and this was held on 23 October. However, although in many respects a success,[77] this conference also underlined many of the problems of organising the left.

Firstly, many of its resolutions called for industrial action by trade unionists, yet the committee had long realised that it had little contact with the union rank and file and enjoyed minimal influence over their leaders.[78] The conference was better supported by intellectuals calling for industrial action than union leaders offering to deliver it.[79] Thus, resolutions calling for the blacking of all shipping to rebel Spain and one-day general strikes made excellent propaganda but had no chance of being implemented. Secondly, the conference confirmed the LSC's support for the Popular Front, which became ever more overt in the following months. In December the LSC advised the Perth DLP to back the rebel Tory MP the Duchess of Atholl in her by-election campaign and in January 1939 fully endorsed the Progressive Alliance campaign of Stafford Cripps after his expulsion from the Labour Party.[80] By espousing the Popular Front the LSC gained new political life but extinguished any remaining chance of influencing the NEC. Finally, the LSC's agitation was conditioned by the fundamental aversion to illegality characteristic of the official labour movement and which was so different from the attitude of French labour or, indeed, that of the British communists whose recruitment for the International Brigades was in open defiance of the law. Although it often toyed with the idea, the LSC never acted illegally.[81]

The inability to change Labour Party policy in the autumn of 1938, and the real need to feel that it was 'doing something' to aid Spain, forced the committee, ineluctably, into launching a purely humanitarian fund-raising campaign to send Food Ships to Spain. Despite earlier hopes of sending anti-aircraft guns, these ships eventually carried food and soap. The final irony was that the LSC had to leave all the arrangements for this operation to the

---

[77] *New Statesman*, October 29 1938.
[78] Churchill College, Cambridge, LSC papers, LSPC 1/5, 11 May 1938 circular to trade unionists. At the previous meeting of the LSC it was felt that although 'on the political side the committee was exerting considerable influence, the industrial field was not at all covered'.
[79] Churchill College, Cambridge, LSC papers, LSPC 1/6, 19 October 1938, G.D.H. Cole to Pole.
[80] Churchill College, Cambridge, LSC papers, LSPC 1/7, 10 December 1938, Pole to Perth DLP.
[81] The attitude of the Spanish ambassador to illegal action was ambiguous: Nuffield College, Oxford, Cripps papers, 773/537, 27 and 30 May 1938, correspondence between Cripps and Brailsford.

TUC and its work became virtually absorbed into the TUC's much larger
Spanish relief effort[82] – a far cry from the committee's original objectives.
Thus, when the Labour Party NEC finally deigned to meet the Labour Spain
Committee, in February 1939, it happily accepted its money while rejecting
its political proposals as 'impracticable'.[83]

A similar progression is visible in the case of a section of the Scottish
labour movement. Scottish labour had consistently taken more advanced
positions on Spain than the British TUC and Labour Party. Matters came to
a head in early 1938 when Glasgow and Edinburgh trades councils, having
failed to win the backing of the STUC and Scottish Labour Party for a co-
ordinated fund-raising campaign decided to take action alone.[84] A meeting
of Scottish trades councils was held on 9 April 1938 which laid the basis for
a conference on 21 May convened under the provocative title of 'Arms
manufacture and Arms for Spain'. Despite official attempts to prevent it,
this conference was attended by 421 delegates from 320 trades councils and
union branches. Alarmingly for the official movement the alleged aims of
this campaign went far beyond mere humanitarian aid. According to
Glasgow Trades Council Secretary Arthur Brady 'this war is not going to be
won with powdered milk alone. It is going to be won with guns, tanks and
airplanes. We know where we can get the munitions if you raise the
money.'[85] The socialist Jane Murray told her husband Tom, serving in the
International Brigades, that the conference was important for the chance it
gave of 'the members breaking away from the rotten leadership and acting
in spite of them'.[86]

Despite such talk, however, it was soon clear that a food ship was a more
feasible goal than a munitions ship, and that the rank and file would need
the assistance of their 'rotten' leaders. The trades councils needed the
backing and expertise of the TUC without which their food ship would
never leave the dock, and the 'official' movement wanted to bring the trades
councils under its own political control while, at the same time, increasing
its own fund-raising potential. Thus, the ensuing weeks saw a process of
mediation and eventual compromise between the STUC (now negotiating
for the trades councils) and the TUC, and a series of conditions were laid
down: namely that the idea of sending munitions would be abandoned, and

---

[82] Churchill College, Cambridge, LSC papers, LSPC 1/7, minutes of LSC 11 November 1938.
[83] NCL minutes, 21 February 1938. Lathan, Noel-Baker and Gillies had met with the LSC.
The LSC proposals were for (1) No co-operation with the government, (2) nation-wide
demonstrations in working hours, (3) co-operation with all progressive forces in aid for
Spain.
[84] Mitchell Library Glasgow, Glasgow Trades Council minutes, 22 February 1938.
[85] *Daily Worker*, 12 April 1938; *New Leader*, 15 April 1938.
[86] NLS, Thomas Murray papers, Box 1, 25 April 1938, Jane to Tom Murray.

that the collection would concentrate on cash rather than clothing or food parcels, with a goal of raising £10,000. A further condition, which was clearly against the spirit of the whole enterprise, was that it was undesirable to 'boost' the food ship idea because 'if adequate cargo is not obtained and the ship is not sent there is a spirit of failure connected with the effort' and they would be left with an awkward amount of cargo.[87]

Therefore, a *modus vivendi* was arrived at which satisfied the aspirations and honour of all parties. However, this should not mask the fact that the final settlement was very much on the terms of the 'official' movement which had forced the trades councils to depoliticise their campaign and, effectively, acknowledge the impossibility of action autonomous of the central institutions of the labour movement. The TUC which had originally been alarmed at the prospect of the Scottish trades councils leading a national movement against its authority and saw in this the hand of its 'old "friends"' the communists, was now happy that the 'necessary safeguards' had been secured even though a communist had been employed as the campaign's organiser.[88]

Even so, the fact that the trades councils were now running a scheme which had been officially endorsed and had received wide local publicity gave them, in practice, a considerable degree of political leverage. As the campaign reached its peak, with no sign of even approximating to the set financial targets, the trades councils put pressure on the NCL to help in finding the balance of the cargo, asking William Elger of the STUC to open negotiations at the TUC Congress in Blackpool. The TUC's Vincent Tewson travelled to Edinburgh and discovered that so far only some £2,500 had been raised, or 300 tons worth of food, and a boat obtained free of charge. The trades councils now wanted a grant to make this up to 500 tons but he had refused on account of the bad precedent this would set. However, he ingeniously suggested that the NCL's fund could take advantage of the free transport to send 200 tons – producing the same result – and he gained Citrine's approval for spending some £2,000 on this'[89] although Citrine was emphatic that publicity should be avoided – 'no reference should be made at all in the press to the participation of the National Council of Labour in this effort'.[90]

It was not surprising that these comparatively weak campaigns should have been blunted by contact with the institutions of the labour movement.

[87] TUC, Fund 3, 21 June 1938, Tewson to Elger; National Library of Scotland, STUC minutes (mf Mss 140), 30 June and 29 August 1938.
[88] TUC, Fund 3, 17 May and 11 July 1938, Tewson to Elger; 8 July 1938, Elger to Tewson.
[89] TUC, Fund 3, 13 September 1938, telephone message from Tewson.
[90] TUC, Fund 3, 16 September 1938, Citrine to Brady.

What was less obvious was that this pattern would be repeated in the trade union movement where some of the most powerful unions favoured strong action against Non-Intervention. Debate over the demand for a special conference of the TUC to discuss Spain reverberated throughout the summer of 1938 but no progress was made. Citrine had a ready fund of, somewhat artificial, reasons for not holding such a conference,[91] yet the real key to his success was that he held up a mirror to the fears and uncertainties of the trade union leaders when it was suggested that they should take political action. Significantly, his most successful tactic was to claim that the advocates of a special conference were really in favour of a General Strike. TUC leaders, he told the building workers' conference, were 'not so childish' as not to understand that 'what we are asked to do by this type of suggestion is to take some sort of action which will compel Parliament elected by the mass of people of this country to depart from a policy which it is now pursuing'. Responsible trade unionists, thus, had to face two main questions – would they be justified in doing this and would such action succeed? 'I do not think', he concluded, 'that we can depart from democratic rule in this country.'[92]

Given that the mass of moderate trade union leaders, for whom the General Strike had been a nightmare, had no intention of taking even limited industrial action, Citrine's insinuation was clearly preposterous. Yet it was also highly effective as it allowed him to plot a chart of trade union action on which there were only three fixed points: a General Strike, conventional political action through the Labour Party and humanitarian relief work. By Citrine's logic, as industrial action over Spain was out of the question on moral and practical grounds, any special conference on Spain would be *ipso facto* redundant. The trade union left never rose to the implicit challenge to devise an alternative form of action. Even so, pressure was still strong enough to force the General Council into granting the limited concession that there should be a private session of Congress to deal with its handling of the whole question and to discuss two resolutions which covered specific

[91] TUC, File 90214, 29 March 1938, Finance and General Purposes Committee circular 494 to General Council members. Citrine answered the specific point that a conference should be called under General Council Standing Order 8 (see above p. 15) on the grounds that it was 'quite impracticable to the present situation' because any vigorous attempt to stem the flow of weapons to rebel Spain would inevitably involve the use of force and thus heighten rather than reduce the risk of war.

His other arguments were that public opinion was not in favour of ending Non-Intervention; that the Labour Party NEC was opposed to a conference; that the 1927 Act made a boycott of exports to 'aggressor nations' illegal; and that the General Council's attitude towards the government's rearmament proposals should be governed by political rather than industrial concerns.

[92] MRC, UCATT records, Mss 78/1/2/13, AUBTW NDC, pp. 62–4.

proposals for changing government policy on Spain. The private session was the last opportunity to effect radical change in the labour movement's policy towards Spain,[93] and the fate of the two separate debates reveals two conflicting currents within the Congress – the authority of Citrine and the General Council and the depth of political and emotional support for Spain in the movement – which allowed apparently contradictory decisions to be taken.

For Citrine, the important task was to defeat the challenge to the authority of the General Council posed by the attempt to refer back its handling of the special conference controversy. He emphasised that the only possible way to enforce a policy of arms for Spain would be through coercive industrial action. Yet would the trade union movement, which professed a belief in democracy, be justified in launching an attack on democratic institutions at a time when 'contempt had been lavishly sprayed' over them?[94] Moreover, any such action would be bound to be unsuccessful as the transport workers had already decided against it, and they were 'the key men'.[95] Finally, the unions had to be aware of their difficult legal position with regard to the 1927 Act, and he referred to a KC's opinion that unions backing their members in such action would doubtless face sequestration.[96] This view was stated even more forcefully in the ensuing discussion by Bevin's deputy Arthur Deakin, who accused the miners of trying to set up his union, the dockers, to bear the brunt of any action. Deakin 'stated clearly they were not prepared to take part in any General Strike for a political issue'.[97] The transport workers were not willing to 'pull the chestnuts out of the fire by refusing to handle goods'.[98] The reference back was heavily defeated on a show of hands.

In spite of this victory, however, Citrine was immediately confounded by unanimous support for a resolution which called on Congress to determine what 'effective steps' should be taken to remove the 'ban on Arms for the duly elected Government of Spain'.[99] This resolution derived from ASLEF's 1938 conference and was moved by its General Secretary Bill Squance,

---

[93] No official report of the private session was ever published, although it is possible to reconstruct the course of the debates from other sources. I was unable to locate in the TUC archive a verbatim report which was apparently circulated to General Council members (Will Paynter, *My Generation*, London, 1972, p. 73).
[94] Lord Citrine, *Men and Work*, p. 360.   [95] *Reynolds News*, 11 September 1938.
[96] ETU *Electrical Trades Journal*, October 1938, p. 266, delegates' report for 1938 TUC. Citrine says that he had consulted both Cripps and Jowitt (both lawyers) 'as to whether there was any way out of this dilemma and they had both replied positively that there was not' (*Men and Work*, p. 360).   [97] *Electrical Trades Journal*, October 1938.
[98] *Manchester Guardian*, 9 September 1938.   [99] *TUC CR*, 1938, p. 363.

inspired by his visit to Spain in May. He argued that there were a number of proposals that should be explored and these included the convening of a conference of trade union executives 'followed by regional conferences and thereafter mass demonstrations at all large centres', as well as a '2 minute silence for the loss of Democracy'.[100] The motion was seconded with an impassioned speech by Will Paynter, then a newly returned International Brigader and member of the South Wales miners' Executive.[101] Citrine later made plain his opposition to the resolution which, in his view, made a farce of the previous proceedings and argued that if it had been taken as an amendment to the General Council's report, as he had recommended, it would have been lost.[102]

After consideration by the Congress General Purposes Committee a series of more concrete proposals, a watered down version of suggestions put forward by the miners' delegation,[103] was accepted without dissent. Firstly, a campaign would be organised nationally and internationally with the IFTU and the LSI. Secondly, the French and British movements, acting through the Internationals, would simultaneously approach their governments calling for the removal of the ban on arms for Spain. Thirdly, the campaign would be linked to a further drive for funds amongst union executives. Fourthly, affiliated unions would report, within a given period, their maximum financial efforts. A report of these efforts would then be made to all affiliates and 'any further suggestions' invited, whereupon the position would be reviewed by the General Council.[104].

Clearly these proposals corresponded to Squance's ideas in name only – in fact, they did little more than enshrine the labour movement's existing policy. Yet even in this attenuated form the proposals were an embarrassment to the General Council and Citrine concludes his brief reminiscences on Spain with the revealing comment that '[Squance's] resolution was discreetly allowed to lapse'.[105] This was not strictly true, although no great urgency was shown in implementing it. By late November 1938 the proposals had been communicated to the Internationals which had in turn approached the CGT and SFIO about simultaneous action. Jouhaux (at the time preoccupied with an abortive General Strike against the French government) was said to be fully in favour of the idea. The approach to the

---

[100] *Locomotive Journal*, November 1938, p. 624.
[101] Will Paynter, *My Generation*, pp. 74–6 gives an abbreviated version of his speech.
[102] Lord Citrine, *Men and Work*, p. 360.
[103] TUC, Correspondence 3, 8 September 1938. The miners' suggestion that there should be a campaign for a £1,000,000 Fund was not included in the final version. According to Paynter this list was drawn up by Horner, Lawther and J.R. Campbell (*My Generation*, p. 76).
[104] *Locomotive Journal*, November 1938, p. 624.
[105] Lord Citrine, *Men and Work*, p. 360.

British unions, however, was delayed by the launch of an appeal for the Czech workers in the wake of the Munich crisis. The replies were finally submitted to the 23 January 1939 F&GP Committee, which again deferred consideration until a fuller report was possible – by which time Catalonia had fallen and the exercise had lost all relevance.[106]

Already, even before the TUC Congress, some of the most important trade unions had begun to divert their energies into more immediate and practical ways of helping Spain. As early as 20 May 1938 the MFGB executive, annoyed at the TUC's failure to respond to their special conference resolution, had been jolted into taking action by the President, Joseph Jones, who had returned from his visit to Spain stressing the need for food, fuel and homes for the orphans of Asturian miners. It was decided to raise a sum of money for humanitarian work equivalent to a levy of 2/6d per member, with Yorkshire, Durham and South Wales becoming immediately responsible for £50,000. Ultimately this appeal raised some £72,000 of which the bulk (£55,961) was spent on homes for Asturian miners' orphans, although significant sums were also allocated to dependants of the International Brigaders and the purchase of 2,000 tons of coal for the Spanish government.[107] The miners' leaders were alive to the fears of their Spanish counterparts that the money would be swallowed up by the TUC's overall relief operation and would not be used where it was most needed by their members.[108] However, they also realised that the expertise of the IFTU was invaluable, especially as they wanted the orphans to be transferred to the relative safety of southern France. Thus the money was channelled through the TUC and jointly administered by a committee that included Walter Schevenels of the IFTU and the French miners' leader. Tragically, by the time that the orphans' home near Tarbes was finally ready in September 1939 France itself was at war.[109]

In spite of the tremendous success of the miners' appeal, the energies of the miners' leaders were increasingly absorbed by the practicalities of administering a massive relief fund and it was assumed that the moment for a political challenge to the government had passed. Instead, they hoped that other unions could be inspired, or forced, to emulate their levy. The MFGB Conference in July called on the TUC to organise 'the maximum practical

---

[106] TUC, Finance and General Purposes Committee minutes, 21 November 1938. The results of the survey were tabulated and bound with the committee's minutes, 20 January and 20 February 1939.

[107] MFGB *Annual Proceedings*, 1938, Executive Council minutes, 20 May 1938. TUC Finance and General Purposes Committees minutes, circular 20 February 1939 gives full details of the MFGB's achievements.

[108] MFGB *Annual Proceedings*, 1938, Executive Council minutes, 22 June 1938.

[109] MFGB *Annual Proceedings*, 1938, Executive Council minutes, 7 September 1938, 4 October 1938, January 12 1939, February 12 1939, 17 August 1939.

assistance for the Spanish people' on lines similar to their own scheme,[110] Horner arguing that a 'million pounds fund is not impossible in a short space of time'.[111] However, the General Council rebuffed the miners' attempt to tack an obligation on other unions to raise 2/6d per member on to their Congress resolution. Instead, the miners were given an opportunity to urge other unions to follow their example, an honour which fell to Will Lawther whose brother had fallen in action with the International Brigades.

However, it was far from clear that the miners' scheme could be applied more generally. The MFGB had not levied money from each member directly, but presented a demand to its constituent districts for a sum of money *pro rata* 2/6d per member, leaving it up to them to recoup this expenditure from their members. The more militant areas which had promoted the idea responded very quickly. In Durham, for instance, members had almost paid their share of the levy within two weeks, while in South Wales, nearly 45% of members contributed to a voluntary 1 shilling levy to reimburse their Executive.[112] Yet the sheer magnitude of the sums involved and the suddenness with which the scheme was implemented placed a heavy strain on the organisation's federal structure. The Nottingham miners, only recently reintegrated into the MFGB, opposed a levy and said that the money should come from the federation's political fund.[113] Similar stresses were apparent in Scotland, where certain counties only paid their share grudgingly and where the National Union of Scottish Mineworkers passed a motion of censure on the MFGB for its high-handed action. The levy also aggravated relations between the MFGB and the T&GWU which jointly represented certain groups of workers.[114] It is perhaps significant that the conservative opponents of the levy were also those who were least inclined to go out and campaign among their members for reimbursement of the money which they had been forced to donate.

Thus, the levy created powerful tensions, and it is a tribute to the miners' discipline and loyalty that the money was raised in the face of the MFGB's strong anti-centralist tendencies. Moreover, as Lawther pointed out at the 1938 TUC – 'I want to observe, in regard to the argument of poverty that

[110] MFGB *Annual Proceedings*, 1938, Executive Council minutes, 11 August 1938.
[111] MFGB *Annual Proceedings*, 1938, conference report, p. 367.
[112] On Durham see the comments by Mr J. Gilliland, MFGB *Annual Proceedings*, 1938, conference report (p. 367); on South Wales see Hywel Francis, *Miners Against Fascism*, pp. 141–6.
[113] TUC, Fund 3, 6 July 1938, report of a meeting of the MFGB Sub-Committee with Schevenels, Citrine and Tewson.
[114] MRC, Mss 126/T&G/1/1/16, T&GWU GEC minutes, 16 August 1938. The most important of these bodies was the 7,553 strong Power Workers Group.

has been used in the past in relation to raising money, that two of our districts classified as special areas contributed £16,600, without any opposition whatever from their members.'[115] Yet the relationship between the miners' Executive and their districts could not be compared to that between the TUC General Council and its affiliates. Citrine and the TUC were glad to see the success of the levy which, after all, greatly increased the amount of money raised in Britain for the International Solidarity Fund and were keen to make sure that the money was channelled through the TUC, yet they realised the impracticality of attempting to extend the scheme on a compulsory basis, if only because such levies were disallowed under most union rulebooks. Thus, the miners' levy had to stand as an isolated example of what could be achieved rather than as a model which could be closely copied by other unions and, although some sought to emulate it, the comparative failure of their attempts serves, in fact, to emphasise the singularity of the miners within the British trade union movement.

The engineering union (AEU) launched an appeal for £50,000 soon after the miners, with the intention of buying lorries for the Spanish government. However, this initiative was hamstrung by a union rulebook which precluded the branches or divisions from contributing directly to the appeal. Instead, all contributions had to be made voluntarily, yet the union's leaders failed to give adequate support to the shop stewards on whom the onus of collection fell. Thus, although a number of lorries were sent, it is apparent that the scheme raised only a fraction of the intended sum. The final amount raised was never revealed.[116] Even so, this appeal was more tangible than that in the building trade. In November 1938 it was reported that the National Federation of Building Trade Operatives (NFBTO) was to launch a £10–15,000 appeal to buy clothes – 'a minimum of 2 shirts, clothing material, shoes and blankets' each – for 45,000 Spanish building workers making defences in very cold weather.[117] However, although the NFBTO President George Hicks had suggested that, in the light of the TUC resolution, there should be workplace collections with the slogan '12 days at a Penny a Day to resist Fascism', nothing came of this until December when an appeal was launched which raised £450 for the Spanish builders.[118] Any hope of a bigger contribution faded in January 1939 when the Amalgamated Society of Woodworkers' executive was disastrously defeated by its own members in a ballot.[119]

---

[115] *TUC CR*, 1938, p. 368.
[116] For a detailed study of the AEU appeal see Tom Buchanan, 'The Politics of Internationalism', pp. 49–52.   [117] *Daily Herald*, 25 November 1938.
[118] University of Manchester, Institute of Science and Technology, NFBTO Archives, General Council minutes, 22 and 23 September 1938.   [119] See below pp. 154–5.

Thus, the miners' efforts failed to generalise throughout the trade union movement – a phenomenon which glaringly highlights both the strengths and weaknesses of British trade union internationalism and, indeed, political activity more generally. For, in spite of the individual feats of fund-raising, the responses of the different unions remained atomised and bureaucratic, opposed to reaching out to involve the rank-and-file membership, let alone forces outside the trade union movement.

The fall of the Spanish Republic in March 1939 discredited the policy pursued by the labour movement not only in this final phase of the conflict but during its entire course. Posterity has smiled kindly on the left's critique: and, indeed, perhaps Spain and Peace could have been saved in the autumn of 1938 if unity had been finally achieved. However, it is by no means apparent that the left had all of the answers. Indeed, this broader failure has served to conceal the real success that Citrine's policy achieved in that, by January 1939, all of the rebels against the NCL's policy in 1938 had been brought into line. In addition to its own relief operations, the TUC was playing a central role in a swathe of projects ranging from the 'unofficial' Labour Spain Committee, to the newly-official Glasgow and Edinburgh food ships and the very respectable miners' and engineers' funds. All had been effectively depoliticised. Demoralised by the long drawn-out defeat of the Spanish Republic and the collapse of collective security, all of these organisations had transferred their energies from political protest to humanitarian relief in a spectacular demonstration of the enduring power of the institutions of the labour movement. The obvious pitfalls that prevented any united radical action, even within the labour movement, must raise the question of whether the Popular Front, which included elements outside of it, was ever more than an irrelevance.

4

'A DEMONSTRATION OF SOLIDARITY AND SYMPATHY ...': THE SPANISH WORKERS' FUND AND ITS COMPETITORS

The scope of the British labour movement's commitment to humanitarian relief work in Spain was undeniable, and by the end of the Civil War, it had contributed some £200,000 worth of supplies to the Republican side.[1] Moreover, major responsibilities were accepted, such as the maintenance of a field hospital in Spain and the care of 4,000 Basque refugee children in Britain. The relief effort was the centrepiece of the movement's response to the war and something which the leaders could readily allude to when challenged by those who claimed that not enough was being done to help Republican Spain. Yet, beyond these bare facts, this area of labour's response was still surprisingly controversial. Critics at the time argued that the labour movement's campaign was politically and organisationally inflexible; that it failed both to mobilise the potential within the movement itself, while also missing the opportunity to work with other political parties and to make inroads into wealthier sections of society beyond the working class. In particular, it was claimed that labour was paralysed by its opposition to communism, which prevented it from developing a more expansive campaign.

This critique has been taken up by historians who have argued that a grouping of organisations occupied the space abandoned by the labour movement and successfully mobilised rank-and-file support, while also involving activists from other parties and social classes. The main organisations of this kind drawing working-class support on a national level were Spanish Medical Aid, the International Brigades' Dependants and Wounded Aid Committee and Voluntary Industrial Aid for Spain. Also, many Aid Spain committees were established locally and from January 1937 the National Joint Committee for Spanish Relief sought to co-ordinate all

---

[1] *TUC CR*, 1939, p. 214. However, over £70,000 of this total came from the miners' 1938 levy for Spain.

national and local relief work. This phenomenon has been presented as a mass movement of solidarity with Spain, dubbed the 'Aid Spain Movement', and as a *de facto* Popular Front: according to Jim Fyrth, 'the Aid for Spain Campaign was the nearest thing to a People's Front that came about in Britain'.[2] Thus, the institutions of labour consigned themselves to the fringes of a broad social movement which embodied the desire for a Popular Front.

However, this interpretation is seriously flawed because it succeeds in inverting the actual relationships. Far from the institutions of labour being a hapless adjunct to a mass movement which most of its members supported, instead it is argued below that the very existence of support for organisations such as Spanish Medical Aid reflected the continuing strength of labour's institutions. Yet this strength had been misspent. It was poured not into creating a vibrant and inspirational campaign, but into creating defensive structures which would not disturb the labour movement and this drove many activists to work with forces outside the movement. This point was obscured because neither the labour movement nor its rivals were willing to recognise publicly that there was no common humanitarian effort for the Spanish people and that there were, in fact, fundamental divisions between them in terms of methods of organisation and objectives.[3] The nature and form of the labour movement's relief work for Spain was conditioned by political rather than humanitarian considerations, with the overriding objective of asserting the distinctive character of its own operation and maintaining total control over all aspects of it. In fact, the relief effort can only be understood as a vital component in the movement's overall political response to the Civil War as well as distinct from any broader campaign in Britain. Accordingly, the emphasis below is not placed on how much money was raised and from which specific sources, but rather on how the organisational structures were created which allowed the movement to control the collection of money in Britain and oversee its deployment in Spain.

The ideological battle between the Popular Front and the labour movement has obscured not only the realities of institutional division, but

---

[2] Jim Fyrth, *The Signal Was Spain*, p.22.

[3] This point is lost in Michael Alpert's, 'Humanitarianism and Politics in the British Response to the Spanish Civil War, 1936–39', *European History Quarterly*, vol. 14, no. 4, October 1984. Alpert rejects any division between politics and humanitarianism: 'People concerned looked back on the time as one where questions were seen in clear black and white terms. To help relieve Spanish suffering was a positive way of reacting, for some in political terms, for many in solely humanitarian ones' (p. 437). The problem with this view is that, at least within the labour movement, many activists were not fully cognisant of the political structures through which their humanitarian aims were being mediated.

also the motives which conditioned the way in which ordinary people opted to express their solidarity for Spain. Labour leaders, for example, were unwilling to accept that party and trade union members could act outside of their control and, thus, still sought to appropriate their members' time and energy even when they failed to participate in the officially sanctioned labour movement campaigns. One union leader paid tribute to 'the service rendered by the rank and file of our movement throughout the country in assisting various voluntary organisations that came into existence to raise funds, to carry on systematic house-to-house collections and to make garments'.[4] William Gillies went even further to state that, in the case of 'unofficial' groups such as Spanish Medical Aid, 'it would not be an exaggeration to say that the sacrifices made by *our* political and trade union membership constitute the principle source of [their] income'.[5] Conversely, the recent advocates of Aid Spain have sought to show that the funds raised by the labour movement can be attributed to the Aid Spain ledger,[6] and that the National Joint Committee for Spanish Relief 'co-ordinated' the activities of the TUC and the Labour Party along with Spanish Medical Aid, the Salvation Army and the Quakers.[7]

In fact, all of these claims were either incorrect or misleading. Rank-and-file members who worked for 'unofficial' organisations often did so in a spirit of rebellion, or at least alienation, from a labour movement campaign that had been devised to restrict their political expression. But, equally, it would be quite wrong to see the 'Aid Spain Movement' as a successful Popular Front driven into the heart of the labour movement. In fact, the very concept of an 'Aid Spain Movement' actually detracts from an understanding of this subject. 'Aid Spain' had no formal national existence and, despite a common leadership including politicians ranging from the Tory Duchess of Atholl to the communist Isabel Brown, the many different organisations remained disunited even after the establishment of the National Joint Committee. Most people who supported them did so on the single issue basis of helping Republican Spain. Politically, these organisations remained much weaker than the sum of their parts would indicate, and there is no evidence that humanitarian work for Spain on a Popular Front basis translated into effective political action.

Where there was a common denominator this was provided by the Communist Party which had militants located in most of the main

[4] MRC, ITF records, Mss 159/3/C/6/13, 15 December 1937, ITF Circular, 'British labour in the Spanish Crisis', by John Marchbank.
[5] Labour Party archives, WG/SPA File 9, 460, 27 August 1938, Gillies to the Spanish Ambassador (my emphasis).   [6] Jim Fyrth, *The Signal Was Spain*, p. 216.
[7] Hywel Francis, *Miners Against Fascism*, 1984, p. 111–12.

campaigns. Communist energy and organisation provided the backbone of committees such as Spanish Medical Aid. However, claims that their involvement was purely altruistic are somewhat disingenuous,[8] for it is apparent that they also sought to direct the campaigns where possible. An indication of the extent of this practice is given by Hywel Francis:

> Isabel Brown ran the Central Bureau for Spain of the CPGB which met before every [National] Joint Committee meeting. It also checked up weekly on all the co-ordinating committees within which it had its own members. The Bureau decided on a line of future action on practical policy and practical ideas.[9]

Even so, the picture of a labour movement paralysed by anti-communism needs to be modified. Certainly there was deep suspicion of and hostility to the communists amongst leaders and if a committee contained communist representatives it was likely to be spurned. But this was not always the case: the example of the Glasgow food ship campaign referred to above and other examples in this chapter show that the prime consideration continued to be one of political control. Communists could be worked with in situations where political control by the labour movement was assured.

However, the communists, too, wanted to exercise political control, and this explains the shift in communist strategy during the Civil War. Initially, the CPGB had endorsed the NCL's fund and urged its members to collect for it, even though this was resented by many communist militants – there was 'uproar' when Isabel Brown told a meeting in the Memorial Hall that the collection 'would be sent to Sir Walter Citrine'.[10] In August 1936 alone the CPGB London District Committee forwarded £169.13.5d to the NCL fund via the London Trades Council.[11] An audit for the period ending 10 March 1937 revealed that just over £1,272 had come from 'known Communist sources'.[12] However, the communists became disenchanted with the lack of recognition which their efforts received from labour leaders,[13] who made it clear that they would happily accept all donations but would not cede control over any aspect of the fund. Moreover, with the failure of the CPGB's attempt to win affiliation to the Labour Party there was less incentive for it to refrain from challenging labour. Thus the CPGB came to

---

[8] Jim Fyrth, *The Signal Was Spain*, pp. 212–13.
[9] Hywel Francis, *Miners Against Fascism*, p. 136, fn 15.
[10] *Manchester Guardian*, 31 July 1936.
[11] BLPES, Film 200, Reel 7, London Trades Council minutes, 13 August 1936.
[12] TUC, Fund 1, Documents section.
[13] *Daily Worker*, 16 September 1936 – challenged Citrine's comments at the 1936 TUC Congress that the Communist Party had given only £600 to the NCL fund, claiming to have given £1,912.18s.5d.

concentrate its energies on campaigns of its own and the appeal for an International Brigade ambulance in November 1936 signalled the abandonment of any pretence of working with the institutions, as opposed to the members, of the labour movement.

The criticism that British labour's humanitarian response to the Civil War was lacking in energy and commitment, and that the actual amount of money raised was disappointing in comparison with the many 'unofficial' responses, has been a persistent one. However, the criticism is based on the premise that the natural course of action for labour's leaders to adopt was to launch a mass campaign that would mobilise the movement's rank and file. In fact, this was the very opposite of what leaders such as Citrine wanted to do, and there were two paramount reasons for this.

One factor was that the Spanish workers' cause was, particularly in the first months of fighting, a profoundly controversial one in comparison with other 'causes' of the 1930s. Citrine claimed in December 1936 that: 'When we raised a Fund for the Austrians [in 1934] the money poured in. We had much greater difficulty in getting money for the Spanish workers.'[14] Some workers, primarily Catholics, were actively opposed to the Spanish Republic, and the collection of money for the humanitarian relief of workers situated in the Republican zone was easily misconstrued as support for the Republican government itself, especially as sections of the press propagated such misinformation. Thus, at least as much attention was often paid to placating hostile members as to collecting money from those who were keen to help, and an aggressive fund-raising campaign could only have polarised such divisions. James Middleton candidly admitted as much in January 1937 when he wrote that: 'Spain has not been made a special issue, frankly on account of the difficulties involved in its presentation.'[15] This factor, however, is analysed in greater depth in the following chapter.

Equally importantly, British labour's relief work clearly reflected the evolution of inter-war internationalism in the premium that was placed on the creation of controlled, bureaucratic structures on the national and international levels and in the perception that the mobilisation of the rank and file was dangerously destabilising. The string of disasters that had so far

[14] TUC, Documents 2, 21 December 1936, report of meeting with 'rank-and-file' delegation, p. 17. This comment is difficult to substantiate. The 'Help for Workers of Austria Fund' raised almost £25,500 in its first five months, and the Spanish workers' appeal some £22,689 in a similar period, with a greater proportion coming not from trade union funds (*TUC CR*, 1934, pp. 58–60, *TUC CR*, 1937, pp. 60–62).
[15] Ruskin College, Oxford, James Middleton papers, MID 59, 22 January 1937, Middleton to Tom Baxter. The difficulties referred to were the position of Blum in France and the Catholic hostility in Britain.

befallen European labour movements in the 1930s had not greatly involved the rank and file. Such crises were short-lived and the response could be contained within the structures created to care for trade union and socialist victims of fascism, the core of which was the International Solidarity Fund (ISF) administered by the IFTU and the LSI. It was envisaged that trade union funds would form the main source of income for these appeals rather than initiatives involving rank-and-file workers. However, this priority had important political consequences at the time of the Spanish Civil War because the legal restrictions on the use of union funds dictated that, irrespective of the Non-Intervention regulations, relief should be for purely humanitarian purposes and directed at an identifiable section of the Spanish working class rather than at the Spanish government or the Spanish people in general.[16]

This framework was ill-suited to respond to the many complexities posed by the Spanish Civil War. For instance, whereas in Austria the ISF had been forced to work in semi-clandestinity through the Quaker 'Friends' Relief Organisation', in Spain a sympathetic government supported by strong workers' organisations was engaged in fighting a brutal war and, ironically, a major difficulty facing the ISF was how to maintain independence from those bodies. Moreover, the ISF was faced with competition from international communism, ranging from the humanitarian activities of its Red Aid to the supply of Soviet weapons and the Comintern's organisation of the International Brigades.[17] Thus, the Civil War posed a challenge to the whole development of labour internationalism because, in terms of what

---

[16] The main restriction on the use of trade union funds was the legal interpretation of their rulebooks, because any union member could challenge a contribution to the ISF, or any other fund, as *ultra vires*. The TUC Research Department studied this problem and concluded that very few trade unions had rules which specifically allowed this kind of grant. However, when rules contained phrases such as 'to pursue any lawful action' and 'to promote the interests of Trade Unions, Trade Unionism or Trade Unionists' there would be less chance of legal action. Courts could also be swayed when a union had a consistent policy of making grants for charitable purposes (TUC, International Brigade, 23 March 1937, memorandum). This latter point was taken into account in January 1937 when the Civil Service Clerical Association (CSCA) was challenged by one of its members after granting £100 to the NCL Fund. The action was based on the argument that the objects of the association were to 'promote the interests of its members; to regulate conditions of employment and to provide benefits at death. The payment of money outside the [British] realm could not be in fulfillment of any of the objects of the body.' The applicant admitted that the CSCA could make contributions for charity, but drew a distinction between the Spanish Workers' Fund and previous contributions to charities such as the King George V Memorial Fund. The judge refused to draw this distinction, and ruled that it was up to the members to judge what was in their own best interests (BLPES, Citrine papers, TUC Research Department memorandum, 24 August 1938; see also Tom Buchanan, DPhil thesis, pp. 241–7).
[17] E.H. Carr, *The Comintern and the Spanish Civil War* (1984) adds little to the work of D. Cattell, *Communism and the Spanish Civil War* (Berkeley, 1956).

was now expected from it, the scope was apparently infinite. Yet Citrine and his colleagues tended towards a more limited perspective, seeing the role of the ISF as an extension of traditional trade union solidarity – putting money aside for fallow times ahead – rather than seeing their effort as a contribution to a Republican victory which would have been the surest way of protecting the long-term interests of the 'Spanish Workers'. In a striking comment at the 1937 TUC Congress Citrine said:

> Whatever we subscribe for Spain is a drop in a bucket. It cannot affect the situation in Spain materially in any sense or form. The few hundreds of thousands of pounds that can be raised in our international movement, compared to the millions which the Spanish Government itself controls demonstrates at once the impossibility of trying to take on our shoulders a policy of that description. *The whole purpose of raising a fund was to make a demonstration of solidarity and sympathy, and desire to help.* But this Congress can never put itself in a position of being able to sustain a major war out of voluntary contributions or even to cope with the distress consequent on a major war.[18]

This passage has been quoted as an example of Citrine 'playing down the importance of the fund',[19] but in fact represents an honest assessment of what the British labour movement could hope to achieve for Spain, while staying within the framework of contemporary internationalism.

The NCL responded to the need for relief very promptly, although clearly spurred on by political considerations. On 25 July 1936 James Middleton, the Labour Party General Secretary, suggested to Citrine that they should set up a fund – 'He mentioned that the Communists would probably institute a fund and it was desirable we should not delay the matter.'[20] Citrine concurred, but felt that the appeal should be launched as part of the ISF. At the 28 July LSI/IFTU meeting, which dealt largely with this matter, Citrine and Gillies were quick to impose their own vision of the nature of the relief effort. When it was suggested that the Internationals should try to organise a medical column for Spain, they argued that they should 'confine themselves to furnish relief. We could open our own food depots in Spain and from this source gain the sympathy of the Spanish workers. We ought to have nothing to do with the belligerent aspects.'[21] It was agreed to contact de los Ríos to see exactly what help the Spanish wanted. Thus, even before his meeting with Eden, where it was agreed that labour could send certain supplies without infringing Non-Intervention, Citrine was already committed to a very limited form of aid.[22]

---

[18] *TUC CR*, 1937, p. 275; my emphasis.   [19] Jim Fyrth, *The Signal Was Spain*, p. 275.
[20] TUC, Documents 1, 11 August 1936, memorandum by Citrine, p. 1.
[21] TUC, Documents 1, 28 July 1936, LSI/IFTU meeting, verbatim report, p. 4.
[22] See above p. 54.

The characteristics of the LSI/IFTU relief effort became clear as it unfolded. Firstly, there was an overriding concern for the strategic use of relief funds. This was because, although relief was only given to the Republican side, the prime commitment was to Spanish (UGT) trade unionists, (PSOE) socialists and their dependants rather than to Republicans more generally, and would continue to apply whatever their fortunes in the war. One of the clearest manifestations of this came at the 21 August 1936 LSI/IFTU meeting where Citrine suggested 'relieving districts in those areas where the fascists had control as well as those in Government hands', possibly working with the Quakers while 'securing that only our friends could be helped'. This idea was swiftly despatched by Adler and de los Ríos who felt that 'it would create a very dangerous situation and it would be impossible to discriminate between the Fascists and the socialist workers who were in distress in such areas. It would lead to great misunderstanding.'[23]

This concern was reflected in a crucial decision that was taken on the use of relief funds. As early as August 1936 Citrine had 'strongly advised' the IFTU not to dispense with its funds too quickly – 'I feel that the conflict may go on for a considerable time.'[24] In December 1936 he drew a comparison with the four-year American Civil War and argued that with Spanish demands continually increasing they must not spend all of the money at once.[25] However, in spite of Citrine's belief that the war would be a long one, the use of funds was also conditioned by fears of an early Republican collapse and by September 1936 a decision had been taken to wait until the war was over to disburse the funds. According to George Hicks 'the Spanish Government have considerable funds in their possession and...the money collected [by the NCL] was being kept in hand at present as it is possible it could be used more effectively later on to assist refugees'.[26] The IFTU feared having to cope with a flood of widows and orphans at a time of 'demoralisation and disappointment' amongst its own members brought on by a heavy Republican defeat.[27] The confidential agreement to keep back the 'greatest possible reserve' in case of a forced Republican exodus lasted until the end of 1937, but due to pressing appeals for food and transport in 1938

[23] TUC, Documents 1, 21 August 1936, LSI/IFTU meeting, verbatim report, p.11.
[24] TUC, Fund 1, 10 August 1936, Citrine to Co-op Wholesale Society (CWS).
[25] TUC, Documents 2, 21 December 1936, report of meeting with 'rank-and-file' delegation, p. 14.
[26] MRC, Mss 273, Constructional Engineering Union, EC minutes, 27 September 1936.
[27] TUC, Fund 1, 5 January 1937, Schevenels to Dubinsky. It should be noted that support for the Spanish Republicans did not collapse when the war finally ended in 1939, as had been feared.

most of this money was then rapidly used up.[28] This decision was the main factor which convinced the French CGT of the need to operate its own relief project independently from the ISF.[29]

Secondly, the aid was never of direct military value. Of course, the distinction between humanitarian and 'lethal' aid has always been a fine one. In September 1936 the ISF had received urgent requests from the Republicans in San Sebastián who appealed for coats and boots for the militia there because, due to the cold, they could not 'hold their weapons' at night. The ISF complied with the request on the understanding that, should the city fall in the interim, the aid would go to the besiegers of the Asturian capital Oviedo.[30] However, despite a short-lived decision to support the British Medical Unit which served on the Republican front line, the ISF relief was usually restricted to food, medicine or tobacco.[31] Cash was never sent and the closest that the ISF came to supplying aid of overt military value was in providing a number of lorries.[32] In January 1937 there were discussions of a plan to build a field hospital in Spain, although Citrine felt that a less adventurous project would be desirable because there was still the prospect of a 'difficult refugee problem'.[33] Caballero, too, dismissed the idea, believing that 'hospitals, food supplies etc. were only of secondary importance' to the purchase of arms which he still vainly hoped the labour movement might supply.[34] Further discussion was pre-empted by the action of the Belgian socialist Camille Huysmans who, Schevenels grumbled, while on a visit to Spain 'had informed the world that the hospital was being provided', so that they were virtually committed to it. However, when Schevenels suggested that the Red Cross might have to help the project, Citrine said that he was 'opposed to any collaboration with them', on the grounds that the ISF must never share the administration of its funds.[35]

Finally, there was a need to target a section of the Spanish population as the recipients of labour movement relief. This was given added urgency by the fact that Caballero, distrusted by the British and international labour

[28] TUC, Fund 3, 4 May 1938, Schevenels to Citrine. This referred to the 21 August 1936, LSI/IFTU meeting, verbatim report, p. 10.
[29] TUC, Fund 1, 18 September 1936, Nathans to Marchbank.
[30] TUC, Correspondence 1, 9 September 1936, Stolz to Citrine.
[31] TUC, Fund 1, 26 August 1936, Citrine to CWS – according to Citrine the tobacco was needed 'for the wounded and for those in the heat of the fight'.
[32] TUC, Fund 3, 29 April 1938, Stolz to Citrine. Stolz argued that the ISF should send lorries rather than food because the main problem in Spain was one of distribution.
[33] TUC, Documents 2, 14 January 1937, LSI/IFTU meeting, verbatim report, pp. 5–6.
[34] TUC, Correspondence 2, 2 February 1937, Schevenels to Citrine.
[35] TUC, Documents 3, 8 February 1937, report of interview, pp. 1–2; TUC, International Brigade, 10 February 1937, Citrine to Brailsford.

leaders, had 'stuck out a claim for the complete administration of the fund'. This was not only opposed by Citrine, on the grounds that it would widen the divisions on the left in Spain,[36] but also by de los Rios who felt that they could not accede to Caballero's request and that the fund should be administered jointly be the UGT and PSOE.[37] Later, when Caballero was prime minister, the international labour movement clashed with him over sending relief to Bilbao. Schevenels reported that

> Caballero was angry when he heard about food going to Bilbao separately, and expressed the opinion that he should be communicated with about the matter. He said 'We are connected with the Basque country and Catalonia, and it is we who must decide what they receive.'[38]

Even after Caballero's fall, however, the suspicion continued that political divisions prevented a proper distribution of relief. In October 1937 Schevenels reported that the food problem had 'lost its acute character' and that where problems persisted this was due to conflicts between the government and other bodies entrusted with food distribution which pursued 'particular political aims rather than feeding the population'. As he had received no requests for food from the ISF committees in Madrid and Valencia for many months, the claims of the threat of starvation must be looked on as 'political polemics'.[39]

Moreover, the aid that initially arrived in Spain had been haphazardly allocated, and this antagonised powerful affiliates. In September 1936 Marchbank of the NUR told Citrine that he had been surprised to learn that the Spanish railwaymen fell outside the scope of the ISF. Apparently Nathans, Assistant Secretary of the ITF, was claiming that on a recent visit to Spain he had discovered that none of the Spanish transport unions had received any aid from the ISF, while 'much fuss was made of the assistance received by the Spanish Government from Soviet Russia'.[40] This matter was a source of some annoyance to the Amsterdam-based ITF, and Edo Fimmen later suggested to a New Zealand affiliate that in future it should donate money to his own organisation rather than the ISF because 'the transport workers receive none of it, and they are constantly appealing to us for assistance'.[41] George Hicks raised this issue at a meeting of the ISF

---

[36] See above pp. 44–5.
[37] TUC, Documents 1, 21 August 1936, LSI/IFTU meeting, verbatim report, p. 11.
[38] TUC, Documents 3, 8 February 1937, report of interview, p. 5.
[39] TUC, Correspondence 2, 29 October 1937, Schevenels to Citrine.
[40] TUC, Fund 1, 22 September 1936, Marchbank to Citrine.
[41] MRC, ITF records, Mss 159/3/c/6/7, 29 September 1937, Fimmen to J. Roberts of the New Zealand Waterside Workers' Union.

Committee in Paris, along with other fears that the amount of money distributed appeared very small and that some of the money was being used to purchase arms – fears that Adler of the LSI was keen to quell.[42] However, Vincent Tewson had to confess to Marchbank that 'we are not aware of the real method adopted by Caballero and Prieto in the distribution of the relief which has been sent'.[43]

The combination of hostility to Caballero, the obvious lack of control over distribution, and the realisation that if the ISF were to enjoy any prestige in Spain it would have to establish a formal presence in Madrid, led to the creation of a mechanism for supervision. In early September 1936 an IFTU/LSI delegation, consisting of George Stolz (of the IFTU), and Delvigne and John Price (both from the LSI), was sent to Spain in order to set up an ISF Committee there. This was given added urgency by the fact that the communist Red Aid was already established and giving press conferences.[44] The delegation was in Spain from 10–21 September and reported that almost nothing was known of the work of the ISF in Spain.[45] However, they were successful in setting up an ISF Committee composed of Deputy Carlos Hernández (UGT) and Enrique Santiago (PSOE), Director of Social Insurance, to which all contributions would be sent for distribution, with an emphasis on material goods to ensure safe arrival.[46] The committee continued to function throughout the war, eventually enlarging its activities to cover the whole Republican zone and successfully resisting pressure to come under Spanish government control. However, although the committee's establishment greatly improved intelligence as to the situation in Spain, one less welcome side-effect was that international relief became unduly reactive to the needs which it could identify. By late 1937, for instance, the NCL was sitting on £5,000 for which no immediate use could be found.[47]

The *mélange* of limitations which hemmed in labour's relief work helps to explain why a storm broke around the Labour Party's decision, in December 1938, to issue a seemingly innocuous appeal for 'Christmas Gifts for Spain'. Part of the problem lay in the Spanish government's decision, in September 1938, to set up a Comité Nacional de Ayuda a España (National Committee for Aid to Spain) with the aim of orchestrating present and future

---

[42] TUC, Fund 1, Documents Section, report of ISF Committee meeting.
[43] TUC, Fund 1, 14 October 1936, Tewson to Marchbank.
[44] TUC, Correspondence 1, 9 September 1936, Stolz to Citrine.
[45] TUC, Fund 1, Documents section, report of delegation, p. 4.
[46] IISG, Amsterdam, IFTU records, Folder 173, IFTU Circulars, 10 September 1936.
[47] TUC, Fund 2, 28 October 1937.

international campaigns. Schevenels told Negrin that the ISF could not tolerate such interference and ordered the British to ignore its demands.[48] Thus, he reacted strongly to the Christmas Gifts appeal, which was arranged through the Spanish embassy, and would distribute the gifts in Spain under the auspices of the Comité Nacional. Schevenels said that the ISF was unwilling to collaborate with the Comité Nacional because it was run by a communist and had 'Communist aims'. He even reprimanded Santiago, the ISF representative in Barcelona for supplying the Labour Party with the addresses of poor families to send presents to![49]

William Gillies, the responsible Labour Party official, replied that he had himself been opposed to the formation of the Comité Nacional, but that this appeal was sponsored by the Spanish embassy, and the Spanish ambassador was hardly a communist agent. He felt that it would have been difficult for the party to repudiate the scheme and their aim was to bring it within the bounds of the ISF.[50] However, this did not satisfy Vincent Tewson who wrote to the Labour Party General Secretary to express his hostility to the appeal which, he felt, was in direct competition with the ISF and had unsavoury political characteristics. He added that this scheme did not have the 'special circumstances' that had recommended the earlier Milk for Spain scheme.[51] However, it is apparent that a further consideration was the growth at this time of many operations on the fringes of official control, such as the Glasgow food ship campaign. Tewson reported 'concern' in the movement at 'the regional efforts which are being made in certain parts of the country for the despatching of food ships which appear to involve the appointment of full-time organisers' and confused the rank and file with a multiplicity of appeals.

However, despite the construction of a well-defined framework for relief, the fear persisted throughout the war that, just as in Britain the labour movement's efforts were failing to win the recognition they deserved, similarly, in Spain, the recipients of ISF aid were unaware of who their benefactors were. In short, the movement was losing the propaganda war with the communists. In January 1937 Schevenels had visited Spain, travelling with an ISF convoy which was delayed *en route* by 'manifest bad will' from the anarchists, in the hope that this would give the Spanish people 'a better understanding of the intense efforts of the Trade Union and Socialist Internationals to do their duty towards Democratic and Republican

---

[48] TUC, Fund 3, 21 October 1938, Schevenels to Tewson.
[49] TUC, Fund 4, 9 December 1938 and 7 January 1939, Schevenels to Tewson.
[50] TUC, Fund 4, 14 December 1938, Bell to Tewson.
[51] TUC, Fund 4, 22 December 1938, Tewson to Middleton. On the Milk for Spain scheme see below p. 156.

Spain'.[52] However, as he confided to Citrine on his return, the Spanish people 'consider the Communists their saviours' because of the supply of Russian arms, and he hinted that it might even be hard to maintain links with the UGT on account of this. So keen was he to check the decline in the IFTU's prestige that he was even willing to suggest that it should make a gesture such as supplying 100 machine guns![53]

Little had changed by January 1938 when Tewson had an interview with Mrs Gwendolen Adams de Puertas, London representative of the Spanish Asistencia Social (a governmental agency). She commented that she had had no idea that the consignments were from the ISF and that while government officials might be aware of this the recipients generally were not. Tewson suggested to Schevenels that labels on the goods might raise the recipients' morale, receiving the reply that all the goods were labelled, but that from the beginning the Spanish people had been unaware of the role of the ISF. Any 'large scale propaganda' came from the communists and Red Aid, but Schevenels found it hard to see how their own work could be better advertised.[54] Tewson wondered whether the labels could be made clearer without becoming a 'propaganda poster'.[55] A few days later Mrs Adams gave Tewson a report on relief work in Spain which concluded that, while the ISF was doing very good work there, many people were unaware of its links with the Labour Party, possibly due to an 'otherwise laudable' lack of propaganda. Indeed, there was the impression that the ISF was simply another communist organisation 'the propaganda of Communist and Anarchist organisations has been so extensive by comparison'.[56]

These episodes reveal two important features of the labour leaders' attitude to their relief work. Firstly, they saw their own efforts as 'genuine' aid, fundamentally different from the gimmicky 'political' aid purveyed by the communists and others, with which they were, however, reluctantly, in competition. This trait was most apparent on the question of publicity. When £3,000 of ISF food supplies were loaded on to the S.S. *Backworth* in

---

[52] IFTU circular, 6 February 1937.
[53] TUC, Documents 3, report of interview between Schevenels and Citrine, 8 February 1937.
[54] TUC, Fund 2, 29 January 1938, Tewson to Schevenels; TUC, Fund 3, 31 January 1938, Schevenels to Tewson.   [55] TUC, Fund 3, 1 February 1938, Tewson to Schevenels.
[56] TUC, Fund 3, 3 February 1938, Mrs Adams de Puertas to Tewson. Mrs Adams was British born but Spanish by marriage to Sr. José Puertas. She was arrested when she attempted to return to Spain in November 1939, and detained until January 1940 facing a charge of carrying out communist propaganda. Citrine wrote to the Foreign Office on her behalf, and described her role during the Civil War as a 'liaison officer' between the ISF and 'bona fide relief machinery in Spain'. He noted that she had been 'keenly opposed' to the tactics of the Communist Party during the war (TUC. 'Spanish Rebellion – Aftermath'; 10 November 1939, José Puertas to Schevenels; 28 November 1939, Citrine to Halifax; 31 January 1940, Halifax to Citrine).

April 1937, for shipment to Bilbao, Citrine was greatly concerned to avoid any publicity which might endanger the vessel and it was decided that only when the ship had been unloaded should this be announced in the labour press.[57] The contrast between this 'responsible' attitude and the more public use which the ILP and the communists were to make of the same ship resulted in a tirade by the mental health workers' leader George Gibson at their 1937 conference. The left-wing parties had, he said

> made a big fuss about sending goods to Spain on the 'Backworth'. Did you know that we had already chartered that boat, which lay in the dock loaded with over £3,000 of food? We did not advertise when the ship was sailing because there were British seamen's lives at stake in that boat. Why should we advertise that a particular boat was leaving on a certain date and would land on a particular date, when we knew that warships were waiting to attack it? But, to our left wingers, sweet are the uses of advertisement. They spread the news broadcast that they were putting goods on board![58]

Yet, in spite of their outrage at such incidents, labour's leaders realised that they were locked in a battle for publicity and used the not inconsiderable means at their disposal to get their own message across. In December 1936 Tewson confided to Citrine that 'at a time when there is a general impression that nothing is being done in regard to Spain, don't you think it might be well to give the *Herald* a general statement'.[59] However, not even the tame and Bevin-dominated *Daily Herald* could always provide the coverage required. Citrine complained to the editor, Francis Williams, about the lack of space given to the launch of the TUC's 'Save the Basque Children' appeal after spending an hour with the *Herald* reporter. He had expected a 'prominent heading' in the paper, he explained, yet was unhappy to see that 'the interview is crowded down, and many material matters are left out completely'. He reminded Williams that the NCL and the General Council were keen for prominence to be given to the appeal.[60] However, they would continue to distinguish between the legitimate publicity given to their own efforts and propaganda which only the communists indulged in.

Secondly, labour's relief work was gravely weakened by the lack of permanent and reliable lines of communication with Spain which would enable it to monitor the situation for itself. Most importantly, no leading TUC or Labour Party official visited Spain in the entire period and it was

---

[57] NCL minutes, 27 April 1937; TUC General Council minutes, 28 April 1937.
[58] MRC, Mss 229/NA/1/1/5, MHIWU July 1937 Conference report, p. 39.
[59] TUC, Fund 1, 8 December 1936, Inter-departmental correspondence, Tewson to Citrine.
[60] TUC, Basque Children 2, 5 May 1937, Citrine to Francis Williams. S. Koss, *Rise and Fall of the Political Press In Britain, Volume 2* (1984), p. 553 covers Bevin's 'intimidation and interference' in reporting of the Civil War.

forced to rely, especially in the tumultuous first months of war, on an array of sources including the often unreliable confidential reports of *Daily Herald* correspondents, IFTU and LSI officials who had visited Spain and meetings with Spanish labour leaders. Yet this problem could have been overcome had greater will been shown.

In December 1936 the ISF Committee offered to fund a full-time British 'observer' in Spain, and the NCL approached two retired trade union leaders, Mr J. Bowen of the postal workers' international, who refused because of the wedding of his son, and the former steelworkers' leader Sir Arthur Pugh, who declined because he did not speak any Spanish.[61] Citrine still favoured sending Pugh, however, with an interpreter if necessary, feeling that the observer would have to be someone 'with standing' in the movement.[62] Attlee suggested Wedgwood Benn, though admitting that the candidate should have knowledge of transport and distribution matters.[63] Citrine later suggested two further candidates – Clutterbuck of the ITF and Price of the LSI, both Spanish speakers and the latter already familiar with the situation in Madrid.[64] However, no attempt was made to secure their services and it was to be an astounding six months before Citrine again contacted the IFTU to admit that, while it would be useful to have an official British representative in Spain, 'there is not much likelihood of our being able to find someone for this purpose'.[65] He added that Dr Morgan, the TUC Medical Advisor, would check on the Onteniente field hospital while on a visit to Spain for Spanish Medical Aid. Even this reply was only in response to specific prompting from Schevenels on the grounds that, with the resignation of Delvigne as LSI/IFTU representative in Spain, he would like to send two Britons to Spain (with one for the hospital).[66] Because inefficiency was the least of Citrine's faults this particular episode can best be explained in terms of a political dilemma, namely that those who would be willing to risk a posting in Spain were precisely those whom Citrine feared would compromise the labour movement by becoming too closely associated with the Popular Front.

This shortcoming denied real substance to the claims of labour leaders to exercise control over the use of the movement's relief in Spain, their

[61] TUC, Correspondence 1, 29 and 31 December 1936.
[62] TUC, Correspondence 1, 4 January 1937, Citrine to David Grenfell MP.
[63] TUC, Correspondence 1, 8 January 1937, Grenfell to Citrine. Grenfell stressed that the job need not be too onerous: 'I do not think our man need to go anywhere but to Barcelona, Valencia, Alicante, Albacete, Cartagena – all places accessible ... from Valencia. He may go to Madrid but need not stay long there.'
[64] TUC, Correspondence 1, 8 January 1937, Citrine to IFTU.
[65] TUC, Correspondence 2, 22 July 1937, Citrine to Schevenels.
[66] TUC, Documents 3, 17 July 1937, A.E. Carthy (International Department) to Citrine.

knowledge of which remained slim. In January 1938, for instance, Tewson suggested that some of the NCL's most recent shipments should be diverted to help refugees in Spain and Schevenels replied that the ISF Committee in Madrid distributed relief 'at its full discretion', but that doubtless the neediest would receive help. The committee gave out relief to the municipalities which in turn distributed it according to need.[67] These incidents reinforce the view that the leaders were mainly concerned with constructing an acceptable image of their relief work for British and international consumption and ensuring the safe arrival of supplies in Spain, yet showed a peculiar lack of curiosity about the actual uses to which that relief was being put.

The relative lack of control which the British labour movement exercised over the use of its relief in Spain contrasted strikingly with the tightness with which it ran the actual fund-raising in Britain. This was expressed both in the nature of the 'official' campaigns and in labour's relations with 'unofficial' organisations. The reason for this strictness was twofold. Labour leaders naturally sought to ensure that the maximum amount of money that was raised would be channelled through their own fund and feared that a mass of overlapping appeals would dissipate this potential.[68] For instance, the NCL's attitude towards the National Joint Committee for Spanish Relief was defined as 'not to associate with the numerous outside bodies which are being constantly set up as it is felt that they compete with the relief work which the movement is undertaking' through the ISF.[69] A similar argument was used against the International Brigades Dependants' Aid campaign, with Tewson admitting to being 'bewildered with the number of *ad hoc* committees being set up which duplicate the efforts being made by the official movement'.[70]

Yet the underlying consideration which restricted labour's relief efforts was political rather than practical. The leadership feared mobilising its membership because this could undermine its own authority, yet it also feared that members would drift into 'unofficial' campaigns beyond their control if their own campaign were not energetic enough. These two

---

[67] TUC, Fund 2, 8 January 1938, Tewson to Schevenels; 14 January 1938, Schevenels to Tewson.
[68] STUC *Annual Report*, 1938, p. 69, details a circular dated 24 January 1938 in which the STUC reminded affiliates that 'it is undesirable to diffuse their energy in the collection of monies for Spanish relief or to encourage any overlapping in the methods by which such monies are administered'.
[69] TUC, Basque Children 2, 31 December 1937, Citrine to Elger.
[70] TUC, International Brigade, 2 November 1939, Tewson to Elger. In fact, there was no 'duplication' here as the NCL refused to allow its fund to be used to support the dependants of International Brigaders, see below pp. 159–61.

considerations were contradictory and the former took precedence over the latter. Ultimately, despite James Middleton's assertion that 'there is ample scope within the possibilities of our own party for all our local comrades to do their share of work on this Spanish issue',[71] the movement abandoned this pretence in practice. It created ideologically pure structures (where it created anything), only to find that many of its members were unwilling to work within them and preferred looser, more imaginative frameworks. Thus, the pursuit of integrity and control often forced the labour leadership to abandon the trade union and Labour Party rank and file to its competitors – a price, however, that it was willing to pay in the short term.

The core of the 'official' response was the NCL's Spanish Workers' Fund which was primarily aimed at securing grants from trade union funds. The TUC was willing to accept money from workplace collections but did nothing to initiate this kind of activity, leaving it entirely up to individual unions or activists. The only occasion when this procedure was broken with was in the specific case of collecting for the Basque refugee children. In February 1938 Mr Harries of the TUC's Organisation Department wrote to Miss Hancock of Bristol T&GWU, explaining that because of the commitment to the children, the TUC was contacting industrial centres to inquire into the possibility of works committees running weekly 1d collections. Miss Hancock replied that she had consulted with the Area Secretary but saw 'little hope' of success – 'we tried it ourselves,' she wrote 'when the Basque children first came to Bristol, but I am sorry to say that we had very little response, and right up to the present moment that is the position'.[72]

However, this style of direct approach was unique and the standard method of collection remained a series of appeals addressed to union executives. Most executives subsequently opened voluntary funds amongst their members for the ISF, but these tended mainly to complement the grants from union funds. Some unions were more imaginative, although these were an exception. The tailors' union, for instance, used its connections within the clothing industry to obtain old stocks of clothes at very cheap prices. However, while it is easy to criticise the standard method of fund-raising for lacking inspiration, there were many difficulties inherent in any alternative.

The most obvious alternative would have been a compulsory levy of trade unionists. For constitutional reasons, however, this could not have been imposed by the TUC and was left, instead, to individual unions to discuss.

---

[71] Labour Party archives, LP/SCW 1/11, 21 January 1937, Middleton to Tom Garnett.
[72] See Tom Buchanan, 'The Role of the British Labour Movement in the Origins and Work of the Basque Children's Committee', pp. 166–7.

At the 1937 conference of the National Union of Clerks a motion calling for branches to decide on a 6d weekly levy for Spain under the union's Rule 58 was fiercely criticised on the grounds that it would be a serious hindrance to the Organiser's recruiting efforts – according to one speaker they 'could not ignore the mentality of the unorganised clerk' on this issue. The motion was withdrawn when the President ruled that it would be enforceable 'only by those branches in which there was a majority in favour of it as a branch levy; and even so it was possible that a dissenter might challenge its legality'.[73] A similar discussion took place at the 1938 General Council of the National Society of Painters, where a compulsory levy was rejected on the grounds that it would be 'objectionable' to the members and produce less income than a voluntary levy.[74] One speaker, while favouring a levy, felt that most members would 'begin to lose their sympathy when any attempt is made to touch their pockets'.[75] In 1938 two major unions, the miners' federation and the AEU launched levy funds with the aim of raising much greater sums than had previously been contemplated. However, in spite of the miners' success in raising some £70,000, almost half of the total amount raised by the British trade union movement during the Civil War, it is significant that the bulk of this money did not come from individual trade unionists but rather from the funds of the federation's constituent unions. The AEU appeal, which called for a voluntary donation from members, was far less successful.[76]

In fact, the evidence for the response of trade union members to direct appeals for levies is conflicting. In September 1936 the National Union of Foundry Workers balloted its members, according to the Rules, on a 2d levy for the NCL Fund and won support by 5,330 to 2,386. Shop stewards were then expected to extract the levy along with the members' monthly union contributions.[77] The Executive took stern action against any member who refused to pay, who had it placed against him as debt.[78] Although some branches failed to contribute, the levy realised £120.10s.6d.[79]

By contrast, in December 1938 the Amalgamated Society of Wood-workers' Executive, inspired by the miners' example, decided to ballot its members for a levy of 2/6d per person and lost by 22,873 to 13,238.[80] In spite

---

[73] APEX records, *The Clerk*, July/August 1937, May 1937 Conference report, pp. 98–100.
[74] MRC, UCATT records, Mss 78/NASOHSPD/4/2/19, NSP General Council minutes, June 1938, p. 99.   [75] *Ibid.* NSP General Council minutes, 30 May 1937, p. 10.
[76] See above pp. 133–5.
[77] MRC, Mss 41/NUFW/4/1, *Quarterly Reports*, October 1936, p. 35; Mss 41/NUFW/1/36, Council minutes, 10 September 1936.   [78] *Ibid.* 3 October 1936.
[79] Results of levy tabulated by branches in *Quarterly Reports*, January 1937, pp. 11–15.
[80] MRC, UCATT records, Mss ASW/11/1/16, NEC minutes, 1 and 2 December 1938; Mss ASW/4/1/19, *Monthly Journal*, January 1939, p. 21.

of the General Secretary's appeal for members to 'take a broad humanitarian view of this matter and make the majority for the levy worthy of the fine international traditions of our society',[81] the ballot produced a welter of criticism from union branches which did not indicate hostility to the ISF so much as anger at the Executive's priorities in the use of union funds. Battersea (#1) Branch said that 'to members at the same time receiving final arrears notices [from the union] this may well be the last straw. These members joined for trade union purposes, not as universal providers.'[82]

The Executive's action was particularly ill-timed coming soon after a cut in member's benefits, for superannuation, sickness and unemployment, which, although sanctioned by a ballot, was still clearly resented.[83] The contrast was emphasised by Shepherds' Bush Branch: 'Why must our leadership send our hard earned money abroad when there is so much want at home in England ... Charity begins at home even if it does not end there.' Similarly Wycombe Branch felt that 'it is time that the Executive Council should turn to and aid our own members. We find that to our detriment union Executives are more interested ... in foreign affairs and are leaving home affairs to fend for themselves.' Other branches protested at what they felt to be 'compulsion' by the leadership. The union's journal published some seventeen condemnatory resolutions, in most cases passed unanimously, and the General Secretary felt compelled to answer the many points raised, concluding that 'it seems to us a grotesque misuse of words for branches to declare that a free vote of our membership is an attempt to compel or force members to contribute to the fund'.[84] Thus, the argument that the trade union rank and file were ripe for a heightened fund-raising effort, but were let down by a lack of bureaucratic initiative, is far from conclusive.

Although it proved difficult to develop new initiatives in the trade unions, there was more scope in the Labour Party and the Co-operative movement. The ISF, for instance, bought quantities of wool which were then knitted into garments by groups of women under the auspices of the Standing Joint Committee of Industrial Womens' Organisations. The co-ordinator, the Labour Party Women's Organiser Mary Sutherland, recorded the 'tremendous enthusiasm' of the volunteers, especially those who could not afford to make further financial contributions.[85] Another notably successful

---

[81] MRC, UCATT records, Mss ASW/4/1/19, *Monthly Journal*, January 1939, p. 21.
[82] *Ibid.* February 1939, p. 115.   [83] *Ibid.* February 1939, p. 115.
[84] *Ibid.* March 1939, pp. 181 and 184.
[85] TUC, Fund 1, 11 January 1937, Sutherland to Citrine. Citrine was scathing about this initiative in private. In December 1936 he told a rank-and-file delegation that: 'You know that one of our Committees has appealed to the wives of Trade Unionists to send woollen

initiative was the Milk for Spain scheme which was launched in November 1937, and gave customers in Co-op stores the opportunity to buy 6d tokens which would be used to send powdered milk. A year later 3d tokens were issued for 'not-so-well-off co-operators in industrial areas'.[86] The trade unions whose members worked in Co-op stores were involved in the appeal from its inception, and NUDAW urged all its members to give generously themselves and to facilitate the operation of the scheme.[87] Admittedly the project encountered initial problems of inertia and conservatism from the managers of some Co-op stores – Harry Pollitt claimed that 'in some important districts it is like drawing teeth to be able to buy the tokens, no attempt [is made] at publicity on the part of the managers to see that the tokens are displayed'.[88] The *Daily Worker* reported that some Co-operative societies preferred to make a single donation rather than handling the tokens, thus defeating the object of the exercise.[89] However, despite these early problems the eventual success of the scheme, which raised over £32,000 was doubtless due to its unalloyed simplicity. The purpose of the appeal was instantly obvious (unlike that of the Spanish Workers' Fund) and the form of collection focussed attention on consumers rather than the workplace. Indeed, back-handed praise for the depth of support in labour strongholds came from a *Catholic Herald* journalist on a mission to the Rhondda valley: 'Tylerstown had a shop window filled with appeals to save the children of Spain; "Milk is a Child's First Necessity – Help to Send Milk to Spain". Some of Tylerstown's children looked as if they had missed that first necessity.'[90]

Of the 'unofficial' responses to the Civil War, probably the most important, and certainly the earliest, was the Spanish Medical Aid (SMA) campaign, launched in August 1936 by the Socialist Medical Association with backing from the communists and rank-and-file Labour Party members.[91] Due to the urgent sense of crisis in which it was born and its avowed humanitarian aims the SMA was never treated as harshly by the labour movement as many other 'unofficial' organisations were. Indeed, initially the SMA was regarded as part of labour's own operations – TUC Chairman Arthur Findlay had been present at the departure of the first

---

goods or knitted goods... We had to grant them from our Fund £1,000 only a few days ago because the response has not been so great' (TUC, Documents 2, 21 December 1936, report, p. 18).   [86] *Co-operative News*, 8 October 1938.

[87] USDAW archives, NUDAW minutes, Industrial General Secretary's report to the Executive Council, 21 November 1937.

[88] Nuffield College, Oxford, Cripps papers, 776/521, 28 January and 16 February 1938, Pollitt to Cripps.   [89] *Daily Worker*, 26 November 1937.

[90] *Catholic Herald*, 10 February 1939.

[91] The best account of the work of the unit is in Jim Fyrth, *The Signal Was Spain*, Part 2.

unit.[92] The SMA was only abandoned when it was plain that it would not be subservient to the NCL.

The prospect of the labour movement sending medical aid had been discussed at the 28 July 1936 LSI/IFTU meeting. Adler of the LSI suggested that they should send medicines by 'a sort of socialist red cross'. It was pointed out that the official Red Cross had already offered medical services and been rejected because the Spanish government felt that they were 'not necessary', although Schevenels later added that the real reason was that the Geneva Red Cross was 'reputed to be anti-democratic'. Citrine and Gillies strongly opposed the idea, not only because it was unnecessary, but also because 'it was only copying the Communists whose assistance in this direction would be very small' and, finally, because this would legitimate similar activity by Germany and Italy in the rebel areas. However, Sr. Airlandis, the Spanish delegate who spoke later at the same meeting, clearly stated that 'they required medical supplies and their stocks were now exhausted'.[93]

On 11 August the NCL officers met a deputation from the newly-formed SMA, and the information received from the IFTU opposing the sending of an Ambulance Unit was presented, although the officers said that the 'most sympathetic consideration' was being given to the project.[94] Soon afterwards, however, Ellen Wilkinson raised the matter at the conference on Spain called in Paris, where the Spanish delegate was, as she told Citrine, 'ready to fling his arms around the necks of the [British] deputation...[a medical unit] was the very moral gesture required'. Citrine felt that this information put him 'in a very invidious position' because 'if they refused aid now it might have been difficult later on'.[95] In fact, Citrine's personal opposition to sending a medical column had been undermined by the lack of agreement between the Spanish representatives in Paris and London, and he was later to comment that ambulances were sent 'more or less in opposition to their will'.[96] Accordingly, the NCL officers decided to grant £2,000 to the unit, to maintain it for at least three months, although they 'didn't want the fact to be made public'. Citrine was also unhappy that a completely independent fund had been set up to support the unit, based at the National Trade Union Club, fearing that it was communist-controlled. However, while he was 'not in a position to say that there were no Communists in it

[92] *Daily Herald*, 24 August 1936.
[93] TUC, Documents 1, 28 July 1936, LSI/IFTU meeting, verbatim report, pp. 4, 6 and 10.
[94] TUC, Documents 1, 13 August 1936, NCL memorandum for GC and NEC members, p. 3.
[95] TUC, Documents 1, 25 August 1936, NCL, verbatim report, p. 6.
[96] TUC, Documents 2, 21 December 1936, report of meeting with 'rank-and-file' delegation, p. 19.

at all...they felt that they would have been grossly misunderstood if they had withheld support from it'.[97] Finally, after a communication from Dr Charles Brook, Secretary of the SMA, the NCL's officers were empowered to liaise with the SMA Committee as it had requested.[98]

However, relations soon soured. The behaviour of the Medical Unit personnel did nothing to allay fears that the labour movement was being duped: in October it was alleged that while passing through Paris some of them had visited the communist headquarters but not those of the socialist party or the IFTU.[99] On 6 November the ISF Committee made a final grant of £1,350 to the SMA, on the understanding that the SMA would seek to maintain the independence of its units from Spanish government control, at least in respect of the ownership of the vehicles.[100] The ISF also granted £1,000 to a separate Scottish ambulance unit, because Citrine thought that it was 'psychologically of the utmost importance' to replace a vehicle already lost in action, although the SMA criticised this decision.[101]

At the 24 November meeting of the NCL, however, it was decided that there could be no direct co-operation, in the sense of an NCL representative on the SMA Committee, so long as communists were involved with it 'in contravention of the original understanding'.[102] Bevin told the General Council that they would no longer support the SMA in any way until communists had been excluded from it.[103] Citrine justified this decision in January 1937 to George Hicks who had sought to clarify the TUC's current relations with the SMA – 'I heard you say that we were no longer working with the British unit.' Citrine said that from the beginning they had

> wanted to assure ourselves that no communists were associated with the unit, and that it would be really representative of the British Labour Movement. I am sorry to say that as time has gone on, although most of the members [of the SMA Committee] are above suspicion, the work has grown more and more in association with the communists.

[97] *Ibid.* p. 5.   [98] NCL minutes, 25 August 1936.   [99] *Reynolds News*, 18 October 1936.
[100] TUC, Fund 1, 10 November 1936, Schevenels to Citrine; TUC, Documents 2, 21 December 1936, report of interview with 'rank-and-file' delegation, p. 19.
[101] TUC, Fund 1, 2 November 1936, Citrine to Schevenels. For an account of the peculiarities of the Scottish Unit see Jim Fyrth, *The Signal Was Spain*, pp. 181–91. TUC, Fund 1, 10 November 1936, Schevenels to Citrine; TUC, Documents 2, 21 December 1936, report of meeting with 'rank-and-file' delegation, p. 19. Soon after this Citrine intervened with the Foreign Office on behalf of two Belfast members of the Scottish unit captured by the rebels, and they were subsequently released, TUC, Correspondence 1, 9 November 1936, telegram from Alderman Midgley in Belfast to Citrine and subsequent correspondence between Citrine and Eden; 16 November 1936, Eden to Citrine.
[102] NCL minutes, 24 November 1936. There is no record in the TUC archives of any formal 'understanding' having been reached on this point. Indeed, it is peculiar that while all of the other 'unofficial' committees had TUC files devoted to them, the SMA, the most important one, did not.   [103] TUC General Council minutes, 25 November 1936.

He added that there had been 'very considerable dissension inside the unit in Spain, and the medical competence and skill of its members, with the exception of the nurses, had been rather adversely commented upon'. A further consideration was the SMA's recent decision to put the Medical Unit at the service of the Spanish government, a much closer relationship than the labour movement was willing to accept. For all these reasons financial support had been ended.[104] However, it should be stressed that here Citrine was apparently conflating the allegations of ill-discipline against the Scottish unit with his political reservations about the British one, which had a good disciplinary record.

Thus, direct relations with the SMA were severed and the experience was to mould labour's future relief activities. In May 1937, for instance, Citrine made it quite clear at the inception of the campaign to care for Basque refugee children that 'we could not be associated with Communist organisations in this work, and we had to be careful as our experience of the Spanish Medical Aid Committee had shown'.[105] In spite of the failure to forge a relationship with the NCL, however, the SMA continued to be enthusiastically supported by many local Labour parties and trade unions – in October 1938 the AEU allowed the committee to use some of the lorries which it proposed to buy with its '£50,000 Fund' to convey aid to Spain.[106] The ambivalence of the relationship was apparent too in that the TUC's Dr Morgan continued to play a prominent role in the SMA. In fact, the NCL's attitude bore an uncanny resemblance to that of the British government which 'neither approved nor disapproved' of the SMA's activities.[107]

The NCL adopted a more intransigent attitude towards the collection of funds for the dependants of members of the International Brigades. With the formation of the British Battalion of the XV Brigade in January 1937 it soon became apparent that the assistance of dependants and wounded would be an expensive task – the estimated weekly cost rose from an initial £70–90 to £700 in November 1937.[108] In February 1937 Citrine had been approached by the socialist journalist H.N. Brailsford who suggested that the labour movement should take responsibility for the 230 trade unionists and 40

---

[104] TUC, Correspondence 1, 4 January 1937, Hicks to Citrine; 7 January 1937, Citrine to Hicks.
[105] TUC, Basque Children 1, 4 May 1937, report of Citrine's meeting with the Basque representative in London, Sr. Lizaso.
[106] MRC, Mss 259, AEU Executive Council minutes, 12 October 1938.
[107] PRO, FO 371, 20542, W12857/62/41, 2 October 1936, Foreign Office minute.
[108] TUC, International Brigade, 22 February 1937, Brailsford to Citrine; 22 November 1937, Charlotte Haldane to Citrine.

Labour Party members currently in the Battalion and Citrine promised to consider the idea.[109] Schevenels, however, was unsympathetic, pointing out that the Brigades were an 'unofficial' communist organisation and 'the responsibility for those who joined...could not be placed on the Trade Unions'.[110] On 23 February the proposal was discussed at the NCL where, significantly, it transpired that some unions had already accepted responsibility for their own members in the Brigades and it was agreed to look into the extent of this practice.[111]

Citrine told Brailsford that union funds could not be used for dependants' aid on legal grounds – money already contributed to the NCL Fund had been earmarked for the Spanish workers and their families and could not be diverted for any other use.[112] However, he promised to look into the use of 'special union voluntary payments' for this purpose. A report prepared by the TUC Research Department analysed a number of union rule books and concluded that only the T&GWU rules 'have a quite certain chance of resisting any action by their members to restrain them from expending money either in support of dependants...or of granting money to the International [Solidarity] Fund'. Referring to this, Bill Alexander notes that Citrine 'in his hostility to doing anything to help the Republic, studied the union donations to check that they were not infringing their own rules'.[113] In fact, it is clear that Citrine was unable to find a serviceable legal reason for not supporting the appeal which would not highlight the problematic legal position of many union contributions to his own fund and, ultimately, the NCL had offer a more overtly political rationale for withholding assistance.

This was made easier by the revelation that Brailsford and others had already issued an appeal in the movement, which was being circulated 'to various Trade Union branches, particularly in Scotland', and that some sections were making weekly donations to it. Thus, although the possibility of a special appeal was discussed by the NCL, it was soon agreed that the responsibility for the International Brigaders was not one which it should accept and that, instead, a further appeal would be issued for the ISF.[114] In June 1937 the dependants' aid campaign was formalised with the appointment of Charlotte Haldane as secretary of a Dependants' Aid

---

[109] TUC, Documents 2, report of meeting.
[110] TUC, Documents 2, 8 February 1937, report of meeting.
[111] NCL minutes, 23 February 1938.
[112] TUC, International Brigade, 1 March 1937, Citrine to Brailsford.
[113] TUC, International Brigade, 23 March 1937, Research Department memorandum; Bill Alexander, *British Volunteers for Liberty: Spain 1936–1939*, p. 142.
[114] NCL minutes, 23 March 1937.

Committee, but a renewed attempt to gain official recognition was rebuffed after Citrine pointed out that contributions to the ISF had ceased 'largely owing to the competing appeals'.[115]

It is, however, important to stress that in refusing to endorse the appeal the NCL was mainly concerned with restricting the donation of grants from trade union funds. In this it was fairly successful as the Executives of such unions as the NUR, NUBSO and the T&GWU rejected International Brigade appeals on the grounds that the cause was 'unofficial', although most unions were willing to pay the union contributions of volunteer members.[116] But, with the withdrawal of the Brigades in late 1938 and the establishment of a National Memorial Fund in their honour this policy began to look increasingly tattered. A notable contribution of some £4,000 was made by the MFGB.[117] Thus, by refusing to sponsor the appeal, the NCL was deliberately distancing itself from the movement's rank-and-file activists, particularly in areas such as South Wales and Scotland where the International Brigades were of central importance. Citrine's injunctions went down particularly badly in Scotland. At the 1938 STUC Congress one speaker attacked

> Mr Citrine [*sic*] with his provincial outlook telling them...that they should not give money to the International Brigade...It really made him sigh for the days before the war when the kaiser was only dictator in Europe, for now they had Hitler, Mussolini, Franco and Citrine to tell them where they should keep their money.[118]

This trait was repeated in the response to the Voluntary Industrial Aid for Spain Committee (VIASC). The committee was the brainchild of Geoffrey Pyke, an eccentric genius with no strong links with the labour movement, who devised and publicised the idea that the value of relief for Spain could easily be vastly increased if voluntary labour was mobilised in reconditioning old vehicles or in manufacturing vital commodities. He set up a committee to develop this project and was joined by two left-wing London trade unionists, Harry Adams of the builders and Joe Scott of the engineers, who

[115] NCL minutes, 23 November 1937.
[116] MRC, NUR records, 1937 *Proceedings and Reports*, May–June Quarterly Meeting, p. 41, #504; UCD, NUBSO records, TU7/108, Council minutes, 21–2 April 1937, p. 137; MRC, Mss 126/T&G/1/1/16, T&GWU minutes, 28 September 1938, p. 311. There was a lengthy struggle over the question of paying International Brigaders' contributions in the National Society of Painters, see MRC, UCATT records, Mss 78/NASOHSPD/4/2/18, General Council minutes, 1937, p. 150; Mss 78/NASOHSPD/4/2/19, General Council minutes, 1938, p. 99.
[117] MFGB *Annual Proceedings*, Executive Council minutes, 7 September 1938, 4 October 1938, 16 February 1938.   [118] STUC *Annual Report*, 1938, p. 152.

were respectively its chairman and treasurer.[119] Pyke felt that it was essential to involve the TUC and to this end met Tewson on 7 April 1937. Pyke claimed to be anxious that the scheme should not fall into communist hands, forcing Tewson to point out that in that case he had chosen his committee rather badly. Pyke acknowledged this but replied that his colleagues had been 'appointed by the unions'. He argued that the campaign now needed official labour movement backing and Tewson concurred that the project would not get far unless it was perceived to enjoy such support. In general, Tewson concluded that the scheme looked 'alright on paper' but he foresaw many practical problems.[120]

Subsequently, Pyke supplied letters from the AEU, the National Union of Vehicle Builders and the Upholsterers' Union pledging their support and added that, as a non-trade unionist, he was willing for a TUC official to take over as secretary of the committee.[121] However, Citrine was worried by the apparent willingness of the unions to accept the principle of voluntary labour and wrote to the eight unions involved pointing out that voluntary industrial aid would involve not only repair and reconditioning, but also the manufacture of goods.[122] Pyke confessed himself baffled at this distinction,[123] and this revealed his naivety in dealing with TUC leaders naturally ill-disposed towards his ideas because of their preoccupation with issues such as the dilution of skills in the government rearmament programme. Moreover, this was a needless mistake to make as, in practice, the VIASC rarely did more than recondition old vehicles. However, the majority of the unions involved shared the TUC's alarm on this point and in May 1937 the Finance and General Purposes Committee decided that, due to the lack of unanimity amongst the relevant unions, the General Council should not endorse the scheme.[124] Subsequently, Pyke's contempt for the arts of political persuasion doomed his attempt to gain the support of the Labour Party's Spain Campaign Committee, despite the support of Stafford Cripps.[125]

However, while not officially backed by the TUC, the VIASC was not actively hindered by it either. When Blackpool Trades Council asked whether the committee was a proscribed body in May 1938, Tewson replied that it was not as it was supported by the AEU and other unions. 'There is,

[119] D. Lampe, *Pyke – The Unknown Genius* (Aylesbury and Slough, 1959), pp. 64–8.
[120] TUC, VIA File, 12 April 1937, report of meeting by Tewson.
[121] TUC, VIA, 7 April 1937, Pyke to Tewson.
[122] TUC, VIA, 14 April 1937, Citrine to Pyke; 14 April 1937, Citrine to Bolton; 15 April 1937, letters to relevant unions.   [123] TUC, VIA, 18 April 1937, Pyke to Citrine.
[124] TUC Finance and General Purposes Committee minutes, 24 May 1937.
[125] See the correspondence in the Cripps papers, Nuffield College, Oxford, Box 773, File 537.

however,' he concluded, 'no close co-operation between the Committee and our own.'[126] The Voluntary Industrial Aid movement continued to thrive in 1937–8 at a rank-and-file level, especially in factories where the engineers' shop stewards' movement was active. In June 1938 the AEU National Committee endorsed the VIASC's work, although the actual degree of support from the union has been greatly over-exaggerated.[127]

All the cases discussed above show the labour movement to have been essentially cautious in its dealings with the 'unofficial' organisations and more concerned with preserving the integrity of its own operations than expanding their scope, thus reinforcing the profoundly negative image of the role of the official movement which had been so prevalent. However, the case of the response to the Basque refugee children suggests that the labour movement could adopt a more positive attitude if structures could be created to protect its interests. In May 1937 the danger to children in the Basque country posed by the Nationalist advance on Bilbao led the NJCSR to petition the British government to allow some 4,000 children to come to Britain for safety. Mrs Leah Manning, an NJCSR activist in Bilbao, wired Citrine asking the TUC to take responsibility for a proportion of the children.[128] Although there was never any dispute that the labour movement should help in this, the matter was complicated by the NCL's earlier decision not work with the NJCSR. After a meeting with Basque and Labour Party officials, Citrine suggested that the TUC could co-operate in the setting up of a central authority to care for the children, on the explicit understanding that no form of 'direct association' was possible.[129] Accordingly, at the 5 May NJCSR meeting a special committee – known as the Basque Children's Committee – was set up, composed of two TUC representatives (one place was later given to the Labour Party), one each from the Society of Friends, the Save the Children Fund, Spanish Medical Aid and the Catholic church, and three officials from the NJCSR.[130]

Although content to leave controversial issues such as the repatriation of the children to the experts on the National Joint Committee, the labour movement played a vital role in the success of the project not only financially with its Save the Basque Children Fund but also organisationally. Vincent Tewson, as labour representative on the committee acted as a vital organisational link with local trades councils, directing them in the setting

---

[126] TUC, VIA, 28 March 1937, Tewson to Mr P. Willis.
[127] See Tom Buchanan, 'The Politics of Internationalism', pp. 49–52.
[128] TUC, Correspondence 2, 2 May 1937, Manning to Citrine.
[129] TUC, Basque Children 1, memoranda by Citrine, 3 May 1937, 4 May 1937; 5 May 1937, Citrine to Grenfell.   [130] TUC, Basque Children 1, 6 May 1937, Grenfell to Citrine.

up of broad-based local Basque Children's Committees which, ironically, closely resembled the model organisations of their Popular Frontist rivals in their kaleidoscopic social content. Tewson often referred to the success of his wife as a model for others to emulate: she had taken the initiative in their locality and involved some forty organisations, including 'three churches, each political party, the Odd Fellows, the British legion and several others' all of whom had agreed to 'adopt' children monetarily.[131] Thus, the case of the Basque children is significant because it shows that the TUC bureaucracy was capable of acting with initiative and imagination in an environment in which it would not feel politically compromised.

Thus, the labour leaders' obsession with control allowed them to achieve their prime objective – they were able to make a genuine contribution to humanitarian relief for their comrades in Spain without surrendering one iota of their own political power or permitting any political change in the labour movement. And it should be noted that within these limitations they did a good job of organising relief, the efficiency of which was implicitly recognised by their critics who made use of their expertise. Yet this was a Pyrrhic victory. Firstly, they had created a fund the purpose and functioning of which was little understood. According to one trade union leader the money was being paid to the Red Cross; according to another all of the money went to support the British Medical Unit (and this at a time when the NCL's support for it had lapsed). No attempt at all was made to explain how the relief work operated, and this left quite senior figures incapable of answering direct questions. Tom Baxter of Birmingham Labour Party told James Middleton that his standard (and incorrect) explanation to his members was that

> the IFTU and the [L]SI was operating its relief mainly through the good offices of the French trade unions, who were much nearer to Spain than Gt. Britain and that entry and exit was easy for the French. Much of all these answers (which quieten the critics and suspicious) are largely of my own imagination but they seem to me to be sensible assumptions.[132]

Secondly, the careful delineations of 'official' and 'unofficial' activities was largely lost on the rank and file. It was not uncommon for Labour Party or trade union branches to make two financial grants at the same time – one to the distant NCL and one to the SMA or some similar fund which would have local meaning. Finally, a fund had been created which operated by

[131] TUC, Basque Children 2, 5 June 1937, Tewson to Sheffield Trades Council; 15 June 1937, Tewson to Rugely and District Labour Party.
[132] Ruskin College, Oxford, James Middleton papers, MID 59, January 14 1937, Baxter to Middleton.

bureaucratic processes at a time when the urgency of Spain's plight demanded vigour, imagination and initiative.

It was these shortcomings which drove so many members of the labour movement to work with 'unofficial' organisations. Although it is impossible to render a full account of personal motivations, the following statements offer a good indication of the prevailing mood of exasperation. For Jim Henson, the ITF representative in Cardiff:

> It seems a great pity over here to see the attitude of some unions and the Labour Party on this question, especially as, on the other hand, the Communist Party are working in all ways to help Spain.
> On the Cardiff Spanish Medical Aid Society we are all working together at assist[ing] and have no time to fall out politically, whilst it seems that our leaders, with a few exceptions such as [Labour MPs] Dobbie, Grenfell and Cocks seem to be waiting...until Franco, Hitler and Mussolini arrive in London.[133]

The case of Southampton is also instructive. In 1937 its Joint Council, organising the local Labour Party, trades council and Co-operative society, had raised over £300 for the ISF; in 1938 nearly £200 was raised for Milk for Spain. However, after that, according to the secretary Leslie Witt, 'I do not appear to have received any plan of campaign for raising money for Food, etc. for Spain, from the National Council of Labour. This may account for the fact that in November, 1938, we felt we must act ourselves.' The Southampton Joint Council then collaborated with many other organisations to raise over £2,700 for a 'Hampshire Foodship', under the auspices of the National Joint Committee. Similar success was achieved by a cross-party coalition which ran a home for Basque children in Southampton. Witt, writing in 1939, argued that

> the best results have undoubtedly been secured where the organisation was on broad lines. It could never have been done solely by Trade Union, Labour and Co-operative effort. In fact, the truth is that consistent support has been forthcoming for our Spanish comrades only from a small number of Labour workers.

He went on to castigate the 'apathy, indifference, and sad to say, even veiled hostility, from some leaders and sections of these movements'.[134]

Thus, labour activists who felt abandoned by their own leaders and were seeking a vigorous campaign on the single issue of Spain were forced into broad alliances on the local level. They often found the results surprisingly

---

[133] MRC, ITF records, Mss 159/3/C/6/17, 13 February 1937, Henson to Fimmen.
[134] TUC, File 946/529, 'Spain, Refugees, 1939', 11 July 1939, Witt to NCL.

rewarding – according to a local Labour Party activist in Southport, Lancashire:

> in a town such as this, where the whole labour movement is extremely backward and weak, much more can be done by a joint, non-political committee, than directly by the Labour party. This is borne out by the fact that the Liberal party is now taking an active part in our committee, and is playing a major part in the organisation of the house-to-house collection.[135]

However, as soon as these alliances were used to introduce a broader criticism of the labour movement this good will could easily evaporate. The Secretary of Cardiff Trades Council told Citrine that the Council's initial decision to co-operate with the local Spanish Aid Committee was revoked when they had received 'a pamphlet from them attacking the official Movement'. He had been surprised, on making enquiries, to find that the Committee was not attached to the TUC.[136]

What these 'unofficial' movements all realised, and what eluded the labour movement leaders, was that successful fund-raising was built on human interest and passion, on a strong local basis and on an awareness of what the public were actually able to donate. The NCL fund seemed distant and uninspiring in contrast with SMA and the other 'unofficial' campaigns. The experience of the campaign for the Basque children suggests that this problem was not insuperable, and that the labour movement could have changed the basis of its operation without losing all control. Thus, one must conclude that the problem in fact went deeper – labour leaders were opposed, on political grounds, to any mobilisation of their rank and file, and were strengthened in this resolve by the existence of hostility to the Spanish Republic within the movement.

[135] Churchill College, Cambridge, LSC papers, LSPC 1/7, 11 December 1938, Colin Pettitt to Pole.
[136] BLPES, Citrine papers, III/1/1, Visit of Trades Council Delegates, 6 February 1937, p. 27.

5

OPPOSITION: CATHOLIC WORKERS AND THE SPANISH CIVIL WAR

If the response of the labour movement to the Spanish Civil War is best explained by its defensive reactions and structures, which placed a greater emphasis on protecting the integrity of its institutions than on mounting a political campaign on behalf of its Spanish comrades, the strength of this imperative was bound to be reinforced by tangible evidence that the unity of the labour movement was endangered by the impact of the Civil War. The best example of a restraining factor of this kind was the effect of the response of Catholic workers upon labour's leaders. The atrocities perpetrated against the Spanish church, mainly by anarchists, in the first months of the conflict left many working-class British Catholics either neutral or thoroughly hostile towards the Spanish Republic and made them question whether the labour movement was truly representing their interests in this matter. This chapter charts the nature, extent and ramifications of such disaffection within the labour movement.

The phenomenon of Catholic workers' opposition has been widely recognised but has received a varied historical treatment for two main reasons. Firstly, the identification of Franco's cause with fascism has been a major obstacle to a proper understanding because it has made Catholic ambivalence towards the Spanish Republic and, in some cases, support for Franco appear aberrant and shameful. Hence historians, especially on the left, have been tempted to ascribe Catholic workers' reactions purely to the power of the pulpit – portraying them as either bullied or indoctrinated into abandoning their duty towards their comrades in Spain. Victor Kiernan compares the 'reckless' Catholic propaganda on Spain in Britain to the speeches of Goebbels (although it should be noted that the labour press was capable of an equally propagandistic presentation of the role of the Catholic church in Spain). A further step has been to suggest that many Catholics saw through the 'lies' which they were being fed on Spain, so that the Civil War resulted in a weakening of the church's authority. Kiernan concludes: 'It may be conjectured that numbers of Catholic workers defied clerical blackmail...and acquired from the experience a more sceptical view of spiritual authority'.[1] Similarly, Michael Alpert has suggested that many Catholic workers were not in sympathy with Franco's cause and that this accounts for the limited success of pro-Nationalist fund-raising by Catholic newspapers.[2] However, although these arguments are certainly valid,[3] they remain largely based on surmise and poorly documented in comparison with the considerable evidence of Catholic workers' hostility to the Spanish Republic.

Secondly, most interpretations agree in seeing labour's Catholic problem as an essentially electoral phenomenon ('the Catholic vote'), which declined in influence within, at the latest, a year of the outbreak of the Civil War. This was certainly an important consideration for the Labour Party which faced municipal elections and Parliamentary by-elections throughout this period. However, the concept of the 'Catholic vote' is unduly limiting, suggesting that the most that the Labour Party had to fear was a protest vote, while Catholics would inevitably stay loyal to labour in the longer term. In fact, the reason why the Catholic response was taken so seriously was that not only was short-term voting behaviour brought into question, but that the Civil War raised fundamental questions of political representation and identity for Catholics which created problems equally for the trade unions, the Labour Party and the Co-operative movement.[4] Thus, the intention here is to ignore tendentious judgements on what should have been the 'natural' response of Catholic workers to Spain and to concentrate on assessing the impact of the Civil War as a genuine crisis of loyalty and identity for many Catholics. In particular, adverse Catholic reactions are treated as a valid critique of labour movement policy towards Spain.

[1] V. Kiernan, 'Labour and the War in Spain', *Journal of the Scottish Labour History Society*, no. 11, May 1977, p. 10.   [2] Michael Alpert, 'Humanitarianism and Politics', p. 429.
[3] The best example of this is the correspondence contained in Labour Party archive file LP/SCW 12, 'Roman Catholics – 1938'. This concerns the attempts by Mr F. O'Hanlon, chairman of Chichester DLP, to bring pressure to bear on the Catholic hierarchy to denounce the Spanish rebels. He argued that: 'For some years Hinsley, Amigo, Woodcock and co. have made the Catholic church in England the instrument of certain reactionary groups' (LP/SCW 12/1, 6 February 1938, O'Hanlon to Middleton).
[4] Although I have not given a sustained treatment in this chapter to the Co-operative movement, it is clear that it shared many problems in this respect with the trade unions and Labour Party. A separate fund was set up, under the auspices of the International Co-operative Alliance, which, in practice, sent relief only to co-operators in the Republican zone and was treated with great suspicion by some Catholics in the movement. In October 1936 opposition to the Bradford Co-operative Society's decision to grant £25 to this fund created problems for Co-operative Party candidates in local elections (*Co-op News*, 31 October and 7 November 1936).

The outbreak of the war in Spain posed a clear threat to the relationship between Catholicism and the labour movement. Catholic communities, primarily the product of nineteenth-century Irish immigration, had long been a mainstay of Labour Party electoral support in areas such as Clydeside, the North-East and North-West of England and parts of London, as well as contributing many leading figures both to the Labour Party and to the trade unions. This process had been accentuated by the partial settlement of the Irish question in 1921 which broke down traditional Catholic support for the Liberals, the party of Irish Home Rule.[5] Yet the relationship remained, at an official level, a pragmatic one, based on mutual convenience. With the decline of Liberalism and with the Conservative party, still identified with Anglicanism, not a viable alternative, the Catholic hierarchy was forced to remain on good terms with the Labour Party so long as it was the political representative of the Catholic working class. However, many points of friction survived. The division of responsibility whereby Catholicism claimed the religious loyalty of the Catholic workers and the labour movement their political and trade union loyalty was fraught with dangers. Catholicism was, after all, staunchly opposed to socialism and preferred to think of Labour not as a socialist party, but rather as a mildly reformist one which should concentrate solely on the improvement of working-class living conditions. The support, however mild, which labour gave to the Spanish Republic forced many Catholics to look afresh at this distinction, and there was no shortage of those who would attempt to exploit the Spanish Civil War as an opportunity to break up the relationship altogether.

Moreover, the discontent over Spain was not an isolated disturbance, but represented the latest of many grievances arising from the position of Catholics within the labour movement, ranging from petty discrimination to alleged political persecution. In November 1936 Archbishop Hinsley claimed to voice the feelings of working-class Catholics when he complained that

> the Labour Movement at times in local situations tended to neglect or to be rather contemptuous of Catholic interests. Catholics were penalised by deprivation of minor honours apparently simply on the ground that they were Catholics in local Labour Parties, and the apportionment of Parliamentary seats, even in constituencies with a preponderant Catholic vote to non-Catholics... showed that the Labour Movement were [sic] not as diplomatic in their handling of the Catholic vote as they might be.[6]

[5] Tom Gallagher, 'Scottish Catholics and the British Left, 1918–1939', *The Innes Review*, vol. 34, no. 1, Spring 1983, pp. 17–19.
[6] TUC, 'Catholic Aspect', 4 November 1936, report, p. 7.

Not only did Catholics feel that they lacked influence in the Labour Party commensurate to their contribution to it, they also feared the rise of an extremist and materialist left in many constituencies which, it was claimed, was seeking to force them out of the party altogether. There was particular friction on questions such as sectarian schooling, birth control clinics and cremation which emphasised the peculiarity of Catholic interests within the party.[7] The Spanish Civil War exposed this division even more starkly because from its outbreak the Catholic church and the labour movement were on opposing sides, with the Catholic hierarchy and press – to differing degrees – siding with the rebels as the saviours of Christianity in Spain. At the heart of the controversy, however, in Britain as elsewhere, was the spate of church burnings and atrocities which followed the military rising and were prominently reported in the Catholic and the populist press. The extent and brutality of these massacres cannot be underestimated: according to one authority some 13 bishops, 4,184 diocesan priests, 2,365 male religious and 283 religious sisters were killed.[8]

The atrocities took on a central importance because to many Catholic workers the question of Non-Intervention (the source of so much debate within the labour movement) was irrelevant so long as labour was perceived to be committed by its resolutions and by its Spanish Workers' Fund to giving political and financial support to an 'Anti-God', 'Red' government. Indeed, suspicion concerning the use that was being made of trade union and Labour Party funds persisted long after the Spanish government had re-established order in the Republican zone and begun to reopen the churches. The excesses of the first few months of the Civil War were, no matter how apologists sought to justify them,[9] an albatross around the neck of the foreign solidarity movement until the end of the war three years later. In the words of Bob Walsh, then editor of the monthly *Catholic Worker*:

> The Spanish Civil War was, I think, one of the most heart-rending things that the Catholic workers ever experienced, because of the numbers of priests and nuns who were killed, and the number of churches which were burnt down...religion was attacked, and that tended to make quite strongly

[7] *Catholic Worker*, October 1937; *Catholic Herald*, 22 October 1937.
[8] The source is A. Montero Moreno, *Historia de la persecución religiosa en España 1936–9* (Madrid, 1961), quoted in Frances Lannon, *Privilege, Persecution and Prophecy: The Catholic Church in Spain, 1875–1975* (Oxford, 1987), p. 201.
[9] The most common apologia for the church-burning was that the fascists had fired from the church roofs. George Elvin, who had recently returned from the Workers' Olympiad in Barcelona, claimed that 'it was for that and not for any anti-religious reason that all the churches in Barcelona except the cathedral were burnt' (*Manchester Guardian*, 27 July 1936). The classic rebuttal of this line is in George Orwell, *Homage to Catalonia* (Penguin edition), p. 52.

motivated workers, who normally never sided with anything that might be called fascism, pro-Franco.[10]

East End dockers admitted, when asked by the *Catholic Herald*, that had they been Spaniards they would have voted for the Spanish 'Labour Party' (i.e. the PSOE) 'because they were Trade Union men and always had been'. However, they would soon have changed their allegiance to Franco: 'As soon as it became clear that the Government was condoning the anti-Catholic outrages in Catalonia...it was time to withdraw their support from the Government, which although it represented their political principles was really out to destroy their Faith.'[11]

A further complication, however, was that the Catholic church was aware of the limitations on its authority over its members and overstated its case partly in a defensive reaction. It was ruefully observed that out of some 500,000 Catholic households only 200,000 received Catholic newspapers, so that in many quarters the 'lies' that Guernica had been bombed flat or that the Republican defenders of Badajoz had been massacred (which, in these cases happened to be the truth) went unchallenged.[12] Moreover, the claim that the Catholic press told the truth on Spain was gravely undermined by the zeal with which its version of the story was taken up by the Rothermere press, which enjoyed little respect amongst the working class after its atrocity stories during the First World War and which, more recently, had endorsed Mosley's Blackshirts. The interest shown by such a tainted source helps to explain how a journalist such as H.N. Brailsford could dismiss the Spanish atrocities as 'inventions' and 'legends'.[13] Thus, Catholic workers were being subjected to two contradictory versions of events in Spain. From many Catholic pulpits and most of the Catholic press came the view that Franco's rising was necessary to pre-empt a well-planned communist revolt against a spineless government, while the labour press portrayed the situation as a conflict between fascism and democracy within which the Spanish church, as opposed to Spanish Catholics, had been drawn into backing the wrong side to protect its vested interests.

In strongly Catholic parts of Britain the conflict between these two views was never satisfactorily resolved in the course of the war. Inevitably this conflict could not be limited to an abstract debate over events in a foreign country and both the Catholic church and the labour movement felt directly threatened by the course of the argument. The intervention by priests such

---

[10] Author's interview with Bob Walsh, 31 January 1985.
[11] *Catholic Herald*, 22 January 1937.   [12] *Catholic Herald*, 8 October 1937.
[13] *Reynolds' News*, 6 September 1936.

as Father Fallon of Bolton and Father Rockcliff of St Helens, who urged
trade union members to protest against 'the use of union money for the
purpose of helping the Red Army in Spain',[14] was clear interference in union
affairs. The *Catholic Times* ran an anti-communist column entitled 'Things
Red' which as late as 1938 was consistently publicising the cases of unions
which supported Spain and urging members to protest. When the NUDAW
conference sent a message of support to the Spanish government it
wrote – 'are the Catholic members of this union intending to raise no
protest at this message to the enemies of God, church and man which has
been sent in their name?'[15] In late 1938 *The Universe* campaigned against
the Co-operative Union's Milk for Spain scheme on the grounds that 'the
co-operative programme is one of the bases of General Franco's whole
programme of reconstruction,' and that the milk should, therefore, be given
to both sides.[16] The sudden interest of pulpit and press in the activities of
the labour movement seemed, from that side, like subversive meddling.

Seen from the other side, however, it could be argued that much of
labour's counter-propaganda came close to attacking Catholicism itself.
Labour sought to blacken the name of the Spanish hierarchy and to draw a
distinction between the bishops and the many ordinary Catholics fighting on
the government side, especially in the Basque country. Yet this subtle
distinction could easily be misconstrued as a more general criticism. William
Gillies informed a constituency agent worried by the impact of Catholic
propaganda on local members that the Spanish church was 'an instrument
of oppression, persecution and ignorance...it has its own party and its
political ideal is that of Austrian Clerical Fascism'.[17] The official NCL
pamphlet *The Drama of Spain, 1931–1936* blamed the church for being 'arm
in arm with the military against the poor. The church launched [a] fanatical
call to war against the Democratic state.'[18]

For many Catholics there was a feeling that the events in Spain were
ushering in a new wave of religious intolerance in Britain, legitimised by the
putative links between Catholicism and fascism. Indeed, many left-wingers
espoused an intolerant anti-Catholicism. The Scottish ILP journalist David
Murray, for instance, supported the Labour MP Josiah Wedgwood in his
campaign against that party's dependence on the 'Catholic vote'. Murray
had visited Spain immediately prior to the rising and had been horrified to
see a bottle of 'Virgin's Milk' on display in a monastery. 'People like that,'

---

[14] *Catholic Times*, 28 August 1936.   [15] *Catholic Times*, 6 May 1938.
[16] *Co-op News*, 26 November 1938, 10 December 1938, 17 December 1938.
[17] Labour Party archives, WG/SPA 128, 17 August 1936.
[18] *The Drama of Spain: 1931–36* (1936), p. 22.

he reflected, 'are incapable of political understanding.'[19] Later he offended local sensibilities in Motherwell when he termed pro-Franco sloganeers 'declassed degenerates'.[20] In October 1936 the Newcastle Trades Council passed a resolution expressing 'disgust with the attitude of the Roman Catholic press to the elected government in Spain' and calling on Catholic trade unionists to repudiate it. When Councillor Norman McCretton criticised this at the Federation of North-Eastern Trades Councils the Newcastle body unsuccessfully tried to force his resignation. Ultimately the Federation accepted a resolution 'regretting that the question of religious belief should be made a matter of Trade Union controversy'.[21]

The Catholic 'problem' amongst trade union and Labour Party members was one which, privately, gave their leaders great concern, not least because the atrocities were held to be the work of the anarchists rather than the section of the Spanish workers which they supported. Of course, the press did not respect such distinctions when apportioning responsibility for the massacres; nor did the Spanish labour leaders go very far in repudiating them. In September 1936, for instance, Pascual Tomás (UGT) had told an LSI/IFTU meeting that the massacres had occurred 'due to the combatant part played by the church'. The murdered priests had carried arms against the people.[22] Similarly, at the March 1937 International Conference, Manuel Cordero (PSOE) attempted to demonstrate that the Republic had not 'turned its back on religion. It has not persecuted religion.' However, 'we feel that distinction has to be made between religion as such and what I describe as clerical fanaticism in the political sphere'.[23] Yet, as early as 25 August 1936, Citrine was willing to recognise that there was more to the situation than a simple contest between democracy and fascism.

> His feeling was that there was atrocities on both sides...it was definitely our duty to protest against those atrocities whoever committed them. It could not be denied that churches had been burned and priests and nuns killed. He only knew that people felt stronger on religious questions than any other.[24]

This view was supported by George Gibson, the mental health workers' leader, who acknowledged that many people 'would be influenced by

[19] National Library of Scotland, David Murray Papers, Accs 7914, Box 3, 29 December 1937, Murray to Wedgwood.
[20] *Ibid.* ILP Motherwell Branch Papers, *The Guide*, February 1938, p. 2.
[21] *Catholic Times*, 30 October 1936; *Daily Herald*, 8 September 1936.
[22] TUC, Documents 2, 28 September 1936, LSI/IFTU meeting, verbatim report, p. 4.
[23] TUC, International Conference 1, verbatim report, p. 21.
[24] TUC, Documents 1, 25 August 1936, NCL, verbatim report, p. 44. The NCL made no formal protest against the atrocities.

religious beliefs rather than political opinions'.[25] Citrine was also aware that, throughout Europe as well as in the USA and Australia, Catholic influence was disrupting labour movement activities for Spain.[26]

In addition to genuine concern, however, the Catholic opposition also provided a convenient debating foil. When Citrine met a rank-and-file deputation on 21 December 1936 their main argument was that a mass campaign should now be launched amongst the unions. Citrine replied that:

> Less than two months ago we considered the question of a mass campaign. I suppose you all know that there is, even in the Transport & General Workers' Union, a considerable reaction from the Catholic elements?
> *Deputation*: We have defeated them.
> *Sir Walter*: I hope you are right.[27]

This was even more apparent at international labour movement meetings where British leaders tended to use the danger of antagonising their Catholic members as a trump card in defence of their actions and in opposition to taking more muscular action over Spain. Moreover, they spoke with a candour on this matter which had not been apparent at earlier meetings. On 4 December 1936 William Gillies defended Non-Intervention as the wisest course available, adding that 'as a repercussion of the events in Spain the Catholics in England were causing difficulties in the unions'. This sentiment was taken a step further by Citrine when he claimed to be able to discern 'the birth within the British Trade Union movement of Roman Catholicism as a political force'.[28] At the International Conference in March 1937 Bevin drew attention to the uphill task that they had faced in rallying an 'apathetic' public to support Spain.

> One very powerful organisation in the country was definitely in favour of Franco. That was the great Catholic organisation right throughout this country. In the Trade Union Movement, when we made grants to your fund very readily, we were met with internal difficulties within the Unions of a very serious character, and they had to be got over.[29]

Symptoms of the problem were apparent from an early stage. Within a month of the rising the *Daily Herald* had run an article by Bernard Sullivan (Secretary of the London Central Branch of the tailors' union and a

[25] TUC, Documents 1, 28 August 1936, Labour Movement Conference, verbatim report, p. 63.   [26] *Ibid.* p. 17.
[27] TUC, Documents 2, 21 December 1936, report of meeting with 'rank-and-file' delegation, p. 16.   [28] IISG Amsterdam, IFTU circulars for 1936, File no. 173, p. 6.
[29] TUC, International Conference 1, verbatim report, pp. 52–3.

Catholic) in reply to unpublished letters from disturbed Catholic readers. Subsequent correspondence was to show that he had failed to reassure many of them.[30] A week later the paper ran an editorial specifically on 'Catholics and Spain' in which it recorded its horror at the atrocities there. However, in an argument that was often to be repeated, it concluded that 'history will fix the responsibility for those destroyed churches and those dead priests on those political elements in Spanish Catholicism which have for many years linked themselves to the forces of darkness and despotism'.[31] Prior to this an editorial in the *Daily Worker* had condemned the atrocity stories as 'an appeal to the humanitarian and religious feeling of the British people, especially the Catholic element, to justify Hitler and Italian Intervention in Spain'.[32]

Electoral considerations clearly were important. Peter Drake has shown how the Labour Party had to direct special attention towards wavering Catholic voters during the Erdington (Birmingham) by-election campaign in October 1936.[33] One informed correspondent noted that Herbert Morrison had 'played up nobly' on behalf of Spain on the NEC, but that 'he won't take any public action until the LCC elections [of March 1937] are over – because of the Catholic vote'.[34] In the most extreme case some Catholic Labour Party councillors, who had been 'de-selected' by their party in Camberwell on account of pro-Franco activities, formed a 'Constitutional Labour Party' which polled some 4,000 votes in the local elections of November 1937.[35] However, the 'Catholic vote' was surprisingly absent from the crucial debates over Non-Intervention in the summer and autumn of 1936, the only real reference being Dalton's comment that 'I am trying to interpret the state of mind of the great mass who voted for us,

---

[30] *Daily Herald*, 22 and 28 August 1936.   [31] *Ibid.* 27 August 1936.
[32] *Daily Worker*, 11 August 1936.
[33] Peter Drake, 'Labour and Spain; British Labour's Response to the Spanish Civil War, with particular reference to the Labour Movement in Birmingham', MLitt, University of Birmingham, 1977, pp. 32 and ff; p. 99.
[34] Churchill College, Cambridge, Noel-Baker papers, NBKR 4/660, letter to Noel-Baker, January 1937. (Signature illegible – possibly Susan Johnson.)
[35] *Catholic Times*, 22 October 1937, 5 November 1937; *South London Observer*, 13 October 1937. The trouble stemmed from the participation of Councillor Egan at a meeting to raise funds in order to rebuild an altar to the English martyrs in Madrid that had been destroyed during the revolutionary unrest at the beginning of the Civil War. According to Egan, a Labour Borough Councillor for twelve years and Chairman of the LCC Works Committee: 'The only question to be considered in connection with the Spanish war is not whether Franco stands for Fascism and Labour for Communism, but which will save religion from extinction. And the only thing we know for certain is that under Franco Catholicism will be allowed to live.' Subsequently Egan, along with his wife and three others, was 'deselected' as a Councillor by North Camberwell Labour party (*Catholic Herald*, 5 March 1937, 17 September 1937; *The Tablet*, 18 September 1937).

including the Catholics. They would not support a policy of going to war directly in respect of the Spanish Comrades.'[36] In contrast, the threat of division in the unions was mentioned much more frequently and openly, and it was here that the Catholic reaction was felt most painfully.

At the Labour Party conference in October 1936 George Hicks said that:

> Inside our own Movement, one would imagine that we would be united to see that everything should be done to supply the Spanish Government with arms, but we have had certain of our Unions definitely challenged by some who have said that the funds which have been raised for relief of the victims of the Civil War have been utilised for arms for Spain. There has been a big division in some of our Unions, and a number of them have resolutions to say that we are intervening on behalf of people who are atheistic and who have engaged in a good deal of religious persecution to which they are opposed. I beg you to think of that when you are examining this problem, if you are going to give the National Council any help in this matter.[37]

These comments reflected the experience of many trade union executives which, in the autumn of 1936, faced vigorous, if largely unco-ordinated, opposition both to grants being given from union funds, and, even, to union funds being used to pay for voluntary appeals at branch level. In late 1936, for instance, the executive of the National Union of Seamen had decided not to partake in a fund-raising scheme due to 'the hostility to such grants made by members of various unions in this country, and the hostility which might be shown within our own ranks by many members, chiefly on religious grounds'.[38] Similarly, an official of the postal workers' union complained to the TUC of 'criticism, particularly from Catholic members of the union who object to the Workers' Party in Spain on religious grounds', and he sought confirmation that the 'right' people were receiving aid.[39] The mental health workers' union generated an 'avalanche' of hostile correspondence from Catholic members when it published an appeal for the NCL Fund, even though it protested that the Civil War was 'not a Communist Revolution... [nor] a fight between religious and irreligious sections of the Spanish people'.[40] Even when unions sought to counter these attacks they often did so half-heartedly. The Railway Clerks Association ran a full-page article in reply to its Catholic critics, but tamely concluded that: 'We support the Spanish Government not because we wholly agree with it, but

---

[36] TUC, Documents 2, 28 October 1936, Labour Movement Conference, verbatim report, p. 36.   [37] *LPCR*, 1936, p. 178.
[38] MRC, ITF records, Mss 159/3/C/6/3, Spence to Fimmen, 20 January 1937.
[39] TUC, Fund 1, 8 September 1936, Paterson to Tewson.
[40] *Mental Hospital and Institutional Workers' Journal*, September–November 1936; MRC, Mss 229/NA/1/1/5, MHIWU National Executive Council minutes, 7–8 October 1936.

because it holds office as the result of an election much freer than Spain has been accustomed to.'[41]

By this time union leaders had had an opportunity to digest the bitter experience of the Civil Service Clerical Association (CSCA), one of whose Catholic members took the Executive to court for granting £100 to the NCL appeal from union funds, on the grounds that this was *ultra vires*. Although this litigation was unsuccessful it highlighted the fact that the use of trade union funds was governed by rules and answerable to the membership. Thus, in challenging the Spanish Workers' Fund, the precise objectives of which were often left deliberately vague, Catholic workers were asking a valid question and, indeed, one which they shared with the left-wing rank and file.[42] If, as the leaders contended in reply to the Catholic critics, the appeal was purely for humanitarian purposes and not intended to support the Spanish government, then the left was bound to wonder what was the point of contributing to it.

Catholic opposition was most visible in the less political craft unions and the unions which had grown most rapidly in the inter-war period (particularly amongst unions organising the 'black-coated' labour force) which lacked the political traditions of older established unions.[43] In such unions specifically Catholic objections could dovetail with the objections of apolitical non-Catholics. The publication of an article in support of the Spanish Republic by E.J. Williams MP in the journal of the Bank Officers' Guild provoked a backlash from members who feared that the union's non-political and non-sectarian stance had been abused.[44] Some Catholic workers felt that their position within their union was compromised because a labour movement which had traditionally turned a blind eye to religious differences was now giving support to what they felt to be an anti-Catholic cause. For example, the Executive of the Typographical Association raised a storm of protest by issuing a leaflet on Spain in its journal. Yet the criticism centred not on the leaflet's contents but on the grounds that members of the association who 'fondly imagined that they belonged to an organisation

---

[41] *Railway Service Journal*, December 1936.
[42] See above, p. 142, fn 16; Tom Buchanan, DPhil thesis, chapter 7, pp. 241–7.
[43] The draughtsmen's union (AESD) received branch resolutions condemning a grant to the NCL Fund (*The Draughtsman*, October and November 1936). There were lengthy correspondences on this issue in the journals of the National Union of Clerks, the Typographical Association and the Amalgamated Society of Woodworkers. Although one might have expected to find evidence of Catholic discontent in the general unions organising unskilled workers, it should be remembered that unions such as the T&GWU and NUGMW provided little formal opportunity for any expression of members' opinions, especially those which were critical of official policy – see chapter 6 below.
[44] MRC, Mss 56/4/1, *The Bank Officer*, November 1936–January 1937.

where every shade of political and religious opinion was represented would have had their opinions rudely shattered'.[45] This perception helped to stimulate the movement for Catholic Guilds as a complement to official trade unionism.[46]

However, in the absence of any general means of organising Catholics within the trade union movement such as the post-1945 Association of Catholic Trades Unionists,[47] such resistance was localised and, beyond writing to the union journal or attempting to pass a branch resolution, there was no further recourse open to Catholic other than dramatically tearing up their union cards. There were, however, economic considerations to be born in mind here, and this form of protest was relatively rare.[48] The same considerations did not apply so pressingly to Labour Party and Co-operative movement membership and there some Catholics – supported by elements in the Catholic press – began to reconsider whether their future lay with these organisations at all. The populist weekly *The Catholic Times* was from the beginning strongly critical of labour's support for the Spanish government, arguing that labour fought communists in Britain but made common cause with them abroad, and it warned that 'if there is not more caution at Labour HQ there will be no more Catholic support for Labour at the polls'.[49] Subsequently it claimed that Attlee and Noel-Baker, on the strength of their statements on Spain, were 'British Kerenskys...bringing the whole Labour movement in this country under the suspicion of being nothing better than a preparation for Red Government'.[50] Nonsensical as this may now sound, the suggestion that labour leaders were at all 'soft on communism' was a damaging one as it struck at one of the main justifications for the Catholic hierarchy's toleration of the labour movement, the assumption that it was a natural ally against communism.

Thus, in the immediate aftermath of the military rising there was the potential for a damaging split. Yet the two main institutions involved, the Catholic church and the TUC, both found this prospect profoundly unwelcome. The TUC had always placed a premium on unity at all costs; the Catholic hierarchy despite its acute differences over Spain, still saw the

---

45 MRC, Mss 39A/TA/4/1/67, *Typographical Circular*, August 1938.
46 See below, pp. 190–1.
47 See R.H. Butterworth, 'The Structure of some Catholic Lay Organisations in Australia and Great Britain', Oxford DPhil, 1959, chapters 8 and 9.
48 In January 1937 the General Secretary of the postal workers' union reported that the union had suffered sixty-five resignations, including the whole staff at Margate and many women telephonists, in protests at a grant to the Spanish Workers' Fund which were 'for the most part on a religious basis' (MRC, Mss 148, UPW Executive Council minutes, 20–1 January 1937, p. 131).   49 *Catholic Times*, 31 July 1936.
50 *Catholic Times*, 14 August 1936.

trade union movement of Citrine and Bevin (even if not the Labour Party) as the most acceptable political representative of the Catholic workers and a bulwark between the British working class and communism. At the same time, the hierarchy must have feared that many Catholics would not obey a demand to withdraw from the labour movement. Thus, some form of reconciliation was mutually desirable and the result was a meeting between a delegation of Catholics prominent in the labour movement and Archbishop Hinsley in October 1936. It is fortunate that a very full account of this meeting survives, compiled by one of the participants, Dr H.B. Morgan, the TUC Medical Advisor and President of the Spanish Medical Aid Committee.[51] Morgan's account shows that the meeting arose from Hinsley's attendance at a Ben Tillett memorial dinner, and certain observations which he made there. Following this a representative body of Catholics associated with the labour movement was chosen to form a delegation by Mr Young, the Buckingham Palace telephonist, and Mr Peacock, the Secretary of the National Trade Union Club. Accompanying them were Miss Somers, a London Labour Party organiser, Tom O'Brien, General Secretary of the theatrical employee's union (NATE) and Bernard Sullivan of the tailors' union (NUTGW). Morgan adds that they were joined by an unnamed member of the T&GWU waiting for them at Archbishop's House, though other sources show that this was Mr F.J. Lavery of the Catholic Transport Guild.[52] His presence is interesting because it suggests that Hinsley was attempting to insinuate the Catholic Guilds, with which he was closely associated, into the 'official' labour movement.

The meeting had before it a document compiled by O'Brien which made the case for those labour movement Catholics who were alarmed by the attitude of the Catholic press and hierarchy on Spain. Firstly, he argued that the atrocities of the early stages of the Civil War had been used by certain newspapers to alienate Catholic workers from the labour movement, and he saw a political motive in this – 'an attempt to connect the orthodox labour movement to communism'. Secondly, many felt that the current situation was the fault of Franco and his allies who used the menace of communism as an excuse for their rising. Thirdly, many Catholic workers felt that the Spanish church was participating in the rising to defend its wealth and that it opposed the Spanish government on economic rather than spiritual grounds. Fourthly, it was felt that the Spanish church had not done enough to remedy the oppression of the Spanish workers and to implement Catholic social teachings. Fifthly, O'Brien claimed that the impression was growing

[51] TUC, Catholic Aspect. Most of the following is based on Morgan's report to Citrine, dated 4 November 1936.   [52] *Catholic Herald*, 6 November 1936.

that the Vatican was aligning itself with fascism against communism. Finally, there was a general feeling that the Spanish government was legitimate, and the time was coming 'when the consciences of Catholics are seriously perturbed as to whether their loyalty to their church and to their Trade Unions and political party are being violated'.[53]

However, for the first hour of the interview Hinsley, in Morgan's words, 'dilated on the communist menace, and his main theme was that communism was a menace to the world which the Catholic Church intended to oppose with all the means at its disposal'. He gave his own version of recent Spanish history, quoting from an allegedly authentic communist document which purported to show that the communists had been planning a revolution in Spain. Moreover, he claimed that the 1936 Spanish election had not returned a representative government, and 'he spoke as if the Premier, Caballero, was definitely acknowledged as a firm communist'. As an aside, 'he stated that he hated the word "proletariat" because it suggested a pagan atmosphere, and the word rather tended to refer to the workers of continental countries as if they were buck negroes from Jamaica'. Hinsley concluded by saying that Spanish democracy was being used as a cloak for the establishment of bolshevism. He denied that the Catholic church in Spain was wealthy and even claimed that, 'previous to the last Government 97% of the Priests were republicans'.

There then followed a 'frank, courageous and unrestricted' discussion. Delegates put the view that there was nothing new in the document which Hinsley had quoted from – this was, they felt, the familiar communist policy which they had resisted for years. The Archbishop was moved to admit that this was 'a source of pride' for the labour movement and that he regarded it as 'quite legitimate, and indeed essential for all workers to be in their appropriate Trade Unions, and quite sound for any Catholic so inclined to be a member of the Labour Party'. When pressed he condemned fascism as vigorously as he had condemned communism. Delegates then drew Hinsley's attention to extreme reactionary utterances in the Catholic press and from the pulpit. In one particular case, in the same Catholic church on the same Sunday, using the same text of the Good Samaritan, two Catholic priests of a preaching order preached entirely different sermons. The Prior of the order in the morning service had supported the rebels and gone so far as to eulogise the *Daily Mail*, while in the evening a well-known broad-minded priest had preached a sermon supporting the Spanish government and democracy.

---

[53] Copy of O'Brien's statement in TUC, Catholic Aspect file. O'Brien's personal views on the Civil War were often more ambiguous – see below p. 189

Finally, the meeting discussed ways of opening lines of communication between working-class Catholics and the church authorities. Hinsley approved of the idea of a 'Catholic Workers' Council' or 'Advisory Catholic Council' so long as it was genuinely representative, and stressed his willingness to meet and talk with such a body. He was less keen on the idea of a 'Catholic Labour League' working within the labour movement, for, while he recognised the need to organise the Catholic workers, 'he was afraid that it might lead to a certain amount of segregation and ostracism to the Catholic worker'. Crucially, Hinsley put the case very strongly that Catholics should remain within their organisations and not leave them because 'that would mean that the enemies of the church would remain in possession'.

A somewhat different version of events appeared in the *Catholic Herald* and, indeed, Morgan's memorandum grew out of the fact that there was no press release following the meeting and that unofficial – and con- flicting – reports trickled out into the Catholic and labour press.[54] This account stressed that the deputation had no official mandate from the labour movement and that it had accepted Hinsley's views on the situation in Spain. The article went on to say that Hinsley had reiterated the right, if not the duty, for Catholics to stay in their unions 'to circumscribe the influence of Communism'.[55] Where the two accounts differ most sharply is that the paper claimed that Hinsley's view was that the time was 'not opportune' to set up a consultative committee. In the same copy of the *Catholic Herald* the editor responded to a statement, similar to O'Brien's, submitted by a Catholic on the Executive of Reading Labour Party. He concluded that an English Catholic had 'a perfect right' to wish to see the traditions of the British labour movement applied to Spain. However, where the choice lay between communism and a corporative state run by a Catholic dictator the immediate choice was obvious.

Although the meeting was essentially an unofficial discussion, to allay fears and establish communications, it is clear that both sides sought to differ amicably on Spain and in this they were helped by being able to restate a joint opposition to communism which allowed a partial veil to be drawn over the points of conflict. This process bore fruit for the Labour Party when the *Catholic Times*, formerly harshly critical, showed a marked change in attitude, stating in an editorial of 6 November 1936 that:

---

[54] TUC, Catholic Aspect, Morgan to Tewson, 10 February 1937.
[55] *Catholic Herald*, 6 November 1936. Internal evidence suggests that this account was written by Lavery of the Catholic Transport Guild.

> To our minds Labour has made a mistake [on Spain], but we recognise that an error of judgement is not proof of bad faith. Labour has not forfeited its right to Catholic support. It continues to share in that watchful tolerance which we accord to all recognised parties ... Catholic Labour men can do good service ... by making known the true facts about the Spanish crisis to all members of the party.

It added that those who had been considering leaving their organisations on the issue of grants to Spain should now wait until their bishops told them to leave. This intervention was particularly useful to the Labour Party coming in the middle of the Greenock by-election campaign and, in the opinion of the *Manchester Guardian* correspondent, 'scotched' an attempt by the Liberal National [government] candidate to start a 'Red scare over Spain in a constituency with many Catholic voters'.[56]

While the 'consultative committee' idea appears to have been taken no further, the links established ultimately led to consultations between the Catholic church and the TUC at the highest level. In late December 1936 Dr Morgan informed Citrine that he had sent Hinsley copies of official NCL publications on Spain, on the strength of which the Archbishop now wanted to meet Citrine to point out certain errors in the literature.[57] On the following day Citrine received a letter from Hinsley himself, laying out his objections to the pamphlets in question, *The Drama of Spain* and *Catholics and the Civil War in Spain* by the London-based Spanish socialist Ramos Oliveira. He objected in particular to the charge of 'Vaticanist Fascism' in Spain, to Acción Popular being dubbed 'the church's political party', and the insinuation that the church was in some way responsible for the actions of Gil Robles and the CEDA. Hinsley called for the former pamphlet to be withdrawn as an erroneous attack which 'cannot fail to have a prejudicial effect against the [Labour] party upon the Catholic masses in England'. However, he had prefaced his remarks by pointing out that the Catholic church in England had 'always tried to forestall any attempt to create conflict between the lawful political and religious allegiances of the faithful', hinting that a truce should now be observed.[58]

Citrine referred these criticisms to Dr Morgan who concluded that, while there was some validity in them, there was no basis for the withdrawal of the publications so long as the Catholic press continued to produce such a biassed view of events in Spain. He felt that it was important for the

---

[56] *Manchester Guardian*, 20 November 1936 and 28 November 1936.
[57] TUC, Catholic Aspect, Morgan to Citrine, 21 December 1936.
[58] *Ibid.* Hinsley to Citrine, 22 December 1936.

Catholic leaders to be made aware of the effect of the Catholic papers supporting Franco which were perceived as having official sanction in the eyes of ordinary people.[59] Subsequently, on 3 February 1937, Citrine met Hinsley and – in Citrine's account – satisfied him that the labour movement did not condone attacks upon religion and that 'he had always endeavoured to exclude sectarian bitterness from its midst'. He added that the disputed pamphlets were a riposte to the bias in the Catholic press and went so far as to apologise for the 'absence of distinction' in *The Drama of Spain*. Hinsley for his part expressed his sympathy for the labour movement – in his original letter to Citrine he had written that, though no politician, he 'should favour Labour being the son of a working man'[60] – and said that he did not want to see divisions between Catholicism and labour.[61] Citrine presented a copy of his *I Search for Truth in the USSR* to Hinsley, for which the Archbishop wrote to thank him, adding: 'I admire your courage and manly straightforwardness.'[62]

The upshot of this episode was that, while both parties maintained their support for opposite sides until the end of the Civil War, these personal meetings allowed the leaders to recognise the common interests that united them. As a sequel the Catholic church and the labour movement co-operated in the operation to care for Basque refugee children from May 1937 onwards. The idea of the Basque Children's Committee was to set up a non-political, humanitarian relief programme behind which all groups could unite. However, the rather unhappy story of Catholic participation in the committee, which ended with the withdrawal of the Archbishop's delegate and his subsequent support for a committee campaigning for the children's repatriation, shows that the whole question of Spain had, by this time, become so emotionally charged that it was impossible to depoliticise any single aspect of the relief work.[63]

Although it is relatively straightforward to chart the immediate political ramifications of the conflict of loyalties amongst working-class Catholics over Spain, it is harder to give an accurate account of the dimensions of this phenomenon. However, this is important when assessing the effect of

---

[59] *Ibid.* Morgan to Citrine, memorandum, 9 January 1937.
[60] *Ibid.* Hinsley to Citrine, 22 December 1936.
[61] *Ibid.* report of interview, 4 February 1937.
[62] *Ibid.* Hinsley to Citrine, 4 February 1937. However, Hinsley continued to complain about *The Drama of Spain*. Speaking at the annual dinner of the London Catholic Transport Guild he said that 'I protest and shall continue to protest more vigorously still against that unfair use of a pamphlet by a political party, many of whose members profess the Catholic faith' (*Catholic Times*, 12 February 1937).
[63] See Tom Buchanan, 'The Role of the British Labour Movement in the Origins and Work of the Basque Children's Committee', pp. 170–1.

Catholic workers' opinion during the whole course of the Civil War. At the meeting in November 1936 both sides had claimed to represent the views of Catholic workers and, presumably, both could provide evidence to support their claim. However, in assessing the scope of the problem there is an immediate difficulty with sources – after all, it was in the interests of the Catholic press to publicise cases of workers' disaffection with labour policy in Spain. Thus, the following account of the problems the labour movement encountered on the local level is drawn mostly from non-Catholic sources. This evidence shows that working-class Catholic discontent with labour over Spain was deep-seated and long-term, and that Labour Party politicians were unwilling to confront the issue politically so long as they felt that they could count on the Catholic vote at the polls. Discontent did, however, diverge from the very active forms discussed earlier, which had largely ended by mid-1937, and this change perhaps reflected the fading impact of the atrocities of 1936 (although the Catholic press did its best to keep their memory fresh). In fact, one of the most striking features of the whole episode is the manner in which a union such as the postal workers could provoke a torrent of criticism from its Catholic members for a £100 grant in the autumn of 1936 and yet grant £500 a year later with barely a murmur of protest.[64] On the national level, one sees the irony of the labour movement coming under attack when it was, in fact, supporting Non-Intervention and failing to mount a significant campaign over Spain, while the adoption in mid-1937 of a policy of more committed support failed to generate much criticism.

Some of the best sources are the reports of the Registration Agents for parliamentary constituencies where the candidates were sponsored by the Manchester-based union NUDAW. In December 1936 Mr Kettle, Agent for Westhoughton, gave a list of possible factors in the defeat in the Preston by-election. These were mainly organisational, but the final one was that 'It is probable that in a town with so large a Catholic population the last minute exploitation of the Spanish situation had a damaging effect on our chances by inducing a number of abstentions'.[65] This assessment corresponded to the prophecy of a Tory MP in the Commons that the Labour Party had 'thrown Preston to the lions' – the by-election would show that 'christian people will stand up and do all they can to fight the Anti-Christs of Spain'.[66]

In January 1937 Mr Griffin, the Agent of another Lancashire constituency, St Helens, wrote that:

---

[64] See Tom Buchanan, DPhil thesis, chapter 9, p. 256.
[65] USDAW archives, NUDAW Political General Secretary's Reports to the Executive, 1936, p. 112.   [66] *Hansard*, 5th series, vol. 316, 29 October 1936, col. 128.

The issues of Spain have deeply disturbed large groups of our Roman Catholic supporters, and of course it is generally known that St Helens has a very large Catholic population. It must be realised that the Catholics of this and of other towns are hearing from certain sources an incessant propaganda against the heroic defenders of Spanish democracy. A great number of small, informal, impromptu meetings have been held inside the clubs in which true perspective is given to the realities of the Spanish peninsular, and I really believe that our efforts are meeting with success. Quiet presentation of fact and argument is meeting with a reward which would be lost to violent declamation, and our Catholic friends are lessening their opposition to the Loyalist forces, and are increasingly appreciative of the menace of what a Fascist victory in Spain would mean.[67]

In February and March he noticed an improvement in the situation with a 'satisfactory' attendance at a showing of the film *Defence of Madrid*, but in April Griffin was disheartened by addressing five trade union branches which

enabled me to see just what effect unscrupulous use by our opponents of the Spanish issue had on the average Trade Unionist. I can confidently state that whilst mis-representation in a matter of this sort cannot be without some effect in a place such as St Helens, it is also clear that our position is winning support from quarters which only a few weeks ago were terribly puzzled and confused. A large amount of rebuilding work is still required, but it is going on.[68]

In May, however, the rebuilding took a knock when Councillor O'Brien resigned from the local party for 'unspecified reasons' which the Agent assumed to be Labour policy over Spain, and the party had to hold four meetings in areas where his influence was strongest to stop the rot.[69] However, despite the opposition's use of the 'Spain factor' in a council by-election, the issue was declining in potency by late 1937[70] while by July 1938 O'Brien had rejoined the party and party members had rallied round to raise money to send an ambulance to Republican Spain.[71] In other areas, however, problems clearly persisted into 1938, as in his first report for the newly-adopted Rutherglen Division (in Glasgow) Mr J. Dean wrote that:

There is a very large Catholic vote in this constituency. On purely 'bread and butter' issues they are with us, but it is obvious to me that their feelings on the Spanish question are being played upon by the Tory machine. It is a most difficult situation to handle, but my view is that it would be folly to endanger democracy in this country by unnecessarily alienating people who have voted

---

[67] USDAW archives, NUDAW Political General Secretary's Reports to the Executive, 1937, p. 6.   [68] *Ibid.* 1937, pp. 13, 27, 33 and 34.   [69] *Ibid.* 1937, p. 40.
[70] *Ibid.* 1937, pp. 52 and 92.   [71] *Ibid.* 1938, p. 82.

Labour for years. Bitterness must be avoided whatever happens, and while Labour stands by the Spanish Government we must not arouse antagonism by showing impatience or disrespect to the other fellow's viewpoint.[72]

However, with the Spanish Republic facing defeat he was able to report that local activity for Spain had massively intensified in February 1939 – 'every affiliated body is selling tickets for the Scottish Food Ship'.[73]

Further evidence of the problems encountered in Lancashire is furnished by the Labour Party NEC minutes, with the analysis of the 1938 local election results. The report drew attention to the party's poor showing in Lancashire with a net loss of seventeen seats. The organisational sub-committee of the regional council gave pride of place to the Spanish factor in its list of reasons for this setback. 'The party's policy on Spain reacted unfavourably throughout the county. The effect varied from place to place but in some boroughs was of a very serious character.' In addition the Secretary of Bootle Trades and Labour Council wrote that, due to the sectarianism of Merseyside politics, Labour now only controlled the mainly Catholic wards and that 'in the wards which are mainly non-Catholic we have lost the Catholics because of the help given to Republican Spain. This has not affected the vote in the Catholic wards, because these wards have not participated in our "Aid for Spain" efforts.'[74]

Thus, the problem was a localised one, limited by the very nature of Catholic working-class distribution in Britain, but even more damaging in that Catholics were often most concentrated where the labour movement was strongest. A good example of this is Glasgow, stronghold of the ILP. Tom Gallagher has argued that the Civil War had 'a destructive effect on the fabric of politics in the West of Scotland' and that a collapse of electoral support for the Labour Party was only averted because, with Liberalism defunct and Conservatism perceived as anti-Catholic, there was no alternative.[75] In September 1936 the ILP's *New Leader* reported how the previous week's ILP Spanish Flag Day there had been met with organised hostility which it blamed on *Daily Mail* and *Daily Express* propaganda whipping up the feelings of Catholic workers. It concluded ruefully that

we regret the innocence of the religious folks who can be convinced by capitalist organs that the Spanish workers are an unruly mob, beset on murder, desecration and vandalism. But it is there, and it means more work for Socialists to press home the truth. For the present we must try to understand the Catholic people while disagreeing.[76]

---

[72] *Ibid.* 1938, p. 82.   [73] *Ibid.* 1939, p. 30.
[74] Labour Party NEC minutes, 23–24 November 1938, p. 467.
[75] Tom Gallagher, 'Scottish Catholics and the British Left, 1918–1939', pp. 35–7.
[76] *New Leader*, 4 September 1936.

The ILP experienced similar disruption in Fife, the seat held by the only Communist Party MP William Gallacher. John McNair reported to David Murray in November 1936 that

> I had 3 meetings in Fifeshire which, the local comrades were good enough to tell me, were successful, but there was a strong Catholic opposition. I understand that Gallacher's meetings in his constituency, which borders Cowdenbeath, were broken up by Catholics. While I was speaking I realised the force of the opposition and its effectiveness as it was led by a local priest, who was no fool, and the secretary of the Young Catholics League...I expect the same opposition again and am naturally collecting material so that the documentation which you have sent me is distinctly useful.[77]

The situation in Glasgow placed local ILP MPs such as John McGovern, himself a Catholic, in a difficult position, and when attacked by the Glasgow Secretary of the Ancient Order of Hibernians for organising the Flag Day he replied, 'I think your condemnation of church burning is quite proper, but your antagonism to collecting funds is quite wrong and I cannot support it.'[78] Subsequently McGovern was sent to Spain by the ILP with a special brief to investigate the role of the church in the Spanish struggle, returning to publish the pamphlet *Why Bishops Back Franco* which claimed to disprove the atrocity stories – 'the truth is that the Spanish Government has shown the greatest consideration to the nuns, providing them with escorts to the frontier and free passes'.[79] His overall conclusion, that the Catholic church in Spain had become 'an institution of Capitalist ownership and exploitation' and that 'the Fascist movement had its birth in the church', was unacceptable to many Catholic workers'.[80] On his return McGovern proceeded to propagandise his views with a series of meetings in Glasgow and London which drew a hostile Catholic reception, in one case marshalled by a Labour LCC Councillor.[81] For McGovern the religious issue had become the crucial one, as he saw it as a test for the fight against fascist propaganda. In the words of his Barcelona Radio broadcast prior to his departure from Spain.

[77] NLS, David Murray Papers, Accs 7914, Box 3, 4 November 1936, McNair to Murray. On 30 October 1936 Murray had written to Murray concerning the 'religious bogey' in the west of Scotland, and had sent McNair his translation of Aguirre's speech in the Spanish Cortes on this question.   [78] *New Leader*, 16 October 1936.

[79] *New Leader*, 11 December 1936. Interestingly his 1960 autobiography *Neither Fear Nor Favour* bears no mention of the vital religious dimension of his visit to Spain, presenting it as a neo-Orwellian investigation into the horrors of Stalinism (the subject which dominated his second visit to Spain in 1938).

[80] John McGovern, *Why Bishops Back Franco*, pp. 7 and 9.

[81] *New Leader*, 19 March 1937 and 26 March 1937.

No-one now has any excuse for being deluded by the lying propaganda of the rebel radio stations, the Fascist press and the *Daily Mail* ... we in Great Britain, and especially in Glasgow have had more than our share of that propaganda from vile gutter papers using and exploiting the Roman Catholic religion for their own material gain.[82]

However, McGovern was rare amongst ILP and Labour MPs in attempting to tackle his Catholic critics head-on, and his case highlights the lack of any coherent stance on Spain by Catholics prominent in the labour movement. In practice there were four main options open to them, of which the first was the outspoken defence of the Spanish Republic adopted by McGovern. This effectively placed the blame for the atrocities on the Spanish church. Albert Wall, Secretary of London Trades Council, convinced himself that the burning of churches was justified on the grounds that they 'ceased to be sacred' if used by the rebels.[83] The busmen's leader Bert Papworth, who visited Spain in January 1937 reported to a mass meeting on his return that he had 'as a Catholic satisfied himself that the democratically elected Government of Spain were not making war on the church'. He had gone out of his way to investigate this question and was shown 'the measures that had been taken to preserve the Tabernacle, the Host and the Vessels intact'.[84] Monica Whatley, the LCC councillor for Limehouse, visited Spain twice during the Civil War (once with a mixed Protestant and Catholic church delegation) and played a prominent role in challenging the official Catholic line on the conflict. This naturally made her the subject of sustained attacks in the Catholic press, forcing her to comment that 'they hate beyond anything that a practising Catholic should support the democratic government of Spain and dare to state that atrocities are a necessary part of the savagery of war'.[85]

A second position was outspoken defence of the Spanish church which identified the Republic with the 'Reds', although examples of this were very rare. In January 1937 David Logan, Labour MP for the Liverpool 'Scotland' constituency, claimed to speak for 90 per cent of his co-religionists in condemning the outrages as 'scandalous'. He asked in a parliamentary question whether

it is a civilised state of society in any land when 50 or 60 nuns can be killed, and 10 bishops who had no fight in them except to fight for the Vatican, which

[82] *New Leader*, 11 December 1936.   [83] *Daily Herald*, 14 August 1936.
[84] *The Record*, February 1937.
[85] See 'What I Saw in Spain' in *Forward*, 1 May 1937. Other important articles by Whatley were in the *Daily Worker* and the *Daily Herald*, both 27 August 1936. The church delegation included Anglicans (the Dean of Canterbury, the Rev. Iredell), Catholics and Free Churchmen (*New Statesman and Nation*, 17 April 1937).

of course is abhorrent these days, or some monk saying paternoster, that they had to be wiped out in the wonderful cause of freedom.[86]

At the 1936 TUC Congress Miss Bertha Quinn of the tailors' union claimed that if free institutions had existed in Spain, as they existed in Britain due to the trade union movement, then the military rising would not have happened. However, the rebel army had been provoked – 'That great outrages have been perpetrated in Spain cannot be challenged from this platform. Red outrages have been perpetrated in Spain.'[87] At her own union's conference a year later she registered her protest at a resolution of fraternal greetings to Spanish trade unionists, much to the delight of the Catholic press who contrasted her to the 'weak-kneed Catholics' holding official positions in the labour movement.[88]

Such frankness was, however, unusual and other leaders who wished to express their doubts tended to speak in more coded terms. For instance at the 1937 TUC Tom O'Brien of NATE decried the 'conspiracy of hypocrisy' over Spain. He felt that he spoke for many in the labour movement who felt that, whatever the outcome of the Civil War, 'democracy will not be the state of society enjoyed in that country for very many days to come'.[89] Yet, however he couched his comments there was little sympathy for his opinions, and as a well-known active Catholic his interventions were inevitably regarded as pro-Franco. At the STUC in April 1937 his defence of Non-Intervention because 'Spanish workers on both sides were offering their blood' was immediately seized upon by an opponent who said that O'Brien had 'revealed himself' as pro-Franco by his comment – 'there was sufficient opposition to peace in the press without having to face it in their own ranks'.[90]

Yet a final, and most popular, position was one of quiescence. F. O'Hanlon, the Chairman of Chichester Divisional Labour Party, had been appalled by the attitude of the Catholic hierarchy to the Civil War and drew up a letter calling on the bishops to denounce the Spanish rebels. However, he was only able to secure the signature of one out of eight Catholic Labour MPs that he approached (David Adams of Newcastle) and two LCC Councillors (Monica Whatley and J.H. MacDonnell). This confirmed his view that the 'reactionary' Catholic hierarchy had been allowed to succeed

[86] *Hansard*, vol. 319, 19 January 1937, cols. 141–5.   [87] *TUC CR*, 1936, p. 432.
[88] *Catholic Times*, 20 August 1937; Miss Quinn was a Labour Councillor in Leeds. The tailors' union was dominated by Catholics in the Leeds branch and when the union launched a campaign to send clothes to Spain the General Secretary met 'unexpected opposition' from that quarter (TUC, Fund 1, 11 January 1937, Conley to Tewson).
[89] *TUC CR*, 1937, p. 274.   [90] STUC *Annual Report*, 1937, p. 146.

because 'the Catholic Labour leaders have utterly failed to lead or even to make any protest'.[91]

One consequence of the absence of any clear Catholic leadership on Spain within the labour movement was a boost to Catholic self-organisation, particularly evident in the unions where this period saw the expansion of Catholic Vocational Guilds alongside established unions in sectors such as printing, transport, the Civil Service and shop work. They reflected dissatisfaction with the established Catholic leaders in the labour movement and the perception that the movement attached no value to a specifically Catholic point of view. Some guilds had been formed in the 1920s and were subsequently designated as organisations for the religious and moral training of Catholic trade unionists, in accordance with Pope Pius XI's encyclical *Quadragesimo Anno* (1931).[92] Numbers remained fairly small, however – the London busmen's guild, one of the longest established, claimed a membership of only 500 in 1937.[93]

The Catholic church was keen to stress that the guilds were not envisaged as Minority Movements rivalling the existing union structure, although informal support was given to Catholic activists in union elections.[94] However, the vast differences between the Catholic church and the labour movement over Spain made such a distinction especially difficult to maintain. For instance, in September 1936 the Manchester Catholic Transport Guild passed a resolution condemning the T&GWU £1,000 grant to the 'Spanish Red Government'.[95] Similarly, in 1938 the *Catholic Herald* explained that the Guilds would endeavour to help their members when unions sought 'un-christian and immoral ends'. Spain was, in its view, a 'test case' because the trade union movement was 'being used for the purpose of helping the Red side in Spain – a cause that does not come within the proper limits of British Trade Union ends... Whatever the truth may be about Spain... it cannot be the proper work of the Trade Unions to run an international class conflict.'[96] Later the paper replied to a pamphlet on *Penetration of the Trade Unions by the Roman Catholic Guilds*. It denied that the Guilds fostered fascism by protesting at 'the interference of Trade Unionism in the Spanish war'. Indeed, Catholics had a right and a duty to

[91] See the correspondence in the Labour Party file LP/SCW 12, 'Roman Catholics – 1938', in particular 15 January 1938, O'Hanlon to Morgan Phillips, and 6 February 1938, O'Hanlon to Middleton.
[92] *Catholic Herald*, 28 January 1938; J.H. Whyte, *Catholics in Western Democracies – A Study in Political Behaviour* (Dublin, 1981), pp. 83–5, summarises the main currents in Catholic social thought.   [93] *The Catholic Times*, 27 November 1936.
[94] *The Universe*, 9 April 1937.   [95] *Catholic Times*, 25 September 1936.
[96] *Catholic Herald*, 28 January 1938.

protest because the unions were involving themselves in affairs 'in which they have no knowledge and no right to interfere'.[97]

Any suggestion of Catholic confessional trade unionism in Britain was greeted with suspicion and hostility by leaders of the labour movement. Citrine for one professed an inability to understand why workers should allow themselves to be divided on political or religious lines as had happened on the continent:[98] at the NCL of 25 August 1936 he argued that 'we had never had Christian unions in this country and we wanted to be very careful not to provoke them' by labour's attitude over Spain.[99] In early 1938 the *Catholic Herald* published letters from Citrine and Bevin in response to calls for an inquiry into the guilds. Citrine pointed out that the General Council had not discussed the matter. However, general policy was to disapprove of the creation within unions 'of groups composed of persons with special interests, having objects other than those appropriate to the membership as a whole'. Bevin too stressed the unions' defence of religious freedoms and deplored 'anything which introduces sectarianism within the union'.[100] However, some of the left feared the guilds as a fascist wedge driven into the labour movement and were keen to bring the matter to a head. The North-East Federation of Trades Councils adopted a resolution calling for an investigation into the guilds which was debated, unsuccessfully, at the Annual Conference of Trades Councils in May 1938.[101]

Difficult as it is to see in the existing Catholic Guilds an alternative trade union movement, it is important to bear in mind that Bevin, Citrine and their colleagues were totally opposed to the establishment of any rival centres of authority in the labour movement on either the left or the right. Moreover, Catholic activism did have the potential to disrupt the trade unions and this was clearly demonstrated in March 1938 when Young Catholics organised a petition against a compulsory stoppage of wages for Spain by the Cadeby Branch of the Yorkshire Miners' Association which led to a protest strike for one shift by the workforce. The management refused to implement a similar stoppage of wages at Maltby colliery. Thus, Catholic

[97] *Catholic Herald*, 17 June 1938.
[98] Interview with Bob Walsh who recalled his conversation with Citrine on this subject at the founding of the World Federation of Trade Unions in 1946.
[99] TUC, Documents 1, 25 August 1936, NCL, verbatim report, p. 44.
[100] *Catholic Herald*, 28 January 1938.
[101] *Catholic Herald*, 18 March 1938; TUC, report of 14th annual conference of trades councils, 28 May 1938, p. 35; *The Universe*, 3 June 1938. After the resolution had been moved the 'previous question' was carried by 48 to 36.

activism could successfully exploit other members' hostility to the imposition of solidarity action.[102]

Although the idea of a Catholic breakaway from the British labour movement remained fanciful, lacking the approval of the Catholic church and a wide basis of support among Catholic trade unionists, a very different situation pertained in Ireland where there was a clear alternative in the existing Irish nationalist trade union movement. After the partition of Ireland in 1921 the British trade unions had preserved their organisation both north of the border in the new province of Northern Ireland and south of it in the Irish Free State. Major unions such as the T&GWU and the NUR retained large memberships in the south, and as late as 1945 British-based unions organised almost 23% of southern Irish trade unionists.[103] However, this situation, which was an affront to Irish nationalism, could only continue so long as the British unions did not draw attention to themselves. The Spanish Civil War, which inflamed Catholic sentiment throughout Ireland, did just that and at a time of particular vulnerability – a section of the indigenous Irish trade union movement, led by William O'Brien of the Irish Transport and General Workers' Union (IT&GWU), was hostile to the British presence and the Irish Trades Union Congress (TUC) had recently set up a Commission of Inquiry to examine the future of trade unions in the South.

The Spanish Civil War caused outrage amongst Irish Catholics, with tangible political consequences. In Ulster, Harry Midgley, a Northern Ireland Labour Party MP who closely associated himself with the Spanish Republican cause, was the victim of a vindictive campaign. The alienation of Catholic voters was primarily responsible for the loss of his Belfast seat in the Stormont elections of February 1938, in the course of which his hustings had to be protected by armoured cars.[104] In the South, De Valera's Fianna Fáil government maintained a strict neutrality in the conflict, but opposition politicians such as Paddy Belton and Eammon O'Duffy (the former leader of the Irish fascist Blueshirt movement who later led a Legion to fight for the rebels in Spain) founded an Irish Christian Front campaigning for the Free State to support Franco. In this deeply Catholic country, with its historic ties with Spain, an attack on Spanish Catholicism was felt by

---

[102] *The Universe*, 4 March 1938; *Catholic Times*, 11 February 1938, 4 March 1938. It has been impossible to verify this incident from non-Catholic sources. I was not granted permission to consult the archives of the Yorkshire Miners.

[103] C. McCarthy, *Trade Unions in Ireland, 1894–1960* (Dublin, 1977), p. 623.

[104] See Graham Walker, *The Politics of Frustration – Harry Midgley and the Failure of Labour in Northern Ireland* (Manchester, 1985), chapter 6, pp. 85–113; *Daily Telegraph*, 5 February 1938.

many as an attack on Irishness itself, with dangerous implications for the British unions.[105]

The isolation of the British unions over Spain was completed by the refusal of either the ITUC, the major Irish trade unions, or the Irish Labour Party to take a stand on the issue. Thus, when unions such as the T&GWU made their financial contributions to the NCL fund, an act which appeared a minimum act of solidarity in the British context, they posed immense problems for their Irish sections. The two unions most affected were the NUR and the T&GWU (known as the Amalgamated T&GWU in Ireland) which suffered widespread condemnation from their Irish branches. Some branches of the Amalgamated T&GWU voted to disaffiliate altogether and the members were readily recruited by the rival Irish T&GWU. Despite subsequent claims that the trade unionists had been intimidated by the Catholic church and the Irish Christian Front, this should also be seen as a mass action by rank-and-file workers who felt that their British-based unions were failing to represent their interests either as Catholics or as Irishmen.[106] The situation was only restored by a personal intervention by Bevin who sent a telegram claiming, with deliberate inaccuracy, that his union's £1,000 grant 'is for medical and humanitarian requirements, with definite instructions that medical supplies are to be available *to either side*, whoever are victims in the awful struggle'. He refused to commit his union to support a particular side in the conflict, hoping merely for a rapid settlement.[107] On 18 September Bevin, ignoring threats of violence, scored a personal triumph by convincing the AT&GWU All-Ireland conference to support the grant by re-emphasising its humanitarian nature.[108]

This episode deserves close attention on a number of counts. Firstly there was a question of timing – in the weeks between the 1936 TUC Congress and Labour Party conference the most powerful trade union leader was concerned to damp down a rebellion amongst his Irish members over Spain and this must have reinforced his commitment to Non-Intervention. Secondly, the Irish dimension directly affected the trade unions rather than the Labour Party and threatened them with the loss of members and branches – a language that union leaders well understood. Thirdly, Bevin's attitude was at the same time courageous and duplicitous. He was willing to mount a dogged defence of internationalist solidarity for Spain when it

---

[105] For the background to this episode see J. Bowyer Bell, 'Ireland and the Spanish Civil War, 1936–1939', *Studia Hibernica*, no. 9, 1969, pp. 137–62.
[106] See Tom Buchanan, DPhil thesis, chapter 6. M. O'Riordan, *Connolly Column*, (Dublin, 1979), p. 36, refers to the 'campaign of intimidation' to force Irish members of the AT&GWU to repudiate their union's grant.
[107] *The Times*, 12 September 1936, my emphasis.   [108] *Irish Times*, 19 September 1936.

was seen to coincide with the interests of his union to do so, and in this he was true to the principles that had consistently guided the labour movement's response to the Civil War. To have surrendered to Irish pressure was not an alternative for him, but was unnecessary anyway given the ease with which he could exploit the ambiguity inherent in labour's internationalism.

Catholic workers' resistance to the labour movement's effort for Spain was more varied and active than has been previously acknowledged, and when an important leader such as George Hicks said publicly 'let us not forget that some organisations had been nearly torn in two by the religious attitude of some of their members [over Spain]'[109] this was more than mere rhetoric. Moreover, it is apparent that, while the passions of the first few months could not be easily maintained, deep scepticism about the Civil War prevailed in staunch Catholic areas right up until the fall of Madrid. Not only was this an electoral hazard for the Labour Party, but it also stimulated independent Catholic organisation in the unions. Although the Catholic factor affected the unions and the Labour Party in somewhat different ways, for both it challenged their paramount functions. For the party it presented problems for the collection of the vote[110] and sowed divisions in local organisations. For the unions it threatened the concept of the British trade unions as organisations that could 'represent the interests of all workers. This was a powerful influence given that union leaders attached more importance to a member's subscription than to a gesture in solidarity with Spain, and one branch resolution opposed to executive policy was taken more seriously than ten in support of it.

However, the impact of this factor on the labour movement's overall response to Spain was far from direct. One contemporary writer, G.T. Garratt, went so far as to argue that the Catholic influence, especially in the north of England, was strong enough to push Labour into backing Non-Intervention in 1936.[111] Harry Pollitt alleged that the reason why labour

---

[109] MRC, UCATT records, Mss 78/AU/1/2/10, report of 1938 AUBTW Conference, pp. 29–36.

[110] This is not, of course, to claim that Catholic hostility was the only electoral problem that the Civil War caused for the Labour Party, but simply the most generalised and consistent. In the Plymouth Drake by-election, in June 1937, the Tories' attempt to play on fears that a Labour government would involve Britain directly in the war found considerable resonance in this naval port. Huge posters were erected saying 'The Socialists would send your husbands, sons and brothers to fight in the Spanish War' (*Daily Herald*, 12 June 1937). In 1938 Citrine was quick to point out that the Labour Party did not regard the Civil War as a vote-catcher: 'it is noticeable that the subject of Spain has not been obtruded by the Labour Party at by-elections', TUC, File 90214, 29 March 1938, Finance and General Purposes Committee circular 494 to General Council members.

[111] G.T. Garratt, *Mussolini's Roman Empire* (Penguin Special, 1938), pp. 107 and 171.

leaders had not 'rushed to give assistance to the Spanish people' was 'a mistaken fear of losing the Roman Catholic vote in elections'.[112] Yet of much more importance than any direct Catholic pressure was the reinforcement which the existence of a significant body of opposition within the labour movement gave to labour's leaders in pursuing a cautious and bureaucratic policy over Spain. James Middleton was able to claim in January 1937 that: 'The Catholic difficulty has obtruded itself in various places, but has not been a factor of much importance so far as policy is concerned.'[113] The reason for this, however, was that policy was already evolving in a direction that could cause the least possible offence to Catholics. Citrine and his colleagues were unwilling to countenance the political mobilisation of the labour movement for Spain and the existence of hostility to Republican Spain in their own ranks coincided happily with their view that there was no clear unanimity of support for a more active policy for Spain as the left-wing critics argued.

[112] *It Can Be Done; Report of the 14th Congress of the CPGB*, (1937), pp. 47–8.
[113] Ruskin College, Oxford, James Middleton Papers, MID 59, 22 January 1937, Middleton to Tom Baxter.

6

⁓

RANK-AND-FILE INITIATIVES

The Catholic workers had attempted to ascertain the degree to which labour movement policy over Spain represented their interests and, to some extent, to change it. In this they shared common goals with the left-wing 'rank and file', formally and informally constituted, within the trade unions whose response to the Spanish Civil War stood as a critique of, and in certain respects an alternative to, existing policy. The activities of the rank and file over Spain took many forms, ranging from participation in and support for the International Brigades to a host of fund-raising initiatives, many of which took place outside of the specific context of trade unionism. Yet there were particular occasions when rank-and-file activists tried to impose their own vision of internationalism on the 'official' leadership. This corresponded to the continuing conflict in the later 1930s within the British trade union movement between 'official' and 'unofficial' structures. Alternative organisations flourished, complementing more traditional forums for rank-and-file opinion such as the trades councils, and it was inevitable that these bodies would hold their own views on the correct response to the Spanish conflict just as they criticised other aspects of official policy. Because of the nature of these movements, however, their response did not present a coherent policy but rather flared up episodically and reflected the vicissitudes of the relationship between the rank and file and the official leadership. Thus, this chapter seeks to explore specific initiatives which challenged the official view of trade union internationalism, and to locate them in the context of relations between trade union leaders and their members more generally.

The concept of the trade union 'rank and file' is, in certain respects, an ambiguous one and requires some initial elaboration. Indeed, in recent years the phrase 'rank-and-filism' has been coined to describe the attitude of historians who, it is argued, have reduced the analysis of internal union relationships to too simplistic a dichotomy of interests between the 'leadership' and the 'rank and file', disregarding the many problems of interpretation and definition which this raises.[1] In its most general application the term defines the ordinary members of a union (including unpaid officials) as distinct from a union's paid leadership and, even in this sense, the term carries connotations of separate interests between the two sides. In this case legitimate rank-and-file pressure is conveyed to the leadership by branch resolutions or union conferences. The term can also refer to the organisation of workers outside of, or parallel to, existing union structures, one example being on the local level through trades councils – the definition used, for instance, by Alan Clinton.[2] Such a definition, however, is less satisfactory for the 1930s, when the independence of the trades councils were being eroded and for rank-and-file initiatives one must look largely to the numerous unofficial 'rank-and-file movements' which developed in that period. These aspired to champion the interests of ordinary workers against not only the perceived class enemies – the employers and the National Government – but also against the trade union leaders who were accused of weakness and betrayal of their members' interests.

At a time of increasing centralisation in the labour movement the influence of these rank-and-file movements, which were deeply rooted in the unions yet independent of them, proved harder to curb than that of the trades councils. Thus, it proved convenient to leaders like Bevin to castigate such movements as communist-inspired, a charge that official histories of the Communist Party have been unwilling to refute.[3] However, it would be unwise to see them simply as communist creations. The eccentricities of communist strategy in the late 1920s and early 1930s damaged the Communist Party's claim to be the sole representative of the rank and file, while the revival in organisation was more the product of tensions within trade unionism than of political manipulation.[4]

The London busmen's movement, for instance, the most prominent of the new wave of rank-and-file movements in the 1930s, grew out of a workforce whose tradition for militancy had reappeared in response to heavy job losses

---

[1] See, for instance, the conference reports in *Bulletin of the Society for the Study of Labour History*, no. 46, Spring 1983, R. Hyman, 'Officialdom and Opposition: Leadership and Rank-and-File in Trade Unions', pp. 4–6; and J. Zeitlin, 'Trade Unions and Job Control: A Critique of "Rank-and-Filism"', pp. 6–7.

[2] Alan Clinton, *The Trade Union Rank-and-File: Trades Councils in Britain, 1900–40*.

[3] See the comment quoted above p. 35, fn 84.

[4] R. Martin, *Communism and the British Trade Unions, 1924–1935* (Oxford, 1969), pp. 168–75.

which their union (the T&GWU) failed to resist. Moreover, the busmen, with their strong local trade union culture based on depot organisation, felt stifled within the confines of Bevin's union which allowed little expression of local autonomy. In mid-1932 an unofficial Rank-and-File Committee was set up with a combined communist and non-communist leadership and took over the journal *Busman's Punch* from the Communist Busworkers. The Committee was soon negotiating on behalf of the London busmen through its control of the Central Bus Committee (CBC) and in 1936 the movement's founder, A.F. (Bert) Papworth, was elected to the T&GWU Executive. The Rank-and-File Committee built mass support amongst London busmen through its ability to win them better conditions and came to exert a powerful influence over the left both in London and nationally, stimulating similar movements in sectors such as printing, the railways and building.[5] However, right until the movement's collapse following the disastrous 1937 bus strike[6] it enjoyed an uneasy relationship with the T&GWU leadership – too powerful to be permitted to survive yet too well-rooted to be easily excised.

By contrast, the other major rank-and-file movement of this period, amongst the engineers, offered an alternative national leadership through shop steward representation. Engineering shop stewards had emerged as radical leaders of the rank and file in the First World War when the need for an intermediate level of shop-floor organisation between the union and its members had become apparent during wartime conditions of production.[7] Much of this organisation had been swept away in the post-war depression which hit the industry, to be revived by the upturn in trade, especially in the aircraft industry, fuelled by rearmament in the later 1930s. From 1935 militant shop stewards were organised in the Aircraft Shop Stewards National Council (ASSNC) and had their own journal, *New Propellor*. Although the ASSNC was 'unofficial' in the eyes of the AEU leaders, the rise of the militants in the union was marked by the election of former Minority Movement activist Jack Tanner to the AEU Executive and, in 1939, its presidency. The left was also strong in the lower echelons of the union's hierarchy, especially in the London region. However, partly due to the greater influence in the ASSNC of the communists, who were now implementing the non-confrontational Popular Front policy, it tended to be

---

[5] The best account is in J. Barrett, 'Busman's Punch: Rank-and-File Organization and Unofficial Industrial Action among London Busmen, 1913–1937', unpublished MA thesis, Warwick University, 1974; the movement is also dealt with in H.A. Clegg, *Labour Relations on London Transport* (Oxford, 1950) and K. Fuller, *Radical Aristocrats* (1985).
[6] See below, pp. 205–6.   [7] J. Hinton, *The First Shop Stewards' Movement* (1973).

a less subversive body than the busmen's movement, and proved more enduring.[8]

Thus, in analysing rank-and-file responses to Spain, this chapter deals with a particular stratum of trade union activists and the organisations to which they belonged. Some of these leaders, such as Bert Papworth and Bill Jones among the busmen, were communists; yet many of them were not, and experienced a particular motivation from embarrassment at the contrast between the well-publicised internationalism of the communists and the apparent failure of the official labour movement to help the Spanish government. However, many of these leaders had a long record of working with communist initiatives such as the 1934 'Co-ordinating Committee for Anti-Fascist Activity'[9] and their politics were permeated with the theory of the united front against fascism.

The main characteristic of the rank-and-file movements' internationalism, as of all their activities, was its directness. Lacking the resources to develop their own international policy they acted as a spur to the official trade union movement, pushing it towards a more active solidarity with the Spanish workers. This attitude was apparent from an early stage amongst the London busmen – at the 17 August 1936 meeting of the Rank-and-File Committee it was agreed, on the motion of the staunchly left-wing Dalston bus depot (T&GWU branch 1/498) to set up a fund to raise £200 for Spanish Medical Aid.[10] In *Busman's Punch* Bernard Sharkey of the CBC addressed busmen on 'What Spain Means to You', urging them to demand through their branches that the NCL should end its support for 'neutrality' and organise 'a powerful campaign to force the British Government to allow the legal Spanish Government to obtain the supplies it needs'.[11] On 16 November 1936 there was an unofficial meeting of the representatives of twenty-eight busmen's branches, backed by the Rank-and-File Committee. Frank Snelling emphasised the need for London trade unionists to send a delegation to Spain to show their moral support and a larger meeting was called for 14 December to discuss this proposal.[12]

Busman's Punch strongly supported the idea of sending a delegation, arguing that it would be 'of immense value for raising financial and material help and would be the spearhead of the United Front campaign to smash the National Government'.[13] Interviewed prior to the second meeting J.W.

---

[8] See R. Croucher, *Engineers at War, 1939–1945* (1982), chapter 1; E. and R. Frow, *Engineering Struggles: Episodes in the Story of the Shop Stewards' Movement* (Manchester, 1982).   [9] N. Branson, *History of the Communist Party of Great Britain*, pp. 121–2.
[10] *Busman's Punch*, September 1936, p. 13.   [11] *Ibid.* p. 11.
[12] *Daily Worker*, 21 November 1936; *Busman's Punch*, December 1936, p. 8.
[13] *Busman's Punch*, December 1936, p. 10.

Jones, acting Chairman and Secretary of the Dalston Branch attacked the 'complete lack of leadership coming from Transport House [which] is causing increasing impatience among the London branches of the union and the great majority of trades unionists generally'. The British trade union leaders had made no effort to carry out their policy on Spain – 'Not one single meeting has been called by the TUC.'[14] At the Memorial Hall on 14 December 103 delegates from 91 London union branches of all trades and five trades councils heard the busmen's leader Bert Papworth move a resolution calling for a delegation to be sent to Spain. This was seconded by R.W. Briginshaw, the printers' leader who had already led a rank-and-file campaign against *Daily Mail* 'lies' on Spain,[15] who urged London trade unionists to force the leadership to take action. The rank and file were not apathetic, he reasoned, but were 'shackled' by the leadership. Subsequently a party of eight was nominated to visit Spain and £45 raised towards their expenses.[16]

The meeting also elected a deputation to put its views to Citrine at the TUC. On 21 December this group quite brazenly entered Transport House without prior appointment and confronted Citrine and Tewson. Citrine was careful to emphasise that he could deal with the deputation only in a personal capacity and pointed out that even if they had approached him by letter he would have had to check with the organisations which they claimed to represent: 'I must always be on my guard to see I don't allow the opinion to be created that because 20 people come down here at a time selected by them, that by reason of their numbers, or something of the kind, I am bound to see them.'[17] The spokesman, J.W. Jones, replied that they did not care in what capacity they saw him – 'What we are concerned with is putting our point of view as active rank-and-filers on why your campaign has not been wide or active enough in this Spanish situation.' He realised that a meeting of the NCL was due and felt that it was important for their views to be heard because 'If it is a question of combatting Fascism we are the people who have got to fight, Sir Walter, and our opinion should be considered.'[18] However, he did apologise for not adopting the 'courteous line' of writing in advance.

The group's case was put by Briginshaw who admitted that the deputation was 'extraordinary', but considered it a necessary response to the alarm felt by rank-and-file trade unionists. This alarm had been increased in the last week by the communists distributing an appeal for help

---

[14] *Daily Worker*, 4 December 1936, p. 10.   [15] See below, pp. 206–9.
[16] *Daily Worker*, 16 December 1936.
[17] TUC, Documents 2, 21 December 1936, report of meeting, p. 3.   [18] *Ibid.* pp. 2 and 4.

'direct from the Spanish trades unionists', which raised the question of why the unions were not able to do this as well? 'We think,' he said, 'the Movement is impotent and too close to the National Government.' His prescription was for Transport House to launch a 'general mass campaign' involving, for instance, an Albert Hall meeting with appeals for volunteers to join the International Brigades and collections for trade union food ships.[19] Mr R. Lee (T&GWU Branch 1/343) drew attention to the almost total ignorance amongst his 600 members as to the extent of the official movements' campaign for Spain. Disarmingly, he welcomed Citrine's agreement to meet them only in a personal capacity because 'I have no hesitation in saying that in your mind I believe you are as dissatisfied with the effort as I am. As the General Secretary of the TUC you would not have sufficient courage to put that into words.'[20] Lee thought that war was wrong when, as in 1914–18, only the capitalists profited from it, but was willing to abandon his objections and fight to save democracy in Spain.[21] Mr J. Course, a member of the printers' union NATSOPA from the *Daily Herald* building, had witnessed continual discussions among his workmates as to what was being done to aid Spain, but was forced to watch the communists make all the running in collections and other practical activities. 'We are asked what we in the Labour Movement are doing to assist them. We say we do all we can from the official organisation [*sic*] – but we don't hear much from them.'[22] Finally, Mr M. Gravit, Branch Secretary of T&GWU 1/305, said that his members who paid the voluntary political levy were unhappy at labour's apparent failure to help the Spanish workers. He felt that the situation called for mass demonstrations – 'you should educate the people in the streets'.[23]

Thus, the deputation presented Citrine with a canvas of grievances based on their own experiences at branch level. In response Citrine fell back on the argument that the labour movement had achieved a great deal for Spain, but had been unable to publicise it, just as 'you would not tell employers in a strike what you are going to do next'. He interspersed his comments with items of 'classified' information which hinted at what the movement might be doing – for instance, the TUC had attempted to purchase arms for the Spanish government prior to the implementation of Non-Intervention, but had been obstructed by the British arms manufacturers.[24] Such revelations, however, were unlikely to impress the deputation and, in fact, reinforced their feeling against what one member called the 'hole and corner methods'

---

[19] *Ibid.* pp. 4–5.   [20] *Ibid.* p. 5.   [21] *Ibid.* p. 6.
[22] *Ibid.* p. 6. NATSOPA organised semi-skilled and clerical workers in Fleet Street.
[23] *Ibid.* p. 6.   [24] *Ibid.* pp. 10 and 12.

of aiding Spain which effectively hid things from the working class.[25] The discussion meandered on, but to little purpose for it was clear that Citrine was unsympathetic to the main aim of the rank-and-file delegates – the invigoration of ordinary trade unionists into activity for Spain through a centrally organised campaign. The almost total lack of empathy on this point was demonstrated by the following exchange:

> *Deputation*: (T&GWU) For the last four months the 'Bus section has been pleading with our own Executive to approach the TUC with regard to a levy on everybody. A levy of 2d per member per week. Nobody has attempted to tackle it.
>
> *Sir Walter*: Your Union gave £1,000. I wish other unions had done as much, but if you can find means of increasing the money we are getting we shall be pleased – we can use it.[26]

The views of the deputation were not put to the NCL.[27] However, the *Daily Worker* made political capital out of the 'successful invasion' of Transport House, claiming that the rank-and-file feeling over Spain was causing 'disquiet even in the most complacent circles of the Labour leadership'.[28]

Meanwhile, this current of rank-and-file pressure was making headway in the London Trades Council (LTC), the prime 'official' forum of London trade unionists. The LTC had, within a month of the outbreak of the Civil War, taken a much more decisive stance than either the TUC or the Labour Party, calling for a four-point national policy of the banning of all arms to the rebels; an open declaration of British government support for the Spanish government; the rendering of aid to the Spanish government and the immediate recall of Parliament.[29] Locally, it campaigned for an official demonstration in central London, pushed into action by the prospect of being outflanked by the communists. On 12 September 1936 the LTC Secretary Alfred Wall had written to Herbert Morrison (in his capacity as Secretary of the London Labour Party) urging on him the need for a mass London meeting – for instance, in the Albert Hall with 'Wells, Shaw and others' – for fear that 'the official movement would lose prestige if unofficial movements were allowed to retain the lead in such activity'. The communists had just raised £600 in Trafalgar Square.[30] Morrison sympathised but pointed out that 'the national bodies had not looked favourably' on the idea.[31]

---

[25] *Ibid.* p. 18.   [26] *Ibid.* p. 17.   [27] NCL minutes, 22 December 1936.
[28] *Daily Worker*, 22 December 1936.
[29] BLPES, Film 200, Reel 7, LTC minutes, Delegates' Meeting, 13 August 1936.
[30] TUC, Correspondence 1, 12 September 1936, Wall to Morrison; 19 September 1936, Morrison to Wall.   [31] *Ibid.* 19 September 1936, Morrison to Wall.

However, this only temporarily deferred the build-up in pressure for a meeting. At the 12 November LTC meeting it was agreed that Wall should request the NCL 'to initiate an intensive campaign in favour of the Spanish workers and to consider the organisation of a central London demonstration'.[32] As Wall confided to Citrine in an accompanying letter, 'My council went "potty" last night on the Spanish situation. I stopped the nonsense by saying that the National Council of Labour was the appropriate body to deal with the problem and that action by local bodies might do more harm than good.' However, he was worried by the spectre of 'unofficial bodies' exploiting Spain – 'it would be well if the official movement could do or say something to counter-act the accusations which are being made to the effect that the Labour Movement is inactive in regard to Spain'.[33] Citrine's eventual reply did little to reassure Wall, as he recorded the NCL's faith in the ability of the PLP 'to press the Government on every possible occasion', and was unwilling to take the initiative in any demonstration.[34]

Prior to the receipt of Citrine's letter, the LTC Executive had successfully staved off a call for a London rally to be convened whatever the reply of the NCL.[35] At a Delegate Meeting on 12 December, however, this decision was referred back amidst acrimonious scenes.[36] The *Daily Worker* portrayed Wall, who put the NCL case against a rally, as the representative of the 'paralysing hand of the official Labour leadership'.[37] Ultimately it was decided to call a demonstration of London trade unionists for 11 January 1937,[38] where two of the prospective delegates for Spain, Miss Olive Beamish and Joseph Jacobs, moved a resolution calling on the NCL to consider 'the convening of a great Congress, representative of the whole Labour movement' to discuss how the movement could help to bring the Civil War to a successful conclusion.[39]

The delegation left for Spain on 18 January 1937, visiting Barcelona, Alicante, Valencia and Madrid before returning to Britain ten days later.[40] Its objectives were manifold. Not only did it serve as a direct expression of

---

[32] BLPES, LTC minutes, Delegates' Meeting, 12 November 1936.
[33] TUC, Correspondence 1, 13 November 1936, Wall to Citrine.
[34] *Ibid.* 27 November 1936, Citrine to Wall; 28 November 1936, Wall to Citrine.
[35] BLPES, LTC minutes, Executive Committee, 26 November 1936.
[36] BLPES, LTC minutes, Delegates' Meeting, 10 December 1936.
[37] *Daily Worker*, 12 December 1936.
[38] BLPES, LTC minutes, Delegates' Meeting, 31 December 1936, for a copy of the leaflet for the meeting.
[39] BLPES, LTC minutes, Delegates' Meeting, 31 December 1936, for a copy of the resolution; *Daily Worker*, 13 January 1937.
[40] *Daily Worker*, 18 January 1937 and 28 January 1937. The full list of delegates was; J. Scott (AEU); R. Sell (ETU); A. Papworth (T&GWU); J. Jacobs (NAFTA); O. Beamish (AWCS); M. Finn (AUBTW); H. Clayden (NUDAW); A. Davis (NATSOPA).

support for the Spanish people from the workers of London, but also, in the words of the engineers' leader Joe Scott, they were 'bringing back a full report of first-hand information for the Trades Unionists of Great Britain'.[41] Moreover, there was the political dimension of how the experience and knowledge gathered could be deployed to influence official labour movement policy. Soon after the delegates' return there was an emotional meeting at Kingsway Hall and cries of 'shame' when they reported that 'leaders in Spain were puzzled because British Trades Unions had done so little to help'. Delegates directed their fire on the movement's leadership – Mr Sell (ETU) argued that 'we have to go to Transport House and turn it upside down' by means of the united front. Joseph Jacobs (NAFTA) said that

> we don't want Sir Walter Citrine to sit on the steps of Downing Street (cries of 'he's gone to sleep there') [a reference to Bevin's comments at the 1936 Labour Party Conference] but we want him to batter down the door and demand the removal of the embargo on arms for Spain.[42]

However, the delegates, following the 'courteous line' eschewed by the earlier deputation, found Citrine an elusive quarry. On the 4 February 1937 J.W. Jones wrote to him on behalf of the 'Trade Union Delegation to Spain Committee' asking for a meeting. Citrine replied that such a request should be made first to the delegates' own unions. Undeterred, Jones wrote again, arguing that this request had 'peculiar circumstances' because the delegation could convey their conversations with Spanish labour leaders and discuss a specific scheme to assist the Spanish workers in the area of transport, which Papworth had already raised with Bevin. Citrine commented that the proposed deputation would 'not serve any useful purpose' in view of the TUC's elaborate contacts with Spain through IFTU delegations, official representatives and conferences. Moreover, he had already been contacted by Bevin on the transport scheme. He concluded that 'the best course would be to approach their own EC's who, no doubt...would bring the matter to the notice of the General Council'.[43] However, given the problems which the TUC was facing in creating lines of communication with Spain at this time, it was clear that Citrine's reasons for not meeting the delegation were political rather than practical.[44]

Prevented from influencing the TUC directly, the delegates set about reporting back to the organisations which had sent them and turned their committee into an 'Aid for Spain' fund-raising body.[45] Beamish and Jacobs

---

[41] *Manchester Guardian*, 18 January 1937.   [42] *Daily Worker*, 4 February 1937.
[43] TUC, Correspondence 2, 4 February 1937, Jones to Citrine, 10 February 1937, reply; 17 February 1937, Jones to Citrine, 22 February 1937, reply.   [44] See above, p. 151.
[45] *Daily Worker*, 5 February 1937.

addressed the LTC and an emergency resolution was carried which called upon the TUC General Council to convene an emergency conference of union executives with the aim of devising 'speedy and necessary actions' in defence of the Spanish workers.[46] Papworth persuaded the T&GWU bus section to raise £250 for the British Battalion of the International Brigades.[47] However, having spent this money on food, clothes and binoculars at a Co-op store he was forced to return the goods, after police intervention and on the advice of the T&GWU,[48] even though none of the items were explicitly covered by the Non-Intervention Agreement. Other delegates addressed union meetings and wrote about their experiences in Spain.[49]

The issue of Spain concentrated the bitterness and alienation which the T&GWU rank-and-file activists felt towards Bevin, particularly in the wake of the March 10–11 1937 International conference where his speech had denied any prospect of active support for Spain. In December 1936 busman Bill Brisky (from T&GWU 1/498) had left to join the International Brigade, disenchanted with the failure of the official movement to respond adequately to Spain's needs. Where he had hoped to see the unions organising levies of their members for Spain 'he saw only, however, the small political parties doing every human thing possible [for Spain], and he knew that these comrades could do little – they lacked the mass membership and organisation of his great labour movement'.[50] After rapidly rising to the rank of Company Commander his subsequent death in action was the occasion for a blistering attack on Bevin by J.W. Jones in *Busman's Punch*, according to which Brisky's death was a lesson

> none more than for his General Secretary with his fat well-fed belly (made possible by the Bill Briskys of the working class), afraid of Fascism as he is of the whole boss class, knowing only 2 words: *unofficial* and *Reds*, who refuses to publish the speech he made at the International conference recently in London – How much longer are the rank and file going to allow their leaders to take them into retreat internationally as they have done nationally.[51]

Matters between Bevin and the rank-and-file movement came to a head in May 1937 when, after the London busmen had been on strike for almost a month demanding a $7\frac{1}{2}$ hour day, Bevin withdrew authority for the dispute

---

[46] BLPES, LTC minutes, Delegates' Meeting, 11 February 1937.
[47] *Daily Worker*, 5 February 1937.
[48] *Tribune*, 2 April 1937; *Daily Worker*, 27 March 1937.
[49] See *Busman's Punch*, February 1937, pp. 8–9, for Papworth's 'Spain as I saw it'; *Daily Herald*, 28 January 1937, for Scott's comments; MRC, UCATT records, Mss 78/AU/4/1/27, AUBTW *Quarterly Journal*, February 1937, p. 135, for Finn's account of his visit to the International Brigade Camp.   [50] *Busman's Punch*, January 1937, p. 5.
[51] *Ibid.* March 1937, p. 3.

from the CBC and got the men back to work. He then suspended the CBC and ordered an inquiry into the rank-and-file movement as a result of which many of the leaders were expelled from the union or debarred from union posts. To make matters worse for the movement, its leaders divided over the foundation of the breakaway National Passenger Workers' Union, which was strongly opposed by the communists.[52] In the aftermath of this fiasco, the current of rank-and-file opposition to official policy on Spain in the trade unions, in the organised sense described above, was largely submerged until the final stages of the Civil War.

Another feature of rank-and-file internationalism was that it was reactive and strongly linked to the specific trade in which workers were involved. Good examples of this are the attitudes of printing workers to so-called 'atrocity stories' in the newspapers and of seamen engaged in trading with Nationalist Spain. The coverage of the outbreak of the Civil War in the Rothermere press, especially in the *Daily Mail* which portrayed the war as a succession of Red atrocities against the Catholic faith, had outraged the labour movement by its alleged misrepresentation (and, incidentally, provided a convenient target against which all sections of the movement could unite). In a typical resolution the Dalston busmen (T&GWU 1/498) dutifully condemned the stories, refusing to believe 'that any workers could be guilty of such things'.[53] Yet, in spite of the chorus of condemnation in the movement, there was little agreement on how the 'atrocity stories' could be combatted. Part of the problem lay in the 'Back to Work Agreement' which had been concluded in the printing industry at the end of the General Strike, one of a number of such deals struck on unfavourable terms at that time to avoid a total collapse of trade unionism. In printing, although remarkably lenient terms were agreed upon, particular emphasis had been placed on protecting the management's right to decide the contents of their papers, a reference to the fact that the General Strike was precipitated by the blacking of an offensive leading article by the *Daily Mail* NATSOPA chapel.[54] Thus, when a committee of rank-and-file printers – led by R.W. Briginshaw of NATSOPA's Odham's Machine Branch – called a meeting to discuss press 'falsehoods' on Spain in September 1936, a demand that had already been raised at a communist rally in Trafalgar Square on 6 September,[55] they were entering into a very sensitive area in union–employer relations.[56]

[52] James Barrett, 'Busman's Punch: Rank-and-File Organization and Unofficial Industrial Action Among London Busmen, 1913–1937', pp. 121–38.
[53] *Busman's Punch*, September 1936, p. 4.
[54] J. Child, *Industrial Relations in the British Printing Industry* (1967), pp. 249–50.
[55] MRC, Mss 39A/TA/4/1/65, *Typographical Circular*, September 1936, p. 294.
[56] *Daily Worker*, 9 September 1936.

On 11 September 1936 there was a well-attended rally (some 1,500 people according to the *Daily Worker*)[57] at the Memorial Hall. Those present were asked to stand in silence for the dead in Spain as well as for the artist Felicia Browning, the first British fatality in Spain and 'known to many workers in Fleet Street where for a period she sold working-class literature outside many shops'. Then, between speeches by Hamilton Fyfe (former *Daily Herald* editor), J.R. Campbell of the Communist Party and Ellen Wilkinson, a motion was passed stating that:

> We printing and newspaper workers in London congratulate the Spanish workers and all fighters for Democracy in Spain on their heroic fight against the military-Fascist attack. We protest against the abuse of the freedom of the press by newspapers with pro-Fascist sympathies.
> The license taken by these newspapers in misrepresenting and falsifying the truth about Spain is, in our opinion, a breach of the spirit of the 1926 'Back to Work' agreement made between the Newspaper Proprietors' Association, the Printing and Kindred Trades Federation and the General Council of the TUC.[58]

An ingenious statement from the meeting stressed that the issue of debate was not interference with the freedom of the press – 'Freedom to express a political point of view and [the] right to present news to suit the view we accept...'. The printers, however, refused to 'accept as legitimate news fit to be printed by Trades Unionists' what they deemed to be 'pure and unsubstantiated atrocity stories, which set class against class in a most vicious form, that inflame sectional passions in the very precarious international situation of today'.[59] At the rally a deputation was elected to visit the Printing and Kindred Trades Federation (PKTF), the co-ordinating body for the printing unions, with the stated aim that the federation should reconsider the 1926 Agreement in the light of recent events and, secondly, that it should consider calling a mass meeting of its affiliates to discuss the situation.[60] Speaking after the rally Briginshaw admitted that 'we have got into the position where we ourselves have raised a certain amount of feeling on the question, but to get any further it will have to be taken up by the Executives of the unions concerned'.[61]

This approach made little impression on the PKTF General Secretary George Holmes who reported to his Executive that the suggested meeting

---

[57] *Daily Worker*, 12 September 1936.
[58] MRC, Mss 43 PKTF/18/3 (the PKTF Subject File on Spain, entitled 'Daily Mail Protest Meeting', has a copy of the agenda for the rally).
[59] *Typographical Circular*, October 1936, p. 323.
[60] MRC, PKTF Subject File, 12 September 1936, Briginshaw to Holmes.
[61] *Newspaper World*, 19 September 1936.

was 'the outcome of an entirely unofficial meeting of printing trade workers'.[62] He informed Briginshaw that he was unable to meet his deputation because no question could be brought before the federation without the backing of a member union. He added that the PKTF was

> unable to take account of political activities such as those alluded to in your letter [i.e. blacking newspaper copy]. Such a course would undoubtedly make confusion worse, compounded by the reactions of one school of political thought against another, even amongst the members of the unions affiliated to the Federation.[63]

In fact, far from alarming the press barons, the rank-and-file initiative only succeeded in arousing a moderate union leadership in defence of the established practices. As early as 7 September Holmes had met with the employers' Secretary, Mr Alton, concerning a report in News Review and elsewhere that 'certain people in the printing trades' wanted to revoke the 1926 agreement. Holmes had 'assured Mr Alton there was not the remotest likelihood that anything would be done and was emphatic that the reports were in no way official'. He emphasised that the agreement would not be cancelled or altered other than through the proper channels, though seeing no good reason why it should not stand uncorrected for a further twenty years. Finally, he urged on the proprietors the need for reciprocity in passing on information pertinent to their respective interests 'rather than that something should be done which would involve the printing trades in a dispute'.[64]

Holmes expanded on this submissive approach in a leading article in the PKTF journal in which he praised the 1926 agreement – 'Nothing finer was accomplished by any industry affected by the General Strike' – and argued that union members should not set themselves up as censors because 'it is not their business'.[65] This comment contrasts eloquently with Briginshaw's view that the 11 September rally was held 'to discuss certain points *affecting us as Printers* in connection with the military-Fascist attack upon the Democratically elected Government of Spain'.[66] However, the key to the failure of this initiative lay not only in the obstruction by the PKTF, but also in the failure of any of the print unions to support it. An editorial in the Typographical Association's journal, for instance, defended the newspapers'

---

[62] MRC, Mss 43, PKTF Executive Minutes, 16 September 1936.
[63] MRC, PKTF Subject File, 14 September 1936, Holmes to Briginshaw.
[64] MRC, PKTF Subject File, Holmes' report on the meeting.
[65] MRC, Mss 43, *Printing Federation Bulletin*, September 1936, p. 1.
[66] MRC, PKTF Subject File, 12 September 1936, Briginshaw to Holmes (my emphasis).

right to print what they wanted, under the aegis of free speech, although warning that 'a mischievous departure from truth is not the best way of preserving loyalty amongst employees and peace in industry'.[67]

Indeed, the only union to take up the issues raised by the printers was the National Union of Journalists which already had its own 'Fascism and the Press Sub-Committee'. On 2 October 1936 this committee reported to the Executive that, while not challenging the rights of newspaper proprietors to choose their own editorial policy for their papers, the union should not yield the right of members to refuse to handle copy containing falsehoods. 'This question,' the report continued

> assumes added importance in relation to press comments and reports on Fascism. The treatment of the Spanish news for example has provided instances of grossly distorted news-presentation which might have been checked had the union spirit and organisations in the offices been strong enough to protest.

The Committee recommended that the union should undertake greater education of members on the value of its 'Code of Professional Conduct'.[68]

Another area of work in which conscience could play an important role in rank-and-file responses was in trade involving Nationalist Spain. Throughout the Civil War one of the unfulfilled ambitions of the British left had been to disrupt this trade, which had continued at a fairly high level,[69] and it has been shown above that British union leaders had already made considerable efforts to prevent the extension of the International Transport Workers' Federation blockade of the Spanish rebels to British workers. In fact, any prospects for solidarity action amongst Britain's seamen were restricted by a number of factors. Most importantly, the National Union of Seamen (NUS) was one of the more reactionary British unions, moulded by its autocratic founder J. Havelock Wilson who had seen his union temporarily expelled from the TUC on the strength of its support for breakaway unions in the wake of the 1926 miners' strike.[70] Moreover, rank-and-file organisation was very limited amongst seamen, who still served under a draconian industrial relations system as defined by the 1888 Merchant Shipping Act. The NUS, which was resolutely 'industrial' in its outlook, had no interest in attempting to take action against the trade with the Spanish rebels on political grounds. Instead, its aim was to negotiate as good a deal as possible for its members engaged on the increasingly

---

[67] *Typographical Circular*, October 1936, p. 325.
[68] MRC, Mss 86/1/NEC/11, NUJ minutes, 2 October 1936.
[69] Jill Edwards, *The British Government and the Spanish Civil War*, pp. 76–81; p. 126.
[70] H.A. Clegg, *A History of British Trade Unions Since 1889*, vol. 2, pp. 458–9.

hazardous voyage to Spanish waters, while at the same time using what legitimate political influence it had to try to persuade the government to afford more protection to British shipping. It was considerably more successful in the former of these objectives than the latter.[71] However, the *quid pro quo* for the relatively high rates of pay which the union extracted from the employers through the National Maritime Board (NMB) was that the NUS had to be able to exercise authority over its members and prevent them from 'breaking articles' other than in the legal way provided.[72] Thus, there was a potential for tension between the seamen and their union, the consequences of which were best demonstrated by the case of the North Shields steamer S.S. *Linaria*.

The *Linaria* arrived in Boston, Massachusetts, in February 1937 carrying anthracite from Marnipol in the USSR. According to one account, while in Russia a charter was offered to carry a cargo to Barcelona, but after telegraphing the owners, the captain reported that the British government would not permit the company to accept. Instead, on arrival in Boston the crew learnt that the ship was to carry a cargo to Seville in the Nationalist zone of Spain and when a deputation met Captain Robinson he showed them an order to proceed to Hampstead, Virginia, to pick up nitrates for Seville. The crew refused to sail for either destination.[73] In the words of the crew's spokesman, Alec Robson:

> We were 75 days crossing the Western ocean and were out of touch with what was going on as regards Spain. When we arrived in Boston...we bought newspapers and read that England had decided on a Non-Intervention policy. We all agreed that this was the right course to take. [On receiving orders] we made inquiries what the Nitrate was for [and] we were told that it was to be used for fertilizer. However we decided that this was not the reason as it is said that Nitrate is 60% explosive and 40% fertilizer. We decided that the only course was to go on strike, which we did.[74]

On 23 February 1937 the men began a 'stay-in strike', Robson announcing that 'we shall not take out the ship if it means helping to kill people in Spain', and cabling a protest to the NUS in London.[75]

Initially the British consul forbade the sailing of the vessel until the Board of Trade had decided whether the cargo contravened the Non-Intervention agreement.[76] A crucial moment came on 26 February when, following a government decision that it did not do so, the NUS advised the crew to

[71] See above, p. 116, fn 29. [72] *The Seaman*, 9 June 1936.
[73] *New Leader*, 26 March 1937, letter from James Martin, a supporter of the crew in Boston.
[74] *The Shieldsman* (South Shields weekly), 22 April 1937, 'exclusive interview' with Robson.
[75] *Manchester Guardian*, 2 March 1937; *Daily Herald*, 24 February 1937.
[76] *Daily Herald*, 26 February 1937.

abandon the action.[77] On the same day Attlee raised the matter in the Commons, asking if the government had sent instructions to the consul in Boston to support the crew. Lord Cranborne replied that nitrates were not prohibited under the Merchant Shipping (Carriage of Munitions to Spain) Act of 1937, and refused to be drawn on Attlee's further question of 'what is the position of sailors... who are asked to load supplies which are obviously war supplies?'[78] Interestingly, in his notes on Attlee's question, Sir. W. Malkin at the Foreign Office admitted that, while it was unclear whether the nitrates would be used for explosives, 'any trade with insurgent territory, whether import or export, may well be regarded as increasing the insurgents' facilities for carrying on hostilities'.[79]

The Foreign Office favoured strong action to discipline the crew 'in view of the importance to the shipping industry of preventing shipping services being interrupted in this way'.[80] However, the problem of how to resolve the dispute was a taxing one for the British government, in spite of the support which it received from an unholy alliance of the shipowners and the NUS. A Board of Trade memorandum[81] revealed that the Shipping Federation

state that the sellers say that this consignment is similar to other consignments which they have been selling to Spanish merchants for the past 30 or 40 years. The consignment is not being sold to insurgent forces but to merchants whose business it is to import chemical fertilizers.

However, they had added the rider that 'it is not possible, of course to say what use will actually be made of the cargo when it reaches Seville'. The report continued that the NUS representative in New York, Mr Dobbyn, had 'strongly advised' the crew to proceed with the voyage, subject to the incorporation in the Agreement of a special clause agreed by the NMB to cover voyages to Spain and providing additional wages and indemnity in the case of injury. (When offered this deal the crew refused it as 'blood money'.)[82] Dobbyn had reported to the government that the men refused to sail with any cargo that could be used for munitions – he kept up his efforts but the men were 'led by Alexander Robson, a well known Communist, and it seems to me unlikely that they will change their attitude'. Further evidence of the NUS attitude is revealed by the Foreign Office discussion of a

[77] *Daily Herald*, 27 February 1937.
[78] *Hansard*, 5th series, vol. 30, col. 2345, 26 February 1937.
[79] PRO, FO 371 21325, W4446/7/41, nos. 78–80, memorandum by Sir W. Malkin on Attlee's parliamentary question.   [80] PRO, FO 371 21325, W4447/7/41, no. 86.
[81] PRO, FO 371 21325, W4447/7/41, nos. 83–4, Board of Trade Report.
[82] *New Leader*, 26 March 1937.

parliamentary question on the *Linaria* on 3 March. The Board of Trade said that the union had 'strongly advised the crew to proceed to Spain and they suggest that use might be made of this fact in the [Foreign Secretary's] reply (the union have informed the Board of Trade that they have no objection to a statement of this kind being made in the House) '.[83]

With the failure of persuasion, means of ending the dispute through coercion were considered. One option was for the consul-general to convene a Naval Court under the 1888 Act, but the British ambassador backed the consul in arguing that this line of action should be avoided on 'political grounds' – 'there would be undesirable publicity and probably H.M. Government would be accused, however unjustly, of assisting one party in the Spanish dispute and of encouraging a violation of the spirit of the neutrality Act'.[84] The favoured course was for the men to be discharged and then to 'take proceedings against the delinquents when they reach this country'.[85] In a further attempt at intimidation the consul warned that they would find it very difficult to get another job – allegedly telling them that 'every British Captain and every British shipping company in the world will known that your are of the *Linaria* crowd'.[86]

This was, in fact, a close approximation to what actually happened. In a hopeless position, abandoned by all but the Boston left,[87] the crew finally decided to leave the ship and be repatriated. They were paid off with five shillings deducted for every day that they had detained the ship in port.[88] On landing in Liverpool seventeen of the crew were charged, under the Merchant Shipping Act, with 'neglect of duty and wilful disobedience of a lawful order'.[89] They were then stranded in Liverpool for some days as the Board of Trade refused to grant them rail warrants home and the NUS denied them help because 'they had refused to obey the orders of the Master of the ship'.[90] Indeed, when Alec Robson went to pay his union dues in his local union office he was initially refused permission to do so.[91] In the face of these charges a Tyneside Defence Committee was set up to pay for their legal and travel expenses, with the Rev John Patton as Treasurer. An appeal was issued which pointed out that the men 'were convinced that what they were asked to do was to effectively support the Spanish rebels, and we believe that they were right in this conviction'.[92]

When the case finally came to court in early May the men scored a victory

[83] PRO, FO 371 21325, W4468/7/41, no. 111, parliamentary question from Mr E. Williams MP.   [84] PRO, FO 371 21325, W4446/7/41, no. 86.   [85] *Ibid.* no. 87.
[86] *New Leader*, 12 March 1937.   [87] *New Leader*, 12 March, 1937; 26 March 1937.
[88] *Manchester Guardian*, 5 March 1937.   [89] *Manchester Guardian*, 6 March 1937.
[90] *Daily Worker*, 25 March 1937.   [91] *Daily Worker*, 27 March 1937.
[92] *The Shieldsman*, 22 April 1937.

following evidence from an analytical chemist that nitrates are essential for the manufacture of munitions. The magistrate declared their action justified, but fined them 40 shillings each for combining to impede shipping between Boston and Hopewell.[93] However, Patton's committee now launched a campaign for an appeal[94] and a month later this was successful. According to the recorder's verdict:

> That they were perfectly entitled to say 'we don't mind risking our lives for what we regard as a good cause' – they were entitled to say that and that is roughly what they did say.

Then, addressing the employer's counsel, he said:

> You are not going to ask me to suppose that the Nitrate in this case was for Agriculture. Were they not entitled to say that they were not prepared to go to a country at war except on specific terms, and that they were not prepared to risk their lives at all carrying vital ingredients of explosives to the insurgent forces against the democratic Government of Spain.[95]

However, the comment in the *Daily Worker* that 'the Recorder showed himself more progressive than the leadership of the NUS'[96] was somewhat misleading, as it is apparent that the court was recognising the crew's right to avoid potential dangers rather than giving crews a charter to black cargoes on political grounds. Yet, although Robson was vindicated in law, he was still under a ban from the Shipping Federation for his actions, and in October 1937 his local union branch carried a resolution that the NUS should support his appeal to have the ban removed.[97] The crew were dragged through the courts again in April 1938, when an attempt was made to quash their appeal ruling. This was thrown out by the judge who, however, made it clear that the crew's case was built solely on the dangers that they would have faced in Spain – if their objection had been based on political grounds alone then 'it would have been quite irrelevant'.[98]

A further sequel to the *Linaria* incident came at the NUS Conference in July 1937, where Provisional General Secretary George Reed stated in his report that the union had advised the crew to proceed 'in accordance with the terms of their agreement and the relevant sections of the Merchant Shipping Act... It appears that the advice was sound because a court decided that they were not justified in refusing to go in the ship. However, on appeal the men won their case... I regret to say that a great deal of capital was made

[93] *Daily Worker*, 8 April 1937.　　　　[94] *Daily Herald*, 8 May 1937.
[95] *Daily Worker*, 8 June 1937.　　　　[96] *Daily Worker*, 15 June 1937.
[97] MRC, Mss 175/6/Br/3, North Shields branch minutes for 7 October 1937.
[98] *Manchester Guardian*, 28 April 1938.

by the Communist Party out of this decision.'[99] Later, a further statement was prised from General Secretary William Spence. He argued that:

> I took it upon myself to advise the men of the 'Linaria'. Where they did wrong in refusing to take the ship to an unloading port. If they had done that and refused to go to Spain that might have put a different aspect on the matter. In my opinion, when they refused to go from Boston to Hopewell they were entirely wrong.

On the subject of the *Linaria*'s cargo he added the following comments which bear interesting comparison with the report from the shipowners' quoted above:

> Some of it was going to be used to make explosives. She was carrying a cargo of Nitrates which had been sent by the same shippers and going to the same consignees for the past 25 years. We got that information. In fact, the refusal of the 'Linaria' crew to carry that cargo to Spain, – well, it was not helping Franco against the workers, that cargo was to be used by small farmers as fertilizer for their orange groves. So that instead of helping Franco they were damaging the workers. I just want to make that explanation.[100]

When viewed as an internationalist gesture by rank-and-file British seamen, the case of the *Linaria* is unique for the Spanish Civil War, and this raises the question of why solidarity action amongst seamen was so limited. Indeed, this question could be posed for the whole of the transport sector for, while there was a rank-and-file dockers' campaign against Japanese shipping from December 1937 to February 1938 in the light of Japanese aggression against China,[101] there was no action of comparable scale against ships trading with Nationalist Spain, in spite of the much greater interest in the Spanish conflict.[102] Part of the answer to this problem lies in the fact that, in many respects, there was nothing unique in the actions of the *Linaria* crew, in refusing to embark on a voyage to Spain, and what set them apart was the political framework in which they located their actions. Indeed, when the men issued an appeal against the charges levelled against them they had adopted a double line of defence;

> a) The Nitrates were material for explosives, and that to carry them to Seville would be intervention on the side of the rebels against the Democratically elected Government of Spain.
> b) That in doing so the ship would be entering a war zone.[103]

[99] NUS records, 1937 AGM report, p. 66.   [100] *Ibid.* p. 75.
[101] Noreen Branson, *History of the Communist Party of Great Britain*, pp. 251–2. PRO, FO 371 22080, F 1360/43/10, F 1694/43/10 and F 1886/43/10 view these events from the government's side.
[102] *Daily Worker*, 17 March 1937 and 26 March 1937, reports some industrial action against ships trading with Nationalist Spain.   [103] *The Shieldsman*, 22 April 1936.

This dual motivation was confirmed by the Board of Trade which reported that the crew refused to proceed 'on grounds based partly on risk of life and partly on an objection to carrying to an insurgent port material which could be used as munitions of war'.[104]

In fact, the danger inherent in sailing to either zone in Spain, and the poor remuneration and conditions, produced a series of rank-and-file actions amongst seamen throughout the Civil War. In December 1936, for instance, the English deck seamen of the *S.S. Thurston* refused to sail their ship from Malta to Spain in view of the dangers involved. The NUS General Secretary informed the Board of Trade that he had advised *Thurston*'s crew that 'if the ship is not carrying materials of war they should proceed'.[105] However, in spite of the Board's confidence that the men would be unlikely to win their case under the Merchant Shipping Act, they were subsequently acquitted in Malta on the grounds that they 'had reasonable cause to refuse to proceed'.[106] This decision went against Foreign Office assurance that 'instructions have been given to His Majesty's ships to resist any interference with British ships on the high seas, and that the *Thurston* is entitled to protection'.[107] At the same time as the *Linaria* strike sixteen crew members from the South Shields' vessel *S.S. Velo* had refused to sign up again for a voyage to Valencia (in Spanish government territory) and the NUS fought a successful court case on their behalf to claim unemployment benefit which had been withheld from them.[108]

Most striking, however, is the case of the liner *Llandovery Castle* which struck a Nationalist mine off the coast of Spain and limped into Port Vendres in France. Subsequently her crew refused to sail her to Genoa for repairs due to the dangers involved, contrary to NUS advice, only to be charged under the Merchant Shipping Act with refusing to obey a lawful command and to receive sentences of up to twelve weeks with hard labour. This manifest injustice sparked off a campaign in the East End of London, where many of the crew came from, for their release and the repeal of the hated Act.[109] These and numerous other incidents suggest that rank-and-file action was more common in the trade with Spain than has been appreciated, but reflected the seamen's understandable preoccupation with personal

[104] PRO, FO 371 21325, W4447/7/41, no. 83.
[105] PRO, FO 371 20588, W17605/9549/41, no. 128, 8 December 1936, telegram from Secretary for Colonies to Governor of Malta.
[106] PRO, FO 371, 20588, W18133/9549/41, no. 218, 14 December 1936, copy of telegram from Malta. [107] PRO, FO 371, 20588, W17605/9549/41, no. 128.
[108] *Daily Herald*, 3 May 1937.
[109] The main sources for this episode are the *Daily Worker*, *The Seaman*, and the NUS AGM report for July 1937 where the union officers defended their handling of the dispute.

safety rather than political principles. Thus, instead of being an isolated incident, the *Linaria* incident was merely separated from these other cases because the crew took their stand primarily on a political principle.

The demise of the busmen's rank-and-file movement in 1937 ushered in a period in which labour leaders had little to fear from the rank and file in propagating their policies on Spain, and the onus fell increasingly on the engineering workers to press for more action. Groups of engineering workers had a long record of activism for Spain. Within a month of the outbreak of the Civil War De Havilland aircraft workers were mobilising against the sale of aeroplanes to the Nationalist side, and threatened the Air Ministry and the management with industrial action unless this traffic ceased.[110] Later, the engineering shop stewards played a leading role in the Voluntary Industrial Aid for Spain movement. However, it was the question of rearmament, and the opportunity that this seemed to create for influencing government policy, which brought them to the fore. Initially the ASSNC was mainly concerned with mobilising support to push the AEU leadership towards a tougher line on rearmament, playing a prominent role, for example, in the 23 April 1938 Emergency Conference on Spain.[111] Later, the De Havilland shop stewards notified the AEU's 1938 National Committee that they would refuse to co-operate with rearmament plans unless the government sent arms to Spain.[112] When the AEU launched its £50,000 Fund for Spain the shop stewards applied pressure for its more active implementation. However, in spite of these efforts, the AEU leaders allowed the rearmament question to lapse inconclusively, and the apparent failure of the 'official' labour movement to take any effective action for Spain after the 1938 TUC Congress, combined with the acute danger facing the Spanish Republic with the fall of Catalonia (Barcelona fell on 26 January 1939) and the imminent prospect of British recognition of Franco, touched off a final outburst of rank-and-file militancy.

Most authors who have mentioned this episode have done so in the context of industrial action for Spain.[113] In fact, however, the level of industrial action involved was largely symbolic and intended as a stimulus to officially sanctioned action. It is more significant to view these events in the context of the 'Arms for Spain' campaign, which the communists had been energetically promoting for some months, to show that the episode did not happen in political isolation. For instance, the route that the engineers'

---

[110] *Daily Herald*, 18 August 1936 and 20 August 1936; Richard Croucher, *Engineers at War 1939–1945*, p. 44.   [111] See above pp. 123–4.   [112] *Daily Worker*, 2 June 1938.
[113] Noreen Branson, *History of the Communist Party of Great Britain*, p. 260; Noreen Branson and Margot Heinemann, *Britain in the Nineteen Thirties* (1970), p. 315; Jim Fyrth, *The Signal Was Spain*, p. 262.

demonstrations followed, from Chenies St to Downing St was well trodden by the 'Arms for Spain' marches, one as recently as 17 January 1939. Moreover, on 31 January there was a particularly eventful demonstration from Chenies St to Parliament Square, where there were rowdy scenes while Spain was being debated in the Commons, provoking a violent over-reaction from the police and garnering wide press coverage.[114]

On 25 January 1939 shop committees from the De Havilland and Handley Page aircraft works and from two engineering factories issued a statement saying that they were no longer prepared 'to remain silent and passive in the face of the crucifixion of Republican Spain's heroic people'. They suggested a programme of actions and the transmission of the following demands to the Prime Minister by elected delegates – firstly, the supply of arms to Spain; secondly, the organisation of convoys to protect shipping to Spain; thirdly, the withdrawal of foreigners (the International Brigades had already been unilaterally withdrawn in the autumn of 1938); fourthly, for the British government to supply food to Spain.[115] On the next day an estimated 600–700 engineers, some of whom had stopped work an hour early, marched from Chenies St (Tottenham Court Rd) to Downing St under the slogan 'We want arms for Spain'. According to one shop steward: 'In the aircraft factories we are making 'planes for the arms programme. We know some of them are going abroad, but we know they are not going to the Spanish Government. We feel they must go there and we are going to have a voice in this.'[116]

On 28 January there was a mass rally for 150 shop stewards from twenty-six engineering and aircraft factories which set up a Shop Stewards Committee and decided to call for a further deputation to the Prime Minister backed by a mass demonstration and industrial action. Moreover, it was hoped to extend the action by mobilising other groups of workers and by asking the executives and district committees of the engineering unions to give official leadership to the movement and to call an All-London Engineers' Demonstration.[117] The question of official support was to prove the main obstacle to the progress of the campaign, although the momentum was maintained by the decision of the 'unofficial' ASSNC to support the

[114] *The Times*, 1 February 1939; The National Council for Civil Liberties archives, Hull University, DCL, 8/6, contain a file on the police actions at the demonstration which gives an interesting sociological profile of the demonstrators.
[115] *Daily Worker*, 26 January 1939; *New Propellor*, February 1939; *Labour Research*, March 1939, p. 66.
[116] *Daily Worker*, 27 January 1939. According to *The Times* of the same day, however, the march was only 200 strong. Moreover, 'at the Handley Page works there was no cessation, and at the de Havilland works the number who stopped was said to be only a small proportion of those employed'. [117] *Daily Worker*, 30 January 1939.

movement and to co-operate with the stewards' committee.[118] On 2
February an estimated 1,000 or more engineers assembled in central
London, having downed tools early, and sent deputations to Prime Minister
Chamberlain, AEU sponsored MPs and the Spanish ambassador prior to
marching on Downing St. Significantly, the men were joined by four
representatives of the AEU London District Committee (DC).[119] There was
a further demonstration on 16 February when the engineers were joined by
rank-and-file builders, and sixteen building job stewards took a resolution
to Downing St calling for arms and food for Spain.[120]

The problem with this kind of action, however, was that, short of
unofficial strike action, it was difficult to develop it without gaining some
form of 'official' impetus. This appeared to be in sight when, on 21
February, the AEU London DC for the first time called an official engineers'
demonstration for the 23 February.[121] On the eve of the rally, Claude
Berridge, DC Chairman, said that 'we stand for unity against Fascism. Part
of the united struggle is our demanding arms and food for our Trade Union
brothers in Spain, who are fighting pro-Fascist Chamberlain, enemy of the
British people, as much as they are fighting the Fascist Franco.'[122] Richard
Croucher has taken this as evidence that 'the AEU as a union was solidly
anti-fascist and was able to mobilise the shop floor to take industrial action
in defence of the Spanish Republic even when the Civil War was almost at
an end'.[123] Such an impression, sadly, was quite illusory.

The AEU Executive, on 23 February, discussed the reports in the *Daily
Worker* that the London DC was calling for members to take part in the
day's demonstration. A motion moved by Brothers Bradley and Kaylor was
carried, with only Jack Tanner dissenting, which authorised the General
Secretary to notify London District Organisers W. Howell and Joe Scott
that 'E.C. instruct that none of our officials must associate himself in any
way with the proposed demonstration and march to the Prime Minister; nor
are they to permit the use of the union's official title or stationery in
connection therewith.'[124] Discussion then turned to earlier correspondence
between the two bodies on the same subject, and a further resolution was
carried (by 4–2) which reaffirmed that 'E.C. disapprove of the London DC
being associated in any way... And further instruct the District Secretary to

[118] *New Propellor*, February 1939, p. 7.
[119] *Daily Worker*, 3 February 1939; *The Times* put the number at 300 marchers.
[120] *Daily Worker*, 13, 15 and 17 January 1939.
[121] *Daily Worker* and *Daily Herald*, 22 February 1939.
[122] *Daily Worker*, 23 February 1939.
[123] Richard Croucher, *Engineers at War, 1939–1945*, p. 65.
[124] MRC, Mss 259, AEU Executive Council minutes, 23 February 1939, p. 219.

take the necessary steps to inform other representatives of the Executive's decision.'[125] The counter-attack by the moderates was only checked on the issue of whether to release a press statement on the matter. Openshaw and Kaylor moved that one should be issued

> intimating that we are not associated in any way – either as a union or as an EC – with the proposed demonstration and march to the Prime Minister...emphasising that, if demonstrations of the kind are deemed advisable, it is the duty of the National Labour Party and for the Trades Union Congress to organise such demonstrations. And to add that, in EC's opinion, the two national bodies in question have done everything possible on behalf of Republican Spain.

The vote was tied 3–3 and the motion lost on the casting vote of Chairman Jack Little, who explained, however, that it had yet to be established whether the London DC and its representatives would participate in the demonstration – had the motion been submitted on the following day he might well have been able to support it.[126] Accordingly, the London District Secretary replied that, in the absence of the District Organisers, he had personally visited the scene of the demonstration and delivered the Executive's letters, adding that the DC Chairman (Berridge) had made it clear to the DC representatives 'that EC had not officially approved of their taking part in the Demonstration'.[127] The Executive agreed to acknowledge this information 'with thanks'. The demonstration which did take place on 23 February elicited little coverage, even in the *Daily Worker*.[128]

The very firm stand taken by the AEU Executive choked off any hope of a significant challenge to government policy even though the rank-and-file agitation continued to spread amongst London trade unionists. Also, time was rapidly running out for Republican Spain. A conference of shop stewards, now representing a wide range of trades, met on 25 February and pledged strike action if the government recognised Franco[129] – yet two days later Franco was recognised. The planning of a march to Downing St on 7 March, called jointly by the engineers' committee and the newly formed All-London Job and Shop Stewards' Action for Spain Committee of the building workers' union (AUBTW), was simply too late to have any effect once that momentous step had been taken and the war, in effect, lost.

The rank-and-file responses were in many respects dissimilar, yet still offered a noteworthy critique of the official response to the Civil War. The attitude of the official leadership, which consistently sought to channel

[125] *Ibid.* p. 220. [126] *Ibid.* p. 220.
[127] MRC, Mss 259, AEU Executive Council minutes, 1 March 1939, p. 237.
[128] *Daily Worker*, 24 January 1939. [129] *Daily Worker*, 27 February 1939.

labour movement internationalism into areas such as humanitarian fund-raising and propagated the view that there was little that ordinary trade unionists could do to offer direct help to the Spanish workers, was contradicted by rank-and-file leaders who asserted that internationalism could actually be built in the workplace where workers should take responsibility for the produce of their labour. Where the TUC and the unions cocooned their response inside an elaborate bureaucratic structure, making it very difficult for the views of ordinary members to be heard through official channels, the rank and file believed in disregarding the formalities and putting their case directly to the relevant party, whether it was Sir Walter Citrine or the Prime Minister. Given the polarity between these viewpoints, which followed the general lines of antipathy between 'official' and 'unofficial' organisation, it is no coincidence that so many of these initiatives were suppressed by the unions involved, irrespective of their political complexion, before troubling the employers or the state. The failure to overcome this problem was doubly frustrating, however, because, in all of these cases, rank-and-file initiatives were seen as a spur to 'official' endorsement rather than as an end in themselves, and collapsed once that endorsement failed to materialise. The rank and file were never strong enough to offer more than a critique of the 'official' policy on Spain, and this should serve as a reminder that when invoking the 'rank and file' in this context, one is in fact dealing with a relatively narrow stratum of activists whose views were, potentially, no more representative of what the real rank and file – the mass of inactive or even actively hostile trade union-ists – thought about Spain than the leaders.

AFTERMATH AND CONCLUSION

With the end of the Spanish Civil War, British labour's internationalism was at last presented with a situation which it could fully control. Here was a defeated foreign labour movement with all the familiar complications of trade union and socialist leaders to be helped to safety, the movements of refugees to be co-ordinated,[1] and intercessions to be made on behalf of those languishing in jail or condemned to death. Franco's obsession with extirpating all vestiges of socialism from Spain ensured that the latter category would be huge. Moreover, there was a continuing humanitarian commitment within Britain where many of the Basque children, for whom secure domestic arrangements could not be made in Spain, were to grow up. The labour movement took on a further responsibility when many crew members of Spanish Republican merchant vessels opted to remain in Britain rather than return to a Francoist Spain. However, the charity of the National Union of Seamen, which acted as the TUC's agent in caring for the sailors, was tempered by trade union considerations – it resisted allowing the Spanish crews to find work on British ships as this would have infringed its long-held principle of 'British Seamen for British Ships'.[2] Crucially for labour's leaders, however, the end of armed Republican resistance marked the end of the 'Spanish problem'. All of them, with the possible exception of Attlee,[3] had felt threatened by Spain; by the demands which Spanish

---

[1] In March 1939 Del Vayo and the Spanish ambassador sought the assistance of the British labour movement in persuading the British government to escort the evacuation of 10,000 Republicans on Franco's 'black-list' from central Spain. Vincent Tewson led a delegation to Halifax on 24 March, but failed to move the government on this point (MRC, Mss 259, AEU Executive Council minutes, 27 March 1939).

[2] TUC, file 946/528, 'Spanish Seamen in British Ports', 21 April 1939, G. Reed to Tewson.

[3] Peculiarly for such an undemonstrative man Attlee, alone of his senior colleagues, opened himself to the passions generated by Spain – witness his visit to Spain and to the International Brigades, and his clenched fist salute on the terrace of the House of Commons

workers had placed on their conception of labour organisation and action;
by the destabilising passions which the conflict had aroused. Now, as the
remnants of Spain's socialist and trade union movement desperately sought
to escape their internment camps in France and find safe haven in Latin
America, where they could engage in a pathetic and fissile exile politics,[4]
that threat had at last been removed.

There were, of course, recriminations at the Labour Party's delayed
conference of Whitsun 1939, where Joseph Pole and Sybil Wingate mounted
vitriolic attacks on the shortcomings of labour's response to the conflict.[5]
But by then, following the collapse of the Munich agreement with Hitler's
annexation of most of the remnants of Czechoslovakia, it was becoming
clear that a European war was looming. Spain's misery was soon to be
generalised throughout a whole continent. Accordingly labour's leaders
were never brought fully to account, nor showed any willingness to accept
criticism or blame, for their contribution to the Civil War. Citrine, in his
memoirs, simply rewrote his role to show that he had opposed Non-
Intervention from the beginning as a 'one-sided arrangement'. During his
visit to Eden, he claimed, he had 'told him flatly' that Non-Intervention
could not succeed.[6] Dalton felt that his own lack of passion for the Spanish
Republic had been justified by the fact that Franco's Spain remained neutral
during the Second World War – a judgement that ignored the presence of
the Spanish 'Blue Division' on the Russian front.[7]

Yet the ritual handwashing and *post-hoc* self-justification contained in
these statements conceal the real success that Citrine, Dalton and the other
leaders had achieved in the course of the Civil War. Most significantly, the
labour movement was virtually unchanged in 1939 in terms of its structure
and concept of political action. Although a few individuals had left the

upon his return. In Parliament he declared himself to be an unashamed pro-Republican, *Hansard*, 5th series, vol. 333, 16 March 1933, col. 491.

[4] TUC archive, file 946/540, 'Spanish Rebellion – Aftermath' contains Citrine's post-Civil War correspondence with Spanish socialists such as Luis Araquistain and Wenceslao Carillo. In 1942 the IFTU reported on the continuing split in the UGT and felt that the group led by Caballero and Carillo was more worthy of support than that of Peña and Pretel. Carillo was seen as 'the most representative trade unionist of the former UGT' and his faction was seen as 'much nearer to the trade union conceptions of the IFTU and...more faithful to its policy' (TUC, File 946/528, 'Spanish Seamen in British Ports', 20 January 1942, Schevenels to Bolton).

[5] LPCR, 1939, pp. 258–61. Ellen Wilkinson spoke for the NEC and rebutted these charges. Although it has often been interpreted as a cunning move on the part of the party leadership to set up such a well-known supporter of Republican Spain in this fashion, her comments suggest that she saw no distinction between the activities of the communists and of the labour movement. For her the SCC was a 'grand record of a working class movement', while the International Brigades were 'a sacrifice the Movement made'. Thus, her position was not as contradictory as some have suggested (LPCR, 1939, p. 257).

[6] Lord Citrine, *Men and Work*, p. 359.   [7] Hugh Dalton, *The Fateful Years*, p. 97.

movement in disgust with labour's support for, or lack of support for, Republican Spain, the numbers were insignificant,[8] and the great potential of the Civil War for destabilising the labour movement had been channelled into harmless areas of activity. Strangely, where individual leaders were discredited in the eyes of activists, the institutions of labour were not. However, more than anything, the response of the movement to the Civil War had been determined by those institutions. Although Citrine and Bevin had regularly and flagrantly misled their members, and got away with it to an extent inconceivable in an age of investigative journalism, they did so in order to protect the institutions of which they were the executives. Thus, the 'failure' of the British labour movement, as perceived from the left, had much deeper roots than the manipulations of individual labour leaders. In the structure and content of its internationalism, the labour movement had long since paid its money and taken its choice.

This was something that the left never realised. Its analysis of the labour movement, as a handful of right-wing leaders exercising a tenuous hold over a mass of members who were simply waiting for an alternative lead, was dangerously deceptive. The consequence was that the left doomed itself to working against the grain of the labour movement, advocating a Popular Front which, whatever its broader political merits, was of little direct help to the people of Spain. The left mistook the widespread disillusionment with labour policy towards Spain, and a yearning for more energetic action, with a political repudiation of labour that simply did not exist. An essential precondition for a successful challenge to labour's policy towards Spain would surely have been a radical critique of the bureaucratic frameworks that underpinned it. However, the left – both communist and non-communist – was unable to provide this critique precisely because it was part of the labour movement and its vision was confined by the limitations that this imposed. Thus, it opted, instead, to pick and choose between the institutions of the labour movement – lionising, for instance, the engineering and mining unions without comprehending that their generous expressions of solidarity with Spain were still mediated through Citrine's brand of bureaucratic internationalism. Where the left was able to establish alternative structures to the 'official' labour movement, these were almost

---

[8] See the letter from J.R. Chancey to Gillies, 26 January 1939; 'the few thousand pounds collected by the party will have little or no effect on the result of the Spanish revolt. The main complaint is that the National Executive have not given this question the attention that it deserved. I write in the past tense, because it seems to me that the Spanish Republic is now beyond hope of saving. I am personally so disgusted that I am resigning from the secretaryship of the Faversham Division[al Labour Party] at the next annual meeting.' Labour Party archive, William Gillies papers, WG/SPA 564.

ineluctably subordinated to the 'official' will. Even so, the united and Popular Fronts were more than mere 'vehicles for the frustration and alarms which the international situation, and above all the struggle in Spain, had created'.[9] They were a legitimate tactic through which the left pursued political power, but an inappropriate one which failed to distinguish between the genuine support that existed for Spain, and the possibilities inherent in that support for radical change in labour movement politics.

These shortcomings were concealed by the rich pickings which the Civil War represented for the Communist Party. The fine example which it set in solidarity with the Spanish people (the level of recruitment for the International Brigades was, alone, a remarkable achievement for such a small party) gave substance to its claim to be the party which truly fought fascism. The Civil War brought a rise in membership which was far from ephemeral – after all, much of it survived the betrayal of anti-fascism evident in the Nazi–Soviet pact and the Communist Party's initial opposition to war with Germany. In historical terms, also, the Communist Party emerged very well from the Civil War. Despite liberal discomfort with the politically repressive activities of the communists in Spain, the party's 'line', that victory in the war and the establishment of 'bourgeois democracy' in Spain had to precede social revolution, is still widely accepted.[10] Similarly, the party's critique of British labour movement policy, in comparison with which the Communist Party's own response seems both undeviating and energetic, has continued to dominate publications on this subject. The Communist Party, it is argued, set the pace on solidarity with Spain either directly, through its own activities, or indirectly, because the imperative of anti-communism moulded labour's own response.

The evidence to support such a view does not come only from communist sources – leading labour movement figures would appear to confirm it in their memoirs. James Middleton, for instance, recollected that the Civil War was an episode in the 'running fight between right and left', within which 'the prime Communist motive was political, to create a sympathetic atmosphere which would smooth their way back to the party, but they overplayed their hand'.[11] According to Attlee: 'The Spanish struggle was the occasion for a determined attempt by the Communist Party to get into the Labour Movement by devious methods, but the majority of the Party were too experienced to fall into the trap.'[12] However, by both of the

[9] Ben Pimlott, *Labour and the Left in the 1930s*, p. 202.
[10] See for example Hywel Francis, *Miners Against Fascism*, p.. 146–8.
[11] Ruskin College, Oxford, Middleton papers, MID 136, unpublished typescript of a biography of Middleton based on interviews by E.H. Robinson, 1960–2, pp. 245 and 250.
[12] Clement Attlee, *As It Happened* (1954), p. 95.

criteria suggested above the role of the Communist Party has been exaggerated. The party's achievements were striking in terms of the amount of money raised or of committees and demonstrations organised, by an active membership a fraction the size of the Labour Party's. Yet, the two main initiatives associated with it, the International Brigades and Spanish Medical Aid, were both symptomatic of the failure to force the labour movement to organise these services itself. The International Brigades placed an almost intolerable strain on the party's slender cadres, but made a much deeper political impact on the rank and file of the labour movement (and the people of Spain) than on the labour leadership.[13] Thus, these heroic achievements should not conceal the Communist Party's failure to force the labour movement to give way on any of the substantive policies that it had propagated from the beginning of the Civil War, most notably the principle of the united front.

Concerning the role of anti-communism as a determinant of labour policy, it has been argued above that this has to be seen as a more complex problem than is generally allowed. Labour's antipathy to communism and to communists was genuine and deep-seated, but was more than a mere knee-jerk reaction. Communism was recognised as a supra-national organisation, of which the CPGB was the British agent, which had to be resisted on the national level. However, in Spain, the Spanish communists were frequently seen as more reliable than the LSI/IFTU affiliates. Similarly, in Britain, the labour movement could work with communists in situations where labour's control was assured. Hence, it is important to locate the problem not primarily in relations between the Communist Party and the labour movement, but rather in the tensions within the labour movement in the 1930s as a centralising leadership sought to fasten a greater discipline upon a fractious membership. The stresses that this created gave the communists the chance to return from their self-imposed sectarian exile and again pose as the champions of rank-and-file interests – yet this also gave the labour leaders an opportunity to castigate genuine expressions of discontent as extremist manoeuvres. The account of labour's response to the Civil War is littered with cases where 'anti-communism' presented labour leaders with

---

[13] One occasion when International Brigaders did make a direct impact on the labour leadership was on 31 March 1938 when a deputation of eighteen wounded volunteers and bereaved women met with Citrine, Dallas and Middleton for the NCL. Dick Springhall of the Communist Party was the group's spokesman and took the opportunity to call for a programme of heightened labour movement solidarity with Spain. After discussion Springhall remained convinced that 'the leaders of the movement did not place the same estimate on the need for an uparalleled effort as they did' (TUC, International Brigade, 31 March 1938).

an excuse not to adopt courses of action which they found naturally unwelcome.[14]

In contrast to the response of the Communist Party, that of the leaders of the labour movement will always appear almost bathetically unheroic. They had organised no 'Labour Legion' for Spain; Citrine had failed to take at least three opportunities to visit Spain during the conflict (in comparison with Pollitt's frequent trips); Non-Intervention had not been challenged until it was too late (and then half-heartedly). However, a semblance of statesmanship is granted to these leaders by the argument that the Spanish Civil War represented the culmination of labour's shift to a more 'realistic' stance on foreign policy and defence. The agony of Spain allowed labour's revisionists to complete their conversion of the party to rearmament and collective security, and prepared the movement as a whole to support another war against Germany. Thus, they tempered their genuine solidarity for Spain with the knowledge that Britain itself needed arms.

However, although the Civil War certainly played a major role in changing attitudes towards war and the use of violence, the interrelationship between this process, the revisionism of the 'Dalton–Bevin–Citrine block'[15] and the Civil War is far from clear. Firstly, it is apparent that these leaders' inhibition in supporting Republican Spain was rooted in a political analysis which, initially at least, suggested that a rebel victory in Spain would not present a threat to British interests that would be on a par with that of Nazi Germany or Fascist Italy. A military dictatorship in Spain would be the natural product of that nation's lack of democratic institutions and the innate tendency of the Spanish (of left or right) to solve political problems by violence. Thus, these leaders were consistently unwilling to prioritise Spain irrespective of their advocacy of rearmament for Britain. Secondly, their attitude towards Non-Intervention was not determined by statesman-like considerations. Admittedly they did not want Britain to be drawn into a war for which it was unprepared, but they were happy to abandon Non-Intervention once it became apparent that they had become dangerously isolated from their own members and from their international colleagues. Thus, the defence of labour movement institutions, both nationally and internationally, took precedence over broader political objectives.

Non-Intervention, however, although justifiably the focus of debate, was in many respects peripheral to, and a distraction from, the question of labour's internationalist response to the Civil War. When Non-Intervention is stripped away it becomes clear that labour's internationalist duty towards

[14] For instance, see above p. 62; pp. 158–9.
[15] J.F. Naylor, *Labour's International Policy*, p. 175.

the Spanish workers was discharged in a consistent fashion which did not waver from the definition given to Anthony Eden in August 1936 – the supply of foodstuffs and medicines to labour's sister organisations in Spain. Thus, where previous historians have tended to ask: 'Why didn't the labour movement do more for Spain?', it is perhaps more pertinent to ask: 'What might the labour movement have been expected to do?' In this sense the limited internationalism practised by Citrine and his colleagues corresponded closely to the legal restrictions on solidarity action, to the dangers of internal disunity arising from such action and, most crucially, to the contours of inter-war labour internationalism. Indeed, there was nothing perverse in their conception of internationalism as bureaucratic and tending to prioritise support for affiliated organisations over broader political goals and, indeed, this conception went almost unchallenged within the labour movement. Although the railmen's leader John Marchbank was to argue in his colleagues' defence that 'More than has been done [for Spain] could not be done in the political circumstances...the initiatives of power are not in our hands',[16] in truth, it was seen as neither necessary, desirable nor practical to attempt to seize them.

Thus, the response to the Spanish Civil War offers a microcosm of the condition of the labour movement in the 1930s. This study makes the case that the 'labour movement', rather than the trade unions or Labour Party in isolation, forms the best framework for studying this kind of subject in this period. The 1930s was a decade of profound imbalance between unions and party because the weakness of the Labour Party in parliament and its scant chance of forming a government contrasted with the stability and strength of the unions. Moreover, the unions, unusually, had a leadership that was equal (if not higher) in calibre to that of the Labour Party, and certainly more experienced and self-confident. This imbalance was finally rectified by the entry of Attlee and others into the coalition government of 1940, by Labour's 1945 electoral landslide, and by Bevin's switch from the industrial to the political wing of the labour movement.

In the particular case of Spain, the unions clearly were the dominant force in determining the labour movement's response. Firstly, since becoming General Secretary Citrine had made himself central to labour internationalism and this allowed him to direct the course of the debate. Secondly, the crucial decisions were taken at the National Council of Labour, or at the Labour Movement Conference, on both of which the unions had a powerful voice. However, brute force did not have to be used

[16] MRC, ITF records, Mss 159/3/c/6/13, 15 December 1937, 'British Labour in the Spanish Crisis' by John Marchbank.

by the unions to get their way. Citrine and Bevin used their authority to produce the result that they required at a time when Attlee was at his least assertive, when Dalton was broadly in agreement with them, when Morrison was a somewhat marginal figure, and when Cripps was at his most enigmatic. Thirdly, in relations with government, the unions and the party had devised a division of responsibility within which the unions had considerable opportunity to infringe on the 'political' sphere. The party's defence of Parliament as its distinctive area of activity was less impressive given its inability to shake the government's majority in the Commons. Finally, the TUC, rather than the Labour Party, controlled the relief work which was the prime area of labour's practical internationalism during the Civil War – the only exceptions to this being the Milk for Spain campaign and the limited humanitarian activity of the Spain Campaign Committee.

Thus, a weakened Labour Party passed the responsibility for Spain to the trade unions, who willingly accepted it. They brought to the Spanish problem an ingrained caution and hostility to the destabilisation that it might cause which was inevitably unhelpful to the cause of the Spanish Republic, as well as a sense that international solidarity was a job that was, in Citrine's words, 'extraneous' to their real duties.[17] These attitudes were, however, no less representative of the contemporary labour movement than the response of the left. Indeed, it would be unjust for Citrine and Bevin to continue to shoulder the burden of opprobrium for the defeat of the Spanish Republic. In the 1930s the trade unions stepped into the breach on a range of political issues, and the Spanish Civil War should stand as an example of constructive trade union engagement in politics, especially in a contemporary political climate in which such engagement is often ridiculed. Ironically, during the Civil War the problem was not that the unions held aloof from foreign affairs as they had done prior to 1914, but that they came down so conclusively on the 'wrong' side in the debate, in the eyes of their critics. Yet, for all its shortcomings the trade union response to Spain compares favourably with the evolution of internationalism in the post-1945 period when it has lapsed ever further into bureaucratic channels, removed from the concerns of ordinary workers.[18]

---

[17] BLPES, Citrine papers, III/1/1, report by Citrine to Trades Council Secretaries, 11 March 1937, p. 7. Citrine told his visitors, in connection with the TUC International Department, that 'it had become almost a full time job doing some of these extraneous things. For example, the Spanish Relief Fund.'

[18] This has been bitterly criticised by Don Thomson and Rodney Larson, *Where Were You Brother? An Account of Trade Union Imperialism* (1978).

BIBLIOGRAPHY

(A) *PRIMARY SOURCES* (INCLUDING TRADE UNION JOURNALS WHERE RELEVANT)

All references are to the period 1936–9 unless specified otherwise.

1 *Archival sources*

Amalgamated Society of Locomotive Engineers and Firemen, 9 Arkwright Road, London, NW3
    Annual Assembly of Delegates reports
    The Locomotive Journal
Amalgamated Union of Engineering Workers, 110 Peckham Road, London SE15
    AEU Reports and Proceedings
    AEU Monthly Journal
Association of Professional, Executive, Clerical and Computer Staff, 23 Worple Road, London SW19
    NUC General Council Minutes
    The Clerk
Bodleian Library, Oxford
    John Johnstone Collection – Street Propaganda Boxes
Bishopsgate Institute, 230 Bishopsgate, London, EC2
    London Co-operative Society archive collection
Broadcasting and Entertainment Trades Alliance, 155 Kennington Park Road, London
    NATE Minutes and reports
Churchill College, Cambridge
    Ernest Bevin Papers
    Labour Spain Committee Papers
    Philip Noel-Baker Papers
Civil and Public Servants Association, 74 Nightingale Lane, London
    CSCA Executive and Sub-Committee Minutes
    CSCA annual reports to Conference

Red Tape
Communist Party of Great Britain, 16 St John Street, London
    Files on the Spanish Civil War
Co-operative Union, Holyoake House, Hanover Street, Manchester
    Co-operative Union, Executive Committee Minutes
    Co-operative Congress reports, 1937 and 1938
    The Co-operative News
    International Co-operative Alliance, Congress report, 1937
General, Municipal, Boilermakers and Allied Trades Union, Woodstock College,
    Long Ditton, Surrey
    NUGMW NEC Minutes
    The General and Municipal Workers' Journal, 1936–9 excluding January
    1937–June 1938
Imperial War Museum, London, Department of Sound Records
    Oral History Recordings on British Involvement in the Spanish Civil War
Inland Revenue Staff Federation, Douglas Houghton House, 231 Vauxhall Bridge
    Road, London, SW1
    Taxes
International Institute of Social History, Amsterdam
    IFTU General Council reports and minutes, 1937
    IFTU circulars, 1936–9
    ITF, *Report for 1935–1937* and *Report for 1938–1946*
    Labour and Socialist International (SAI) archives
Labour Party, Walworth Road, London
    William Gillies' Overseas Correspondence, Spain 1931–9
    Subject Files on Spain
    NEC Minutes
London School of Economics, Library
    London Trades Council, Minutes
    Walter Citrine papers
    Hugh Dalton papers
Marx Memorial Library, Clerkenwell Green, London
    Busman's Punch, August 1936 to June 1937
    New Builders' Leader
    New Propellor, November 1936 to March 1939
Mitchell Library, Glasgow
    1 *Glasgow Collection*
    Glasgow Trades Council, Executive Committee Minutes
    2 *Scottish Labour History Society collection*
    Miners' Federation of Great Britain, *Annual Proceedings*, 1936–9
    STUC, *Annual Reports* 1937–8
    STUC *Bulletin*, 1937–9
National Library of Ireland, Dublin
    William O'Brien Papers
    Thomas Johnston Papers
National Library of Scotland, Edinburgh

Minutes of the Ayrshire; Lanarkshire; West Lothian; Mid and East Lothian; Fife, Clackmannan and Kinross miners' unions
David Murray Papers
Thomas Murray Papers
Edinburgh Trades and Labour Council, Minutes
National Union of Scottish Mineworkers, Executive Committee Minutes
Scottish TUC, General Council Minutes
National Union of Seamen, Maritime House, Clapham, London, SW4
AGM Minutes
The Seaman
National Maritime Board, Minutes
National Union of Tailors and Garment Workers, 16 Charles Square, London, N1
Executive Board Minutes
The Tailor and Garment Worker
Nuffield College, Oxford
Stafford Cripps Papers
Public Record Office, Kew, London
General Foreign Office Correspondence in the FO 371 series
Ruskin College, Oxford
James Middleton papers
Technical, Administrative and Supervisory Section, Onslow Hall, Richmond, Surrey
Association of Shipbuilding and Engineering Draughtsmen (AESD) Executive Council Minutes, 1937–9
AESD Circulars
The Draughtsman
Trades Union Congress, Congress House, London
Subject files on Spain
General Council Minutes
Finance and General Purposes Committee Minutes
International Committee Minutes, 1930–9
National Council of Labour Minutes.
Union of Shop, Distributive and Allied Workers, 188 Wilmslow Road, Fallowfield, Manchester
NAUSA AGM reports, 1937 and 1938
The Shop Assistant
NUDAW Annual Delegate Meeting, Minutes, 1937
NUDAW Executive Council Minutes, and Industrial and Political General Secretaries' Reports to Executive Council
The New Dawn
University College Dublin, Archive Department
NUBSO Council Minutes
NUBSO *Monthly Report*
University of Manchester, Institute of Science and Technology, Library
NFBTO Minutes, 1936–9
Warwick University, Modern Records Centre
(a) *Amalgamated Engineering Union*

Executive Council Minutes
(b) *International Transportworkers' Federation*
General Council Minutes, 1937–1939
Spain subject files
Press Reports
(c) *Mental Hospital and Institutional Workers' Union*
NEC Minutes, including Annual Conference Minutes
Mental Hospital and Institutional Workers' Journal
(d) *National Union of Foundry Workers*
Council Minutes
Quarterly Reports
(e) *National Union of Journalists*
NEC Minutes
(f) *National Union of Railwaymen*
Annual Reports and Proceedings
Railway Review
(g) *National Union of Seamen*
Executive Committee Minutes
North Shields Branch, Minutes
(h) *Printing and Kindred Trades Federation*
Executive Committee Minutes
Subject File on '*Daily Mail* – Protest Meeting'
Printing Federation Bulletin
(i) *Railway Clerks' Association*
Annual Delegate Conference, report, 1937
(j) *Society of Lithographic Artists, Designers, Engravers and Process Workers*
National Council Minutes, 1937–9
Executive Committee Minutes
The Process Journal (excluding June–December 1938)
(k) *Transport and General Workers' Union*
General Executive Council and Finance and General Purposes
Committee, Minutes
(l) *Typographical Association*
Minutes
Typographical Circular
(m) *Union of Post Office Workers*
General Purposes Committee Minutes
Quarterly Executive Council Minutes
Conference Minutes (typescript)
The Post
(n) *Union of Construction, Allied Trades and Technicians* deposit
(o) *Amalgamated Union of Building Trade Workers*
Executive Council Minutes
Circulars to branches
National Delegate Conference Minutes, 1936–8
AUBTW Quarterly Journal

District Committee No. 1 (London), Minutes, 1937–8
(p) *Amalgamated Society of Woodworkers*
   NEC Minutes
   Monthly Journal
(q) *National Federation of Building Trades Operatives*
   Conference reports, 1937–9
(r) *National Society of Painters*
   Executive Committee Minutes
   General Council Minutes, 1937 and 1938
   Monthly Journal

2 *Official reports*

Trades Union Congress Annual Reports
Reports of the Annual Conference of the Labour Party
It Can Be Done: Report of the 14th Congress of the CPGB (1937)
For Peace and Plenty! Report of the 15th Congress of the CPGB (1938)
Parliamentary Debates

3 *Newspapers and periodicals*

Catholic Herald
Catholic Times
Catholic Worker
Daily Herald
Daily Worker
Electrical Trades Journal (ETU)
Forward
Irish Independent
The Irish Times
Labour
Labour Research
Labour's Northern Voice
Left Review
Man and Metal (ISTC)
Manchester Guardian
Ministry of Labour Gazette
The New Leader
The New Statesman
The News Chronicle
The Railway Service Journal (RCA)
The Record (T&GWU)
Reynolds' News
The Tablet
The Times
The Tribune
The Universe

The Week

4 Pamphlets

Amalgamated Engineering Union, *To All Members of the AEU* (1938)
Brailsford, H.N. *Spain's Challenge to Labour* (Socialist League, 1936)
Brockway, Fenner. *The Truth About Barcelona* (ILP, 1937)
Brown, Isabel. *Spain: Durango – A Martyred City* (Relief Committee for the Victims of Fascism, 1937)
Burns, Emile. *Spain* (CPGB, 3 editions, 1936)
Campbell, J.R. *Spain's Left Critics* (CPGB, 1937)
Labour Spain Committee. *Labour and Spain*, official report of the 23 October 1938 LSC conference
Labour Party. *Agony of Spain* (1936)
—— *A Catholic Looks at Spain* (1937)
—— *Madrid – The 'Military' Atrocities of the Rebels* (1937)
—— *What Spanish Democracy is Fighting For* (1938)
London Trades Council. *The Truth Behind the Spanish Rebellion* (1936)
McGovern, John. *Why Bishops Back Franco* (ILP, 1936)
—— *Terror in Spain* (ILP, 1938)
MFGB. *Spain and Ourselves* (1938)
National Council of Labour. *An Appeal to Every British Citizen Who Loves Fair Play – Spain, Labour's Call to the Nation* (1938)
National Emergency Conference on Spain. *Report* of 23 April 1938 conference
Noel-Baker, Philip. *Franco Bombs British Seamen: Labour Condemns Chamberlain's Surrender* (1938)
Oliveira, Ramos. *The Drama of Spain* (NCL, 1936)
—— *Catholics and the War in Spain* (NCL, 1936)
Pollitt, Harry. *Spain and the TUC* (CPGB, 1936)
—— *Arms for Spain* (CPGB, 1936)
—— *Spain – What Next?* (CPGB, 1939)
TUC. *The Spanish Problem* (1936)
Voluntary Industrial Aid for Spain Committee. *Spain and the TUC* (1937)
—— *Spanish Army Fund* (1938)

5 Published memoirs

Attlee, C.R. *As It Happened* (London, 1954)
Azcárate y Flores, Pablo de. *Mi embajada en Londres durante la guerra civil española* (Barcelona, 1976)
Brown, W.J. *So Far...* (London, 1943)
Citrine, Lord. *I Search for Truth in the USSR* (1936)
—— *Men and Work: The Autobiography of Lord Citrine* (London, 1964)
—— *Two Careers – A Second Volume of Autobiography* (London, 1967)
Dalton, Hugh. *The Fateful Years: Memoirs 1931–1945* (London, 1957)
Horner, A. *Incorrigible Rebel* (London, 1960)
McGovern, John. *Neither Fear Nor Favour* (London, 1960)
McNair, John. *Spanish Diary* (Leeds, n.d.)

Manning, Leah. *What I Saw in Spain* (1936)
Morrison, Herbert. *Autobiography* (London, 1960)
Orwell, George. *Homage to Catalonia* (London, 1974 edition)
Paynter, Will. *My Generation* (London, 1972)

(B) SECONDARY SOURCES

Books

(Published in London unless otherwise stated)

Aldgate, Anthony. *Cinema and History – British Newsreels and the Spanish Civil War* (1979)
Alexander, Bill. *British Volunteers for Liberty: Spain 1936–1939* (1982)
Allen, V.L. *Trade Unions and the Government* (1960)
—— *Sociology of Industrial Relations* (1971)
Arnot, Robin Page. *The Miners – In Crisis and War* (1961)
Bagwell, P.S. *The Railwaymen: The History of the National Union of Railwaymen* (1963)
Bolloten, Burnett. *The Spanish Revolution* (Chapel Hill, 1979)
Boyd, A. *The Rise of the Irish Trade Unions, 1729–1970* (Tralee, 1970)
Bullock, Alan. *The Life and Times of Ernest Bevin, Volume 1, Trade Union Leader, 1881–1940* (1960)
Brademas, John. *Anarcosindicalismo y revolución en España, 1930–1937* (Barcelona, 1974)
Branson, Noreen. *History of the Communist Party of Great Britain, 1927–1941* (1985)
Branson, Noreen and Heinemann, Margot. *Britain in the Nineteen Thirties* (1970)
Brenan, Gerald. *The Spanish Labyrinth: An Account of the Social and Political Background of the Spanish Civil War* (Cambridge, 1943)
Briggs, A. and Saville, J. (eds.) *Essays in Labour History, 1918–1939* (1977)
Cahm, E. and Fisera, V.C. *Socialism and Nationalism in Contemporary Europe*, 3 vols. (Nottingham, 1980)
Calhoun, Daniel. *The United Front – The TUC and the Russians, 1923–1928* (Cambridge, 1976)
Carr, E.H. *The Comintern and the Spanish Civil War* (1984)
Cattell, David. *Communism and the Spanish Civil War* (Berkeley, 1955)
—— *Soviet Diplomacy and the Spanish Civil War* (Berkeley, 1957)
Child, John. *Industrial Relations in the British Printing Industry* (1967)
Claudin, Fernando. *The Communist Movement, From Comintern to Cominform* (1975)
Clegg, Hugh Armstrong. *Labour Relations in London Transport* (Oxford, 1950)
—— *A History of British Trade Unions Since 1889; Volume 2, 1911–1933* (Oxford, 1985)
Clinton, Alan. *The Trade Union Rank-and-File: Trades Councils in Britain, 1900–40* (Manchester, 1977)
—— *Post Office Workers – A Trade Union and Social History* (1984)

Cloud, Yvonne. *The Basque Children in England – An Account of their Life at North Stoneham Camp* (1937)

Cole, G.D.H. *British Trade Unionism Today – A Survey* (1939)

—— *A History of the Labour Party From 1914* (1948)

Corkill, D. and Rawnsley, S. *The Road to Spain. Anti-Fascists at War, 1936–1939* (Dunfermline, Fife, 1981)

Coverdale, John. *Italian Intervention in the Spanish Civil War* (1975)

Cronin, James. *Labour and Society in Britain, 1918–79* (1984)

Croucher, Richard. *Engineers at War, 1939–1945* (1982)

—— *We Refuse to Starve in Silence: A History of the National Unemployed Workers' Movement* (1987)

Cunningham, Valentine, (ed.) *The Penguin Book of Spanish Civil War Verse* (1980)

—— *Spanish Front: Writers on the Civil War* (Oxford, 1986)

Dewar, Hugo. *Communist Politics in Britain: The CPGB From its Origins to the Second World War* (1976)

Donoughue, Bernard and Jones, G.W. *Herbert Morrison: Portrait of a Politician* (1973)

Edwards, Jill. *The British Government and the Spanish Civil War, 1936–1939* (1979)

Ehrmann, H.W. *French Labor – From Popular Front to Liberation* (New York, 1947)

Foot, Michael. *Aneurin Bevan, A Biography. Volume 1, 1897–1945* (1962)

Fox, Alan. *A History of the National Union of Boot and Shoe Operatives* (Oxford, 1958)

—— *History and Heritage – The Social Origins of the British Industrial Relations System* (1985)

Francis, Hywel. *Miners Against Fascism: Wales and the Spanish Civil War* (1984)

Frow, E. and R. *Engineering Struggles: Episodes in the Story of the Shop Stewards' Movement* (Manchester, 1982)

Fuller, Ken. *Radical Aristocrats* (1985)

Fyrth, H.J. and Collins, H. *The Foundry Workers* (Manchester, 1959)

Fyrth, Jim. *The Signal was Spain: The Aid Spain Movement in Britain, 1936–39* (1986)

—— (ed.) *Britain, Fascism and the Popular Front* (1985)

Garratt, G.T. *Mussolini's Roman Empire* (Penguin Special, 1938)

Gordon, Michael. *Conflict and Consensus in Labour's Foreign Policy, 1914–1965* (Stanford, 1969)

Greene, Nathanael. *Crisis and Decline: The French Socialist Party in the Popular Front Era* (Ithaca, New York, 1969)

Gupta, P.S. *Imperialism and the British Labour Movement, 1914–1964* (1975)

Harris, Kenneth. *Attlee* (1982)

Haslam, Jonathan. *The Soviet Union and the Struggle for Collective Security in Europe, 1933–39* (1984)

Hinton, James. *The First Shop Stewards' Movement* (1973)

—— *Labour and Socialism. A History of the British Labour Movement, 1867–1974* (Brighton, 1983)

Hoskins, Katherine. *Today the Struggle* (Texas, 1969)

Hutt, Allen. *The Post-War History of the British Working Class* (Left Book Club, 1937)

—— *British Trade Unionism: A Short History* (1975 edn)

Jackson, Julian. *The Popular Front in France: Defending Democracy 1934–38* (Cambridge, 1988)

Jefferys, J.B. *The Story of the Engineers* (Letchworth, 1946)

Jupp, James. *The Radical Left in Britain, 1931–1941* (1982)

Kleine-Ahlbrandt, William Laird. *The Policy of Simmering: A Study of British Policy during the Spanish Civil War 1936–1939* (The Hague, 1962)

Koss, Stephen. *Rise and Fall of the Political Press in Britain*, Vol. 2 (1984)

Lampe, David. *Pyke – The Unknown Genius* (Aylesbury and Slough, 1959)

Lannon, Frances. *Privilege, Persecution and Prophecy: The Catholic Church in Spain, 1875–1975* (Oxford, 1987)

Legarretta, Dorothy. *The Guernica Generation, Basque Refugee Children of the Spanish Civil War* (Reno, Nevada, 1984)

Lerner, S. *Breakaway Unions and the Small Trade Union* (1961)

Leventhal, F.M. *The Last Dissenter: H.N. Brailsford and His World* (Oxford, 1985)

Logue, John. *Towards a Theory of Trade Union Internationalism* (University of Gothenburg, 1980)

Lovell, J. *British Trade Unions 1875–1933* (1977)

McCarthy, Charles. *Trade Unions in Ireland, 1894–1960* (Dublin, 1977)

MacDougall, Ian. *Voices from the Spanish Civil War: Personal Recollections of Scottish Volunteers in Republican Spain 1936–39* (Edinburgh, 1986)

Mahon, John. *Harry Pollitt – a biography* (1976)

Marquina Barrio, A. *La diplomacia vaticana y la Espana de Franco (1936–1945)* (Madrid, 1983)

Martin, Roderick. *Communism and the British Trade Unions, 1924–1935 – A Study of the National Minority Movement* (Oxford, 1969)

Martin, Ross. *TUC – The Growth of a Pressure Group, 1868–1975* (Oxford, 1980)

Miller, K.E. *Socialism and Foreign Policy* (The Hague, 1967)

Milotte, Mike. *Communism in Modern Ireland – The Pursuit of the Workers' Republic Since 1916* (Dublin, 1984)

Moloney, Thomas. *Westminster, Whitehall and the Vatican – The Role of Cardinal Hinsley, 1935–43* (Tunbridge Wells, 1985)

Morgan, Kenneth, O. *Labour People: Leaders and Lieutenants, Hardie to Kinnock* (Oxford, 1987)

Mortimer, J.E. *History of the Engineering and Shipbuilding Draughtsmen* (1960)

Naylor, J.F. *Labour's International Policy – The Labour Party in the 1930s* (1969)

Newton, Douglas. *British Labour, European Socialism and the Struggle for Peace, 1889–1914* (Oxford, 1985)

Nicholson, Marjorie. *The TUC Overseas: The Roots of Policy* (1986)

O'Riordan, Michael. *Connolly Column* (Dublin, 1979)

Pelling, Henry. *A Short History of the Labour Party* (1961)

—— *A History of British Trade Unionism* (1963)

Pike, David Winegate. *Conjecture, Propaganda and Deceit in the Spanish Civil War: The International Crisis over Spain as seen in the French Press* (Stanford, 1968)

Pimlott, Ben. *Labour and the Left in the 1930s* (Cambridge, 1977)
—— *Hugh Dalton* (1985)
Pimlott, Ben and Cook, Chris (eds.) *Trade Unions in British Politics* (1982)
Preston, Paul. *The Coming of the Spanish Civil War: Reform, Reaction and Revolution in the Second Republic* (1978)
—— (ed.) *Revolution and War in Spain, 1931–1939* (1984)
Price, John. *The International Labour Movement* (Royal Institute of International Affairs, 1945)
Puzzo, Dante A. *Spain and the Great Powers, 1936–1941* (Columbia University Press, 1962)
Robinson, Richard. *The Origins of Franco's Spain: The Right, the Republic and Revolution, 1931–1936* (Newton Abbot, 1970)
Saville, John. *The Labour Movement in Britain: A Commentary* (1988)
Saville, J. and Briggs, A. (eds.) *Essays in Labour History 1918–39* (1977)
Schevenals, Walther. *A Historical Precis: Forty Five Years. International Federation of Trade Unions* (IFTU, 1955)
Southworth, H.R. *Guernica! Guernica! A Study of Journalism, Diplomacy, Propaganda and History* (University of California, 1977)
Thomas, Hugh. *The Spanish Civil War* (1961)
Thomson, Don and Larson, Rodney. *Where Were You, Brother? An Account of Trade Union Imperialism* (1978)
Vernon, Betty. *Ellen Wilkinson, 1891–1947* (1982)
Walker, Graham S. *The Politics of Frustration – Harry Midgley and the Failure of Labour in Northern Ireland* (Manchester, 1985)
Waterman, Peter. (ed.) *For a New Labour Internationalism* (The Hague, 1984)
Watkins, Kenneth W. *Britain Divided: The Effect of the Spanish Civil War on British Political Opinion* (1963)
Whiting, R.C. *The View From Cowley: The Impact of Industrialization Upon Oxford, 1918–1939* (Oxford, 1983)
Whyte, J.H. *Church and State in Modern Ireland, 1923–1979* (Dublin, 1980)
—— *Catholics in Western Democracies – A Study in Political Behaviour* (Dublin, 1981)
Windrich, E. *British Labour's Foreign Policy* (Stanford, 1952)
Wood, Neal. *Communism and British Intellectuals* (1959)

Theses

Barrett, James. 'Busman's Punch: Rank-and-File Organization and Unofficial Industrial Action among London Busmen, 1913–1937', unpublished MA thesis, Warwick University, 1974
Buchanan, T.C. 'British Trade Union Internationalism and the Spanish Civil War', unpublished DPhil thesis, University of Oxford, 1987
Davis, Samuel. 'The British Labour Party and British Foreign Policy, 1933–1939' unpublished PhD thesis, London University, 1950
Drake, Peter. 'Labour and Spain: British Labour's response to the Spanish Civil War

with particular reference to the Labour Movement in Birmingham', unpublished MLitt thesis, Birmingham University, 1977

Heywood, Paul. 'Marxism and the Failure of Organised Socialism in Spain', unpublished PhD thesis, LSE, 1988

Errock, Heather Mary. 'The Attitude of the Labour Party to the Spanish Civil War', University of Keele, unpublished MA thesis, 1980

Lancien, D.P.F. 'British Left Wing Attitudes to the Spanish Civil War', unpublished BLitt thesis, University of Oxford, 1965

Mueller, Marja Lynne. 'The British Labour Party's response to the Spanish Civil War', unpublished PhD thesis, University of Alabama, 1979

Reid, Huw. 'The Furniture Workers from Craft to Industrial Union, 1865–1972', unpublished PhD thesis, Warwick University, 1982

Shepard, George W. 'The Theory and Practice of Internationalism in the British Labour Party, with Special Reference to the Inter-war Years', unpublished PhD thesis, London University, 1951

Articles

Alpert, Michael. 'Humanitarianism and Politics in the British Response to the Spanish Civil War, 1936–39', *European History Quarterly*, vol. 14, no. 4, October 1984

Bowyer Bell, J. 'Ireland and the Spanish Civil War, 1936–1939', *Studia Hibernica*, no. 9, 1969

Buchanan, Tom. 'The Role of the British Labour Movement in the Origins and Work of the Basque Children's Committee, 1937–39', *European History Quarterly*, vol. 18, April 1988

—— 'The Politics of Internationalism: The Amalgamated Engineering Union and the Spanish Civil War', *Bulletin of the Society for the Study of Labour History*, vol. 53, Part 3, 1988

Carlton, David. 'Eden, Blum and the Origins of Non-Intervention', *Journal of Contemporary History*, vol. 6 (3), 1971

Eatwell, Roger. 'Munich Public Opinion and the Popular Front', *Journal of Contemporary History* (1971)

Exell, Arthur. 'Morris Motors in the 1930's, Part 2 – Politics and Trades Unionism', *History Workshop Journal*, no. 7, Spring 1979

Gallagher, Tom. 'Scottish Catholics and the British Left, 1918–1939', *The Innes Review*, vol. 34, no. 1, Spring 1983

Fleay, C. and Sanders, M.L. 'The Labour Spain Committee: Labour Party Policy and the Spanish Civil War', *The Historical Journal*, 28, 1, 1985

Francis, Hywel. 'Welsh Miners and the Spanish Civil War', *Journal of Contemporary History*, vol. 5, no. 3, 1970

Gallagher, M.D. 'Leon Blum and the Spanish Civil War', *Journal of Contemporary History*, vol. 6 (3), 1971

Graham, Helen. 'The Spanish Socialist Party in Power and the Government of Juan Negrín, 1937–9', *European History Quarterly*, vol. 18, 2, April 1988

Green, Nan. 'The Communist Party and the War in Spain', *Marxism Today*, 14, 1970

Green, Nan and Elliott, A.M. 'Spain Against Fascism 1936–39', *Our History*, pamphlet 67

Haworth, Jolyon. 'French Workers and German Workers – The Impossibility of Internationalism, 1900–1914', *European Studies Quarterly*, vol. 15, no. 1, January 1985

Heywood, Paul. 'De las dificultudes para ser marxista: el PSOE, 1879–1921', *Sistema*, 74, September 1986

Hyman, R. 'Officialdom and Opposition: Leadership and Rank-and-File in Trade Unions', *Bulletin of the Society for the Study of Labour History*, no. 46, Spring 1983

Kiernan, V.G. 'Labour and the War in Spain', *Journal of the Scottish Labour History Society*, no. 11, May 1977

Little, Douglas. 'Red Scare, 1936: Anti-Bolshevism and the Origins of British Non-Intervention in the Spanish Civil War', *Journal of Contemporary History*, vol. 23, April 1988

Macfarlane, L.J. 'Hands off Russia – British Labour and the Russo-Polish War, 1920', *Past and Present*, 38, December 1967

McKinlay, Alan. 'From Industrial Serf to Wage Labourer: The 1937 Apprentice revolt in Britain', *International Review of Social History*, vol. 21, Part 1, 1986

Moran, W. 'The Dublin Lockout – 1913', *Bulletin of the Society for the Study of Labour History*, 27, Autumn 1973

Newman, Michael. 'Democracy versus Dictatorship: Labour's Role in the Struggle against British Fascism, 1933–1936', *History Workshop Journal*, 5, Spring 1978

Parker, R.A.C. 'British Rearmament, 1936–1939: Treasury, Trade Unions and Skilled Labour', *English Historical Review*, 379, April 1981

Samuel, Raphael. 'The Lost World of British Communism', *New Left Review*, 154, December 1985

—— 'Staying Power; The Lost World of British Communism, Part 2', *New Left Review*, 156, March/April 1986

Samuels, Stuart. 'The Left Book Club', *Journal of Contemporary History*, vol. 1, no. 2, 1966

Stone, Glyn. 'Britain, Non-Intervention and the Spanish Civil War', *European Studies Review*, vol. 9, 1979

Swain, Geoffrey. 'Was the Profintern really necessary?', *European History Quarterly*, vol. 17, no. 1, January 1987

White, Stephen. 'Labour's Council of Action 1920', *Journal of Contemporary History*, vol. 9, no. 4, October 1974

Zeitlin, Jonathan. 'Trade Unions and Job Control: A Critique of "Rank-and-Filism"', *Bulletin of the Society for the Study of Labour History*, no. 46, Spring 1983

—— 'Debating "Rank-and-Filist" Labour History' with Richard Price and James E. Cronin, *International Review of Social History*, vol. 34, 1, 1989

INDEX

Acción Popular, 182
Adams, David, 189
Adams, Harry, 161
Adams de Puertas, Gwendolen, 149
Adler, Friedrich, 76, 92, 105, 144, 147, 157
'Aid Spain Movement', 5, 138, 139
Aid Spain/Spanish Aid Committees, 74,
   118, 137, 166, 204
Aircraft Shop Stewards' National Council,
   124, 198, 216–19
Airlandis, Sr, 43, 48, 157
Alcázar, Toledo, 29
Alexander, A.V., 40n5, 101, 112
Alexander, Bill, 160
Allen, V.L., 8
Almería, 91
Alpert, Michael, 138n3, 168
Amalgamated Engineering Union, 30, 49,
   62, 96–7, 110, 122, 125, 135, 154, 159,
   162, 163, 198; ('£50,000 Fund') 135,
   216; (and rank-and-file workers'
   movement) 216–19
Amalgamated Engineering Union, London
   District Council, 62, 218–19
Amalgamated Society of Woodworkers,
   135, 154–5, 177n43
Amalgamated Union of Building Trade
   Workers, 47, 130, 219
Anarchism, Spanish, 24, 25, 27, 28, 30, 43,
   44n24, 45, 68, 75, 76, 114, 148, 173
Ancient Order of Hibernians, 187
Anglo-Russian Joint Advisory Committee,
   20
Anschluss, 108, 123
Associated Society of Locomotive Engineers
   and Firemen, 125, 131
Association of Engineering and Shipbuilding
   Draughtsmen, 177n43

Asturias, (1934 revolt in) 27, 31, 46;
   (conquest of) 103, 106; (attempt to
   save miners from) 103–6; (orphans
   from) 133
Atholl, Katherine Duchess of, 74, 123, 127,
   139
Attlee, Clement, ('Clam' Attlee) 14; 40n5,
   41n8, 55, 65, 69, 87, 90, 94, 104n154,
   104n155, 111n8, 112, 119, 123n59, 178,
   221, 224, 227, 228; (and the
   International Brigades) 14, 221n3;
   (interventions on Spain in Parliament)
   84, 100–1, 211
Auden, W.H., 18n47
Auriol, Vincent, 57
Austria, fund-raising for the workers of,
   141, 142
Azcárate, Pablo de, 125n72, 127n81
Aznar, Sr, 101
Azorín, Francisco, 91

Backworth, S.S., 100, 101, 149–50
Badajoz, 28, 171
Baldwin, Stanley, 37, 59
Balliol College, the Master of, 120
Barcelona, 25, 28, 43, 44n24, 76, 115,
   170n9, 187, 210, 216
Basque children, care of in Britain, 5,
   31n74, 80n32, 102, 137, 150, 153, 159,
   163–4, 165, 166, 183, 221
Basque Children's Committee, 163–4, 183
Basque country, 26, 28, 91, 100–3
Basque Government, 101, 102–3
Basques, 100n139, 101, 115
Batista i Roca, Sr, 115
Baxter, Tom, 164
Beamish, Olive, 203, 204
Belgium, and the Spanish Civil War, 3

Belin, René, 57n96
Berridge, Claude, 218, 219
Bevan, Aneurin, 68
Bevin, Ernest, xii, xiii, 9; (career of) 10–11; (relations with Citrine) 11n22; 13, 22, 30; (and internationalism) 40; 42, 45, 59, 71, (and mediation in Spain) 77; (and the political use of industrial action) 80–1; 82, 83, 87, (speech at March 1937 International Conference) 88–9; 119, 125n72, 131, 150n60, 174, 179, 191, (and Irish Branches of the T&GWU) 193–4; 204, (role in Spanish Civil War assessed) 228
(and the British Government) 51, 64, 69, 88, 90, 93, 103n150
(and Communism and the Popular Front) 5, 34, 35–6, 47n36, 75, 88, 93, 158, 197
(and controversy over his speech at International Conference) 94–5, 205
(and the Labour Party) 13, 15, 60
(and Non-Intervention) 18, 56, 60, 61, 63–4, 65, 67, 68, 69, 88–9, 90
(and rearmament) 4, 15, 226
(and Spain) 4, 46, 58
(and union members) 11, 62, 197, 205, 223
Bilbao, 91, 100, 101, 102, 149, 163
Birmingham, 6, 96, 164, 175
Blum, Léon, 42, 46, 56, 58, 64, 65, 68, (resigns) 79; 100–1, 103, (second administration of) 107; 141n15
(and Non-Intervention) 17, 37–8, 48, 52, 80n28
Board of Trade, 210, 211, 212, 215
Bolton, W., 78
Boston, Massachusetts, 210–15
Bowen, J., 151
Bracke, Alexandre, 57, 70
Brady, Arthur, 128
Brailsford, H.N., 159–60, 171
Bramley, Fred, 9
Bridgewater, by-election in, 121
Bright, John, 17–18, 18n46
Briginshaw, R.W., 200, 206, 207, 208
Brisky, Bill, 205
Britain, impact of Spanish Civil War on, 3, 30, 36, 74–5, (opinion poll findings) 107n1; 111, 141, (attitudes of British Catholics) 167–91
Broadbent, C., 112n15
Brockway, Fenner, 115
Bromley, J., 2n3
Brothers, Mr, 69n166
Brown, Isabel, 67n155, 74, 139, 140

Brown, W.J., 9n17
Browne, Capt. R.F., 78n21
Browning, Felicia, 207
Brunete, battle of, 75
Bullock, Alan, 4
Busman's Punch, 198, 199, 205

Cádiz, 116, 116n29
Calvo Sotelo, Jose, 28
Cambon, M., Minister at the French Embassy in London, 55
Campbell, J.R., 132n103, 207
Campbell Bannerman, Sir Henry, 18n46
Cardiff, 82, 165, 166
Carrillo, Wenceslao, 222n4
Casado, Colonel, 109
Catalonia, 24, 25, 26, 28, 34, 43, 44n24, 75, 76, 103, 107, 108, 109, 115, 171, 216
Catholic Church, in England, Wales and Scotland, 168n3, 170, 171, 178–9, 180, 183, 189
Catholic Church, in Spain, 26, 172, 173, 175, 180, 187, 188, 192, (atrocities against) 28, 170–1
Catholic Herald, The, 156, 171, 181, 190, 191
Catholic Times, The, 172, 178, 181
Catholic Worker, The, 170
Catholic Vocational Guilds, 178, 179, 183n62, 190–1
Catholics, in Britain, 3, 36, 46, 62, 80n32, 141, 163, 167–91 *passim*, 194–5; (position of in the British labour movement) 169; (fears of during the Spanish Civil War) 172–3; (the 'Catholic vote') 175–6; (in the unions) 176–8; 179–81, (evidence for the attitudes of working-class Catholics) 183–8; 188–9
Catholics and the Civil War in Spain, NCL pamphlet, 182
Central Bus Committee, 198, 199, 206
Chalmers-Mitchell, Sir Peter, 123
Chamberlain, Neville, 34, 69, 79, 102–3, 108, 110, 218
Chatfield, Admiral, 52
Chautemps, Camille, 80
China, attacked by Japan, 83, 214
Church of England, 169, 188n85
Churchill, Viscount, 66
Citrine, Sir Walter, xii, xiii, (career of) 9–10; (relations with Bevin) 11n22; 39, (criticises Largo Caballero) 44–5; 48, (attempts to procure arms) 49; 57, (suppresses CGT resolution) 65n142;

67, 77, (and the International Brigades)
78; 81, (and crisis in the LSI) 91–3; 95,
(concept of political action) 99–100;
(and Northern Front of the Civil War)
100–6; (and split in the UGT) 113–14;
124, 132, 140, 146, 149, (and atrocities)
173–4; 179, (meets Archbishop
Hinsley) 182–3; (and Catholic Guilds)
191; 195, (and rank-and-file
delegation) 200–2; 220, 225n13
(assessment of role in the Spanish Civil
War) 136, 222–3; 227–8
(and the British Government) 40–1, 46,
50–1, 53–4, 59, 62–3, 89–90, 94, 100–6,
108–9, 116–17
(and Communism and the Popular Front)
34–5, 85, 91, 93, 113–14, 115, 157–8, 159
(criticism of) 41, 161, 204, 222
(and industrial action for political
purposes) 111, 118, 130–1
(and internationalism) 21–2, 40
(and the Labour Party) 7n13, 10, 84, 89,
101, 194n110, 203
(memoirs of) xi, 132, 222
(and Non-Intervention) 40–2, 46, 49, 50,
52–3, 55, 56, 58, 59, 60–1, 62–3, 66,
70–1, 73, 81, 84, 87, 93, 112, 117, 143,
201
(and rearmament) 15, 162, 226
(and relief work) 54, 129, 135, 141, 143,
144, 145, 149–50, 151, 155n85, 157,
160, 162, 202
(and Spain) 10, 31, 42–3, 44–6, 58, 75, 76,
115
Civil Service Clerical Association, 142n16,
177
Civil Service, trade unions in, 9n15
Clegg, Hugh, 11
Clerk, Sir George, 38
Clinton, Alan, 197
Clive, Lewis, 112n15
Clutterbuck, J., 151
Cockburn, Claud, a.k.a. Frank Pitcairn,
94n116, 95
Cole, G.D.H., 120
Comintern (The Third International), 20,
22, 25, 29, 32, 77, 83, 91–2, 93n112,
142
Comité Nacional de Ayuda a España, 147–8
Communist Party of Great Britain, 4n6, 5,
6, 8, 12, (history of) 32–3; (adopts the
Popular Front) 33; 34, 35, (and Non-
Intervention) 47; 62, 120, 120n44, 122,
126, 129, (and relief work) 139–41;
(London District of) 140; 150, 157–9,

165, 187, 197, 198, 202, 207, 214,
('Arms for Spain' campaign) 216–17;
(role in Spanish Civil War assessed)
224–6
Communist Solar System, The, Labour
Party pamphlet, 34
Comorera, Juan, 43, 44
Confederación Española de Derechas
Autónomas, 26, 27, 34, 182
Confederación Nacional del Trabajo,
10n21, 24, 25, 113, 126
Confédération Général du Travail, 20, 44,
48, 56, (alleged communist influence
over) 57–8; 58, 64, 65, 68, 132; (Relief
work independent from the ISF) 57n92,
145
Conservative Party, the British, 7, 41n8, 52,
169, 184, 185, 186, 194n110
Co-operative Movement, the British, 16, 36,
119, 120, 155, 156, 168n4, 172, 178
Cordero, Manuel, 87n74, 88, 173
Cot, Pierre, 37–8
Council of Action, 1920, 18, 19
Cranborne, Lord, 62–3, 93n110, 103, 116,
211
Cripps, Sir Stafford, 14n37, 33, (and Non-
Intervention) 47; 55, 61, 118–19, 122,
124, 127, 131n96, 162, 228
Croucher, Richard, 218

Daily Herald, 44 (and Non-Intervention)
47; 55, 58, 64, 68n164, 76, 91, 116, 119,
150, 174, 201, 207
Daily Mail, 171, 180, 188, 200, 206
Daily Worker, (and Non-Intervention) 47;
88, 94, 121, 123, 156, 175, 202, 203,
207, 213, 218, 219
Dallas, George, 58n101, 64, 225n13
Dalton, Hugh, xii, 4, 11, 14–15, 31, 40n5,
41, (attitude to Spanish socialism) 42;
45, (and Portugal) 52; 59, 60, 64, 80,
80n28, 90n96, 111–12, 114, 175, 222,
226, 228
Darlan, Admiral, 52
Deakin, Arthur, 131
De Asúa, Jiménez, 68, 69
De Brouckère, Louis, 43, 49, 52, 76, 86, 91,
92, 94, 105
Defence of Madrid, (film), 185
De Havilland, workers for, 216–17
Delbos, Yvon, 52, 53, 101, 103
De los Ríos, Fernando, 48, 49, 60, 64, 143,
144, 146
Del Vayo, Álvarez, 68, 90n96, 94n116, 103,
104, 221n1

Delvigne, M., 147, 151
De Palencia, Isabel, 69, 71
Deutsch, Julius, 111–12
Dmitrov, Georgi, 91–2
Dobbie, William, 67, 165
Dobbs, Alfred, 98, 98n132
Drake, Peter, 6, 175
Drama of Spain, The, NCL pamphlet, 172, 182, 183
Dukes, Charles, 68, 125n72
Durutti, Buenaventura, 24

Ebro, battle of the, 107–8
Eden, Anthony, 37, 50–1, 52, 53–5, 63, 68, 79, 89–91, 93, 94n116, 100, (and Northern Front of the Civil War) 101–5; 108, 143, 222, 227
Edwards, Ebby, 61, 104, 105, 117
Edwards, Jill, 79
Egan, Councillor, 175n35
Electrical Trades Union, 9
Elger, William, 129
Elliott, Sydney, 120, 123n58
Elvin, George, 170n9
Elvin, H.H., 123n59

Federación Anarquista Ibérica, 24, 44n24
Fallon, Father, 172
Faure, Paul, 56
Ferrer, Francisco, 30
Fifeshire, Scotland, 187
Fimmen, Edo, 21, 77, 81–3, 146
Findlay, Arthur, 156
Foreign Enlistment Act, 1870, 78
Foreign Office, the British, 41, 42, 47, 50–1, 52, 54, 62–3, 77, 78n21, 89–91, 93, 93n110, 100, 103, 104, 105, 116–17, 149n56, 158n101, 211, 215
France, and the Spanish Civil War, 37–8, 56, 93, 98
Francis, Hywel, 6, 22, 140
Franco, Francisco, (role in the Spanish Civil War) 28, 61, 78, 89, 90, 103–4, 105, 107, 109, 219, 221, 222
(British attitudes towards) 102, 111, 117, 161, 167, 171, 172, 175n35, 179, 182, 192, 214
Franco–Spanish Treaty, 1935, 50n48
Friends of New Spain, 31
Fyrth, Jim, 5, 138
Gallacher, William, 187
Gallagher, Tom, 186
Garrett, G.T., 78, 78n18, 194
General Federation of Trade Unions, 7–8, 20

General Strike, 1926, 9, 10, 18, 130, 206, 208
Germany, (and Non-Intervention) 48, 63, 79, 91
(exploits minerals in Spain) 87–8, 90
(intervenes in the Spanish Civil War) 38, 66, 77, 93, 94, 97, 99, 157
(German warship shells Almería) 91
Gibson, George, 99, 150, 173
Gijón, attempts to rescue miners from, October 1937, 103–6
Gillies, William, 31, 40, 41, 44n24, 48, 51–2, 53, 54, 58, 64, 70, 77, 90n96, 92, 111, 128n83, 139, 143, 157, 172, 174
Giral, José, 28
Glasgow, 185, 186–8
Greene, Ben, 95
Greenwood Arthur, 40, 50–1, 54, 55, 58, 62, 68, 69, 70, 79, 84, 111n8
Grenfell, David, 60, 68, 87, 121, 123n58, 151n63, 165
Griffin, Mr, Labour Party Parliamentary Agent for St Helens, 184–5
Griffiths, James, 124
Grumbach, Solomon, 70
Gollancz, Victor, 104n155, 123n58
Guadalajara, battle of, 75, 91n97
Guernica, 77, 100, 171

Haldane, Charlotte, 160
Halifax, Lord, 54, 108, 109, 117–18, 221n1
Hann, Maurice, 59n109
Harris, Oliver, 105
Hastings, Lord, 67n155
Hayday, Arthur, 91–2
Henderson, Arthur, 7, 17
Henson, Jim, 82–3, 165
Hernández, Carlos, 147
Hicks, George, 40, 64, 67–8, 111, 135, 144, 146, 158, 176, 194
Hinsley, Archbishop, 168n3, 169, (meets labour delegation) 179–81, (relations with Citrine) 182–3
Hoare, Sir Samuel, 101
Hoare–Laval Pact, 1935, 101n145
Holmes, George, 207
Homage to Catalonia, 76, 170n9
Home Counties Labour Association, 95–6
Home Office, the, 69n166, 86
Horner, Arthur, 32, 35, 106, 120, 122, 124, 132n103, 134
Howell, W., 218
Huysmans, Camille, 85, 145

Independent Labour Party, 13, 19, 20, 115, 120, 120n44, 150, 172, 186, 187

Inskip, Sir Thomas, 117
International Brigades, xiii, 6, 33, 77–9, 89, 108, 126, 127, 132, 142, 201, 217, 221n3, 222n5, 224, 225
International Brigades, British Battalion of, 14, 74–5, 90, 112, 128, 132, 133, 134, 159, 205
International Brigades Dependants and Wounded Aid Committee, 75, 137, 152, 159–61, 225n13
International Brigades, National Memorial Fund, 161
International Committee for the Co-ordination of Aid to the Spanish Republic, 57
International Conference, London, 10 March 1937, 86–9, 92, 94, 173
International Federation of Trade Unions, (formation of) 20; (in the 1930s) 21–2; 29, (and pre-Civil War Spain) 31; 40, 43, (first response to Civil War) 48; 49, 57, 64, 74, (assessment of Spanish political situation, 1937) 76; (boycott of Spanish rebels) 81; 83, 85, (and crisis in the LSI 91–3; (and split in the UGT) 113–14; 116, 132, 133, 149, 158, 204, 222n4, 225
(General Council of) 92, 93, 111
(and relief work) 29, 142, 144–7, 151, 157, 164
International Federation of Trade Unions, Joint meetings with the LSI, (28 July 1936) 43, 48, 52, 143, 157; (21 August 1936) 52, 56, 58, 144; (28 September 1936) 67–8, 173; (26 October 1936) 56, 69–70; (4 and 5 December 1936) 81, 84, 174; (14 January 1937) 85; (9 March 1937) 79, 86–7; (25 May 1937) 77; (16 June 1937) 91–2; (24 June 1936) 92–3; (13–16 September 1937) 94, 114; (14 April 1938) 112
International Solidarity Fund, of the LSI and IFTU, 29, 135, 142, 142n16, 143, (nature of) 144–7; 148, 149, 152, 155, 160, 161, (Madrid Committee of) 147, 151, 152
International Transport Workers' Federation, 21, 22, 77, (boycott of Spanish rebels) 81–3; 146, 165, 209
Internationalism, in the labour movement, (history of) 17–23; (and the Spanish Civil War) 29–30; 40, 41, (centrality of humanitarian relief work to) 54; 65–6, 71–2, 135, 141–2, 199, 220, 221, 223, 226–7, 228

Ireland, xii, (1913 Dublin lockout) 18–19, 62, (and Spanish Civil War) 192–4
Irish Christian Front, 192–3
Irish Labour Party, 193
Irish Trades Union Congress, 192
Irish Transport and General Workers' Union, 192–3
Italy: (and Non-Intervention) 38, 48, 54, 79, 90, 91n97
(and the British Government) 108–9
(intervenes in Spanish Civil War) 38, 66, 75, 77, 93, 99, 116, 157

Jacobs, Joseph, 203, 204
Japan, aggression against China, 83, 214
Jarama, battle of the, 75
Jolly George, S.S., 18
Jones, J.L., 112n15
Jones, Joseph, 125, 133
Jones, W.J. (Bill), 199, 200, 204, 205
Jouhaux, Léon, 43–4, 48, 49–50, 52, 53, 56, 64, 68, 70, 81, 85, 92, 94, 100–1, (and split in the UGT) 114; 132
Jowitt, Sir William, 131n96

Kaylor, Mr, 218–19
Kiernan, Victor, 167–8
Krier-Becker, Lily, 113n19

Labour and Socialist International, (formation of) 20; (in the 1930s) 21; (and fascism) 29; (and pre-Civil War Spain) 31; 40, 42, 43, (initial response to the Spanish Civil War) 48; 57, 64, 74, 76, 83, 85, 86, (crisis in) 91–3; 105, 111, 116, 132, 151, 164, 225, (and relief work) 142, 144–7
Labour and Socialist International, Joint meetings with the IFTU: *see under* International Federation of Trade Unions, Joint meetings with the LSI
Labour movement, British, xiii, 2, 3, 4, 5, (defined) 6; (history of) 7–17; (debate on nature of in the 1930s) 15–17; (internationalism of) 17–23; (and anti-communism) 34–5; 36, (origins of attitude to Non-Intervention) 39–48; (attitudes to Spanish labour) 42–6; (first delegation to Eden) 50–1; (second delegation to Eden) 53–4; (policy on Non-Intervention) 61; (delegation to Foreign Office) 62–3; (delegation to Paris) 64; (changes position on Non-Intervention) 70–1; 73, 74, (and Spanish politics) 75–6; (and the

International Brigades) 78–9;
(international ill-feeling towards) 83;
(and communism) 85; 89, 92, (secrecy
of response to Civil War) 95; 104, 106,
(policy in 1938–9) 110; (attitude to
Spanish labour in 1938–9) 112–16; (and
the Popular Front) 121–2; (relief work
of) 137; (and the 'Aid Spain
Movement') 138; (and the
International Solidarity Fund) 144–52;
(and 'unofficial' campaigns) 156–63;
(and care for Basque children) 163–4;
(and working-class Catholics) 169,
171–2; (success of leaders during
Spanish Civil War) 222–3; 226; (in the
1930s) 227

Labour Movement Conference, 16, 40, 45,
55, 227; (28 August 1936) 60–1; (4
September 1936) 63–4; (9 September
1936) 65–6; (28 October 1936) 71, 80;
(9 March 1937) 87–8; (23 June 1937)
93

Labour Party, xi, xii, 2, 4, 5, (and 1931)
crisis) 7; 9n15, 10, 11, (in the 1930s)
12–17; (constituencies movement)
13–14; 23, (pre-Civil War aid to PSOE)
31; 40, (defence policy criticised) 60;
62, 87–8, (rank-and-file discontent)
95–6; 97, 100, 107, 111, (criticised by
the UGT) 112; 118, 119, 120, 123, 125,
126, 127, 128, 150, 159, 193, 194n110,
219, (role in Spanish Civil War
assessed) 227–8

(and British Catholics) 168–70, 175–6,
178, 180, 181–2, 184–7, 188, 189, 194
(and the British government) 50–1, 53–4,
58, 59, 62–3
(and communism and the Popular Front)
32, 33, 34–6, 92, 121, 140, 148, 225–6
(and the International Brigades) 78, 112,
126
(and internationalism) 17–18, 19, 22, 40
(and Non-Intervention) 61, 68–9, 79, 96,
97
(performance on Spain in Parliament),
84–5, 100–1, 116, 124
(and relief work and fund-raising) 139,
147–8, 149, 155–6, 163, 165, 166
(and the trade unions) xiii, 8, 9n15, 13,
15–17, 89, 98, 122, 130, 227

Labour Party, Conferences, (1936) 68–9,
176; (1937) 73, 118, 126; (1939) 222

Labour Party International Department, 67,
228n17

Labour Party, London, 110n7, 121, 179, 202

Labour Party National Executive Committee,
1n1, 11, 13, 15, 16, 48, 64, 93, 98, 119,
120, 123n58, 126, 127, 130n91, 175,
186, 222n5, 223n8

Labour Party National Executive
Committee, Spain Campaign
Committee of, 96, 118–19, 126, 162,
222n5, 228

Labour Spain Committee, 96, 119, 121,
126–7, 136

Lansbury, George, 7, 14, 15, 59

Largo Caballero, Francisco, 25, 27,
(becomes Prime Minister) 29, 31, 42,
44; (criticised by Citrine) 45; 46, 47,
75, 76, 77, 86, 94, 112–14, 145, 146,
147, 180, 222n4

Laski, Harold, 120, 126

Lathan, George, 128n83

Lavery, F.J., 179, 181n55

Lawther, Will, 66, 132n103, 134

League of Nations, 17, 18, 73, 86, 90,
92n101, 93, 94, 99, 103

Left, the British, (defined) 119–20; (divisions
within) 120–3, 126; (failure of)
223–4; (in the Labour Party) 13, 33,
62n126, 95–6

Left Book Club, 33

Lerroux, Alejandro, 26, 27, 46

Linaria, S.S., 210–15

Listowel, Lord, 31, 104n155

Little, Jack, 50, 67, 125, 219

Lizaso, Sr, 102

Llandovery Castle, S.S., 215

Lloyd Thomas, Hugh, 53n66

Logan, David, 188

London County Council, 175, 187, 188, 189

London Trades Council, (and Non-
Intervention) 47; 123n59, 188, 202–3,
205

Longuet, Jean, 56, 94

McCretton, Norman, 173

MacDonald, Ramsay, 7, 10, 17

MacDonnell, J.H., 189

McGovern, John, 120n44, 187–8, 187n79

McNair, John, 187

Madariaga, Salvador de, 77

Madrid, 25, 28, 43, 76, 78, 107, 109, 116,
146, 147, 151

Maisky, Ivan, 90n96, 111n8

Manchester Guardian, 54, 64, 182

Mander, Geoffrey, 123n59

Manning, Leah, 31n74, 163

Marchbank, John 63, 66, 83, 125n72, 146–7,
227

Mental Health and Institutional Workers' Union, 99, 150, 176

Merchant Shipping Act, 1888, 209, 212, 213, 215

Merchant Shipping (Carriage of Munitions to Spain) Act, 1937, 211

Mexico, 54n70, 93

Middleton, James, 50, 62n126, 96, 111, 112, 115, 123n58, 141, 143, 153, 164, 195, 224, 225n13

Midgley, Harry, 158n101, 192

'Milk for Spain' scheme, 118–19, 148, 156, 172, 228

Miners, (in South Wales) 6, 22, 62n125, 105, 120, 124, 125, 132, 133, 134; (in Durham) 62n125, 124, 125, 133, 134; (in Yorkshire) 133, 134, 191; (in Nottinghamshire) 134; (in Scotland) 134; (in Asturias) 27, 103–6, 133

Miners' Federation of Great Britain, (and Northern Front of Civil War) 104–6, 122, (special conference of) 124–5, 132, ('levy' fund for Spain) 133–5, 136, 137n1, 154, 161

Minority Movements, 8, 32, 190, 198

Morgan, Dr H.B., 151, 159, 179–82

Morocco, use of soldiers from by Spanish rebels, 28, 61

Morrison, Herbert, 14–15, 41, 59, 80, 175, 202, 228, (opposes Non-Intervention) 14n37, 60, 61, 71

Mosley, Sir Oswald, 33, 34, 171

Mounsey, George, 54, 63

Munich, agreement, 108, 109, 111n8, 120, 133, 222

Murray, David, 172–3, 187

Murray, Gilbert, 123

Murray, Jane, 128

Murray, Thomas, 112n15, 128

Nathans, N., 77, 146

National Amalgamated Furnishing Trades Association, 66, 67, 120

National Amalgamated Union of Shop Assistants, 23, 98

National Council of Civil Liberties, 217n114

National Council of Labour, (formation of National Joint Council) 8; (revived in 1932) 13; 14, 15, 55, 59, 62, 64, 68, 95, 97–8, 111n8, (discusses armistice in Spain) 112n17; 127, 136, 151, (and Spanish Medical Aid) 157–9; (and International Brigades Dependents Aid) 159–61; 163, 172, 199, 200, 202, 203, 225n13, 227;

(controls international contracts) 42, 57 (important meetings of) (25 August 1936), 16, 40, 52, 60, 191; (27 August 1936) 40, 42, 54; (21 October 1936), 69; (22 June 1937) 92–3 (and its relief fund) 19, 129, 140, 143, 144, 147, 150, 152, 160, 164, 166

'National Emergency Conference', London, 23 April 1938, 123–4, 216

National Federation of Building Trade Operatives, 135

National Government, 2, (formation of) 7; 15, 34, 40, 49, 60, (and the 'blockade' of Bilbao) 100; 104, 106n167, (and the Anglo-Italian Agreement) 108–9; (foreign policy in 1938–9) 108–9; (and rearmament) 110; (and Spanish Medical Aid) 159; 199, (recognises Franco) 219

(and Non-Intervention) 37–8, 51, 52, 63–4, 80–1, 97

National Joint Committee for Spanish Relief, 74, 137, 139, 140, 152, 163

National Maritime Board, 210, 211

National Society of Operative Printers and Assistants, 201, 206

National Society of Painters, 154, 161n116

National Trade Union Club, 157, 179

National Unemployed Workers' Movement, 32

National Union of Boot and Shoe Operatives, 97–8, 161

National Union of Clerks, 154, 177n43

National Union of Distributive and Allied Workers, 69n168, 98, 156, 172, 184–6

National Union of Foundry Workers, 154

National Union of General and Municipal Workers, 23, 68n164, 125n72, 177n43

National Union of Journalists, 209

National Union of Railwaymen, 63, 83, 99, 125n72, 146, 161, 192, 193

National Union of Scottish Mineworkers, 134

National Union of Seamen, 82n49, 83, 116n29, 176, 209–15, 221

National Union of Tailors and Garment Workers, 153, 179, 189n88

National Union of Vehicle Builders, 162

Naylor, J.F., 4n6, 85

Negrín, Juan, 75, 76, 77, 108, 109, 111, 112, 115, 148

Nenni, Pietro, 42, 58n101, 76

Newcastle, 82

New Leader, 65n142, 186

New Propeller, 198

New Statesman and Nation, 65n142
News Chronicle, 52, 65n142, 105, 121
Newspaper Proprietors Association, 207–8
Noel-Baker, Philip, 18, 35n83, 40, 41n8, 65, 84–5, 87, 104n155, 112, 123n59, 128n83, 178
Non-Intervention, international policy of, 2, 11, 16, 17, 29, 36, 41, (initial ambivalence towards on left) 46–8; 48, 51, (and Portugal) 53; (attitude of French communists) 56; 61, (1936 TUC Congress debate) 66–7; 68, 70, 71, 73–4, 79, 80n28, 92, 107, 109, 110, 112, 175, 184, 205, (and Nitrates) 210–11; 222, 226
    (and humanitarian relief) 54, 143
    (labour movement support for) 55–9, 61, 68, 83–5, 86–7, 88–9, 90, 95, 97, 99, 174, 189, 193, 194
    (opposition to) 14n37, 60, 61, 63, 66–7, 71, 88, 96, 97, 98, 116, 117, 122, 124, 222
    (origins of) 37–9, 52–3
Non-Intervention Supervisory Committee, 38, 63, 79, 86, 93
Northern Ireland Labour Party, 192
Norway, seamen from boycott Spanish rebels, 82
Nyon conference, 79

O'Brien, Tom, 179–80, 181, 189
O'Brien, William, 192
O'Duffy, Eammon, 192
O'Hanlon, F., 168n3, 189
Orwell, George, 76, 170n9
Oviedo, 145
Oxford, 1938 by-election, 120

Pacifism, 15, 18, 59–60
Page Arnot, Robin, 122
Palme Dutt, Rajani, 32
Papworth, A.F. (Bert), 188, 198, 199, 200, 203n40, 204, 205
Parliamentary Labour Party, 13, 16, 64, 89, 116, 203
Parti Communiste Français (and Non-Intervention), 56, 58, 64, 65
Pardito Comunista de España, 25, 46, 75–6, 77, 88, 109, 112–15
Partido Obrero de Unificación Marxista, 28, 44, 44n24, 75, 76, 77, 115, 120
Partido Socialista Obrero Español, 1, 21, (origins of) 24–5; (left-turn under Largo Caballero) 27; 29, 30, 31, 76, 79, 84, 87, 87n74, 88, 91, 113, 126, 144, 146, 147, 171, 173

Partit Socialista Unificat de Catalunya, 43
Patton, Rev. J., 212–13
Paynter, Will, 132
Pelling, Henry, 15–16
Peña, Ramon Gonzáles, 113–14, 222n4
Pimlott, Ben, 15–16
Pitcairn, Frank: *see* Cockburn, Claud
Pivert, Marceau, 56
Plymouth, Lord, 38, 116
Pole, Joseph, 96, 119, 222
Pollitt, Harry, 32, 47n36, 118, 121n50, 123, 156, 194, 226
Populaire, Le, 57
Popular Front, in Britain, 4n6, 5, 6 (in South Wales), 33–5, (problems of) 120–2, 123–4, 127, 136, 138, 139, 223–4
Popular Front, in France, 37, 38, 70, 79–80
Popular Front, in Spain, 1, 27, 30, 34
Portugal, 38, 47, (despised by Dalton) 52; 62, 68n164
Preston, by-election in, 184
Preteceille, Ogier, 114n23
Price, John, 21, 147, 151
Prieto, Indalecio, 25, 27, 42, 43, 45, 76, 77, 113, 115, 147
Primo de Rivera, José Antonio, 22, 32
Primo de Rivera, Miguel, 25
Printing and Kindred Trades Federation, 207–8
Pugh, Sir Arthur, 151
Pyke, Geoffrey, 161–2

Quadragesimo Anno, 190
Quakers, 139, 142, 144, 163
Quinn, Bertha, 189

Radical Party, in France, 48, 61, 80
Railway Clerks' Association, 80, 176
Ramos Oliveira, Antonio, 49, 49n44, 104n155, 182
Rank-and-file movements, 12, 35, 35n84, 62, 163, 174, 196–220 *passim*, ('rank-and-filism') 196–7; (delegation to TUC) 200–2; (and the 'official' movement) 220; (rank-and-file of the Labour Party) 13–14, 95–6, 139; rank-and-file movements amongst: London busmen, 197–8, 199–206; engineering workers, 198–9, 216–19; printing workers, 206–9; dockers, 214
Rearmament, 4, 15, 60, 110, 117, 122, 162, 198, 216, 226
Red Aid, 147, 149
Red Cross, the, 145, 157, 164
Reed, George, 213–14
Reynolds' News, 120

Rio Tinto, mines, 87, 90
Roberts, Wilfred, 74, 123n59
Robinson, W.A., 69n166
Robles, Gil, 26, 182
Robson, Alexander, 210–13
Rockliff, Father, 172
Rutherglen, Glasgow, 185–6

St Helens, Lancs., 184–5
Salazar, Dr Antonio, 38
Salengro, Roger, 57
Salvation Army, 139
San Sebastián, 145
Santander, 102
Santiago, Enrique, 147, 148
Schevenels, Walter, 43, 48; (and Paris
    Conference, August 1936) 49–50; 67,
    (assessment of political situation in
    Spain, 1937) 76; 77, 90n96, 95, 100,
    105, 113, 133, 145, 146, 147–8, 151, 152,
    157, 160; (visits Spain) 76, 85–6
    (and international communism) 115, 148,
    160
Schiff, Victor, 44, 45, 77
Scotland, 97, 127–9, 160, 161, 185–8
Scott, Joe, 161, 203n40, 204, 205n49, 218
Scottish Ambulance Unit, 158
Scottish Trades Union Congress, 97, 128–9,
    161, 189
Section Française de l'Internationale
    Ouvrière; 20, (tendencies within) 56;
    (divisions over Non-Intervention) 57;
    70, 132
Sell, R., 204
Seymour Cocks, Frederick, 67, 165
Shipping Federation, 211, 213
Snelling, Frank, 199
Socialist League, 13, 33, 120
Socialist Medical Association, 156
Somers, Miss A., 179
Southampton, Joint Council, 165
Southport, Lancs., 166
South Wales, 6, 22, 62n125, 82–3, 101, 118,
    125, 131, 156, 161
South Wales Miners' Federation, 35
Soviet Union, (policy towards Spanish Civil
    War) 39; 58, 65, 75–6, 85, 92, 93, 146
Spain, Civil War in, 1936–9, 1, (origins of)
    23–8; (first months of) 28–9; (British
    attitudes to) 30; 75, 91, (Northern
    Front of) 100–6; (final phase of) 107–8;
    (possible armistice in) 111; (British
    recognition of Franco) 219; (aftermath
    of) 221–2
Spain, Second Republic, 1931–9, 1, 2, 4, 25,
    (conflicts within) 26; (Asturias revolt)

27; (*coup* of 17 July 1936) 28;
    (wartime politics in) 75–7; 93,
    (political tensions within) 109, 112–15
Spain Campaign Committee: *see under*
    Labour Party National Executive
    Committee, Spain Campaign
    Committee of
Spanish Medical Aid, 33, 74, 118, 121n50,
    137, 138, 139, 140, 151, 156–9, 163,
    164, 179, 199, 225
Spanish Problem. The, TUC pamphlet, 3
Spanish Workers' Fund, of the NCL, 19,
    141n14, 142n16, (publicity for) 149–50;
    153–6, 170, 176, 177, 178n48, 193,
    228n17
Special Branch, The British, 49n44
'Special European Conference', Paris, 13
    August 1936, 49–50, 157
Spence, William, 83, 116n29, 214, 215
Springhall, Dick, 225n13
Squance, William, 125, 131, 132
Standing Joint Committee of Industrial
    Women's Organisations, 155
Stolz, George, 76, 145n32, 147
Stott, W., 80
Sullivan, Bernard, 174, 179
Sutherland, Mary, 155
Swan, J., 120n42, 125
Sweden, seamen from boycott Spanish
    rebels, 81

Tanner, Jack, 30, 50, 96, 120, 198, 218
Teruel, battle of, 107
Tewson, Vincent, 115, 129, 147, 149, 150,
    151, 152, 162, (and care for Basque
    children) 163–4; 200, 221n1
Tomas, Pascual, 67–8, 84, 86, 88, 92, 173
Toole, Joseph, 80
Townley, Mr, 98
Trade unions, British, 10, (in the 1930s) 12;
    23, (and communism) 32; 34, 35,
    (threat from fascism to) 60; (and
    politics) 81; (and the Labour Party) 89;
    94, (changing response to Spanish Civil
    War) 95–9; 107, (and rearmament)
    116–17; (and the Popular Front) 121;
    (campaign for special conference on
    Spain, 1938) 130; 133, (use of trade
    union funds) 142n16; (and Catholic
    Guilds) 190–1; 194, (and rank-and-file
    movements) 196–7; (dominate labour
    movement response to Spain) 227–8;
    (fund-raising for Spain) 132–6, 153–6;
    (and Catholics) 169, 172, 176–8, 180,
    185, 191
Trades Councils, (in the 1930s) 12; 123,

163, 191, 196–7; (Blackpool) 162; (Cardiff) 166; (Glasgow and Edinburgh) 128–9, 136, 140, 148; (Newcastle) 173; (North East Federation of Trades Councils) 173, 191; (Southampton) 165
Trades Disputes and Trades Unions Act, 1927, 9, 9n15, 111, 130n91, 131
Trades Union Congress, 7, 10, (and Trades Councils) 12; (and the IFTU) 20; 22, 30, 49, 50, (and the International Brigades) 78; 85, 89, 94, 97, 100, 105, 108, 110, 115, 117, 124, 125, 127, (and the Scottish food ship) 128–9; 135, 139, 150, 153, 162, 163, 178–9, 200, 201, 204, 209, 219, 220, 228
Trades Union congress, annual congresses of, (1936 Congress), 3, 11, 61, 62–3, 66–7, 193; (1937 Congress) 73; (1938 Congress) 119, 129, 130–2, 134
Trades Union Congress, Finance and General Purposes Committee, 8, 97, 108, 132, 162
Trades Union Congress, General Council, (formation of) 8; 9, 11, (and the NCL) 13; 14, (and war) 15; 16, 18, 35, 41, (initial response to the Civil War) 48; 64, 65n142, 66, (delegation to Eden, March 1937) 89–91; 93, (telegram to Chamberlain) 102; 123n59, 124, 130n91, (authority of) 130–2; 133, 150, 158, (and Voluntary Industrial Aid) 162; 191, 204, 205, 207
Trades Union Congress, International Department, 67, 78, 228n17
Trades Union Congress, Organisation Department, 153
Trades Union Congress, Research Department, 142n16, 160
Transport and General Workers' Union; 10, 21, (branches and Non-Intervention) 62; 81, 82, 125n72, 131, 134, 153, 160, 161, 174, 177n43, 179, 190, (Irish branches and the Civil War) 192–3; 198, 201, 202, 205; (T&GWU Branch 1/498) 199, 206; (T&GWU Power Workers' Group) 134n114
Trevelyan, Sir Charles, 73

Typographical Association, 177, 208

Unión General de Trabajadores, 20, 20n52, 24–5, 29, 31, 43, 48, 67, 76, 85, 108, 112, (split in) 112–14, 115, 125, 144, 146, 147, 149, 173, 222n4
Union of Democratic Control, 17
Union of Post Office Workers, 176, 178n48, 184
United Peace Alliance, 33, 119, 120
United Textile Factory Workers' Association, 69n166
'Unity' campaign, 1937, 33, 99, 120
Universe, The, 172

Valencia, 146
Vandervelde, Emil, 89
Vansittart, Sir Robert, 52, 90n96, 100, 102, 105
Vega, José Rodríguez, 113
Velo, S.S., 216
Voluntary Industrial Aid for Spain, 137, 161–3, 216

Walker, James, 60, 71, 80, 125n72
Wall, Albert, 188, 202–3
Walsh, Bob, 170, 191n98
War and Peace, Labour Party document, 15
Ward, Bert, 30
Watkins, K.W., 3
Wedgwood, Benn, William, 151
Whatley, Monica, 188, 189
Why Bishops Back Franco, ILP pamphlet, 187
Wilkinson, Ellen, 10, (visits Spain in 1934) 31; 42n12, (at Paris conference, August 1936) 50; 104n155, 118, 121, 121n50, 123n59, (and Spanish Medical Aid) 157; 207, 222n5
Williams, E.J., 177, 212n83
Williams, Francis, 150
Wingate, Sybil, 118, 222
Witt, Leslie, 165
Workers' Travel Association, 106

Zak, Bill, 66, 73
Zilliacus, Konni, 40, 96
Zyromsky, Jean, 53, 56, 68

THE SPANISH CIVIL WAR AND THE BRITISH LABOUR MOVEMENT

This book draws on a mass of previously unstudied documentary material to provide a major reinterpretation of British labour's response to the Spanish Civil War, and is the first full-length study of this controversial subject to be published. It challenges the prevailing view that the labour leadership 'betrayed' the Spanish Republic, and that this polarised the movement along 'left' versus 'right' lines. Instead, it argues that the overriding concern of the major leaders was to defend labour's institutional interests against the political destabilisation caused by the conflict, rather than to defend Spanish democracy. Although the main advocates of this position were trade union leaders associated with the labour right such as Walter Citrine and Ernest Bevin, the book argues that their dominance reflected the centrality of the trade unions to labour movement decision-making rather than the abuse of union power to achieve political goals. Hence, labour's response to the Civil War was fully in step with the bureaucratic evolution of inter-war labour internationalism. To support this argument Dr Buchanan makes the case that the British working class was by no means united in its support for the Spanish Republic: many Catholic workers, for instance, were alienated by the persecution of the church at the outbreak of the Civil War and forced to reassess their allegiance to the British labour movement in consequence. Moreover, even within the left, the conflict between institutional and political interests prevented coherent action against the leadership's policy. Hence, the book argues against the relevance of the left's 'Popular Front' strategy, which failed to address the problem of how to overcome the institutional resistance to radical policies. Thus this book offers an important new interpretation of a subject of considerable historical and political interest, and suggests new ways of studying political action within the labour movement in the 1930s.